Aldham Robarts LRC

Liverpool John Moores University

THE
SINO-AMERICAN
ALLIANCE

WITHDRAWN

ID0322448

LIVERPOOL JMU LIBRARY

3 1111 00849 7776

THE
SINO-AMERICAN
ALLIANCE

Nationalist China
and American
Cold War Strategy
in Asia

John W. Garver

An East Gate Book

M.E. Sharpe
Armonk, New York
London, England

An East Gate Book

Copyright © 1997 by M. E. Sharpe, Inc.

First paperpack printing 1999.

All rights reserved. No part of this book may be reproduced in any form without written permission from the publisher, M. E. Sharpe, Inc., 80 Business Park Drive, Armonk, New York 10504.

Library of Congress Cataloging-in-Publication Data

Garver, John W.
The Sino-American alliance : Nationalist China and American Cold War strategy in Asia / John W. Garver
p.   cm.
"An East Gate book."
Includes bibliographical references and index.
ISBN 0-7656-0025-0 (cloth : alk. paper).
ISBN 0-7656-0053-6 (pbk : alk. paper).
1. United States—Foreign relations—Taiwan.
2. Taiwan—Foreign relations—United States
3. United States—Foreign relations—1945–1989.
4. Cold War.
I. Title.
E183.8.T3G37   1997
327.73051249—dc21
97-5056
CIP

Printed in the United States of America

The paper used in this publication meets the minimum requirements of the American National Standard for Information Sciences— Permanence of Paper for Printed Library Materials, ANSI Z 39.48-1984.

BM (c)   10   9   8   7   6   5   4   3   2   1
BM (p)   10   9   8   7   6   5   4   3   2   1

To Alexander and Vanessa and the children of my friends
on both sides of the Taiwan Strait in the hope that they will
all find a way to live together in peace.

JOHN MOORES UNIVERSITY
AVRIL ROBARTS LRC
TEL. 0151 231 4022

Contents

Figures and Tables

Figures

Tables

Abbreviations

AGE	Aerospace Ground Equipment
AFB	Air Force Base
AFRT	American Forces Radio, Taiwan
AID	Agency for International Development
ARVN	Army of the Republic of Vietnam
ASPC	Asian and Pacific Council
ASW	Antisubmarine warfare
AVG	American Volunteer Group
BCP	Burma Communist Party
CAA	Civil Aeronautics Administration (ROC)
CAF	Chinese Air Force (ROC)
CAL	China Air Line
CAT	Civil Air Transportation company
CATM	Chinese Agricultural Technical Mission
CCK	Ching Chuan Kang (air base in central Taiwan)
CCP	Chinese Communist Party
Chicoms	Chinese Communists
Chinats	Chinese Nationalists
CIA	Central Intelligence Agency
CINCFE	Commander in Chief, Far East (Tokyo)
CINCPAC	Commander in Chief, Pacific (Pearl Harbor)
CMC	Central Military Commission (PRC)
CNO	Chief of Naval Operations
COD	Continental Operations Department (ROC)

COMPACAF	Commander, Pacific Air Forces
COMTDC	Commander, Taiwan Defense Command
CPSU	Communist Party of the Soviet Union
CPV	Chinese People's Volunteers
DOD	Department of Defense
ECA	Economic Cooperation Administration
G-2	Intelligence section of staff
GNP	Gross national product
GOB	Government of Burma
GRC	Government Republic of China
GVN	Government of (South) Vietnam
IAEA	International Atomic Energy Agency
ICA	International Cooperation Administration
INR	Intelligence and Research (U.S. State Department)
JCRR	Joint Committee on Rural Reconstruction
JCS	Joint Chiefs of Staff
JIC	Joint Intelligence Committee
JSPC	Joint Strategic Planning Committee
LST	Landing ship tank
KMT	Kuomintang, Nationalist Party of China
MAAG	Military Assistance Advisory Group
MAP	Military Assistance Program
MDAP	Mutual Defense Assistance Program
MND	Ministry of National Defense (ROC)
MSTA	Military Sea Transportation Service
NATO	North Atlantic Treaty Organization
NEFA	North East Frontier Agency
NIE	National Intelligence Estimate
NSA	National Security Agency
NSAM	National Security Action Memorandum
NSC	National Security Council
NVDA	National Volunteer Defense Army
OCB	Operations Coordinating Board
OPC	Office of Policy Coordination (CIA)
OSS	Office of Strategic Services
PCT	Presbyterian Church of Taiwan
PLA	People's Liberation Army
PLA-N	People's Liberation Army-Navy
POW	Prisoner of War
PRC	People's Republic of China
PT boats	Patrol torpedo boats

RAW	Research and Analysis Wing (Indian Intelligence Board)
ROC	Republic of China
RVN	Republic of Vietnam
SACO	Sino-American Cooperative Organization
SCAP	Supreme Commander Allied Powers
SEATO	South East Asia Treaty Organization
SFF	Special Frontier Force (India)
SNIE	Special National Intelligence Estimate
SOG	Studies and Observation Group
TDC	Taiwan Defense Command
TO&E	Table of Organization and Equipment
UN	United Nations
USAF	United States Air Force
USIA	United States Information Agency
USG	United States Government
USSR	Union of Soviet Socialist Republics
VFW	Veterans of Foreign Wars

1

Introduction

This book is about the ways in which the United States' relationship with Nationalist China served U.S. policy interests in Asia during the 1950s and 1960s. It attempts to weigh the various components of the U.S.-Nationalist relation in terms of their utility, or their disservice, to U.S. policy objectives. The thesis of this study is that the United States' relationship with the Nationalist regime on Taiwan was an important and valuable element of U.S. strategy in Asia during the two decades between 1950 and 1971. U.S. leaders of that era believed that this was the case, and a dispassionate retrospective judgment leads to a similar conclusion. The multifaceted U.S. alliance with the Nationalist regime on Taiwan played an important role in U.S. strategy for splitting the Sino-Soviet bloc and containing the revolutionary expansion of China during the early Cold War era in Asia.

The utility of Nationalist China to U.S. strategy was multifaceted. Utilization of Taiwan by U.S. military forces and denial of it to the military forces of the Sino-Soviet bloc maintained the integrity of the offshore island chain along the eastern coastline of the Eurasian continent. This allowed the United States to secure threatened sea lines of communication between North America and forward positions around the periphery of the Sino-Soviet bloc in East Asia. Once Nationalist military forces had been reorganized by the mid-1950s, the mobilization of the military resources of Nationalist China made a major contribution toward offsetting the Sino-Soviet bloc's superiority in ground forces, and provided a means of containing the enemy land offensives expected to characterize the beginning of a general East-West war. In peacetime, the existence of a militarily potent

LIVERPOOL
JOHN MOORES UNIVERSITY
AVRIL ROBARTS LRC
TEL. 0151 231 4022

and potentially aggressive Nationalist regime off the coast of the People's Republic of China (PRC) compelled Beijing to divert resources away from economic development and improvement of popular living standards, thereby fostering dissent and possibly accelerating the long-term delegitimization of the regime. Of course, the Nationalist-U.S. threat also worked the other way as well, helping to legitimize the repression of the Chinese Communist Party (CCP). The Nationalist regime also provided a useful way of isolating the People's Republic of China internationally, since relations with the former automatically precluded relations with the latter.

The existence of a non-Communist and prosperous Chinese polity off the coast of the PRC also contributed to undermining the Communist model of development among the people of China and of Asia. While the effects of the Taiwan development model were not fully felt until the 1970s and 1980s, well after the time frame of this book, much of the basic architectural design work for that model was done during the 1950s and 1960s. From a long-term perspective, the amorphous power of example generated by a successful modern, democratic *Chinese* polity on Taiwan may well prove to be the most durable benefit deriving from the U.S.-Nationalist alliance of the 1950s and 1960s. It therefore behooves us to consider the early U.S. midwifery of what later became the Taiwan model. Finally, cooperation with Nationalist China offered the United States effective intelligence assets with which to penetrate the veil of state secrecy in Communist China. In sum, cooperation with Nationalist China gave the United States important advantages in dealing first with the hostile combination of the Union of Soviet Socialist Republics (USSR) and the PRC and, after 1960, with the PRC alone.

The premise of this book is that, during the decades between 1950 and 1971, the United States and the People's Republic of China engaged in a protracted political struggle, with each side using all means short of outright war to injure and punish the other side. The leaders of both countries chose to keep this confrontation below the level of declared belligerency, but the conflict was nonetheless bitter. Men fought and died. Whatever means could be used to hurt, weaken, demoralize, or confuse the other side were used. Both sides deemed the use of all means short of war legitimate.

From one perspective, this book constitutes a study of the secret history of Sino-U.S. relations during the 1950s and 1960s. In their long political war, both Beijing and Washington mobilized whatever forces were available within and beyond their national boundaries. Sometimes this was done with the consent of governments exercising sovereignty over that territory, sometimes without. Because of the political costs associated with violation of the sovereignty-based norms of the international order, and because of the sentiments of public opinion in the Western democracies, both Washington and Beijing kept much of their activity secret. Many of the battles of this two-decade-long political war were sub rosa—and many of them are elucidated in the following pages. What follows is only a partial history of the "secret war," however, as the Chinese side of the ledger is absent. A *balanced* history of the secret Sino-U.S. war would include Beijing's clandestine campaigns against the United States in Asia, Africa, Latin America, and Europe.

This book assumes that the U.S. link with Taiwan, and even more generally the strategy of containment from which that link derived, was not itself the primary cause of the U.S.-PRC confrontation during the 1950s and 1960s. Were the Sino-American confrontation during that period essentially about the U.S. presence on Taiwan and U.S. involvement with the Nationalist competitor to the Chinese Communist Party, then whatever advantages the United States might derive from its links with Taiwan, in terms of a favorable structure of power vis-à-vis a hostile China, would be illusory. If U.S. nonengagement with Nationalist China on Taiwan would have ended PRC hostility toward the United States, there would have been no need to contain China. Indeed, U.S. engagement with Nationalist China would have produced the very problem—a hostile China—that it was intended to address.

PRC historiography insists that this was, in fact, the case; the roots of U.S.-PRC confrontation lay in President Harry S. Truman's 27 June 1950 interposition of the Seventh Fleet into the Taiwan Strait, and U.S. support for Nationalist China over the subsequent twenty years was the major cause of Sino-American hostility.

I view the problem differently. During the U.S.-PRC ambassadorial talks in Geneva and Warsaw in 1955–56, and again during the Sino-American discussions leading up to the Shanghai Communiqué of 1972, the Taiwan issue was indeed the most sensitive and difficult one. But beneath that issue lay an array of issues having to do with the global balance of power. In 1955–56 Washington and Beijing recognized few if any convergent interests in these areas: the growth of Soviet global power, decolonization and its aftermath, the Japan-U.S. alliance, Soviet control over Eastern Europe, and so on. Given these divergent interests, there was no impetus to compromise. In 1971–72 the two sides were able to set aside the Taiwan issue because they now agreed on a wide range of major global issues: global strategy for dealing with the Soviet Union, U.S.-Japanese relations, the Indian Subcontinent, the Indochina war, arms control, Soviet-European relations, and so on. One striking aspect of the rapprochement of the early 1970s was the rapidity with which robust cooperation on a range of important issues replaced conflict over Taiwan. The conclusion is inescapable: multiple convergent interests pushed Washington and Beijing to compromise over Taiwan. Which was more fundamental, the Taiwan issue or the degree of divergence or convergence of interests on other global issues? It seems to me that the latter was the more fundamental. Until the tight bipolar world disintegrated with the collapse of the PRC-USSR alliance, there would be no impetus for Beijing and Washington to compromise over Taiwan. Once that occurred and Chinese and U.S. interests began to converge, the Taiwan issue was easily set aside. The global balance of power was the most important element.

The Sino-American confrontation of the 1950s and 1960s was about far more than Taiwan. It was about the fate of East and Southeast Asia. Were the countries of that region to develop under the tutelage of elites committed to Leninist socialism, or under the tutelage of elites committed to liberal capitalism? For reasons of both ideology and the security of the new revolutionary Chinese state they had founded, China's Communist leaders sought the former.

A recent study by Professor Chen Jian mines newly available Chinese sources to analyze CCP perceptions in 1949.[1] Chen stresses the revolutionary aspirations of CCP leaders. Mao Zedong's overriding objective as the revolutionary movement he led approached nationwide victory, was to sustain the momentum of that movement. Now that the first stage of the revolution was nearly complete, it was imperative to move the revolution into its second, socialist stage. The social and political structures of the old order had to be destroyed, and structures of a new socialist order established. The revolution could not be allowed to stall because the goals of its initial stage had been achieved. There was bound to be strong internal opposition to transition to socialism. The resistance of the bourgeoisie and the petite bourgeoisie, especially sections of the intelligentsia, would have to be crushed. Mao's foreign policies were an extension of these domestic imperatives. A policy of militant, revolutionary struggle internationally was conducive to overcoming internal opposition to the revolutionization of China's society.

Internationally, Mao viewed world affairs through the prism of Marxism-Leninism. The confrontation under way between the USSR and the Western countries led by the United States was a manifestation of class struggle. The United States led the world's reactionary forces. The hostility of U.S. imperialism to the Chinese revolution was inevitable, while New China could look to the USSR for necessary assistance in economic, military, and political construction.[2]

Mao was especially concerned with the success of revolutionary movements in areas around China's periphery. Indochina and Korea had been tributaries of China before wars by France and Japan in the 1880s and 1890s. But Mao and his comrades also paid great attention to revolutionary struggles elsewhere in East and Southeast Asia. If those movements were successful, China's new revolutionary state would be more secure against threat and pressure by U.S. imperialism. Chinese assistance to those movements would thus enhance PRC security. It was also in accord with Marxism-Leninism's prescription of proletarian internationalism. In addition, it provided a way for New China to play a more important role in Asian affairs.[3]

Alliance with the USSR followed from this analysis. During a visit by a CCP delegation to Moscow in July–August 1949, Stalin and CCP leader Liu Shaoqi discussed cooperation in support of world revolution. Stalin proposed that while the USSR was to remain the leader of the world proletarian revolution, China should play a more active role in advancing the rising tide of revolution in East Asia. Liu agreed and said China would try to do more to support Asian revolutionary movements.[4] Shortly afterward, the People's Liberation Army (PLA) transferred several divisions of ethnic Koreans to Kim Il Sung and began large-scale military assistance to Ho Chi Minh's Viet Minh forces in Indochina.

For reasons of ideology and the security of the state they led, U.S. leaders concluded they should seek to thwart the revolutionary efforts of the new Chinese state. American liberal ideology deemed repugnant the system of Communist Party dictatorship and command economy extolled by Communism. U.S. leaders of the late 1940s also generally believed that American power ought to serve the cause of freedom in the world. In terms of security, U.S. security would be enhanced if the territories and resources of various East Asian states were controlled by elites sympathetic to the United States and its values. It would be diminished were those lands and resources mobilized under the direction of elites dedicated to antithetical values and institutions.

Two decades of confrontation through all means short of war was the result of the clash of these ideological and state security perspectives. It is necessary to reiterate this key assumption: the U.S.-PRC confrontation was, in large part, about the future of Asia. Conflict over Taiwan was secondary to this broader struggle between Leninist-led and non-Leninist-led development throughout East Asia.

There was widespread revolutionary ferment in post–World War II Asia. In the words of one study, there was "nearly ubiquitous" regime collapse in that region, with elites and political structures widely discredited by association with Western colonialists and Japanese occupiers. Government's hold on the countryside had weakened, and political situations were highly fluid.[5]

The contest between China and America was fought out in two geographic zones. The first zone included Korea, Taiwan, and Indochina, the second zone the Philippines, Malaysia, Indonesia, and Japan. In the first zone there was sharp and direct confrontation between the United States and the People's Republic of China. In the second zone the conflict was less intense and less direct but nonetheless quite real. Throughout the region, both the United States and the PRC mobilized and applied national power to direct development along the desired lines, working with sympathetic local elites in the process.[6]

A corollary of this view is that the national power of one great power was constrained and checked by that of the other. Many important factors other than the relative power capabilities of China and the United States were, of course, involved. The argument here is *not* that either American or Chinese power was the sole or necessarily the most important factor that determined the destinies of various regions and countries. Some extremely important variables emerged out of the historic and social processes internal to the countries of these two zones. Yet the relative power capabilities of the United States and China also played a very important role. The power of the United States and China checked each other along the thirty-eighth parallel of the Korean peninsula and down the Taiwan Strait. China's national power played an extremely important role in defeating the American effort in Indochina and directing that region along the socialist path of development. Had the relative application of either American or Chinese power been substantially greater or less in Korea, Taiwan, or Indochina, the outcomes could well have been different. In the second zone, China supported revolutionary movements in Malaysia, the Philippines, and Indonesia, and "anti-imperialist" movements in Japan. But American power was too great in this region, and Chinese power too weak, for Chinese policy to win.

It follows from this analysis that the construction of a relatively more powerful position for the United States benefited that nation and the goals sought by American power. In other words, the U.S. alliance with Nationalist China played an important role in constructing a structure of power favorable to the attainment of U.S. interests in Asia. Nationalist China was, of course, only one element of this structure. Focusing on this one element does not imply that it was *the* most important element. Rather, the proposition is merely that it was *one* important element.

The interpretation of the U.S.–Nationalist China relation developed in this book and summarized above differs somewhat from previous U.S. scholarship on this issue. This study constitutes the first in-depth look at the

United States' relationship with Nationalist China during the 1950s and 1960s. Several other scholars have, however, dealt with that relationship as part of broader studies. Warren I. Cohen, in his seminal study of Sino-U.S. relations, touched on the U.S.-Nationalist relationship of that era, emphasizing almost exclusively the costs of that relationship to the United States. U.S. support for Nationalist China isolated the United States "almost as much as it did the People's Republic," according to Cohen.[7] It also greatly increased Beijing's hostility toward the United States; Beijing no longer required "ideological reasons for its virulent hostility to the United States."

In a recent and impressive study of U.S. policy toward Taiwan and Hong Kong, Nancy B. Tucker also stresses the debit side of the account. The Nationalist regime was a discredited dictatorship which tarnished the United States by association. Chiang Kai-shek tried to maneuver the United States into conflict with the PRC and defied U.S. efforts to reduce tension with Beijing. U.S. ties with the Nationalists created problems for the United States with friendly and allied countries in Asia and in Europe. The United States accepted this because of its "anti-Communist crusade."[8] Tucker's analysis, like Cohen's, gives no sense of the major benefits that the United States derived from its association with Nationalist China. Michael Schaller goes further, judging the U.S.-Nationalist link an unmitigated catastrophe: "The most significant and ultimately disastrous aspect of the American response to the North Korean attack [of June 1950] was the decision to draw a military barrier around Communist China and become uninvolved in the civil war. . . . Not only would South Korea be defended, but now Taiwan would be shielded from invasion."[9]

The problem with these earlier studies is not that they are wrong, but that they are one-sided. They place nearly exclusive stress on conflicts within the U.S.-Nationalist alliance, on the unattractive aspects of the Nationalist regime, and on the failure of various Nationalist operations on the mainland. These scholars presented a one-sided view, overlooking the many substantial gains the United States derived from association with Nationalist China. No policy is without costs, difficulties, and risks. Certainly the U.S. alliance with Nationalist China was fraught with these. Several of the cooperative efforts undertaken by Nationalist China and the United States failed—sometimes monumentally, as in Burma and Tibet. Nor did the U.S.-Nationalist alliance represent some sort of invincible weapon. It neither deterred China from supporting Hanoi nor kept Hanoi from overwhelming Saigon with Chinese and Soviet support. Yet, the United States gained substantially from its alliance with Nationalist China. Until Chinese leaders disassociated themselves from the USSR and indicated a willingness to align with the United States against Moscow, U.S. leaders concluded that the gains of the alliance with Nationalist China outweighed the costs and risks associated with that alliance.

As the above suggests, the focus of this book is on the role of the U.S. alliance with Nationalist China *in U.S. policy.* The absence of consideration of the Nationalist perspective on the interactions between Nationalist China and the United States will disappoint some people. Indeed, I myself find this lack disappointing, and should confess that this is not the book I initially set out to write. When I began research for this book in 1993, I planned to focus on the dynamics of U.S.-Nationalist intra-alliance bargaining—a topic in which I became interested as the result of a conference organized by Harry Harding in the summer of 1987. Primary documentation on the U.S. side of the alliance through the late 1950s was abundant with the progressive publication of the *Foreign Relations of the United States* series by the U.S. State Department. Initially I hoped to secure access to similar materials on the Nationalist side, and then to compare how each side viewed the two countries' conflicts and cooperation. Unfortunately, this was not possible. During a visit to the Kuomintang Committee on Party History, I found that the archives for the post-1949 period remain closed. I was thus confronted by a basic asymmetry of evidence. There was no way of knowing with any degree of confidence (that is, from primary policy documents) what Nationalist perceptions and objectives were, while I could reach solid conclusions about these things regarding the American side. I was thus confronted with a choice. I could write a lopsided study of U.S.-Nationalist interactions, or I could shift my focus to U.S. strategy. I chose the latter, in the belief that a study with this focus could make a useful contribution to our understanding, since no previous study had focused on this topic. Moreover, as indicated above, the overall interpretation of the utility of the U.S.-Nationalist alliance developed in this study is contrary to that reached by most other studies of the topic.

I wish to thank various people who assisted me with this book. Steven I. Levine soldiered his way through an early draft nearly twice the length of the present one. Steve's criticisms resulted in a much tighter, somewhat less turgid work. Michael Hunt, Allen Whiting, William Stueck, and James Lilley also gave me their valuable suggestions. I should also thank Harry Harding for inviting me to participate in the 1987 conference on "China as an ally" which gave rise to my interest in the U.S.–Nationalist China alliance. The Chiang Ching-kuo Foundation subsequently provided support that allowed me time to write substantial portions of the text and to make a research trip to Taipei during the summer of 1993. Special thanks is due to Dr. Hsing-wei Lee, then the director of the Chiang Ching-kuo's Washington, D.C., office. Thanks is also due for the generous help of Dr. Martin Goren, librarian for the U.S. Drug Enforcement Agency in Washington, D.C., of Dr. Hanna Zeidlick, archivist at the Center for Military History in Washington, D.C., and of General Kai-nan Ma, deputy director of the Bureau of Military History of the Ministry of Defense in Taipei. Dr. Ed J. Marolda at the Naval Historical Center assisted with the identification of individuals in various photographs and facilitated my research at his center. Wo Li-chong, then a graduate student at the East Asian Institute of National Cheng Chi University in Taipei, served diligently as my research assistant. Thanks is also due to several anonymous participants in U.S. intelligence operations in the 1950s and 1960s, who agreed to discuss their activities.

At Georgia Institute of Technology, Joy Daniell assisted in seemingly endless editorial revisions. Ms. Daniell should also be given an award for competence in deciphering professorial cursive scrawl. Final thanks is due to Georgia Tech's chair of the School of International Affairs, Linda P. Brady, for facilitating juggling of teaching schedules to make free substantial blocks of time for research and writing.

One bit of advice from several of my friends and critics that I have chosen to ignore has to do with use of the word "thalassocracy." One of my readers' comments was: "What the hell does this mean?" While this word is admittedly rarely used and not widely known, it conveys, I believe, an important strategic concept—maritime supremacy. It is also a concept rich with history, originating in the Athenian League's maritime paramouncy and continuing through the maritime base of the British Empire of the nineteenth century. It is thus a concept with which Americans, with their "continental island" nation, *ought* to be familiar. It also seems particularly appropriate to a discussion of the role of Taiwan in U.S. strategy in the Pacific region.

As regards the Latinization of Chinese words, this book follows the guidelines of *The China Quarterly,* the premier English-language China studies journal. Pinyin is used without tone marks except for the following, which use the Wade-Giles system: names such as Chiang Kai-shek, Sun Yat-sen, Taipei, Kuomintang, and the names of individuals living outside mainland China. The offshore islands of Quemoy and Matzu are referred to by their pinyin names, Jinmen and Mazu.

Notes

1. Chen Jian, *China's Road to the Korean War: The Making of the Sino-American Confrontation,* New York: Columbia University Press, 1994.
2. Ibid.
3. Ibid.
4. Ibid., pp. 74–75.

LIVERPOOL
JOHN MOORES UNIVERSITY
AVRIL ROBARTS LRC
TEL. 0151 231 4022

5. Michael H. Hunt and Steven I. Levine, "The Revolutionary Challenge to Early U.S. Cold War Policy in Asia," in *The Great Powers in East Asia, 1953–1960,* Warren I. Cohen and Akira Iriye, eds., New York: Columbia University Press, 1990, pp. 13–31.

6. I develop this theme in John W. Garver, "Polemics, Paradigms, Responsibility, and the Origins of the U.S.-ROC Confrontation in the 1950s," *The Journal of American-East Asian Relations,* vol. 3, no. 1 (Spring 1994), pp. 1–34.

7. Warren I. Cohen, *American Response to China: An Interpretative History of Sino-American Relations,* New York: Wiley and Sons, 1971, p. 218.

8. Nancy B. Tucker, *Taiwan, Hong Kong, and the United States, 1945–1992: Uncertain Friendships,* New York: Twayne, 1994.

9. Michael Schaller, *The United States and China in the Twentieth Century,* New York: Oxford University Press, 1979, p. 133.

2

Contradictory Policies: Encouraging Chinese Titoism and Consolidating the Offshore Perimeter

**Encouraging Chinese Titoism and Consolidating
the Offshore Perimeter**

The accelerating collapse of China's Nationalist regime in late 1948 raised fundamental questions for the United States. Previously, Harry S. Truman's administration had hoped that, despite its deep flaws, the Nationalist regime might be able, with U.S. support, to prevent China's Communist forces from completely prevailing through force of arms. Following the devastating Nationalist defeats of late 1948, however, U.S. leaders concluded that the Nationalist regime was doomed. A prudent U.S. policy, therefore, should focus on achieving American interests vis-à-vis China's new Communist rulers. By early 1949 the Truman Administration had concluded that the United States should disengage from the Chinese civil war and the Nationalist Chinese regime, "let the dust settle," and then attempt to work out some sort of accommodation with the new Communist China.[1]

Several factors produced this policy. One was a profound revulsion toward the ineptitude of the Nationalist elite and a belief that events in China were part of a broader wave of profound political ferment sweeping post–World War II Asia. Calculations regarding the power interests of the United States also pointed toward the rapidly developing Cold War with the USSR.

Key members of the Truman Administration, because of their experience with the Nationalists during the late 1940s, developed an extremely jaundiced view of the Nationalist elite. Corruption and incompetence reigned in the Nationalist leadership.

Another premise of the Truman policy of disengagement was a belief that profound revolutionary forces were shaking Asia, and that a prudent U.S. policy had to accommodate those forces, not oppose them.[2] Age-old passivity and acceptance of poverty and oppression were giving way to popular aspirations for economic development and freedom from foreign domination. Those popular aspirations translated into nationalism which, in China, the Communists had succeeded in appropriating. This, most fundamentally, explained the Communist victory over the Nationalists. If the United States was to avoid alienating the nationalist sentiments arising in China and other Asian countries, it should not become entangled with the discredited Nationalist elite that fled to Taiwan, any more than it should become associated with European colonialism or with opposition to aspirations for economic development. Prudent U.S. policy must build on the hopes of the awakening masses of Asia, rather than thwarting these hopes. From this perspective, the Nationalist regime was part of the old order. U.S. association with the unpopular and repudiated Nationalist elite would not improve the standing of the United States in the eyes of the Chinese and other Asian peoples.

In terms of calculations regarding U.S. power interests, the centers of gravity for the rapidly emerging Soviet-U.S. contest were in Europe and the Middle East. U.S. forces were already spread very thin, and new undertakings in the Far East would divert them from more critical areas. Most important, the overriding strategic interest of the United States was in countering the power of the USSR, and there existed the possibility of exploiting Chinese Communist differences with Moscow so as to minimize Soviet influence with China. Guided by the State Department, Truman doubted that Moscow controlled the CCP, was aware of previous tensions between the CCP and Moscow, and anticipated new tensions over such issues as Soviet special rights in Manchuria and Xinjiang. The Joint Chiefs of Staff (JCS) rejected these notions of "Chinese Titoism." These military voices won wide support in Congress, but did not determine U.S. policy throughout 1949 and into early 1950.

Late in 1948, the Truman Administration formulated two broad strategies in response to the accelerating collapse of the Nationalist regime. First,

Chinese Titoism was to be encouraged in order to draw the emerging Communist-led China away from the USSR. Second, a defense perimeter was also to be established through the chain of islands running along the coast of East Asia, from the Aleutians through Japan and the Ruyukyus to the Philippines. There was a consensus among U.S. leaders that this island chain now formed a vital defense frontier for the United States. Because of U.S. naval supremacy, that chain could be held relatively cheaply by U.S. forces in the event of war, containing Soviet and Soviet-allied forces, while the United States rushed in reinforcements, mobilized its national strength, and planned future strategic counteroffensives. If, as seemed likely, the United States decided to adopt the strategic offensive against the USSR in Europe, the western Pacific perimeter could be held with minimal forces, thereby allowing the concentration of maximum forces elsewhere for offensive operations.[3]

There was a serious contradiction between the two strategies. That contradiction focused on Taiwan, which was an important link in the new offshore defense perimeter. Yet U.S. prevention of a CCP takeover of Taiwan would work contrary to exploitation of Beijing-Moscow contradictions. From the standpoint of exploiting Chinese "Titoism," the United States should distance itself from Nationalist Formosa, even perhaps sacrificing it to Beijing if the PRC's response was right. From the standpoint of the offshore defense perimeter, however, Taiwan occupied an important position at the center of the offshore chain.

Geography underlay this dilemma. The fact that Taiwan was a fairly large island separated from the Asian mainland by a hundred miles of sea made it both defensible by the United States at a modest cost and valuable for the maintenance of U.S. thalassocracy in the western Pacific Ocean. The United States' decision of late 1948 to wash its hands of the Nationalist regime was motivated partly by the fact that the costs of trying to keep the Nationalists in power were simply too great. Only the commitment of large numbers of U.S. troops to fighting the Communists in China, along with unlimited amounts of U.S. military and economic assistance to the Nationalist government, would suffice, at great cost, to keep the Nationalists in power, the Truman Administration concluded. The fact that Taiwan was an island, together with the fact that U.S. air and naval forces held supremacy over the western Pacific Ocean, created the possibility that the United States might deny Taiwan to the emerging Communist Chinese regime at a modest cost to itself.

Recent history had also demonstrated that Taiwan's location made it valuable to maintenance of U.S. naval supremacy in the Pacific. During World War II Taiwan had figured prominently in U.S. Navy strategy. As the American offensive campaign in the Pacific gathered steam in mid-1944, U.S. military leaders debated the best geographic approach to Japan. Chief of Naval Operations Admiral Ernest J. King strongly advocated seizing Taiwan and using it as a staging area for the final campaigns against Japan. Navy leaders argued that the blockade of Japan by air, by submarines, and by surface ships would force Japan to surrender without invasion of the home islands. Control of Taiwan would greatly facilitate this blockade by allowing U.S. forces to dominate the sea lanes over which Japan received essential supplies of oil, rice, and raw materials from Southeast Asia. Control of Taiwan would "put the cork in the bottle" of Japanese sea communications to the south, choking off all Japanese traffic in and out of the South China Sea.

During a pivotal strategic debate in Honolulu in July 1944, Pacific commander Admiral Chester W. Nimitz conceded that bases on Luzon would also serve this purpose, but he felt that Taiwan was better. Were blockade alone insufficient to defeat Japan, Taiwan would serve as a base for an invasion of Japan's Kyushu Island. General Douglas MacArthur, then the Supreme Commander, Southwest Pacific Area, argued strongly in favor of an advance through the Philippines rather than Taiwan, largely on the basis of political considerations having to do with American moral obligations to liberate its good friends on the Philippines. These political concerns persuaded Roosevelt during the July 1944 Honolulu conference. The issue was not decided, however, until September, when Japanese conquest of U.S. air bases in southwestern China eliminated the air support deemed essential for a successful assault on Taiwan.[4] In 1949–50, as in 1944, the U.S. Navy viewed Taiwan as extremely valuable because of its particular location.

While the U.S. Navy felt more strongly about the importance of Taiwan than did the other armed services, or the State Department, concern about the security of sea lanes between North America and forward areas abroad was not a parochial concern of the U.S. Navy. Indeed, as the U.S.-USSR confrontation intensified, this became a grave concern shared by most U.S. defense planners. After 1945, the USSR had embarked on a large-scale submarine construction program based on captured German U-boats, technology, and engineers. The resulting Soviet submarines (three new classes were introduced into the Soviet navy in the late 1940s) were superior boats with high underwater speed and endurance, depth capability, and torpedo reload interval. A rubberized coating reduced their vulnerability to sonar detection. Soviet engineers also advanced German torpedo technology—already the most advanced in the world in 1945—to produce reliable acoustic homing torpedoes.

By 1948, the Soviet submarine fleet numbered 210 boats, making it five times the size of the Nazi submarine fleet in 1939. Over half of these boats were long-distance types. Of the USSR's four submarine fleets, the Pacific fleet was the largest. The Soviet submarine fleet was also growing rapidly. U.S. Navy intelligence estimated in the late 1940s that the annual production rate would climb to 100 boats per year by 1960. In fact, that rate was reached by 1955.[5] By the late 1940s, U.S. military planners faced the possibility that, in the event of war, hundreds of modern Soviet submarines would attack U.S. vessels carrying soldiers and war materials from North America to forward positions in Europe and the Far East, and raw materials between Southeast Asia and Japan.

The U.S. Navy responded to the Soviet submarine challenge by developing antisubmarine warfare (ASW) capabilities. The major weakness of the Soviet submarine strategy was geographic. Soviet boats had to pass through narrow and shallow straits before they could reach the open seas where U.S. convoys would be. The Soviets attempted to surmount this difficulty by acquiring forward bases beyond U.S.-controlled straits—in Turkey, Libya, Albania, and China. U.S. strategists sought to counter Soviet efforts to break out to the high seas. Access to Taiwan's harbors and airfields would have been a major gain for Soviet submarine warfare capabilities in the Pacific. Denial of that access conversely made a major contribution to the American ability to restrict Soviet submarine access to the sea lanes between North America and U.S. forward positions.

The Tortured Decision to Sacrifice Taiwan

In spite of the value of Taiwan to the maintenance of U.S. thalassocracy in the western Pacific, the U.S. government decided to sacrifice Taiwan, so as to achieve broader political objectives. This was not an easy decision. Initially, U.S. leaders sought to balance the contradictory requirements of encouraging Chinese Titoism and consolidating the offshore perimeter by relying on indirect economic and diplomatic means to deny Taiwan to the CCP.

On 8 November 1948, the secretary of defense directed the JCS to assess "the strategic implications to the security of the United States should Formosa and its immediately adjacent islands come under an administration which would be susceptible to exploitation by Kremlin-directed Communists."[6] The JCS replied, on 24 November 1948, that a Communist takeover of Taiwan would be "seriously unfavorable" to the security of the United States. Since a Communist takeover of mainland China would probably result in the unavailability of harbor and rail facilities there for use by U.S. military forces in the event of war, the JCS said, "the potential value to the

United States of Formosa as a wartime base capable of use for staging of troops, strategic air operations and control of adjacent shipping routes would be enhanced." Control of Taiwan by an "unfriendly," "Kremlin-directed" power "would be of even greater strategic significance." In the event of war, the JCS memo asserted, hostile control of Taiwan would give an enemy the "capability of dominating to his advantage and our disadvantage the sea routes between Japan and the Malay area, together with a greatly improved enemy capability of extending his control to the Ruyukyus and the Philippines, either of which could produce strategic consequences very seriously detrimental to our national security." The JCS urged that "It will be most valuable to our national security interests if, in spite of the current Chinese situation and its obvious trends, Communist domination of Formosa can be denied by the application of such diplomatic and economic steps as may be appropriate to insure a Formosan administration friendly to the United States."[7]

These recommendations fed into NSC 37/2 of 4 February 1949. The analysis underlying an initial draft of this decision memorandum asserted that "The basic aim of the United States should be to deny Formosa and the Pescadores to the Communists without ourselves taking any open unilateral responsibility for them or power over them." This was to be done by "diplomatic and economic" means, not military means. The document stressed the political costs of going beyond diplomatic and economic means to hold Taiwan. The greatest of these costs would be intensifying Chinese hostility toward the United States. Occupation of Taiwan by U.S. military forces "would galvanize all mainland Chinese opinion in support of the Communists, the very thing we must avoid if our political warfare is to have any degree of success in China." There was no costfree way of isolating Taiwan from the mainland, the NSC report warned, but the least costly way of doing so was to encourage and support "*local* non-communist Chinese control over Formosa" (emphasis in original) through diplomatic and economic means.[8] "Local" meant "non-Nationalist," or at least "Nationalist but not too closely associated with Chiang Kai-shek."

This policy of denying Taiwan to the Communists via "local" control was threatened by "the increasing tendency of a great many Nationalist officials and their families to seek refuge on the island," and by the absence of a viable "alternative to National Government leaders." The newly appointed governor of Formosa, General Chen Cheng, showed some promise, the precursor to NSC 37/2 declared, but future developments were clouded by the "influx of refugee politicians and militarists from the mainland—many of them men whose gross incompetence has played into the hands of the Communists in China." This was the "greatest obstacle" to development of a "stable non-Communist Government" on Taiwan. The report explicitly ruled out the course that became U.S. policy after June 1950: support on Formosa of the Nationalist government "or a rump thereof *as the recognized Government of China.*" Such an approach "would be the worst policy for the United States to follow" (emphasis in original). U.S. association with the Nationalists would "greatly complicate our position on the mainland and hamstring our tactical flexibility toward China proper."[9]

Use of diplomatic and economic means to encourage "local" control over Taiwan as a way of denying Taiwan to China's new Communist rulers was the central thrust of National Security Council (NSC) 37/2, approved by Truman on 4 February 1949. In order to "develop and support a local non-Communist Chinese regime" on Formosa, NSC 37/2 said, the United States would use its "influence whenever possible to discourage the future influx of mainland Chinese" to the island, while maintaining "discreet contact" with "potential native Formosan leaders with a view at some future date to being able to make use of a Formosan autonomous movement should it appear to be in the U.S. national interest to do so." The United States would also use a combination of threats and inducements to pressure the authorities on Taiwan to implement reforms increasing the "efficiency" of their regime, contributing to the "welfare and economic needs of the Formosan people," and encouraging "active Formosan participation in positions of responsibility in Government."[10] Progressive reforms plus stabilization of Taiwan's economic situation through injections of U.S. assistance would, it was hoped, reduce the ability of the CCP to take the island through subversion and internal disorder.

NSC 37/2 recognized the possibility that diplomatic and economic means alone might prove inadequate to deny Taiwan to the CCP. The day after Truman approved NSC 37/2, the NSC asked the JCS to estimate "the extent of the threat to U.S. security in the event that diplomatic and economic steps to deny Communist domination of Formosa prove insufficient." The JCS replied, on 10 February 1949, that the increasingly likely Communist takeover of mainland China made it "more apparent than ever that the United States faces the prospect of strategic impotence on the continent of Asia, [and that] our military capabilities in the Western Pacific must rest primarily on control of sea lanes and maintenance of strategic air potential from strategically tenable island position[s]." "Enemy control of Formosa would seriously jeopardize our capabilities in these respects while constituting a major contribution to enemy capabilities." The loss of Taiwan to a hostile China would thus constitute a "serious" threat to the security of the United States. In spite of Formosa's "great strategic importance," the JCS recommended only some minor moves to strengthen Taiwan, and ruled

JOHN MOORES UNIVERSITY
AVRIL ROBARTS LRC
TEL. 0151 231 4022

out an "overt military commitment" to Formosa's defense. U.S. military resources were simply too limited. In the words of the memo,

> In spite of Formosa's strategic importance, the current disparity between our military strength and our many global obligations makes it inadvisable to undertake the employment of armed force in Formosa, for this might, particularly in view of the basic assumption that diplomatic and economic means have failed, lead to the necessity for relatively major effort there, thus making it impossible then to meet more important emergencies elsewhere. In this connection the distinction between the Formosan problem and the Iceland situation, where direct action is contemplated, if necessary to prevent Communist control, lies in the fact that Iceland is directly vital to our national security while the importance of Formosa cannot be said to be in that category.[11]

The contrast with Iceland elucidates JCS thinking about Taiwan's relative geopolitical value at this juncture. Iceland's significance lay in its potential role in the NATO effort to keep Soviet submarines out of the North Atlantic and, conversely, in Moscow's plans to use its submarine fleet to disrupt the movement of men and material across the North Atlantic in the event of an East-West war in Europe. Taiwan was important as a central component of a chain of offshore island positions, but it was not a strategic choke point like Iceland.

Truman, at the urging of the State Department, rejected a JCS proposal for military aid for the Nationalists and the deployment of U.S. ships to Taiwan on the grounds that a "show of military force" would impose a "heavy political liability" on the United States. It "would have serious political repercussions throughout China" and "might create an irredentist issue just at the time we may wish to exploit Soviet action in Manchuria and [X]inkiang."[12] In lieu of the dispatch of "minor fleet units" as proposed by the JCS, the NSC decided that the State Department "would strengthen and increase its representation on Formosa, and to that end should immediately detail a high ranking officer to Taipei" who was to press Chen Cheng (the Nationalist governor and military commander of Taiwan) for economic and political reform.[13] The decision to rely solely on diplomatic and economic means to deny that island to the CCP was thus reaffirmed.

By the middle of 1949, it was increasingly apparent that this policy would not succeed. Talks between Livingston T. Merchant, counselor to the U.S. Embassy, and prominent Chinese politicians about limiting Nationalist authority in Taiwan went nowhere. Nationalist officials and soldiers began to flee to Taiwan by the hundreds of thousands after the PLA crossed the Yantgze on 20 April. By May 1949, there were between 500,000 and one million Nationalist refugees on Taiwan. By August, Canton, the last major port not yet in Communist hands, was under threat from the PLA. Demoralized and dispirited remnants of the Nationalist armies gathered on Taiwan, where they imposed harsh military rule over a sullen and restive population. U.S. policy had to be rethought. According to NSC 37/6 of 4 August, there was now little hope for "installation of an effective and liberal administration" on Taiwan." Because of this, "the ultimate passage of Formosa under Communist control, by external or internal action, appears probable." According to a Central Intelligence Agency (CIA) estimate, without U.S. military intervention, Taiwan would probably be under Communist control by the end of 1950.

On 4 August 1949, Truman asked the JCS once again to "reexamine" its earlier recommendation against U.S. military intervention, assuming "conditions short of war" and that "in the absence of military measures Formosa and the Pescadores will sooner or later come under Communist control." Assuming such conditions, Truman asked whether the JCS now regarded Taiwan and the Pescadores "as of sufficient military importance to the United States to commit U.S. forces to their occupation."[14] Two weeks later the JCS reaffirmed their earlier opinion "that the strategic importance of Formosa" did not justify "overt military action." "So long as the present disparity between our military strength and our global obligations exists," the JCS said, undertaking additional obligations on Taiwan simply was not prudent. Significantly, however, the JCS insisted that "incipient or actual overt war" in the Far East might lead it to change its recommendations and justify military action to hold Taiwan.[15]

In November 1949, Secretary of State Dean Acheson apprised Truman of the results of a broad reevaluation of U.S. Far Eastern policy by a group of three special consultants. According to Acheson, this Group of Three had concluded that "Broadly speaking there were two (possible) objectives of policy: one might be to oppose the Communists' regime [in China], harassing it, needle it, and if an opportunity appeared to attempt to overthrow it. Another objective of policy would be to attempt to detach it from subservience to Moscow and over a period of time encourage those vigorous influences which might modify it." The Group of Three unanimously recommended the second alternative. Acheson concurred.[16]

The JCS still pushed for military aid to Taiwan. On 23 December the JCS recommended initiation of a "modest, well-directed, and closely supervised program of military aid to the anti-Communist government in Taiwan." Such a program, together with stepped-up political, economic, and psychological measures, would suffice to hold Taiwan, the JCS insisted.[17] The State Department argued strongly against the JCS recommendation. The United States needed, Acheson said, to take a "long view not of six or twelve months but of six or twelve years."

JOHN MO....
AVRIL ROBARTS L...
TEL. 0151 231 40..

On 30 December, Truman approved NSC 48/2. This pivotal document embracing Acheson's view defined U.S. Far Eastern policy in the aftermath of the establishment of the PRC and was intended to bring to a close the wrenching debate of 1948–49 over policy toward Taiwan. It implicitly provided for the sacrifice of Taiwan to the CCP by limiting U.S. support for the Nationalists to diplomatic and economic means, even though it was clearly understood that such means were inadequate and that without U.S. military intervention Taiwan's fall to the PLA in the immediate future was virtually certain.

NSC 48/2 provided that "The United States should exploit, through appropriate political, psychological and economic means, any rifts between the Chinese Communists and the USSR and between the Stalinists and other elements in China, while scrupulously avoiding the appearance of intervention." Regarding Formosa, the United States should continue "attempting to deny" that island to the CCP through "diplomatic and economic means within the limitations imposed by the fact that successful achievement of this objective will primarily depend on measures of self-help." The document explicitly reaffirmed that the strategic importance of Formosa did not justify overt U.S. military action.[18]

To minimize the impact of the anticipated Communist takeover of Taiwan on U.S. reputation and third-country morale, the same day NSC 48/2 was approved, the State Department issued a directive to U.S. embassies abroad telling them how to handle Taiwan's anticipated fall. U.S. representatives should stress, the directive said, that Taiwan "politically, geographically, and strategically, is part of China in no way especially distinguished or important." The island had no "special military significance." "China has never been a sea power," the directive stated, and the island of Taiwan had "no special strategic advantage to the Chinese Communist armed forces." Nor had the United States assumed any "responsibility or obligation, actual or moral," for the island.[19]

On 5 January 1950, Truman publicly announced the U.S. decision to pursue a hands-off policy toward the Chinese civil conflict. Regarding Formosa, Truman said that the United States would not "pursue a course which will lead to involvement in the civil conflict in China." Nor would it provide military aid or advice to Chinese forces on Formosa.[20]

Several days later, Acheson delivered his subsequently famous (perhaps infamous) remarks to the National Press Club. Speaking on 12 January Acheson specified, quite in line with NSC 48/2, that the U.S. defense perimeter in the western Pacific ran through the Aleutians, Japan, the Ryukyus, and the Philippines. Taiwan and South Korea were pointedly excluded. Acheson went on to say that, regarding areas outside the U.S.

defense perimeter, "No person can guarantee these areas against military attack." Such a guarantee would not be "sensible," "necessary," or "practical." Were such an attack to come, it would have to be resisted by the people attacked and then by "the entire civilized world under the Charter of the United Nations."[21] The point was clear. There was no U.S. commitment to Taiwan or to South Korea.

The Sino-Soviet Alliance and the United States' Scrapping of Its Hands-Off Policy

By early 1950, the Truman Administration had written off Taiwan. It was only a matter of time, U.S. leaders felt, until that island fell to the PLA, destroying the remnants of the Nationalists and finally ending the Chinese civil war. This policy choice was made in the face of strong pressure from the JCS, and especially the Navy, and over strong criticism from the Congress and the media. Truman responded to these pressures by making concessions at the margins—by allowing the Navy to deliver arms previously contracted for to Taiwan and by approving limited economic aid—but he held firm on the central principle of no U.S. military relation with or military action on behalf of the Nationalists.

Two events in early 1950 radically changed the international situation in East Asia. One was the formation of the USSR-PRC alliance in February. The other was the North Korean invasion of South Korea in June. Two recent studies have analyzed these two critical events on the basis of newly available ex-Soviet archives. Fortunately, these two studies broadly agree in their conclusions. Joseph Stalin and Mao Zedong came together with deep suspicions of each other. They were able to overcome those suspicions and form a thirty-year treaty of "friendship, alliance, and mutual assistance" largely because of the advantages each anticipated from that treaty vis-à-vis the United States. The two leaders agreed that prospects for further revolutionary advances in Asia were good, and that the newly formed socialist camp should support those advances.

Stalin apparently saw revolutionary offensives in Asia as a way of diverting U.S. strength and attention from Europe (the critical theater for Stalin as for the Americans) and driving a wedge between the PRC and the United States. Mao, deeply committed to revolutionary ideology, saw further revolutionary gains in Asia as a way of driving back U.S. imperialism and thereby enhancing the security of China's new revolutionary state. Moreover, by demonstrating solidarity with the revolutionary elites emerging in countries around China's periphery, China would build its prestige with those elites.[22]

The Sino-Soviet treaty was a military alliance. Article I of the treaty provided that "In the event of one of the High Contracting Parties being attacked by Japan or States allied with it, and thus being involved in a state of war, the other High Contracting Party will immediately render military and other assistance with all means at its disposal." This phraseology was designed to give Stalin, especially, some flexibility. While he was anxious to embroil China in confrontation with the United States, Stalin was apprehensive about himself becoming embroiled in a war with the United States at a time and a place not of his own choosing. Thus he insisted that a "state of war" (meaning, presumably, a state of *declared* war) must exist. Moreover, the attacking state had to be *allied* to Japan. If this required a formal treaty of alliance, such did not exist between Japan and the United States until 1952. Thus, Stalin hoped to retain discretion in deciding the question of war and peace between the USSR and the United States. In the event of war, however, the obligation of the PRC to help the USSR, and vice versa, was sweeping.

Agreements ancillary to the February treaty extended the USSR's naval basing rights at Port Arthur and its special rights vis-à-vis Manchurian railways through the end of 1952. No time limit was placed on the right of the Soviet Union, "at the proposal" of the Chinese government, to use Port Arthur in the event of war.[23] These provisions meant that in the event of a USSR-USA war, Manchuria would become a staging area for Soviet forces. They also meant that Soviet submarines would operate out of the naval base at Luxun, leapfrogging the narrow straits out of the Sea of Japan. The two sides also pledged in the treaty to consult on all important international problems, to "participate in all international actions aimed at ensuring peace and security throughout the world." What such cooperation might mean was indicated several weeks before the conclusion of the PRC-USSR treaty, when both countries recognized Ho Chi Minh's insurgent North Vietnamese government and proclaimed their support for its struggle against France. Large-scale, covert Chinese assistance to Ho Chi Minh's military forces was beginning about the same time.[24]

The CCP's decision for alliance with the USSR was linked to the planned invasion of Taiwan. The PLA had minimal air and naval capabilities as it began planning for the invasion of Taiwan in mid-1949. Success required the rapid acquisition of these capabilities. Thus acquisition of Soviet assistance in these areas was one of the highest priorities during Liu Shaoqi's visit to Moscow in July–August 1949.[25] Stalin agreed to provide assistance, and a large-scale Soviet effort to build PLA air and naval capabilities was under way by the end of 1949. Stalin rejected, in mid-1949, a proposal by Liu that Soviet assistance be used for the invasion of Taiwan. Such a course, Stalin told Liu, would risk a new world war.[26]

Mao again raised the matter with Stalin in December 1950. The Soviet leader again refused. Following the agreement to form an alliance and, more important, following Truman's 5 January 1950 announcement that the strategic importance of Taiwan did not justify U.S. military intervention, Stalin agreed to the Chinese request. Stalin also agreed that half of the $300 million loan the USSR was extending to China could be used to purchase naval equipment for the Taiwan invasion.[27]

The logic of the situation also strongly suggests that a key Chinese purpose in entering the February 1950 alliance was to further reduce the likelihood of U.S. intervention to thwart the upcoming Taiwan invasion. Early in 1949 CCP leaders were greatly concerned with possible U.S. military intervention against the CCP. By the middle of that year, they had concluded intervention *on the mainland* was unlikely. They continued to worry, however, about U.S. intervention when the PLA assaulted Taiwan. According to Chen Jian, by early 1950 CCP leaders had concluded the United States would not intervene on Taiwan. The United States was too weak politically and militarily to intervene.[28] Certainly the fact that the USSR stood behind Beijing was an important factor weakening U.S. aggressiveness. At the end of January 1950, General Su Yu told a conference discussing the Taiwan invasion that he was now confident that Washington would not risk *a third world war* by sending its military forces to protect Taiwan.[29]

By allying with Moscow, Beijing greatly increased the gravity of the threat confronting the United States in the burgeoning Cold War. The United States now confronted a vast Eurasian combination ranging from Central Europe to Southeast Asia. Large numbers of veteran soldiers were added to the enemy order of battle confronting the United States. It also became much more likely, indeed virtually certain, that any conflict with the USSR would be global, imposing on the United States simultaneous major wars in Europe and the Far East.

The Sino-Soviet treaty also increased the likelihood that Taiwan, were it to come under Beijing's control, would be made available to Soviet air and naval forces. This was the clear implication of Beijing's solemn pledge to "immediately render military and other assistance with all means at its disposal" in the event of war. Moreover, China's subjugation of Taiwan would have been accomplished with large-scale Soviet support and Soviet consent. While it is tempting to dismiss the prospect of Soviet military use of Taiwan with our knowledge of subsequent disputes between Mao and Khrushchev, we must be wary of this sort of historical presentism. In 1950, prudence required U.S. leaders to take Moscow and Beijing at their word, and those words promised intimate cooperation in the global struggle against U.S. imperialism.

Even with the advantage of forty years hindsight, it is difficult to say that, had a war between the Soviet-led and the U.S.-led alliance systems broken out in the 1950s, the PRC would have remained neutral. The PRC's top leaders said repeatedly and clearly that they would not remain neutral in the global struggle against the United States. They were bound by treaty to support the USSR. Moreover, Mao Zedong and other Chinese leaders had a strong sense that if the New China was to be respected, the imperialists had to be made to understand that, unlike the Old China, the PRC would not be pushed around, but would do what it said it would, including following through on threats to use military force. All of this suggests that there is little reason to conclude that China would not have stood by its obligations under the 1950 treaty in the event of a U.S.-Soviet war. Figure 2.1 depicts the strategic situation in the Pacific following the conclusion of the Sino-Soviet treaty.

The Sino-Soviet treaty virtually eliminated prospects for Chinese Titoism for the foreseeable future. By committing the PRC to close alliance with the USSR, the 1950 treaty dissolved the key factor working against U.S. intervention in Taiwan. For the foreseeable future, U.S. efforts to exploit "Chinese irredentist sentiment with respect to Soviet actions in Manchuria, Mongolia, and Xinkiang," as Acheson had characterized earlier U.S. strategy, seemed certain to fail. It also increased the geopolitical significance of Taiwan in countering the new Sino-Soviet bloc. The prospect of Soviet forces operating out of Luxun, let alone Chinese ports farther south, greatly increased the importance of maintaining the integrity of the offshore perimeter. The 360-mile gap between Okinawa and Taiwan and the 100-mile gap between Taiwan and the Philippines would be very difficult to close if Soviet air forces operated out of Taiwan, providing an umbrella for Soviet submarines heading for the open Pacific. With Taiwan under U.S. control, Soviet submariners could be bottled up in the East China Sea. With Taiwan in PRC hands, the cork was out of the bottle. Even U.S. leaders who had previously advocated sacrifice of Taiwan in order to better encourage Chinese Titoism now concluded that maintaining the integrity of the barrier chain of offshore islands was highly important to U.S. security interests.

The impact of the PRC's alliance with the USSR on U.S. policy was apparent in NSC 68 promulgated in April 1950. This was one of the seminal documents of U.S. post–World War II strategy, setting the United States on a worldwide struggle against Communism. While the NSC 68 examination of the United States' "strategic plans and its objectives in peace and war" was prompted mainly by the imminent Soviet test of an atomic bomb and its probable capability of producing hydrogen bombs, the underlying

Figure 2.1 The Western Pacific Defense Perimeter

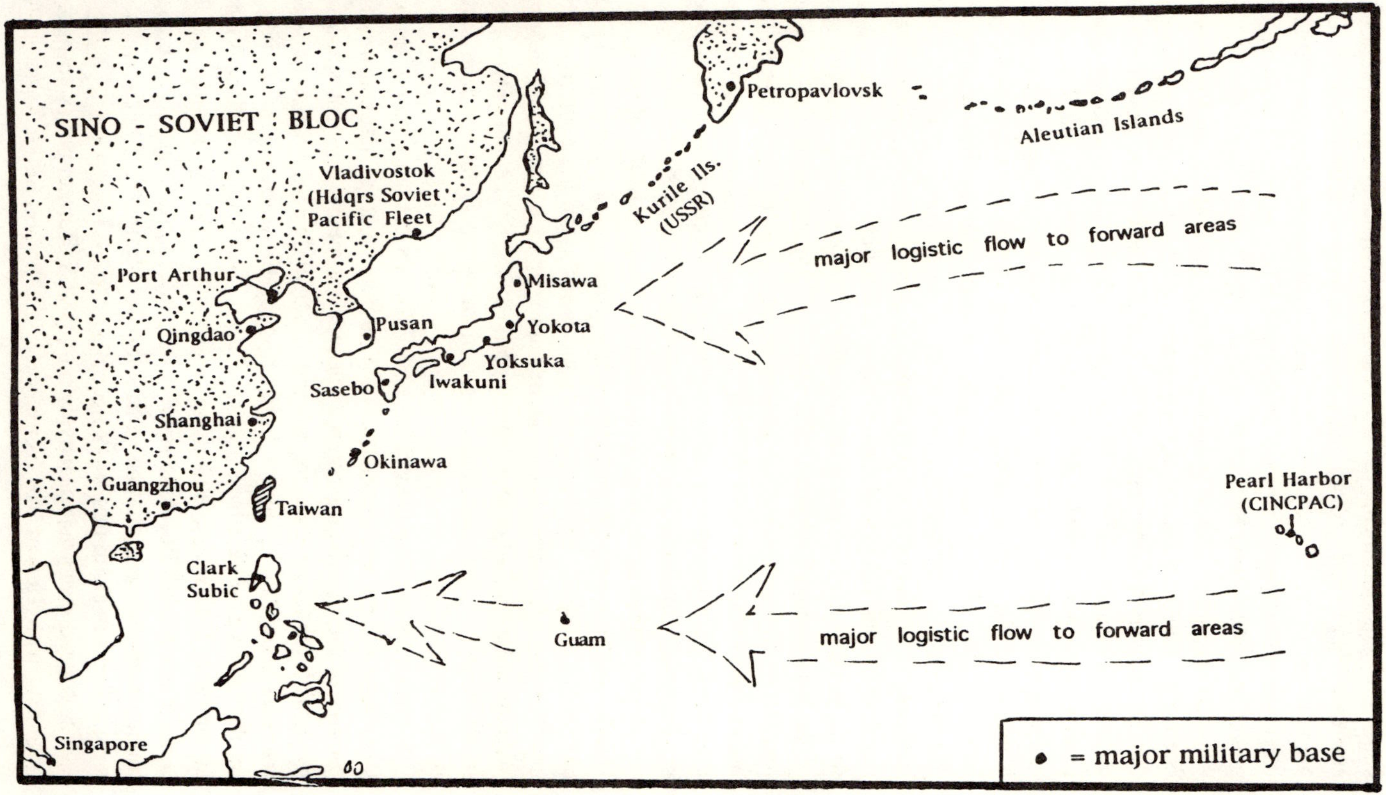

SINO - SOVIET BLOC

Petropavlovsk

Aleutian Islands

Kurile Ils. (USSR)

Vladivostok
(Hdqrs Soviet
Pacific Fleet)

Port Arthur

Qingdao

Shanghai

Guangzhou

Pusan

Sasebo

Misawa
Yokota
Yoksuka
Iwakuni

Okinawa

Taiwan

Clark
Subic

Singapore

Guam

Pearl Harbor
(CINCPAC)

major logistic flow to forward areas

major logistic flow to forward areas

● = major military base

concern of this document was with the global balance of power. "For several centuries it had proved impossible for any one nation to gain such preponderant strength that a coalition of other nations could not in time face it with greater strength," the document read. This "historical distribution of power" had now been "basically altered" by several factors. One was the Chinese revolution. Power was increasingly gravitating into two centers, one led by the United States and the other by the USSR. Soviet policy was directed "toward the domination of the Eurasian land mass." Soviet efforts in this regard, if successful, "would raise the possibility that no coalition adequate to confront the Kremlin with greater strength could be assembled."[30]

Europe was the center of Soviet aspirations, according to NSC 68, with Moscow hoping to bring all of Europe under its domination. It was in Asia, however, that Moscow had the greatest opportunities. Soviet ideals had "found a particularly receptive audience in Asia, especially as the Asiatics have been impressed by what has been plausibly portrayed to them as the rapid advance of the USSR from a backward society to a position of a great world power." China was clearly a major example of the "Asiatic" appeal of the Soviet model of rapid advance. The Communist success in China, together with the "political-economic-situation in the rest of South and South-East Asia, provides a springboard for a further incursion in this troubled area." "Throughout Asia the stability of the present moderate governments, which are more in sympathy with our purposes than any probable successor regimes would be, is doubtful." From its position of strength, the USSR was "pursuing the initiative in the conflict with the free world." "Its atomic capabilities, together with its successes in the Far East, have led to an increasing nervousness in Western Europe and the rest of the free world. We cannot be sure, of course, how vigorously the Soviet Union will pursue its initiative. . . . There are, however, ominous signs of further deterioration in the Far East."

Unlike NSC 48/2 of December 1949, NSC 68 did not speak of drawing Communist China away from the USSR. It noted that the nationalism of the peoples of the satellite countries "still remains the most potent emotional-political force," and that the "excessive demands of the Kremlin" on its satellites could "be made good only through extreme coercion," with the result that "if a satellite feels able to effect its independence of the Kremlin as Tito was able to do, it is likely to break away." NSC 68 did not apply this concept to PRC-USSR relations, however. Since the conclusion of the Sino-Soviet treaty, the exploitation of Sino-Soviet tensions had become a long-term rather than an immediate project.[31]

The second event that decisively moved U.S. Taiwan policy toward engagement with Taiwan was North Korea's attack on South Korea in June

1950. U.S. leaders believed (correctly, as recently available ex-Soviet archives make clear) that this attack was launched with the approval and support of Stalin and Mao Zedong. The North Korean attack convinced U.S. leaders that the newly formed Sino-Soviet bloc was committed to aggressive moves to expand the frontiers of the Communist camp in Asia. Voluntary retreat before this offensive would be disastrous to the unity of the Western alliance. American views in this regard were deeply influenced by the fiasco of Western appeasement of Nazi aggression in the 1930s. The North Korean invasion tapped strong beliefs of U.S. leaders—beliefs derived from the failure of the Western attempt to appease Nazi Germany in the 1930s. According to these beliefs, the Western failure to stand up to Hitler's limited aggressions of 1935–38 helped produce World War II. Appeasement had emboldened Hitler and convinced him that the Western democracies were too weak and cowardly to fight. It would have been better, according to this image of history, had the Western democracies stood firm early on, been prepared to meet force with counterforce; and, above all, refused to abandon to aggressive tyrants peoples willing to fight for their freedom. These beliefs and images were seared deeply into the minds of America's leaders of 1950 and structured their perception of events surrounding Korea. Through these cognitive mechanisms, the Taiwan of 1950 became the Czechoslovakia of 1938.[32]

These cognitive dynamics were made clear during the Anglo-American discussions of Korean War strategy in December 1950, after China had thrown its military weight behind North Korea's effort. Secretary Acheson, previously the foremost advocate of sacrificing Taiwan, rejected a British proposal to conciliate Beijing by offering concessions such as admission to the United Nations and recognizing China's claim to Taiwan. He could not believe, Acheson said, that the Chinese Communists would "become calm and peaceful if we gave them Formosa and made other concessions. On the contrary, if we gave concessions, they would only become more aggressive." "It would be like offering a reward for aggression."[33] So long as Beijing pursued a course of aggression, there could be no weakening of U.S. support for or disengagement from Nationalist Formosa.

In the new international context of June 1950, the geopolitical importance of Taiwan was brought again to the attention of Washington decision makers by the long "Memorandum on Formosa" by Commander in Chief, Far East (CINCFE) Douglas MacArthur, written on 14 June 1950—eleven days before North Korea's attack on the South.[34] Because of the pivotal role MacArthur's memorandum played, and because its analysis differed substantially from the November 1948 JCS analysis of Taiwan's geopolitical value, reviewing it at some length will be useful. The domination of

Taiwan by a power unfriendly to the United States "would be a disaster of utmost importance," MacArthur warned. Formosa was "geographically and strategically" an "integral part" of the "western strategic frontier of the United States . . . extending from the Aleutians through the Philippine Archipelago." Control of this offshore frontier "in the event of hostilities can exercise a decisive degree of control of military operations along the periphery of Eastern Asia." From positions along this offshore line, U.S. forces "would have the capability to interdict the limited means of communication available to the Communists and deny or materially reduce the ability of the USSR to exploit the natural resources of East and Southeast Asia."[35] Possession of Taiwan by an unfriendly power, on the other hand, would create "an enemy salient in the very center" of the United States' western strategic perimeter. From bases on Taiwan, enemy forces would be 100 miles closer to Okinawa and 150 miles closer to Clark Field and Subic Bay in the Philippines than from any point on the Chinese mainland. This would double the intensity of the air effort an enemy force could mount against Okinawa, and would bring U.S. Philippine bases within range of enemy fighters (which were all land-based), a situation which did not then exist, according to MacArthur's memo.

If Soviet air and naval forces had access to Taiwan, Moscow would stockpile military supplies on Taiwan prior to the outbreak of hostilities. It would then be in a position to provide forward-operating facilities for the short-range coastal submarines which were predominant in the Soviet Pacific Fleet. Because of its central location and its base potential, MacArthur warned, "Formosa in the hands of the Communists can be compared to an unsinkable aircraft carrier and submarine tender ideally located to accomplish Soviet offensive strategy and at the same time checkmate counter-offensive operations by U.S. forces based on Okinawa and the Philippines." To demonstrate the importance of Taiwan, MacArthur reviewed the important role bases on Taiwan had played in Japan's offensive campaigns in Southeast Asia in 1942–44 and in its defensive operations in the western Pacific in 1944–45.

In Senate testimony shortly after his relief from command in April 1951, MacArthur elaborated on the assumptions underlying his views on Taiwan's geostrategic value. MacArthur assumed that facilities on a PRC-controlled Taiwan would be available to Soviet military forces. Pressed by Senator Russell Long about how a Red China with very weak air and naval forces could pose a threat to Japan from Taiwan, MacArthur replied that Beijing "would probably make bases [there] available for the Russian submarine power and air power." The great danger, MacArthur said, was that Taiwan would become a platform for *Soviet* submarines and airplanes threatening U.S. bases on the Philippines and in Okinawa. Taiwan's significance lay not primarily in the fact that it was several hundred miles farther east than points along the mainland, though this was important, but in its position just north of the Philippines and south of Japan. From that position, Soviet forces would threaten U.S. bases and their supply lines from Pearl Harbor and Guam. Confronted by a buildup of *Soviet* air and submarine forces on Taiwan, the United States would have to position substantial counterforces to defend its Philippine and Okinawa bases. These defensive requirements would tie down a considerable portion of U.S. forces in the Pacific, substantially reducing U.S. strategic flexibility—the ability to shift and concentrate U.S. forces elsewhere.[36]

Another of MacArthur's assumptions had to do with the impact of modern technology on war. Weapons had become so lethal that the day of the frontal assault was over. A winning strategy thus required maneuver, envelopment, and the bypassing of enemy strong points. "Good commanders do not turn in high casualties," was MacArthur's famous aphorism. In the Pacific campaigns of World War II, the United States had used such a strategy to foil Japan's plan of imposing on the United States a war of attrition which would be too costly for the American people to bear. The same strategy should now be applied to dealing with Communist China, MacArthur urged. In a war with China, the United States should not attack enemy strong points or commit large forces to a land war on the continent of Asia. Rather, it should use its superior air and naval forces, along with relatively small and highly mobile ground forces, to wage envelopment campaigns. Naval blockade should also be employed to isolate China from the outside world. Effective naval blockade was an "immensely powerful weapon," MacArthur felt. Denial of Taiwan to Communist China would be very useful in imposing an effective blockade on China. Conversely, PRC possession of that island would greatly facilitate protection of China's vital coastal traffic.

Broadly conceived, MacArthur was proposing a maritime strategy for dealing with the Sino-Soviet bloc in Asia. That bloc dominated the Eurasian continent and enjoyed interior lines of communication. On the other hand, those lines of communication were primitive, and the United States enjoyed exterior lines of communication as well as superior air and naval forces. The United States should utilize the superior mobility deriving from its technological and geographic advantage to isolate and weaken China, minimizing its ability to concentrate forces against the United States in Korea or elsewhere. Moreover, the United States should use its maritime supremacy to isolate China, stunting and disrupting its economic and military development. In short, the United States should maintain mastery over the seas and airspace of the western Pacific, and should use its thalassocracy to defeat the vast land armies of China. Such a strategy fit with the domestic political imperatives confronting U.S. military planners. Government based on the consent of the governed required that casualties in a future war be kept low. In this context, Taiwan as the center of the offshore island chain was important.

MacArthur's maritime strategy was adopted, ipso facto, under Truman after Chinese entry into the Korean War and more deliberately by Dwight Eisenhower's administration in 1953. Harry Truman, George C. Marshall, and Dean Acheson, the earlier architects of the policy of sacrificing Taiwan, demonstrated their new conversion to the geopolitical thinking outlined by MacArthur's 14 June memo by urging many of MacArthur's arguments, sometimes nearly verbatim, on British leaders at the Anglo-American conference in December 1950. Following the Chinese Communist entry into the Korean War, British leaders were extremely concerned that the conflict would escalate into a general war with China. Entanglement with Chiang Kai-shek, especially military involvement in Taiwan, made this more likely, British leaders felt. American leaders disagreed. Acheson told Prime Minister Clement Attlee that "If . . . we permitted Formosa to be attacked and fall, we would raise the gravest dangers in Japan and the Philippines . . . where [are located] the bases from which our operations [in Korea] were being conducted and upon which our whole Pacific position rested."[37] Marshall, supported by JCS Chairman Omar Bradley, said that he had "very strong feelings in the matter from a military point of view." The United States "could not afford to have our chain of island outposts split by a Formosa in hostile possession," Marshall said. The United States could not now afford to let Formosa go, he maintained. Formosa was of no particular strategic importance in U.S. hands, but it "would be of disastrous importance if it were held by an enemy." At that point, Truman added: "We can't open our whole flank by giving up Formosa."[38] When Attlee said that encouraging a breakdown of the Sino-Soviet alliance should be the West's major aim, Acheson did not challenge this, but explained that there were immediate, short-run concerns, such as military threats to Japan, the Philippines, and other countries, that had to be met. In this situation it would not be wise, Acheson explained, to weaken present security for the sake of long-term possibilities.[39] Once the United States was at war and confronted by an undeniable Sino-Soviet bloc, even the most ardent advocates of sacrifice of Taiwan were persuaded of the geopolitical value of Taiwan.

On 26 June 1950, the U.S. military command ordered the Seventh Fleet to "take stations to prevent invasion of Formosa and insure Formosa not to be used as a base of operations against Chinese mainland." This order was subsequently revised to include the Pescadores and to stipulate that naval surface and air operations could be conducted from "anchorages in Formosan waters."[40] The next day, 27 June, Truman informed the world of the shift in U.S. policy toward Formosa. U.S. military forces quickly inserted themselves into the Taiwan Strait, following Truman's declaration. An aircraft carrier task group based around the 27,100-ton *Valley Forge* left Subic Bay and headed northward. On 29 June it passed Taiwan, with its planes patrolling the Strait.[41] The State Department also upgraded its representation on Taiwan, transferring the Counsel General in Hong Kong, Karl Rankin, to Taipei as First Secretary. Previously the U.S. mission in Taipei had been headed by a chargé d'affaires, Robert G. Strong.[42]

The Truman Administration's June 1950 intervention in the Taiwan Strait was intended for the duration of the Korean conflict. (This is discussed in chapter 3.) After the Korean War was transformed into a Sino-American war with China's entry at the end of 1950, the chances were virtually nil that the United States would go back to the June 1950 policy and voluntarily sacrifice Taiwan after peace was restored in Korea. The advantages of a maritime strategy to the United States in confronting the Sino-Soviet bloc, and of the role of Taiwan in such a strategy, were simply too great.

Beijing's Policy Choices and U.S. Engagement with Formosa

The major argument against engagement with the Nationalists on Formosa prior to February 1950 was that fundamental U.S. interests would best be served by trying to draw Communist China away from the USSR. The February 1950 treaty demolished this argument. During the several months between the signing of that treaty and the North Korean invasion of the South, Acheson continued to hammer away at the inequities of Soviet treatment of China. Indeed this was a major thrust of his comments during this period.[43] The increasingly apparent closeness of the Sino-Soviet relation, culminating in the two countries' joint effort to support North Korea's conquest of the South, made these arguments increasingly untenable. At least for the foreseeable future, the PRC was joined in close military-political cooperation with the USSR. In this new situation, efforts to draw Beijing away from Moscow had little chance of success. In fact, with Beijing allied with Moscow, efforts to conciliate Beijing could even be counterproductive, convincing Beijing and Moscow that Washington was unwilling to stand up to the new Sino-Soviet combination. Moreover, the Soviet challenge had become much greater via the augmentation of China's strength. The question now facing U.S. leaders was how to deal with the new, undeniable Sino-Soviet bloc. It was this question, most fundamentally, that led to U.S. engagement with Nationalist Formosa.

In terms of impact on U.S. foreign policy, there seems to be a strong similarity between the Sino-Soviet treaty of February 1950 and the Japanese-German-Italian treaty of September 1940. Each treaty joined together the major powers of Europe and Asia in a common effort to overturn the established structure of power upheld by the United States. By doing this, both treaties precipitated vigorous U.S. countermeasures against the anti-U.S. alliance. Prior to both the 1940 and the 1950 treaties, U.S. diplomacy strove to detach the Asian power from the European power, the latter being deemed in both cases as the more powerful and dangerous of the two challengers. Between the disjuncture of German and Japanese policies brought about by the Soviet-German nonaggression pact of August 1939 and the ascension of Hideki Tojo to power in Tokyo in July 1940, Washington sought to work out a modus vivendi with Japan as a way of detaching that power from Germany. This would allow the United States to concentrate on dealing with the German challenge. Once Japan moved into alliance with Germany, however, U.S. policy rapidly hardened. As much as any other Japanese action, it was Tokyo's decision to ally with the Third Reich that set the country on a course leading to Pearl Harbor. A decade later, in 1950, the Sino-Soviet alliance, by uniting the PRC and the USSR in a common effort to overturn the U.S.-dominated international order, had a similar effect.

Notes

1. This discussion follows Nancy B. Tucker's *Patterns in the Dust: Chinese-American Relations and the Recognition Controversy, 1949–1950,* New York: Columbia University Press, 1983. See also William W. Stueck, *The Road to Confrontation, American Policy Toward China and Korea, 1947–1950,* Chapel Hill: University of North Carolina, 1981.

2. See Dean Acheson's 12 January 1950 speech to the National Press Club in *Department of State Bulletin,* 23 January 1950, pp. 111–19, and Acheson's defense of the administration's China policy to the Senate "MacArthur hearings" in June 1951, in *Hearings Before the Committee on Armed Services and the Committee on Foreign Relations, United States Senate, Eighty-Second Congress, First Session, to Conduct an Inquiry into the Military Situation in the Far East and the Facts Surrounding the Relief of General of the Army Douglas MacArthur from His Assignments in That Area* (hereafter cited as *Military Situation in the Far East*), part 3, 1951, pp. 1837–59.

3. John Lewis Gaddis, "The Strategic Perspective: The Rise and Fall of the 'Defense Perimeter' Concept, 1947–1951," in *Uncertain Years, Chinese-American Relations, 1947–1950,* Dorothy Borg and Waldo Heinrichs, eds., New York: Columbia University Press, 1980, pp. 77–93. See also John Lewis Gaddis, *Strategies of Containment: A Critical Appraisal of Postwar American National Security Policy,* New York: Oxford

University Press, 1982. David Allan Mayers, *Cracking the Monolith: U.S. Policy Against the Sino-Soviet Alliance, 1949–1955,* Baton Rouge: Louisiana State University Press, 1986. Gordon H. Chang, *Friends and Enemies: The United States, China, and the Soviet Union, 1948–1972,* Stanford University Press, 1990.

4. Samuel E. Morrison, *History of United States Naval Operations in World War II,* vol. XII, *Leyte, June 1944–January 1945,* Boston: Little, Brown, 1970, pp. 4–11. Ernest J. King, *Fleet Admiral King: A Naval Record,* New York: W.W. Norton, 1952, pp. 566–67. Chester W. Nimitz, *Triumph in the Pacific: The Navy's Struggle Against Japan,* Englewood Cliffs, N.J.: Prentice Hall, 1963, pp. 96–97.

5. Norman Polmar and Jurrien Nost, *Submarines of the Russian and Soviet Navies, 1718–1990,* Annapolis, MD: Naval Institute Press, 1991, pp. 137–48.

6. JCS memorandum for the Secretary of Defense, 24 November 1948, NSC 37, National Archives.

7. Memoir of Secretary of Defense, 24 November 1948, Record Group 273, NSC 37.

8. Draft report by NSC on the position of the United States with respect to Formosa, 19 January 1949, NSC 37/1.

9. NSC 37/1, 19 January 1949.

10. NSC 37/2, 3 February 1949, Record Group 273, National Archives.

11. Memorandum for Secretary of Defense, "The Strategic Importance of Formosa," 10 February 1949, NSC 37.

12. Draft report by the NSC on supplementary measures with respect to Formosa, 3 March 1949, NSC 37/5.

13. NSC 37/4, 18 February 1949.

14. NSC 37/6, 4 August 1949.

15. JSC to Secretary Johnson, 17 August 1949, in *Foreign Relations of the United States (FRUS),* 1949, vol. IX, pp. 376–78.

16. Gaddis, *Strategies of Containment,* pp. 68–69.

17. Edward John Marolda, *U.S. Navy and the Chinese Civil War,* doctoral dissertation, George Washington University, 1990, p. 103.

18. NSC 48/2, 30 December 1949, RG 273, NSC 48, National Archives. Regarding the evolution of the strategy of using Titoism to contain the Soviet Union, see Gaddis, *Strategies of Containment,* pp. 68–71.

19. *New York Times,* 2 June 1951, p. 4.

20. *Department of State Bulletin,* 16 January 1950, p. 79.

21. *Department of State Bulletin,* 23 January 1950, pp. 111–18.

22. Sergei N. Gancharov, Xue Litai, and John W. Lewis, *Uncertain Partners: Stalin, Mao and the Korean War,* Stanford University Press, 1993. Chen Jian, *China's Road to the Korean War: The Making of the Sino-American Confrontation,* New York: Columbia University Press, 1994

23. Aitchen K. Wu, *China and the Soviet Union,* London: Methuen, 1950, pp. 415–19.

24. Qiang Zhai, "Transplanting the Chinese Model: Chinese Military Advisors and the First Vietnam War, 1950–1954," *Journal of Military History,* no. 57 (October 1992), p. 692.

25. Chen Jian, *China's Road,* pp. 97–98.

26. Goncharov et al., *Uncertain Partners,* p. 69.

27. Ibid., pp. 99–100.

28. Chen Jian, *China's Road,* pp. 101–2.

29. Ibid.

30. NSC 68, *FRUS,* 1950, vol. I, pp. 234–61.

31. This interpretation of NSC 68 differs from that of Gaddis, *Strategies of Contain-*

ment, pp. 89–109, 116. Gaddis finds NSC 68 a "deeply flawed document" that erroneously lumped all Communists together. "Fragmentation of the Communist world might be a desirable objective, but treating communists everywhere as equally dangerous was not the way to achieve it," Gaddis says. Gaddis traces NSC 68 to the influence of Paul H. Nitze, who succeeded Kennan as director of policy planning at the end of 1949. Gaddis identifies Kennan as the major proponent of drawing the PRC away from the USSR, and correctly argues that NSC 68 lumped the Chinese and the Soviet Communists together. He ignores, however, the treaty and ancillary documents of February 1950 which joined Chinese and Soviets together.

32. There is no space here to debate whether these perceptions were accurate. The mainstream scholarly interpretation in the United States is probably that they were inaccurate. I would argue, however, that a policy of *sic vis paxum parra bellum* (an ancient Roman maxim meaning "He who desires peace prepares for war") did, in fact, help prevent a general, hot East-West war during the post-1945 decades. Nor does new evidence confirm the proposition that Stalin would not have attempted to fill power vacuums that continued to exist around the Soviet periphery in the postwar period.

33. Harry S. Truman, *Memoirs of Harry S. Truman,* vol. II, *Years of Trial and Hope,* Garden City, NY: Doubleday, 1956, p. 398.

34. James F. Schnabel, *United States Army in the Korean War, Policy and Direction: The First Year,* Washington: Office of the Chief of Military History, U.S. Army, 1972, p. 367.

35. General Douglas MacArthur, "Memorandum on Formosa," 14 June 1950, NSC 37/10.

36. *Military Situation in the Far East,* part 1, p. 181–85.

37. Truman, *Years of Trial and Hope,* p. 403.

38. Ibid., p. 408.

39. *FRUS,* 1950, vol. VII, pp. 1397–1403.

40. Marolda, *U.S. Navy,* pp. 117–18.

41. Ibid., p. 119.

42. *FRUS,* 1950, vol. VI, p. 418.

43. In addition to the comments by Acheson during this period cited above, see his "United States Policy Toward Asia," a speech delivered on 15 March 1950, in *Department of State Bulletin,* 27 March 1950, pp. 467–71.

3

Nationalist China and the
Korean War

The Strategic Debate over Nationalist China
and the Korean War

Policy toward Nationalist China was a key dimension of the clash between President Harry S. Truman and General Douglas MacArthur in 1950–51. The conflict between Truman and MacArthur over who was to set foreign policy for the United States played out against the background of differing conceptions of the United States' relationship with Nationalist China. Prior to China's entry into the Korean War in November 1950, policy toward Nationalist China was the major point of substantive disagreement between MacArthur and the Truman Administration. After China's entry, the focus of substantive difference shifted to limited versus an expanded war, yet even then, differing concepts about the utility of Nationalist China continued to figure prominently in the debate. Focusing on the substantive background of the Truman-MacArthur debate causes the limits of the Truman Administration's reengagement with Nationalist China to become clear. The subsequent policy of Dwight D. Eisenhower's administration is also best seen against the backdrop of the Truman-MacArthur debates over policy toward Nationalist China.

MacArthur viewed Truman's 27 June 1950 order deploying the Seventh Fleet to protect Formosa as reflecting a fundamental shift in the estimated strategic importance of Formosa. From MacArthur's perspective, Formosa

LIVERPOOL
JOHN MOORES UNIVERSITY
AVRIL ROBARTS LRC
TEL. 0151 231 4022

would now play an important role in maintaining American supremacy over the Pacific Ocean. To Secretary of State Dean Acheson, however, this "was not the idea at all."[1] From Acheson's perspective, the U.S. engagement with the Nationalists and Taiwan was a temporary expedient, a function of the conflict in Korea. Although the policy of exploiting Sino-Soviet tensions was deeply modified by the Sino-Soviet alliance and the Korean War, Acheson and Truman were not willing to discard it entirely. Military necessity had forced the neutralization of Taiwan, but the United States should be aware of the substantial costs associated with this, and the relationship should be kept to the minimum required by military exigencies.[2] This meant that while protecting Nationalist Formosa from Communist attack, the United States would keep it at arm's length. Once peace was restored in Korea, the United States should be prepared, if Beijing's response was right, to disengage from Nationalist China.

MacArthur had a very different view both of Chiang Kai-shek and of the United States' relationship with Nationalist China. For MacArthur, the central political fact of Chiang's career was his unalterable opposition to Communism in China. Whatever other shortcomings Chiang may have had, MacArthur believed, he had stood in uncompromising opposition to the growth of Communist power in China. MacArthur was convinced that the large majority of ordinary Asians were opposed to Communism, and were therefore inclined to look with sympathy on Chiang and his life's effort. Moreover, in its effort to rally Asia's anti-Communist forces, the United States should encourage and support such staunch anti-Communists as Chiang.

Soon after Truman's declaration of 27 June engaging U.S. forces to "neutralize" Taiwan, the administration began signaling the provisional nature of that action. This was largely in response to British and Indian pressure and motivated by a desire to secure the political support of those two countries for the effort in Korea. London had grave doubts about the wisdom of the Korean intervention and deeply feared that the fighting would spread beyond Korea, perhaps becoming a general war which would detract from the Western effort to defend Europe against the USSR.[3] India too urged Washington to avoid associating with the rump Nationalist regime and to signal U.S. willingness to accept the PRC's claim to that island. In response to these diplomatic pressures, the Truman Administration signaled that U.S. intervention in Formosa was a temporary measure associated with the conflict in Korea. On 19 July 1950 Truman sent a message to Congress, saying:

> In order that there may be no doubt in any quarter about our intention regarding Formosa, I wish to state that the United States has no territorial ambitions whatever concerning that island, nor do we seek for ourselves any special

position or privilege on Formosa. The present military neutralization of Formosa is without prejudice to the political questions affecting that island. Our desire is that Formosa not become embroiled in hostilities ... and that all questions affecting Formosa be settled by peaceful means as envisaged in the Charter of the United Nations.

With peace reestablished, even the most complex political questions are susceptible of solution. In the presence of brutal and unprovoked aggression, however, some of these questions may have to be held in abeyance in the interest of the essential security of all.[4]

Twelve days after Truman's statement to Congress, General MacArthur arrived in Taipei for discussions with Chiang Kai-shek. He left the next day. MacArthur was impressed by the quality of the Nationalist military forces he saw during his visit to Formosa. Although lacking equipment and in definite need of training, they were "excellent," with good morale and good overall quality, MacArthur later testified to Congress. In sum, they represented a "potential of a half million first-class fighting men."[5]

Acheson saw MacArthur's visit as a deliberate attempt to associate the United States with Nationalist China just as the administration was striving to stress the arm's-length nature of that relationship. According to Acheson's memoir, "Official Washington was startled to read in the press on August 1 that General MacArthur had arrived in Formosa, kissed Madame Chiang's hand, and gone into conference with her husband."[6] Acheson believed that MacArthur's visit to Taiwan, with its high-profile meeting between MacArthur—who had now added Commander of United Nations (U.N.) forces in Korea to his list of positions—and Generalissimo Chiang would inevitably be interpreted as a sign of new cordiality and cooperation in U.S.–Republic of China (ROC) relations. MacArthur's subsequent explanation of his visit was that Truman's 27 June statement had charged him with responsibility for the effective defense of Formosa, and that this task required that he understand the situation on that island and make arrangements for the effective cooperation of U.S. and Nationalist forces. This required, in turn, a personal inspection of the island and discussions with Chiang Kai-shek. While MacArthur's rationale for his Taiwan visit was impeccable, he certainly understood its broader political implications as well as Acheson. MacArthur felt that signals of new U.S.-ROC cordiality and cooperation were exactly what was needed.

At the time, it was widely reported that MacArthur had gone to Taipei without authorization from, or even against orders from, Washington. This was not the case. A 1 July 1950 letter from Acheson to Ambassador Wellington Koo had asked the Nationalist government to consult with a representative of MacArthur's headquarters regarding the defense of Taiwan. A week later the State Department's political adviser to CINCFE, William J. Sebald, informed Washington that MacArthur planned to visit Taiwan at the first available opportunity to investigate the situation there.[7] Later, when Army Chief of Staff General J. Lawton Collins visited MacArthur's Tokyo headquarters in mid-July, MacArthur told him that he intended to visit Formosa for talks with Chiang Kai-shek as soon as the situation in Korea was stabilized. Collins did not object. Shortly after Collins's visit, the JCS informed MacArthur of Beijing's continuing declarations of intent to invade Formosa, and warned that such an invasion would probably succeed unless the Nationalists took swift and vigorous defensive measures. In reply, MacArthur informed the JCS that he intended to visit Formosa about 31 July to survey the situation there. The JCS answered with a suggestion that, pending the issuance of new instructions on policy issues regarding Formosa by Washington, it might be wise for MacArthur to send a senior officer to Taipei rather than going there himself. The JCS added, however, that if MacArthur felt it necessary, he should feel free to go to Formosa, as the responsibility was his own.[8]

But if MacArthur's visit to Taipei did not involve subordination, his efforts to keep the State Department in the dark certainly exacerbated suspicions in Washington. MacArthur declined to let his State Department adviser, William Sebald, accompany him to Taiwan, on the basis that only military matters would be discussed.[9] The U.S. Embassy in Taipei also knew nothing of MacArthur's mission to Taiwan until a member of the general's entourage telephoned from Taipei's Songshan Airport after his arrival there. The technicalities of interdepartmental communications could not, however, obscure the broader issue: what was at stake was the nature of the U.S. relationship with Nationalist Formosa. Below the quibbles over the adequacy of bureaucratic coordination was a basic difference in perspective toward U.S. links with Formosa. MacArthur saw his visit as a perfectly acceptable way of consolidating America's vital strategic defense perimeter into the western Pacific, while Acheson wished to keep Nationalist Formosa at arm's length pending some sort of accommodation with Communist China once the fighting in Korea stopped.[10] Again, it is necessary to keep in mind that this debate was prior to China's entry into the Korean War. After China's entry, the terms of debate changed, and Acheson moved much closer to MacArthur's position.

Following his conferences with MacArthur, Chiang Kai-shek issued a statement reporting that agreement had been reached "on all problems discussed," and that "The foundation for the joint defense of Formosa and for Sino-American military cooperation has thus been laid."[11] Several aspects of Chiang's statement were objectionable to the State Department: the implication that broad political questions had been discussed; the assertion that the United States and Nationalist China were joined in "common cause" against Communism in Asia; the idea that ROC armed forces were now under the "determined leadership" of CINCFE; and, most of all, the implication that some sort of U.S.-ROC military alliance was being established. Acheson was most alarmed by what he perceived to be MacArthur's and Chiang's joint effort to determine U.S. policy. A report by the State Department's Office of Chinese Affairs surmised that Chiang Kai-shek was encouraging MacArthur in his efforts to move the United States closer to Formosa. Chiang was "playing Tokyo and Washington as two separate, competing entities," the report said.[12] The Pentagon shared the State Department's apprehension that independent actions by MacArthur might create a new de facto relationship with Nationalist China. To exclude the possibility that MacArthur might create a U.S.-Nationalist military relationship by deploying U.S. military units to Taiwan under his authority to neutralize that island, the JCS informed MacArthur that it was the president's intention to limit the defense of Taiwan to operations carried out without committing U.S. forces to the island itself. MacArthur was therefore to make no commitment to place U.S. forces there even in the event of attack. No U.S. forces were to be deployed to Formosa without specific JCS approval.[13]

The confusion surrounding MacArthur's conference with Chiang Kai-shek led Truman to dispatch his special assistant W. Averell Harriman to Tokyo to convey presidential views on Formosa. MacArthur and Harriman were old friends. The two discussed the Formosan issue in Tokyo on 6 August and 8 August 1950. From his talks with Harriman, MacArthur gained the "very definite impression" that:

> There was no fixed and comprehensive United States policy for the Far East; that foreign influences, especially those of Great Britain, were very powerful in Washington; that there was no apparent interest in mounting an offensive against the Communists; that we were content to attempt to block their moves, but not to initiate any counter-moves; that we would defend Formosa if attacked, just as we had done in Korea; that President Truman had conceived a violent animosity toward Chiang Kai-shek; and that anyone who favored the Generalissimo might well arouse the President's disfavor. He left me with a feeling of concern and uneasiness that the situation in the Far East was little understood and mistakenly downgraded in high circles in Washington.[14]

For his part, Harriman reported back to Truman that MacArthur "has a strange idea that we should back anybody who will fight Communism" even though U.S. association with Chiang Kai-shek would create more difficulties than positive contributions. Harriman explained to MacArthur that unity in the United Nations over the Korean issue was of "overwhelming importance." Association with Chiang could create a split in UN ranks. Many countries were opposed to association with Chiang: Britain, India, "and such countries as Norway, who although stalwart in their determination to resist Russian invasion, did not want to stir up trouble elsewhere." Harriman pointed out to MacArthur the fundamental conflict between the United States' interest in military neutralization of Taiwan and Chiang Kaishek's interest in using Taiwan as a steppingstone for return to the mainland. Yet MacArthur simply could not understand that Chiang was a "liability." MacArthur felt that the United States was not improving its situation by "kicking Chiang around" and "undermining" him. In spite of his manifold disagreements with Washington's perspectives on Chiang Kaishek, MacArthur said he accepted President Truman's position and would act accordingly. Yet Harriman left with a sense of unease: "For reasons which are rather difficult to explain, I did not feel that we came to a full agreement on the way we believed things should be handled on Formosa and with the Generalissimo."[15]

On 17 August 1950, nine days after he met with Harriman, MacArthur received a letter from the commander of the Veterans of Foreign Wars (VFW), inviting him to send a message to that group's forthcoming annual encampment. According to MacArthur's memoir, he routinely received and answered many such invitations. The general drafted a message which he felt, so he later claimed, fully supported President Truman's policy on Taiwan. He sent it to the Army Department for clearance ten days before the encampment. The Army found nothing objectionable in it. More politically attuned quarters did, however. Three days before the VFW encampment, MacArthur received a cable from Secretary of Defense Louis Johnson directing him in the name of "the President of the United States" to withdraw the message on the grounds that "various features with respect to Formosa are in conflict with the policy of the United States."[16]

The thrust of MacArthur's VFW address ran counter to administration policy toward Taiwan. On 25 August, Truman sent a letter to U.N. Secretary-General Trygve Lie as part of an effort to placate London, New Delhi, Beijing, and other concerned capitals by indicating the provisional nature of the new U.S. relationship with Nationalist China. Responding to Beijing's charges of aggressive U.S. actions toward China's territory, Taiwan, Truman's letter said that the United States' actions toward Formosa were impartial, addressing both the forces on Formosa and those on the mainland. The United States neither had designs on Formosa nor desired to acquire a "special position" there.[17] In a further effort to ease tensions arising from the Formosan issue, Truman told a press conference on 31 August that "It will not be necessary to keep the Seventh Fleet in the

Formosa Strait if the Korean thing is settled. That is a flank protection on our part for the United Nations forces."[18] U.S. engagement with Nationalist China was provisional and might be undone once the fighting in Korea stopped.

The same day Truman sent his letter to Secretary General Lie, 25 August 1950, the 1 September issue of *U.S. News and World Report* went to press. It contained MacArthur's VFW address, in spite of the fact that MacArthur subsequently professed to have complied with Johnson's order of 20 August. Acheson was "outraged" by the article's "effrontery and damaging effect at home and abroad."[19] Aside from running counter to the purposes of Truman's letter to Lie, Acheson saw the letter as a "very gratuitous attack on what *had been* the policies of the administration before the Korean War," for example, not protecting Taiwan. Truman believed the publication of MacArthur's VFW speech "could only serve to confuse the world as to just what our Formosan policy was."[20]

The arguments in MacArthur's VFW address were the same as those in the general's 14 June 1950 memorandum, which had played a pivotal role in prompting the decision to neutralize Taiwan; but while the geopolitical logic of neutralizing Taiwan had impelled the administration to protect Taiwan, it was unwilling to allow that objective to completely override broader diplomatic objectives. This MacArthur's VFW address threatened to do so by stressing the geopolitical importance of Formosa. The threat was best encapsulated by the memorable phrase that Taiwan was "an unsinkable aircraft carrier and submarine tender," from which a hostile power could "overshadow the strategic importance of the central and southern flank of the United States front-line position" in Asia. This statement implicitly conflicted with Truman's policy that U.S. protection of Taiwan was a temporary expedient deriving from the conflict in Korea. If Formosa was as vital to the overall U.S. position in East Asia as MacArthur's VFW address suggested, it was hardly likely that the United States would abandon it merely because the fighting stopped in Korea. MacArthur's address also asserted that "Nothing could be more fallacious than the threadbare argument by those who advocate appeasement and defeatism in the Pacific that *if we defend Formosa we alienate continental Asia*" (emphasis added). As we saw in chapter 2, this approach happened to be the direction approved by President Truman prior to June 1950.

Following the publication of MacArthur's VFW speech, Truman discussed with his advisers the possibility of relieving MacArthur of his commands, but decided against it. The question of who would determine U.S. policy toward Nationalist China was an important consideration, but MacArthur was an immensely popular and prestigious general and his removal would give ammunition to critics of the administration's policies. Truman determined to handle his deepening conflict with MacArthur with great forbearance and patience.

During their meeting at Wake Island on 15 October 1950, Truman and MacArthur discussed the role of Nationalist China. MacArthur apologized for any embarrassment his VFW address had caused Truman. He had thought, MacArthur explained, that his letter to the VFW was "right down the line" of the president's policy on Formosa; otherwise, he would not have sent it. The president then said that he considered the whole matter closed. MacArthur concurred.[21]

Nationalist China's Role Following PRC Entry into the Korean War

The entry into the Korean War of several hundred thousand Chinese People's Volunteers (CPV) on 28 November 1950 created, in MacArthur's phrase, an "entirely new war." This led MacArthur to reverse an earlier endorsement of Washington's rejection of a Nationalist offer of troops for Korea. Shortly after North Korea's invasion of the South, Nationalist Chinese authorities had offered 33,000 "seasoned troops" for the common effort. The administration had declined this offer because of its desire to secure British and Indian support in the United Nations over Korea. MacArthur had concurred in this decision largely because he believed that Nationalist forces should concentrate on the vital defense of Taiwan. Large-scale Chinese intervention in Korea now altered the situation in the Taiwan Strait, according to MacArthur. With forces committed in Korea, it was unlikely that China would attack in the Taiwan Strait. This conclusion was tied to MacArthur's larger strategic vision. It was in China's interest, he concluded, to limit the new war to Korea so that China could concentrate its forces there. It was in the United States' interest, however, to utilize its exterior lines of communication and its superior air and naval forces to confront China with multiple, geographically disparate challenges, thereby compelling China to divide its forces and taxing its weak transportation system.

Truman was committed to limiting the war to the Korean peninsula. Europe—not Asia—Truman, Acheson, and Marshal felt, was where the United States should concentrate its strength. There was also the possibility that Moscow might enter an expanded Sino-American war, possibly throwing its weight against the United States in some theater other than the Far East. The February 1950 treaty obligated the USSR to assist China "with all means at its disposal" if China became "involved in a state of war" with the United States. An expanded Sino-U.S. war, Truman feared, might touch off World War III.

On the morning of 29 November 1950, Washington received a message from MacArthur, recalling Chiang's earlier offer of 33,000 troops and reporting that these troops represented "the only source of potential trained reinforcement available for early commitment" to Korea. These forces could be moved to Korea in approximately fourteen days, MacArthur reported. He also predicted that Chiang would be willing to provide a much larger force, and proposed that he negotiate directly with the Nationalist government to this end.[22] A joint State-Defense meeting considered MacArthur's proposal. George Marshall (who replaced Louis Johnson as Secretary of Defense on 19 September 1950[23]) argued against MacArthur's proposal on the grounds that "Our position of leadership is being most seriously compromised in the United Nations," and that "The utmost care will be necessary to avoid disruption of the essential Allied line-up in that organization." Acheson agreed, adding that deployment of Nationalist forces to Korea "would leave us isolated" in the U.N. Moreover, involvement of Nationalist forces might extend hostilities to Formosa and "other areas." Truman endorsed Marshall and Acheson, and an appropriate message was dispatched to MacArthur the evening of 29 November.[24]

When Army Chief of Staff J. Lawton Collins met with MacArthur in Tokyo on 7 December, MacArthur renewed his proposal for utilization of Nationalist forces. The situation of the U.N. Command was dire. If the enemy offensive continued and substantial reinforcements were not forthcoming, and if the present restrictions on the U.N. Command were continued, MacArthur said, it would soon be necessary to evacuate Korea. MacArthur listed four major "restrictions," the last of which was no reinforcement of Korea with Chinese Nationalist forces. If he could secure 50 to 60,000 Nationalist troops he could secure a defensive line across Korea, MacArthur told Collins.[25]

In his Senate testimony in May 1951, shortly after his recall, MacArthur elaborated on the logic of using Nationalist forces for diversionary actions. When the U.S. government had considered and rejected use of Nationalist forces in June 1950, MacArthur explained, two Communist Field Armies had been concentrated for invasion of Taiwan. In those circumstances, Nationalist forces were needed for the defense of Taiwan. Redeployment of Chinese Nationalist forces outside the Taiwan theater would have weakened Taiwan in the face of a strong invasion threat. By late 1950, however, the situation was different. The strong Chinese Communist armies previously concentrated against Taiwan had been redeployed to Manchuria or Korea. In these circumstances, a substantial portion of Nationalist forces could be freed from defense of Formosa. If the Nationalists were allowed to undertake offensive operations against the Chinese Communists, Nationalist attacks would force Beijing to deploy forces to guard the coastal areas. If the United States enhanced Nationalist military capabilities by providing weapons, training, and advice, the diversionary effect of such Nationalist offensive operations would be increased. "The slightest use" of Nationalist troops would have "taken the pressure off my troops" in Korea, MacArthur told the Senate.[26]

The main grounds for rejecting overt use of Nationalist forces, either in Korea or against the mainland to relieve pressure on U.N. forces in Korea, was fear that such action might lead to a general war with China, which would redound to the benefit of the USSR. George Marshall most frequently and forcefully raised this concern. Marshall strongly felt that Europe was and must remain the center of gravity for U.S. strategy. At a top-level meeting convened immediately after word of China's massive intervention reached Washington, Marshall argued that if the United States became engaged in a general war with China in Asia, it would be less able and willing to deploy forces to Europe to deal with the Soviet threat. If, as Marshall believed likely, Moscow remained a nonbelligerent in Korea while supporting its Chinese ally by all means short of war, Moscow would be able to achieve overwhelming superiority in Europe. A U.S.-Chinese war would also strengthen the USSR-PRC alliance, rather than undermining it as U.S. interests required.[27] Western European governments shared these concerns.[28]

Exclusion of an *overt* Nationalist role was, in other words, part of the administration's strategy of limited war. MacArthur disagreed with this strategy, and his differing prescriptions regarding employment of Nationalist forces followed from this. The potentialities that MacArthur believed to be presented by Nationalist Chinese forces played an important role in his efforts to force Truman to abandon the strategy of limited war. While Nationalist military and political potential was less important to MacArthur's proposed alternate strategy of expanded war than U.S. technological superiority and the advantages of exterior lines of movement, those potentialities nonetheless played an important role in the general's proposed strategy. From Truman's perspective, MacArthur's proposal to overtly utilize Nationalist potential was likely to contribute to the onset of a general U.S.-PRC war.

One contingency in which the Truman Administration was apparently prepared for *overt* employment of Nationalist forces was if U.N. forces were forced out of Korea. Following China's entry and the retreat of U.N. forces before the Chinese advance, U.S. leaders recognized the possibility that U.N. forces might be forced out of Korea. In such an eventuality, the United States would seek to continue the struggle through other means.

Nationalist forces might play an important role in such an eventuality.[29]

MacArthur's discontent with the "restrictions" imposed upon his command led Washington to fear that he might withdraw from Korea in circumstances short of sheer military necessity as a way of forcing an expanded war. This led to issuance of new directives to MacArthur on 29 December 1950, making it clear that he was expected to fight the war with forces on hand, that the United States intended to avoid a "major war," that he was to defend successive positions in South Korea inflicting maximum casualties on advancing Chinese forces, and that he was to withdraw from Korea only if physically compelled to do so by the enemy.[30] MacArthur replied the same day with a call for the lifting of restrictions on his command:

> It is quite clear now that the entire military resource of the Chinese Nation, with logistic support from the Soviet, is committed to a maximum effort against the United Nations Command. In implementation of this commitment a major concentration of Chinese force in the Korean-Manchurian area will increasingly leave China vulnerable in areas whence troops to support Korea operations have been drawn. Meanwhile under existing restrictions our naval and air potential are being only partially utilized and the great potential of Chinese Nationalist force on Formosa and guerrilla action on the Mainland are being ignored. Indeed as to the former we are preventing its employment against a common enemy by our own Naval Force. . . . [As long as these restrictions continue] the concentration of China's military forces solely upon the Korean sector would seem to be sound.[31]

Rather than allowing the Chinese Communists to concentrate their strength in Korea, the United States should use its air and naval superiority to compel China to disperse its forces. Other than air bombardment, all MacArthur's proposed measures involved the Nationalists. Blockading the Chinese coast would require the use of bases on Taiwan. Nationalist forces were to be used in Korea and for "diversionary action (possibly leading to counterinvasion) against vulnerable areas of the Chinese Mainland." "I believe," MacArthur told the JCS, "that by the foregoing measures we could severely cripple and largely neutralize China's capability to wage aggressive war," and "at once release the pressure upon our forces in Korea." MacArthur recognized that "this course of action has been rejected in the past for fear of provoking China to a major war effort," but argued that since Beijing had already committed itself to an all-out effort against the United States, there was "nothing we can do that would further aggravate the situation as far as China is concerned."[32]

On 9 January 1951 the JCS again ordered MacArthur to defend successive positions in Korea and to inflict maximum losses on enemy forces. MacArthur's primary mission was the safety of his forces and the defense of Japan, the JCS said, and if MacArthur felt that withdrawal from South Korea was necessary to achieve this, such a move was authorized. Regarding his proposal to use Nationalist forces in Korea, the JCS told MacArthur that this had been ruled out because they would probably not have a "decisive" effect on the "Korean outcome," while they would be of "greater usefulness elsewhere." The JCS told MacArthur that his suggestions for expanded operations against China were under consideration, but also noted the major difficulties regarding those proposals.[33] As we shall see in chapter 6, Washington was, in fact, moving forward with a plan of *covert* action along the lines of MacArthur's proposal for "expanded operations."

MacArthur replied the next day, 10 January, warning that under current circumstances his forces could not hold a position in Korea *and* defend Japan from attack. The U.S. government would have to choose between holding Korea and defending Japan. If U.N. forces stood in Korea, they would be destroyed, leaving Japan vulnerable to invasion. "Under the extraordinary limitations and conditions imposed upon my command in Korea," MacArthur told the JCS, "its military position is untenable, but it can hold, if overriding political considerations so dictate, for any length of time up to its complete destruction. Your clarification requested."[34] This was read in Washington as an implicit threat to withdraw from Korea unless MacArthur's strategy of expanded war against China was adopted. Acheson's estimate was: "Nothing further was needed to convince me that the General was incurably recalcitrant and basically disloyal to the purposes of his Commander in Chief."[35]

As United Nations forces retreated before the CPV onslaught in January 1951, U.S. leaders gave serious consideration to the overt use of Nationalist forces in the contingency that U.N. forces were forced out of Korea. The high tide of the Chinese advance was reached on 25 January 1951. Thereafter, United Nations forces succeeded in stabilizing a defensive front line south of Seoul and began to slowly push the Chinese northward. Had U.N. forces been thrown out of Korea, the Truman Administration could well have embraced an overt Nationalist attack on the mainland as part of the U.S. response. As it was, the battlefield situation was already beginning to improve on 6 February, when civilian and military leaders met to discuss JCS recommendations for actions to weaken China's war-making ability. The meeting noted that the JCS had drafted its recommendations, which included offensive operations by the Nationalists, when it appeared that United Nations forces would be forced into a beachhead around Pusan. Now, however, circumstances were different: "It appears now that from a military viewpoint circumstances do not warrant using Chinese Nationalist forces on the mainland of Asia. Our actions now are based on the premise that we should do nothing to spread the war outside of Korea," noted the memorandum of the meeting.[36] The NSC decided to move forward with moves to strengthen Nationalist military capabilities, including its offensive capabilities, without *overtly* utilizing those capabilities at present. In mid-March 1951, National Security Agency (NSA) intercepts of transmissions from the Spanish and Portuguese embassies in Tokyo to their home governments, reporting recent discussions with General MacArthur, convinced Truman that MacArthur was deliberately attempting to precipitate a war with Communist China. The general had told the ambassadors of the staunchly anti-Communist governments of Madrid and Lisbon that he was confident that he could dispose of the "Chinese Communist question" once and for all. When this happened, the Soviet Union could either keep out of the war or face destruction itself. These intercepts convinced Truman that MacArthur was playing a dangerous double game of reassuring Washington of his obedience while provoking China—perhaps in collusion with Chiang Kai-shek—to expand the war. Truman could not divulge the contents of these ultrasecret intercepts, since this would let U.S. allies know that the United States was spying on them. Instead, Truman had to rely on public evidence to build a case against MacArthur.[37]

MacArthur was not long in providing the needed justification. The final straw came on 5 April 1951 when Congressman and Republican House leader Joseph Martin read a letter from MacArthur. The letter had been written on 20 March—the same day on which Washington had informed MacArthur of a decision to begin cease-fire negotiations, and on which the general had responded with a public démarche to the commander of the CPV, designed to undermine that initiative. Fittingly, the issue targeted by MacArthur's letter to Martin was the Nationalist role in Korea. Responding to an earlier letter from Martin, which had proposed using Nationalist forces to open "a second Asiatic front to relieve the pressure on our forces in Korea," MacArthur told the congressman that "Your view is in conflict with neither logic nor this tradition [of meeting force with maximum counterforce]." MacArthur's letter also contained the memorable phrase, "There is no substitute for victory," and implicitly criticized those Europe-centered people in Washington who would accept less than victory in Asia.[38] On 11 April, Truman relieved MacArthur of all his commands.

MacArthur's views about the efficacy of an expanded war against China were not shared by the mainstream of the U.S. military leadership. His views about the potential military utility of Nationalist forces and of the utility of Taiwan as a central component of the offshore perimeter were, however, representative of mainstream military opinion. On 11 December 1951, nine months after MacArthur's removal, CIA Director Walter Bedell

Smith warned that Nationalist forces would have to be utilized "within the immediate future, if we are to get any benefit from them." Smith suggested that Nationalist units might be rotated through Korea or used in "temporary thrusts onto the mainland."[39] The JCS concurred with Smith's observation and proposed organization of a two-division Nationalist force for offensive operations. Matthew Ridgway's replacement as commander in Korea, General Mark W. Clark, also favored asking the Nationalists to provide two divisions for Korean service to test their fighting ability against Chinese Communist forces. This time, South Korean President Syngman Rhee nixed the idea.[40] In April 1952 the NSC again debated the wisdom of large-scale offensive use of Nationalist forces.

As before, State Department opposition succeeded in overruling this. There was a consensus at the NSC meetings, however, that Nationalist China constituted a valuable asset, and that the United States should increase Nationalist capabilities, holding them in readiness for use against Communist China should circumstances make this desirable. State Department Counselor Charles Bohlen, an opponent of offensive employment of Nationalist forces, summarized the sense of the NSC meetings: "We clearly want an instrument which will be ready to use if circumstances make its use desirable. We might want at some time, perhaps before long, to take Hainan, to make hit-and-run raids along the mainland, or even to secure a lodgement on the mainland."[41]

The military also chaffed at the Truman Administration's arm's-length approach to Nationalist China in preparation for a post–Korean War modus vivendi with China. In July 1950 the JCS had urged upon Truman the view that the strategic importance of Taiwan was so great that it should be denied to any enemy of the United States regardless of the situation in Korea.[42] During 1951 and 1952, the recommendations of the new CINCFE, General Matthew Ridgway, for the defense and military utilization of Taiwan were repeatedly vetoed by Truman as part of his arm's-length policy.[43]

Nationalist China and the Peace Settlement in Korea

During the first six months of the U.S.-PRC war that began in November 1950, differences over Taiwan were one issue preventing cease-fire negotiations. Beijing insisted that U.S. agreement to withdraw from Taiwan was a precondition for the beginning of talks, while Washington insisted on excluding Taiwan. Washington insisted that talks deal only with stopping the fighting in Korea. Discussion of political issues was separate from stopping the Korean conflict, Washington insisted, and Beijing's insistence on including political issues was tantamount to rejection of negotiations.[44] Beijing, however, insisted that withdrawal of U.S. forces from Taiwan and the Taiwan Strait, and recognition of the Cairo Declaration and the Potsdam Declaration, were necessary for peace in Korea, and would have to be included on the agenda of any cease-fire talks.

As the CPV offensive petered out in early 1951 and then changed to near collapse under the mounting hammering of U.N. forces, Beijing's position on negotiations shifted. Beijing dropped its earlier insistence on inclusion of Taiwan and agreed that negotiations would be limited to strictly military questions. This shift opened the way for the beginning of negotiations. The U.S. negotiating team was under explicit orders not to discuss political issues such as Formosa or U.N. representation. The sole objectives of the talks were to stop the fighting in Korea and to set up a mechanism for ensuring that the armistice agreements were carried out.[45]

Once armistice talks were under way, the question quickly arose of the relation of those talks to subsequent discussion of Taiwan and other "political issues." By September 1951, U.S. leaders had decided that discussions of various "Far Eastern problems" could take place only after achievement of a *political* settlement of the Korean issue, defined to mean achievement of a unified Korea with maximum assurances against renewed invasion or subversion.[46] Moreover, once "Far Eastern political problems" were discussed, the United States would insist that all interested nations would participate. The ROC government, for instance, would be invited to participate in the discussion of the Formosan issue.[47] These decisions meant that U.S. strategy was increasingly directed toward a long-term confrontation with China. Beijing was not to be rewarded with Taiwan for its "aggression" in Korea. And Taiwan was too important an asset in countering Communist China to be abandoned merely because the first round in what promised to be a long contest was over.

Notes

1. Dean Acheson, *Present at the Creation: My Years in the State Department,* New York: W.W. Norton, 1969, p. 422.

2. In March 1950, for example, Acheson warned the Senate Foreign Relations Committee that "everyone who has talked with [Chiang] comes back with one thought, and that is that he believes World War III is absolutely inevitable, that the United States will have to go back and conquer China, and that he will come riding in on our coat tails."

3. See discussion between British ambassador Oliver Franks and U.S. officials in August 1950 in *Foreign Relations of the United States (FRUS), 1950,* vol. VI, pp. 464–66, 467–68. Also, pp. 431–33, 444–46.

4. *Department of State Bulletin,* 31 July 1950, p. 166.

5. *Military Situation in the Far East, Hearings Before the Committee on Armed Services and the Committee on Foreign Relations, United States Senate, Eighty Second*

Congress, First Session, to Conduct an Inquiry into the Military Situation in the Far East and the Facts Surrounding the Relief of General of the Army Douglas MacArthur from His Assignments in That Area, Part I, Washington: Government Printing Office, 1951, p. 23. (Hereafter cited as *Military Situation in the Far East.*)

6. Acheson, *Present at the Creation,* p. 422.

7. *FRUS,* 1950, vol. VI, p. 370.

8. James F. Schnabel, *United States Army in the Korean War, Policy and Direction: The First Year,* Washington: Office of the Chief of Military History, U.S. Army, 1972, P. 368.

9. William Sebald, *With MacArthur in Tokyo,* New York: W.W. Norton, 1965, pp. 122–24.

10. *FRUS,* 1950, vol. VI, p. 439.

11. *New York Times,* 2 August 1950, p. 6.

12. *FRUS,* 1950, vol. VI, p. 486.

13. James F. Schnabel and Robert J. Watson, *The History of the Joint Chiefs of Staff, The Joint Chiefs of Staff and National Policy,* vol. III, *The Korean War* (hereafter cited as *The Korean War*), part I, Wilmington, DE: Michael Glazier, 1979, p. 513.

14. Douglas MacArthur, *Reminiscences,* New York: McGraw Hill, 1964, p. 341.

15. *FRUS,* 1950, vol. XIV, pp. 427–30.

16. MacArthur, *Reminiscences,* p. 341.

17. Ibid., p. 342.

18. *Public Papers of the Presidents of the United States: Harry S. Truman, 1950,* Washington: Government Printing Office, 1965, p. 607.

19. Acheson, *Present at the Creation,* p. 423.

20. Harry S. Truman, *Memoirs of Harry S. Truman,* vol. II, *Years of Trial and Hope,* Garden City, NY: Doubleday, 1956, pp. 354–55.

21. *FRUS,* 1950, vol. VI, pp. 533–34.

22. *FRUS,* 1950, vol. VII, p. 1253.

23. Louis Johnson had balked at ordering MacArthur to withdraw his VFW address, as he was ordered to do by Truman. This confirmed Truman's growing beliefs regarding Johnson's incompetence and his disloyalty to the administration. See Joseph C. Goulden, *Korea, The Untold Story of the War,* New York: McGraw Hill, 1982, pp. 157–63.

24. Walter S. Poole, *The Joint Chiefs of Staff and National Policy, 1950–1952,* Washington: Historical Division, Joint Secretariat, Joint Chiefs of Staff, 1979, p. 397.

25. *FRUS,* 1950, vol. VII, p. 1469 n.

26. *Military Situation in the Far East,* part I, p. 22.

27. *FRUS,* 1950, vol. VII, p. 1243.

28. Ibid., p. 1087.

29. Truman, *Years of Trial and Hope,* p. 400.

30. Acheson, *Present at the Creation,* pp. 514–15.

31. *FRUS,* 1950, vol. VII, pp. 1631–33.

32. Ibid., p. 1631.

33. Poole, *The Joint Chiefs of Staff and National Policy,* p. 398. Acheson, *Present at the Creation,* pp. 514–15.

34. Poole, *The Joint Chiefs of Staff and National Policy,* p. 398.

35. Acheson, *Present at the Creation,* p. 516.

36. *FRUS,* 1950, vol. VII, pp. 1567–68.

37. Joseph C. Goulden, *Korea, the Untold Story of the War,* New York: McGraw Hill, 1982, pp. 477–78.

38. MacArthur, *Reminiscences,* p. 386.

39. Poole, *The Joint Chiefs of Staff and National Policy*, p. 407.

40. Report by JSPC to JCS, 10 March 1958. RG 218 (JCS), Geographic File 1957, 381 Formosa, box 9, sec. 35, JCS 2118/97, National Archives.

41. *FRUS,* 1952–54, vol. XIV, p. 35.

42. Schnabel and Watson, *The Korean War,* pp. 506–8.

43. Poole, *The Joint Chiefs of Staff and National Policy,* pp. 403–7.

44. See statement by Secretary of State Dean Acheson in *FRUS,* 1951, vol. VII, pp. 88–93.

45. William H. Vatcher, *Panmunjom, The Story of the Korean Military Armistice Negotiations,* NY: Praeger, 1958, pp. 14–15, 21, 28. Walter G. Hermes, *Truce Tent and Fighting Front,* Washington: Office of the Chief of Military History, U.S. Army, 1966, pp. 13–17.

46. *FRUS,* 1951, vol. VII, pp. 887–88, 914–15.

47. Ibid., pp. 218, 867.

4

Formation of the
U.S.-Nationalist Alliance

Nationalist Formosa and Eisenhower's New Look

The views of the incoming Republican administration in 1953 led to a much more prominent role for Nationalist China in U.S. strategy. In May 1953 Dwight Eisenhower directed his newly appointed chiefs of staff to reevaluate U.S. global strategic military orientation.[1] Several broad considerations drove this review. One was the belief that U.S. forces were mal-deployed, with too many stationed at forward positions overseas, leaving too small a strategic reserve in the continental United States. Redeployment of U.S. forces to the United States also had budgetary advantages. Eisenhower and the JCS feared, however, that too large or too rapid a withdrawal of U.S. forces from overseas would embolden the Communist powers, while undermining the confidence of countries friendly to the United States in America's ability and willingness to protect them. Thus, the strategic redeployment of U.S. forces back to the United States was to be matched by increases in the capabilities of "indigenous forces." In Asia, Taiwan offered some of the most promising "indigenous forces."

A second broad consideration driving Eisenhower's strategic review was a belief that the United States had to seize the initiative in the Cold War through a more aggressive orientation toward the Sino-Soviet bloc. The United States should no longer merely respond to Communist advances, Eisenhower felt. Unless the United States seized the initiative, the Soviet

Union would have little incentive to negotiate seriously with the United States. In line with this, the United States should pursue overt and covert activities designed to undermine the power, prestige, and unity of the Communist powers. There was, of course, a contradiction between this desire for a more aggressive orientation toward the Sino-Soviet bloc and the desire to redeploy U.S. forces to the continental United States. One way in which this contradiction was addressed was through the buildup of the capabilities of U.S. allies in forward areas. Again, this pointed toward Nationalist China.

The result of Eisenhower's strategic review was NSC 146/2, approved by Eisenhower on 6 November 1953. NSC 146/2 formally incorporated Formosa into the western Pacific defense perimeter. The Truman Administration's NSC 48/5 of May 1951 specified "the off-shore defense line" to include "Japan-Ryukyu-Philippines-Australia and New Zealand," with the addendum that the United States would "Deny Formosa to any Chinese regime aligned with or dominated by the USSR." In other words, under Truman, Formosa, not being a part of the United States strategic perimeter, might *not* be "denied" to a China *not* "aligned with or dominated by the USSR." Eisenhower's NSC 146/2 altered this by providing that the United States would "Effectively incorporate Formosa and the Pescadores within U.S. Far East defense positions by taking all necessary measures to prevent hostile forces from gaining control thereof, *even at grave risk of general war,* and by making it clear that the United States will so react to any attack" [emphasis added].[2] In spite of these seemingly severe words, this implied a lower level of U.S. commitment than that given to the other components of the western Pacific offshore chain. Aggression by Sino-Soviet bloc forces against Japan, South Korea, the Philippines, Australia, and New Zealand would *automatically* involve the United States in war. For Taiwan and Indochina, the U.S. commitment was not "automatic," but U.S. interests were so great that an attack on them would probably compel the United States to react with military force, either locally at the point of attack or generally against the military power of the aggressor. There were two major reasons for this more flexible level of U.S. commitment to Formosa. First, the state of civil war that still existed between Nationalist China and Communist China, and that made Nationalist Formosa so useful for limited offensive operations against China, involved certain risks. Second, and relatedly, there were basic disagreements between the United States and the Nationalists regarding the "return" of the Nationalists to the mainland.[3] Throughout its alliance with Nationalist China, the United States was compelled to deal with dilemmas arising out of a fundamental divergence of objectives. While the United States viewed maintenance of Taiwan in the western Pacific perimeter as vital to U.S. security, and was prepared to risk general war to attain this objective, it was not prepared for war to liberate the Chinese people from Communism. That was China's own struggle. The Nationalist objective, however, was nothing less than destruction of the Communist regime and emancipation of the Chinese people from Communist tyranny. Out of this divergence of objectives arose troublesome dilemmas.

The Mutual Security Treaty

The decision to formally incorporate Formosa into the western Pacific off-shore defense perimeter laid the basis for the conclusion of the U.S.-ROC mutual defense treaty of December 1954. The initiative for that treaty came from Taipei. Taipei wanted a mutual security treaty because it would stabilize U.S. policy toward Taiwan, making it more difficult for Washington to radically shift policy toward Taiwan, perhaps embracing Taiwan independence, creating a U.N. trusteeship over Taiwan, or abandoning Taiwan for the sake of a modus vivendi with Beijing. Once the United States signed a formal mutual security treaty with the government in Taipei, it became politically and legally more difficult for the United States to alter course, adopting a new orientation that might ignore its treaty partner, the government in Taipei. A treaty with the United States would also enhance the domestic and international respectability of the Nationalist regime.[4]

From Washington's perspective, the mutual security treaty served several purposes. It helped deter PRC military action against Taiwan by eliminating any ambiguity as to the American commitment to Taiwan's defense. Formal extension of U.S. military protection to Taiwan might also encourage Beijing to accommodate the de facto separation of that island from the mainland. De facto acceptance might then gradually move toward de jure recognition. Incorporation of Taiwan and its assets into the common security effort of the Free World would strengthen that effort. A mutual security treaty would also provide a political and legal basis for utilization of bases in Taiwan by U.S. military forces, should that become necessary. Greater Free World strength would deter Sino-Soviet adventurism. Washington was also cognizant of the positive effects a treaty would have on the Nationalists' domestic and international position, and it approved of those effects. A legitimate partner in Taipei was a more effective partner.

Until late 1954, the Eisenhower Administration rejected a mutual defense treaty with Nationalist China for two not entirely consistent reasons. First, such a treaty might involve the United States in hostilities with Communist China through Nationalist actions. Second, it might "tie the hands" of the Nationalists in conducting limited offensive operations against Communist China.[5] U.S. leaders saw substantial utility in Nationalist "limited offensive operations" against the mainland. They feared, consequently, that those operations would need to be restricted if the United States was formally associated with the ROC. The U.S. military, ever concerned with matching its commitments to its limited resources, also opposed a treaty with Formosa, favoring the more flexible status quo instead.[6]

These objections were pushed aside in October 1954, when Eisenhower decided to use conclusion of a mutual security treaty as a quid pro quo to secure Nationalist acceptance of a plan to achieve U.N. action neutralizing the Taiwan Strait. This was an old problem. As early as August 1950, barely a month after Truman engaged the Seventh Fleet to neutralize Taiwan, the State Department began seeking a diplomatic means of relieving the United States of the burden inherent in this responsibility. The United Nations was a focus of these efforts. Secretary Dean Acheson proposed to the General Assembly an international solution of the Formosan issue that would take into consideration the legitimate interest "of all concerned and interested parties," but would require them meanwhile to abjure the use of military force. Pending the final resolution of the Formosan issue, the United Nations would assume responsibility for the neutralization policy. The JCS had opposed this plan on the basis that it would restrict future U.S. freedom of action vis-à-vis Taiwan, while improving the Communist ability to concentrate forces in Korea by removing the threat of Nationalist invasion. These issues were still being debated when Chinese Communist forces entered the Korean War in November 1950. At that point the administration promptly laid aside the neutralization proposal.[7] U.N. sponsorship of neutralization of the Taiwan Strait represented an effort to institutionalize the separation of Taiwan from the political entity ruling on the mainland of China—and vice versa. It was this, of course, which made it so objectionable to both Chiang Kai-shek and Mao Zedong.

U.S. handling of the peace treaty with Japan, signed in San Francisco in September 1951, worked in a similar direction, helping persuade Chiang and Mao that the true purpose of U.S. policy was in fact two Chinas. John Foster Dulles (who handled the negotiations for the Truman Administration) saw the treaty with Japan as an opportunity to create a legal basis for Taiwan's separate status from China. Thus the United States overrode Britain's proposal to have Japan cede Taiwan in favor of "China." Instead Japan simply renounced claim to the island without specifying the new possessor. Neither the PRC nor the ROC was a signatory to the peace treaty with Japan. London and Tokyo were unwilling to sign with Taipei, and Washington did not insist. The United States told Taipei, however, that it would persuade Tokyo to sign a separate treaty with Taipei along the general lines of the San Francisco treaty if Taipei would accept restriction of that treaty's application to Taiwan and the Pescadores. Taipei was extremely reluctant to do this, but eventually agreed in order to get a treaty with Japan and not be excluded from the broad Allied settlement with Japan. Dulles thus secured the ROC's self-recognition, at least in a legal sense, that its jurisdiction did not extend to the Chinese mainland, but was confined to Taiwan and the Pescadores.[8]

The Korean armistice of July 1953 revived the question of measures that might reduce U.S.-PRC tensions while not undermining Taiwan's integration into the Pacific strategic perimeter. U.S. leaders again began to hope that it might be possible to secure U.N. endorsement of Taiwan's neutralization. The initiation of heavy PLA artillery bombardment of the Nationalist-held offshore islands on 3 September 1954 added further urgency to the push to secure the "neutralization" of the Taiwan Strait. A major trouble with all proposals to neutralize Taiwan was that Chiang Kai-shek adamantly rejected them. This conundrum was addressed by Secretary of State John Foster Dulles at an NSC meeting on 6 October 1954. A purely defensive treaty between Taiwan and the United States would have many advantages for U.S. policy, Dulles argued. Unfortunately, Chiang Kai-shek wanted to go beyond defensive arrangements to offensive actions against Communist China. Chiang would oppose "neutralization" since this would "reduce the chances of spreading the present conflict [over the offshores] into a war with Communist China in which the United States would be involved." This, after all, Dulles reminded the meeting, was Chiang's only hope of returning to the mainland. Eventually, however, the NSC developed the idea of winning Chiang's acceptance of a neutralization scheme by offering him the mutual security treaty he so craved. This concept was endorsed by Eisenhower at another NSC meeting on 28 October 1954.[9]

Chiang was interested in the proposed tradeoff. Differences remained, however, over the geographic scope of the treaty. Should the treaty support, implicitly or explicitly, Nationalist aspirations of returning to the mainland to liberate the Chinese people from Communist rule? Taipei argued that the treaty should indeed recognize the ROC government as the sole, legitimate government of all of China. This was, after all, the U.S. position on the question of Chinese representation at the United Nations. The United States should be consistent, Taipei argued, and not have one policy for the U.N. and another as the basis of political relations between the two countries. Moreover, as the leader of the Free World, Taipei argued, how could the United States fail to support the aspirations of Free China to liberate the Chinese people from Communism? The conclusion of these arguments, and of U.S. acceptance of Taipei's claim to sovereignty over the mainland, was that the United States should support the Chinese Nationalist effort to recover the mainland, and that this should be at least implicit in the mutual security treaty. This Washington was not prepared to do.

A compromise was eventually reached. Article VI of the treaty, signed by Secretary Dulles and Foreign Minister George Yeh in Washington on 2 December 1954, provided that the clauses regarding joint efforts to resist armed attack and obligating the signatories to "act to meet the common danger" applied only to "Taiwan and the Pescadores," along with "such other territories as may be determined by mutual agreement." The latter caveat provided an elastic clause, permitting the application of the treaty to defense of the Nationalist-held offshores or even the Chinese mainland—if the United States so agreed. Nationalist leaders were extremely unhappy with the phraseology of the elastic clause, but accepted it because they wanted a treaty and the United States would go no further.

U.S. leaders recognized that the more formal commitment to Nationalist China, implicit in the 1954 treaty, increased the risks of Chiang Kai-shek's maneuvering the United States into conflict with mainland China. Conse-quently, as the United States began moving toward a formal security treaty with the ROC, the feeling mounted that Nationalist guarantees of 1953 not to "radically alter the pattern or tempo of operations hitherto undertaken" against the mainland were inadequate. U.S. leaders feared that once the United States was obligated by treaty to come to Taiwan's assistance, Tai-pei might provoke a conflict with the PRC by initiating large-scale offen-sive operations against the mainland or by stationing large concentrations on Jinmen and Mazu, thereby triggering a Communist attack against those islands. To prevent this, U.S. representatives insisted that Taipei agree that all Nationalist military actions against the mainland be initiated only after joint consultation and U.S. consent. The U.S. side also insisted that it should have authority to approve Nationalist deployments to Jinmen and Mazu. Initially, Nationalist representatives adamantly rejected these de-mands. The liberation of the mainland from Communist rule was a sacred mission, they said, which could not be shelved or abridged. No sovereign government could concede to another the control over its armed forces, especially where such a fundamental national mission was involved. More-over, if the ROC accepted these U.S. demands, this would be tantamount to public abandonment of the mission of recovering the mainland. Nationalist morale would thereupon collapse. U.S. representatives were sympathetic to Taipei's dilemma, but insisted on terms that they felt were essential to guaran-tee U.S. control over questions directly linked to U.S. involvement in war.

Eventually, Taipei accepted the U.S. demands, because it wanted a treaty and because the United States would not waive these requirements. To address the problem of Nationalist domestic legitimacy, however, the

United States accepted an ROC proposal to exclude these matters from the body of the treaty, handling them instead in ancillary notes to be exchanged in private a week after the signature of the treaty itself. Moreover, the United States would not contradict Nationalist efforts to restrict dissemination of knowledge of the notes within Taiwan. As late as the early 1980s, these notes had not been published in Taiwan, thereby sparing the Nationalists the embarrassment of having it generally known that their main ally had the power to veto a return to the mainland.[10] The notes exchanged privately by Yeh and Dulles on 10 December read:

> The Republic of China effectively controls both the territory described in Article VI of the Treaty of Mutual Defense . . . and other territory. It possesses with respect to *all territory* now and hereafter under its control *the inherent right of self-defense*. In view of the obligations of the two Parties under the said Treaty and of the fact that the use of force from either of these areas by either of the Parties affects the other, *it is agreed that such use of force will be a matter of joint agreement,* subject to action of an emergency character which is clearly an exercise of the inherent right of self-defense [emphasis added].[11]

The two sides subsequently disagreed over the meaning of these words. Taipei pointed to the acknowledgment of its "inherent right of self-defense" over "all territory now and hereafter under its control" as recognition of its right to do whatever necessary to defend the offshore islands. Moreover, Taipei insisted that it was obligated to secure "mutual agreement" only for the movement of "military elements which are a product of joint effort and contribution." This allowed Taipei to maintain that units being assigned to the offshore islands were not the product of such "joint effort and contribution." Finally, the note did not clearly say that the ROC would launch no military operations against the mainland without U.S. approval—or at least, so Taipei maintained. From the U.S. perspective, such arguments were sophistry. The clear intent of the note, Washington felt, was to prevent large-scale Nationalist offensive operations against the mainland, or a buildup of Nationalist forces on the offshores without U.S. consent.

Below these disagreements was another, more fundamental one about the treaty itself. From Taipei's perspective, since the treaty was a defensive arrangement, it simply was not applicable to the ROC's "sacred mission" of recovering the mainland. The 1954 treaty applied only to a Communist attack on Taiwan. It did not apply to, and imposed no restrictions upon, the ROC's right to recover the mainland from Communist usurpation, Taipei argued. The United States' view was different. The quid pro quo for the United States' obligating itself to come to Taiwan's defense, Washington felt, was Taipei's agreement not to launch an effort to recover the mainland without U.S. consent. Without such a commitment, Washington argued, the United States would never have entered into a binding obligation to defend Taiwan, for to have done so would have deprived the United States of the power to determine whether it would assume the burden of war with Communist China. These divergent perspectives would give rise to deep anger that rocked the newly forged alliance during the second Taiwan Strait crisis of 1958.

The chief purpose of the 1954 treaty was, according to its preamble, to "declare publicly and formally" the unity of the two countries, "so that no potential aggressor could be under the illusion that either of them stands alone in the West Pacific Area." To this end, Article V of the treaty provided that "an armed attack in the West Pacific Area against the territories of either of the Parties would be dangerous" to the "peace and safety" of the other party, and consequently, each party "would act to meet the common danger in accordance with its constitutional processes." This particular choice of words left the United States with considerable flexibility in choosing whether, when, and how to respond to a clash between PRC and ROC forces.

Operation Oracle and the Geneva Talks

Once Washington and Taipei reached agreement on the terms of their treaty, the United States could proceed with its scheme for U.N. neutralization of Taiwan. In January 1955 the United States supported a New Zealand proposal for a U.N. Security Council resolution opposing the use of force in the Taiwan Strait. This effort was code-named Operation Oracle.[12] According to New Zealand's plan, the Security Council was to call upon "the People's Republic of China and the Republic of China" to "terminate hostilities" forthwith in the Taiwan Strait. The use of the formal name "People's Republic of China" was suggestive of possible U.S. recognition of that entity. Simultaneously, however, the use of the name "Republic of China" was repugnant to Beijing, suggesting dual representation of "China" in the U.N. For purposes of debating the adoption of the New Zealand resolution, Beijing was to be invited to send a representative to participate in the Security Council's debate. If Beijing's endorsement or at least acquiescence to a cease-fire in the Taiwan Strait could be secured, a majority of the Security Council would probably approve the resolution. In this fashion, United Nations authority would be used to lessen the probability of military confrontations over the offshores in the Taiwan Strait.[13] Stripped of diplomatic ambiguity, Washington's plan was to use Beijing's desire for admission to the United Nations, along with vague suggestions that PRC participation in the Security Council debate might lead to PRC admission to the U.N., to secure Beijing's acceptance of the New Zealand proposal.

As promised, Taipei did not block the New Zealand proposal when it came before the Security Council. The proposal to invite a representative of the "Central People's Government of the People's Republic of China" to participate in the scheduled Security Council debate was approved 9 to 1. Taipei voted against the motion, but did not exercise its veto.[14]

Beijing's rejection of the proposal to participate in Security Council debate was swift. The purpose of the resolution, Zhou said on 3 February, was "to intervene in China's internal affairs and to cover up the acts of aggression by the United States against China." The PRC would attend the Security Council only if the Chiang Kai-shek clique was expelled from it and the PRC attended in the name of China.[15]

Several months after the failure of Operation Oracle, Washington decided to open direct talks with Beijing in an effort to persuade it to renounce the use of force against Taiwan. The venue for this effort was the U.S.-PRC ambassadorial talks in Geneva during 1955 and 1956. The United States initially agreed to these talks largely as a way of circumventing British and Indian pressure to include the PRC at the big-power conference at Geneva in July 1955. But there were also hints that Beijing might be willing to modify its unremitting hostility toward Taipei. At the Bandung conference of African and Asian countries in April 1955, Zhou Enlai had said: "The Chinese people do not want to have a war with the United States of America," and "the Chinese Government is willing to discuss the question of relaxing tension in the Far East and especially the question of relaxing tension in the Taiwan area."[16] U.S. leaders feared that these and similar words were intended as bait to entice the Americans into contacts that would lead to the erosion of the ROC's international position. Yet, the possibility that Beijing might be persuaded to renounce the use of military force against Taiwan was worth exploring. Beijing's diplomacy seemed to be moderating in a number of areas.

Against these modest hopes were set deep suspicions that Beijing would use the ambassadorial talks to enhance its international stature, perhaps even achieving de facto U.S. recognition. This Washington was determined to avoid. Thus, once the ambassadorial talks began in August 1955, the United States refused a meeting of U.S. and PRC foreign ministers which Beijing repeatedly proposed. U.S. leaders calculated that such high-level contacts would be widely interpreted as de facto U.S. recognition of the PRC, a development that might undermine international support for the ROC, perhaps even leading to the PRC's admission to the United Nations.

Beijing's estimate in this regard was probably not too different. Achieving such a foreign ministerial meeting was one of Beijing's top objectives at the ambassadorial talks.[17]

By October, it was clear to Dulles that Beijing would not agree to the nonuse of force against Taiwan except, perhaps, as part of a larger package entailing PRC admission to and ROC expulsion from the United Nations. This Dulles would not accept. He thus decided to swap the deadlocked talks for something Washington desired very much—Nationalist withdrawal from the offshore islands. Taipei had always adamantly opposed the U.S.-PRC ambassadorial talks. Dulles told Foreign Minister George Yeh that if Taipei "considered it more important to break off the [Geneva] talks than to retain Jinmen and Mazu, we would arrange to terminate the talks as soon as you were prepared to evacuate the island."[18] Chiang Kai-shek rejected the proposal. Instead, Chiang stepped up the deployment of Nationalist forces to those islands, while the U.S.-PRC talks continued.

Taipei strongly opposed the U.S.-PRC ambassadorial talks because such talks might permit Beijing to divide the United States from Nationalist China. Taipei feared that Beijing might agree to the nonuse of force in the Taiwan Strait as a quid pro quo for U.S. military and political disengagement from Taiwan.[19] Two results could then follow. One would be the indefinite continuation of "Two Chinas," along with the corollary that the Chinese on the mainland would continue to live under Communism. The Nationalist dream of returning to the mainland to destroy the Communist regime would evaporate. Chiang Kai-shek and other Nationalist leaders would live out their lives as the rulers of a small island, instead of going down in the annals of Chinese history as the creators of a great, united, and free China. The second result would be a gradual weakening of Nationalist China's political-military position, along with a corresponding growth of Chinese Communist strength. Then, when conditions were appropriate, the Chinese Communists would find some pretext to set aside any previous pledge not to use force against Taiwan, and would attack and seize Taiwan.

A deep Nationalist fear in the mid-1950s was that the United States would return to its 1949 policy of dropping Nationalist China for the sake of encouraging Chinese Titoism. While Chinese Nationalist leaders probably were not aware that driving a wedge between Moscow and Beijing remained a top U.S. objective even under Eisenhower (such matters were, of course, top secret), the Truman Administration had been fairly open about its objective. U.S. policy changed substantially after China entered the Korean War, but the logic underlying the earlier policy remained.[20]

Taipei's apprehensions regarding the U.S.-PRC ambassadorial talks were ill founded. Washington and Beijing remained far apart over Taiwan and the nonuse of force. Beijing's objective was indeed to secure withdrawal of the Seventh Fleet from the Taiwan Strait and the termination of U.S. support for Nationalist China. Beijing's invariant position was that since tension in the Taiwan area was due fundamentally to U.S. military intervention there, beginning in June 1950, the "relaxation and elimination" of that tension required the withdrawal of U.S. military forces from the region. Beijing agreed to the principle that the United States and the PRC should abjure the use or threatened use of force in bilateral relations or in the solution of other *international* problems, but adamantly refused to apply that concept to relations between the PRC and Taiwan. Taiwan was entirely and exclusively an *internal* affair of the PRC, Beijing insisted, and had no place in negotiations between the United States and China. The United States, on the other hand, insisted that since the Taiwan issue was clearly a source of potential military conflict between the United States and the PRC, refusal to apply the principle of nonuse of force to the Taiwan area made agreement to apply that principle elsewhere meaningless. Moreover, Washington insisted that any renunciation of the use of force would be without prejudice to the right of individual or collective self-defense against armed attack. This was an attempt to ensure that a non-use-of-force agreement would not be tantamount to nullification of the 1954 ROC-U.S. mutual security treaty. Beijing rejected all such arguments as American attempts to compel China to accept the status quo of "U.S. occupation of China's territory, Taiwan." The United States rejected the proposition that it was "occupying" Taiwan or that Taiwan was or had ever been part of Communist China.

By January 1956, the U.S.-PRC ambassadorial talks were deadlocked over the Taiwan issue. The exchange of draft proposals had reached a state in which PRC representatives routinely kept any mention of Taiwan out of their draft proposals, while U.S. representatives routinely put it back in. The essence of the deadlock was that the PRC was not going to accept any sort of restriction on its right to seize Taiwan by any means necessary, while the United States was not willing to countenance a substantial upgrading of the PRC's international position until it did just that. The U.S.-PRC ambassadorial talks continued until 1971, with Taiwan remaining the main source of tension.

The Nationalist Military Contribution to the Alliance

Eisenhower, like Truman, sought to avoid war with China, but both presidents considered general war with China a possibility that might arise out of Chinese actions in Korea, the Taiwan Strait, or Indochina. Indeed, by the mid-1950s, China was seen as a more likely source of aggression than the

Soviet Union.[21] In order to deal with the contingency of war with China, to deter it, or, if need be, to defeat China, the Eisenhower Administration sought to strengthen the non-Communist world's collective defense effort in the Far East. The need for allies in the global contest with the Sino-Soviet alliance was reaffirmed by Eisenhower's broad review of U.S. strategic orientation in 1953. In the April 1954 issue of *Foreign Affairs,* Dulles explained:

> The cornerstone of security for the free nations must be a collective system of defense. They clearly cannot achieve security separately. No single nation can develop for itself defensive power of adequate scope and flexibility. In seeking to do so, each would become a garrison state and none would achieve security. . . . Security for the free world depends, therefore, upon the development of collective security and community power rather than upon purely national potentials.[22]

The existence of a militarily potent Nationalist regime was viewed by U.S. strategic planners as a major asset in deterring and/or defeating aggression by the Sino-Soviet bloc in Asia.[23] One reason for this was the dearth of strong and willing allies in the Far East. The United States had allies in Europe who were able and willing to make major contributions to Free World strength: Britain, France, Germany, etc. In the Far East, however, U.S. allies were weaker, and, in the case of Japan, unwilling to assume a substantial military burden. This put a premium on those Asian allies, such as Nationalist China, that were willing and able to carry a heavier military load.

When Nationalist forces first withdrew to Taiwan, they did not constitute a potent fighting force. After several years of reorganization, training, and U.S. assistance, U.S. military leaders rated ROC military capabilities highly. By the early 1960s, Nationalist China was one of America's major military partners in the Far East. As Table 4.1 indicates, the five major allies of the United States in the European theater contributed 2.6 million soldiers and $26 billion in military expenditures during the year 1963. This represented 84 percent and 409 percent, respectively, of total Soviet military manpower and expenditures. In the Far East, however, the relative allied contribution was much smaller, equaling only 31 percent of Chinese military expenditures and 75 percent of Chinese military manpower. Moreover, only the forces of Japan, Taiwan, and Thailand constituted a strategic reserve, in the sense that, in the event of a general war, their forces could be available for deployment outside their boundaries. South Vietnam's resources were, of course, directed toward meeting the challenge from Hanoi, while South Korea's preoccupation in the event of a general war would be

Table 4.1

Burden Sharing by Major U.S. Alliance Partners*

	Military Expenditures (Constant $ Millions)	Military Expenditures as Percent of GNP	Size of Armed Forces (Thousands)	Armed Forces per 1,000 Population
European Allies				
West Germany	8,974	5.2	425	7.4
Britain	7,390	6.1	450	8.4
France	6,767	5.6	735	15.4
Italy	2,623	3.3	515	10.1
Turkey	439	4.9	475	16.0
Total Allied contribution as percent of Soviet total	409%		84%	
Asian Allies				
Japan	1,235	1.0	243	2.5
Taiwan	303	10.2	557	45.7
South Korea	180	4.2	627	23.1
South Vietnam	288	13.5	425	27.8
Thailand	96	2.4	85	2.9
Total Allied contribution as percent of Chinese total	31%		75%	

*The five major alliance partners in each theater; all figures for 1963.

Source: World Military Expenditures and Arms Trade, U.S. Arms Control and Disarmament Agency, 1975.

defense against North Korea's potent army. Taiwan's forces represented 63 percent of all military forces that might be used throughout the region. The heavy burden shouldered by Taiwan is indicated by figures for military expenditures as a percent of GNP and number of soldiers per 1,000 population. Taiwan's relative defense spending was ten times as great as Japan's and surpassed only by South Vietnam. In terms of military manpower, the burden assumed by Taiwan was far greater than any allied country.

One reason for the relatively smaller allied role in Asia, and for the greater importance of Nationalist China as an ally, was the reluctance of the Japanese political elite to rearm as Germany was then doing. By 1963, West Germany's defense spending was over seven times that of Japan's, with nearly double the military manpower. A more fundamental factor had to do with China's historic dominance in Asia. Europe was, for centuries, divided into independent nations of roughly equal power. While this situation was deeply modified by the emergence of the USSR in the mid-1940s, the disparity between the resources of the Western European powers and the USSR was not so great as the gap between the PRC and the other East Asian countries (exclusive of Japan). Because of a pattern of historical development very different from Europe's, a single nation of continental proportions, China, emerged in Asia to dwarf its neighbors in power. This combination of relative preponderance of Chinese power in East Asia with Japan's decision to opt out of the great power game put a premium on what allies were available to the United States in Asia. Nationalist China was one.

That Taiwan was an island also greatly increased the strategic flexibility of Taiwan's forces, and hence of their potential utility to allied commanders in the event of a general war. Taiwan's insularity, combined with the U.S. thalassocracy over the western Pacific, meant that Taiwan could be fairly easily defended in the event of a major war and that a large percentage of its forces would consequently be available for deployment elsewhere.

Nationalist China's relatively high level of military spending was directly related to its receipt of military assistance from the United States. It makes sense to think of U.S. military assistance to Taiwan and other countries as "matching funds" akin to those given by the U.S. federal government to encourage state spending in particular areas. Table 4.2 shows levels of U.S. military assistance to various countries during the period 1950–65. Taiwan was the top-ranking Asian recipient of U.S. military assistance, and indeed was outranked globally only by France and Turkey.[24] During the 1960s, of course, U.S. assistance to South Vietnam would far exceed the earlier levels extended to either South Korea or Taiwan.

Table 4.2

U.S. Military Assistance, 1950–66 (Recipients of over $900 Million; Millions of Dollars)

France	4,236
Turkey	2,570
Taiwan	2,411
South Korea	2,391
Italy	2,289
Greece	1,428
Belgium and Luxembourg	1,256
Netherlands	1,221
United Kingdom	1,035
Japan	902
West Germany	901

Source: Statistical Abstract of the United States 1966, Department of Commerce, p. 257.

Successive statements of U.S. policy toward Taiwan gave high priority to maintaining and strengthening its military potential. NSC 5503 of January 1955, for example, listed, as the second U.S. objective, "continued development of the military potential of GRC armed forces." Missions assigned Nationalist forces by NSC 5503 included assisting in the defense of Formosa and the Pescadores, "taking action" to defend Jinmen and Mazu, and contributing to "collective non-Communist strength in the Far East."[25] NSC 5723 of 4 October 1957, which superseded NSC 5503 on that date, reiterated these objectives.

The air force was the Nationalist armed service rated highest by U.S. military advisers. Between 1953 and 1973, the United States transferred 1,549 warplanes to Taiwan. These deliveries, listed in Table 4.3, included virtually all advanced U.S. air-superiority fighters. Along with the aircraft went extensive training by U.S. personnel in Taiwan, at U.S. bases on Okinawa, and in the United States. Thousands of Nationalist pilots were trained in flying and tactical skills, along with more esoteric subjects such as night fighting, instrument flying, low-altitude bombing, long-distance patrolling, sea rescue, naval air defense, and electronic warfare and electronic countermeasures. U.S. technicians helped the ROC air force set up an air control system, a combat command and control system, training programs including the utilization of electronic training systems, and repair and maintenance programs.[26]

Taipei tried repeatedly to leverage its important role in U.S. Far Eastern strategy into U.S. support for substantial enhancement of Nationalist *offensive* capabilities. The United States refused because such an enhancement

Table 4.3

U.S. Aircraft Deliveries to Taiwan[*]

Type of Aircraft	1953	1954	1955	1956	1957	1958	1959	1960	1961	1962	1963	1964	1965	1966	1967	1968	1969	1970	1971	1972	1973	Total
F-47N	150																					150
T-33A	7	18	4		16	22										15	2	2	6	4		96
F-84G	76	81	11		46	31																245
P4Y	22	7	6																			35
PBY5A		7	4																			11
F-86F, D		25	104	51	89	111	5	48														433
H-19B			4																			4
SA-16					2																	2
C-119					16	6	3							12			42	36				114
F-100F, A								81										19	21	2	5	132
T-28								20	2	4												26
F-104A, B, G								26			6	27	21			4		22			3	109
TF-104G									6							3						9
F-5A, B													9	10	34	22	2	21	4			102
T-38A																				38		38
O-1G																				19		19
SA-16																						2
H-19B																						4
HU-16, A/B				6	2	1										2						11
HH-1H																			9			9

[*] Exclusive of reconnaissance aircraft, which are listed in chapter 10.

Source: Meijun zai Hua gongzuo jishi (kongjun guwen zu) (Record of U.S. military activities on Taiwan, Air Force Advisory Group), Taipei: Air Force Headquarters, 1981.

JOHN MOORES UNIVERSITY
AVRIL ROBARTS LRC
TEL. 0151 231 4022

would weaken U.S. control over the conduct of large-scale Nationalist offensive operations against the mainland. American support for the development of Nationalist military capabilities was limited by the U.S. desire to deny Taipei the capability to autonomously initiate and/or sustain large-scale offensive operations against the mainland. Taiwan was thus denied the ability to initiate large-scale amphibious operations against the mainland without U.S. air, naval, and logistic support. Nationalist capabilities were kept commensurate with the mission U.S. planners wished them to perform. In line with this, the United States supplied only limited numbers of transport aircraft to the ROC. Limited logistic capabilities meant that Nationalist forces would be dependent on U.S. support for any large-scale offensive operations on the mainland. By limiting the Nationalists' logistic capabilities, Washington not only avoided an unnecessary expense, but also limited Taipei's ability to independently launch large-scale operations that might entangle the United States in conflict with Communist China.

The United States also supported extensive construction of air base facilities on Taiwan for the use of both the ROC air force and, in the event of war, the U.S. Air Force. Large-scale construction of airfields began during the Korean War and continued through the mid-1950s. The ROC navy received the least emphasis under the U.S. military assistance program, but here too there were substantial developments. The ROC navy received 383 craft of various sorts from the United States during the years 1952–78. The major vessels are listed in Table 4.4. With U.S. assistance, the Nationalists developed significant but modest amphibious capabilities. Forty-five landing craft of various sorts were transferred to Taiwan. It is significant that a large portion of these vessels were supplied about the time of the 1958 strait crisis; these vessels gave the ROC the ability to supply Jinmen and Mazu. They also gave Nationalist forces the capability of conducting small-scale offensive operations against the mainland. They were inadequate, however, for large-scale or sustained operations on the mainland. Landing craft could also be used to move men and material around the island of Taiwan. Given the topography of Taiwan, and the limited development of Taiwan's rail and highway system in the 1950s and 1960s, movement by sea was often the fastest and cheapest way to conduct such deployments. Antisubmarine warfare capabilities was another focus of ROC naval development. The submarine chasers, destroyers, escort, and patrol escort ships provided by the United States all contributed to this. U.S.-supplied mine sweepers also had ASW missions, since many Soviet and Chinese submarines were designed for mine laying. The P47 and PBY5A Catalina seaplanes supplied by the United States were also used for long-range sea patrol. The United States also provided the ROC navy with 72 sonar sets and 236 radar sets

Table 4.4

U.S. Transfer of Naval Vessels to Taiwan

1952	2 landing ships, medium
1954	2 support landing ships, large; 2 destroyers; 10 submarine chasers
1955	6 utility landing craft; 2 mine sweepers, coastal; 1 landing ship, tank; 1 destroyer
1956	3 landing ships, medium
1957	1 landing ship, tank; 1 landing craft repair ship; 5 submarine chasers; 1 utility landing craft
1958	3 utility landing craft; 1 infantry landing ship, large; 7 landing ships, tank
1959	1 destroyer; 2 landing ships, tank; 2 landing ships, medium; 1 auxiliary floating dry dock; 7 landing craft, utility; 2 coastal mine sweepers
1960	1 submarine chaser; 2 landing ships, tank
1961	1 gasoline tanker; 1 dock landing ship
1962	1 landing ship; tank; 1 landing ship, medium
1963	1 auxiliary ocean tug
1965	3 escorts; 2 patrol escorts; 2 coastal mine sweepers; 1 fleet ocean tug
1966	6 patrol escorts; 1 mine sweeper, coastal
1967	2 patrol escorts; 1 destroyer
1968	1 escort; 1 floating derrick; 1 destroyer; 1 escort vessel; 1 auxiliary floating dry dock
1969	1 patrol escort; 1 surveying ship
1970	6 destroyers; 7 mine sweepers, coastal
1971	1 internal combustion engine repair ship; 1 auxiliary floating dry dock; 1 gasoline tanker; 1 auxiliary ocean tug; 1 light cargo ship; 2 destroyers
1972	1 auxiliary ocean tug; 1 gasoline tanker; 1 surveying ship; 2 destroyers
1973	3 destroyers; 2 submarines
1974	1 internal combustion engine repair ship; 1 fleet ocean tug
1977	3 destroyers; 1 salvage vessel
1978	1 destroyer; 1 fleet ocean tug

Source: Meijun zaiHua gongzuo jishi (haijun guwenzu) (Record of U.S. Military Activities on Taiwan, Naval Advisory Group), Taipei: Navy Headquarters, 1981.

used for monitoring the movement of surface and submarine traffic in the Taiwan area.[27] Some of these radars were placed on the offshore islands.

With American support, Taiwan became a bastion of substantial but carefully limited strength in the western Pacific defense perimeter. Its air and naval forces and bases contributed substantially to the maintenance of U.S. thalassocracy in the Pacific. In the event of war with the Sino-Soviet bloc, or after about 1963 with China alone, Nationalist forces would have made a significant contribution to preventing enemy air and naval forces from breaking into the Pacific Ocean. In the event U.S. leaders had been forced to decide on offensive operations on the Asian continent, Nationalist forces would have figured prominently in those plans.

U.S. leaders considered the use of Nationalist forces several times during the 1950s. In the fall of 1951 the JCS developed contingency plans for U.S. military action (short of deployment of U.S. ground forces) in support of the French position in Indochina. In the event of overt Chinese intervention in response to these U.S. moves, the JCS projected a number of counter-moves including naval blockade of China's coast, air bombardment of Chinese military facilities, and deployment of Chinese Nationalist forces.[28] Again, following the fall of the French position at Dien Bien Phu in 1954, when U.S. leaders were considering the possibility of loss of all of Indochina to Communist forces, the substantial augmentation of Nationalist forces was one option laid before the NSC, in the following words:

> Further need for a re-examination of U.S. policies [toward Nationalist China's military missions and requirements] may arise out of developments which appear imminent in Southeast Asia. Depending upon the nature of the settlement which is reached in Indochina, it is possible that Free World capabilities in SEA may be severely curtailed while those of Communist China are expanding. In such an eventuality it might become desirable to (a) strengthen the imbalance of military potential thus created; and, (b) to strengthen the constraining forces which can be brought to bear on the Communist flank. . . . Specifically, with reference to Formosa, considerations might have to be given to raising force levels . . . and otherwise greatly enhancing the offensive potential of GRC forces. The foregoing should be considered in the light of Japan's slow progress in building up military potential.[29]

The major factor weighing against, and ultimately ruling out, use of Nationalist forces overtly and under conditions short of war was a fear that use of Nationalist forces might precipitate counterintervention by Communist China. Early in 1958, for instance, ROC Defense Minister Yu Dawei proposed the organization and equipment of a GRC "fire brigade," including one marine and three army divisions. This quick-reaction force was to be kept ready for use outside the Taiwan defense area in the Far East and the Middle East.[30] After detailed consideration, the JCS eventually advised against Taipei's proposed "fire brigade." While recognizing the "desirability, particularly in general war, of the indigenous augmentation of U.S. ground forces in the Pacific area," and while appreciating "the increasing psychological problems confronting the GRC with respect to the maintenance of morale in their armed forces, and their natural desire to bolster their prestige in the eyes of their own citizens and to maintain their position among other world powers," the JCS concluded that substantial difficulties made acceptance of Taipei's proposal inadvisable. First among these difficulties was the fact that "The commitment of such a force in contingency operations elsewhere in the Far East would almost certainly be followed by Chinese Communist military intervention on the other side as well as renewed aggression against the Taiwan defense area." This would be detrimental to the United States' desire to avoid general war.[31]

Fear that utilization of Nationalist China's military capabilities would trigger, or at least increase the prospects of, PLA entry ultimately proved decisive in the case of the two hot wars the United States fought during the long Cold War in Asia: the Korean War and the Vietnam War. There is no way of knowing whether the fears of American leaders charged with making these decisions were justified. This author's guess is that such fears were *not* justified, but that neither was the probable contribution derived from Nationalist participation large enough to justify the increased risk of general war with China run in the fog of an ongoing limited war. I doubt whether Chinese leaders would have accepted general war with the United States because Nationalist forces were introduced into South Korea or South Vietnam during the wars in those countries. But neither would the contributions of Nationalist forces in those theaters have been decisive. In Korea, U.N. forces won without the Nationalists. In Vietnam, the United States would have lost, I suspect, in spite of any Nationalist contribution.

Notes

1. Robert J. Watson, *History of the Joint Chiefs of Staff,* vol. V, *The Joint Chiefs of Staff and National Policy, 1953–1954,* Washington: Historical Division, Joint Chiefs of Staff, 1986, pp. 14–26. The exception to Eisenhower's clean sweep of the JCS was Chief of Naval Operations (CNO) Admiral William Fecteler, whose tenure dated only from 1951.

2. NSC, Progress Report on NSC 146/2, 16 July 1954.

3. Watson, *JCS and National Policy, 1953–1954,* p. 25.

4. Much of this analysis of the 1954 treaty is from Shao Yu-ming, *Zhong Mei guanxi yanjiu wenji* (Collected research on Sino-American relations), Taipei: Chuanji wenxue chubanshe, 1980, pp. 111–16.

5. Regarding the first, see Watson, *JCS and National Policy, 1953–1954,* p. 263. Regarding the second, see NSC, Progress Report on NSC 146/2, 16 July 1954.

6. See oral statement by JCS to Secretary of Defense, 13 October 1954, in National Archives, RG 218, JCS, Geographic File 1954–56, 381 Formosa, box 18, sec. 15.

7. Walter S. Poole, *The Joint Chiefs of Staff and National Policy, 1950–1952,* Historical Division, Joint Secretariat, JCS, December 1979, p. 396.

8. Su-Ya Chang, "The United States and the Long-Term Disposition of Taiwan in the Making of Peace with Japan, 1950–1952," *Asian Profile,* vol. 16, no. 5 (October 1988), pp. 459–70.

9. Watson, *JCS and National Policy, 1953–1954,* p. 263.

10. Shao Yu-ming, *Zong menhu kaifang dao Zhong Mei duanjiao* (From the open door policy to the severing of Sino-American relations), Taipei: Danjiang daxue chubanshe, 1983, p. 27.

11. *United States Treaties and Other International Agreements,* vol. 6, part 1, Washington: Government Printing Office, 1956, p. 454.

12. *FRUS,* 1955–57, vol. II, pp. 44–45.

13. Ibid., p. 131.

14. Ibid., pp. 178–79.

15. Ibid., pp. 202–3.

16. Quoted in Kenneth T. Young, *Negotiating with the Chinese Communists, the U.S. Experience, 1953–1967,* New York: McGraw Hill, 1968, p. 44.

17. Regarding the U.S.-PRC ambassadorial talks see Young, *Negotiating.* Also see Robert G. Sutter, *China Watch, Towards Sino-American Reconciliation,* Baltimore: Johns Hopkins University Press, 1978, pp. 47–62.

18. *FRUS,* 1955–57, vol. III, pp. 110–12.

19. See communications from Yeh to Dulles and Rankin, October 1955 and January 1956, in *FRUS,* 1955–57, vol. III, pp. 175–76, 279–82.

20. Ibid.

21. A briefing paper prepared for the U.S. delegation to the 1954 Geneva Conference, for example, said that while Soviet leaders essentially sought to preserve the status quo, China's leaders were still "on the make," driven by revolutionary élan, and that they sought to restore China's traditional domination of Asia. "The Sino-Soviet Relation and Its Potential Sources of Differences," *FRUS,* 1952–54, vol. XIV, part I, p. 404.

22. John Foster Dulles, "Policy for Security and Peace," *Foreign Affairs,* vol. 32, no. 3 (April 1954), pp. 355–56.

23. See the September 1954 NIE, p. 629.

24. A substantial portion of U.S. assistance to France actually went to Asia. The United States paid for much of the French military effort in Indochina from 1950 to 1954.

25. NSC 5503, 15 January 1955, National Archives.

26. *Meijun zai Hua gongzuo jishi (kongjun guwen zu)* [Record of American military activities on Taiwan (air force advisory group)], Taipei: Air Force Headquarters, 1981, pp. 65–66.

27. Ibid., pp. 245–46.

28. *From Pearl Harbor to Vietnam: The Memoirs of Admiral Arthur W. Radford,* Stephen Jurika, ed., Stanford, CA: Hoover Institution Press, 1980, p. 346.

29. Progress Report on NSC 146/2, 16 July 1954.

30. CNO to CINCPAC, 9 January 1958, RG 218 (JCS), Geographic File 1957, 381 Formosa, box 9, sec. 35.

31. JCS memorandum for Secretary of Defense, 17 March 1958, RG 218, Geographic File 1957, 381 Formosa, box 9, sec. 35. Acceptance of Taipei's "fire brigade" proposal would also have entailed diversion of U.S. aid from other countries, such as South Korea, which the United States was then requiring to reduce its forces from 720,000 to 630,000. "The repercussions resulting from this inconsistency could well have serious effects on the United Nations Command [in Korea] and cause the ROC to take unilateral action which would upset the armistice agreement in Korea."

5

Containment Versus Liberation

Divergent Perspectives Within the Alliance

Throughout the U.S.-ROC alliance there was a fundamental conflict of perspective about the basic purpose of the alliance. U.S. leaders were generally committed to the strategy of containment, according to which Communist China was to be surrounded by a political-military zone intended to thwart Beijing's efforts to extend Communism into areas adjacent to China, and which would keep the Sino-Soviet alliance under pressure until that alliance broke apart. Communist China's diplomatic and propaganda offensives were to be countered and defeated, and various political, economic, and military instruments would be used to harass, pressure, and weaken Communist China. But unless Beijing imposed a major war on the United States through aggression against neighboring countries, the United States would not seek to overthrow or destroy China's Communist regime. The objective was to modify the behavior of China's Communist government, to weaken and isolate that regime, and to draw it away from the USSR, *not* to destroy the regime itself. From the American perspective, Nationalist China was a link in the system of containment. The purpose of the U.S.-ROC alliance was to consolidate Nationalist China within that system, using its assets as part of the countervailing structure of power in Asia.

Nationalist leaders, on the other hand, sought nothing less than the destruction of China's Communist regime and the state founded by that regime, the People's Republic of China. From the Nationalist perspective, the Communist-led government on the mainland was an illegitimate "bandit" clique that had temporarily usurped control over a large part of China's national territory, thereby disrupting the authority of China's legitimate, legally constituted government, the Republic of China. The regime ruling over the mainland was a regime that systematically negated China's traditions—for example, those regarding the family, respect for learning, and the private ownership of land. Nationalist leaders believed that, because of its oppressive nature, the CCP regime was extremely unpopular and maintained itself in power largely by coercion. Given this, it was the sacred duty of Free China to "recover" the mainland, liberating the Chinese people from the terrible yoke of Communist oppression. Taiwan was a "revolutionary base" on which the forces of the Chinese people's anti-Communist revolution could gather strength. The purpose of the U.S.-ROC alliance was to guarantee the security of that base until the moment the Nationalist return to the mainland arrived. When that moment arrived, the alliance should also, the Nationalists believed, provide the basis for U.S. support for the recovery of the mainland.

Washington was unwilling to found U.S. policy on the objective of overthrowing Communist rule in China. U.S. leaders recognized, however, that Nationalist commitment to that objective made Nationalist China more useful to the American strategy of containment. Because of the Nationalist commitment to the destruction of the CCP, Nationalist forces could be used to weaken and disrupt Communist China. Its intense hostility to the CCP made Nationalist China a particularly valuable asset both for protracted struggle via means short of war, and for the contingencies of limited or general war. Yet utilization of Nationalist capabilities entailed serious risks, the greatest being that utilization of Nationalist capabilities might allow the Nationalists to maneuver the United States into a war with China.

Not all Nationalist leaders were equally committed to the doctrine of returning to the mainland. Among the Nationalist elite, no one dared to openly challenge Chiang Kai-shek's belief that return to the mainland was the supreme mission for which all could be sacrificed. But there were some Nationalist leaders who understood that the reality of Communist China's immense power made such an outcome unlikely—at least short of a major U.S.-PRC war. Some Nationalist leaders felt that the primary duty was construction and defense of Free China *on Taiwan,* and understood that this objective might be endangered by efforts to recover the mainland. Again, given the authoritarian political system of Nationalist China under Chiang Kai-shek, such views could not be openly expressed. Their adherents could, however, subtly support American proposals predicated on such views.

Among the American elite, too, there were differing degrees of commit-ment to the dominant doctrine, containment. During the Truman Adminis-tration, U.S. leaders took an extremely jaundiced view of Chiang's vision of return to the mainland. Having watched the Nationalist regime on the main-land crumble after 1945, such individuals as Truman, Marshall, and Ache-son simply had too low an estimate of Nationalist abilities to believe that notions of return were anything more than self-delusion and fantasy. Even under Truman, however, and following China's entry into the Korean War, U.S. leaders took a supremely pragmatic approach to the use of Nationalist forces against Communist China, usage which the Nationalists invariably framed in terms of return to the mainland. As we shall see in chapter 8, the Truman administration undertook the earliest and one of the largest U.S.-ROC operations "returning" Nationalist forces to the mainland in the border regions of Yunnan Province.

U.S. leaders were generally open to exploring the possibility that Nation-alist military activity might provide the catalyst for effective resistance to Communist rule on the mainland. U.S. leaders also saw a standing and credible threat of Nationalist return as an instrument of psychological war-fare against Communist China, and as a factor enhancing the esprit de corps and fighting potential of Nationalist forces. On the other hand, U.S. leaders were apprehensive about being maneuvered by the Nationalists into a war with Communist China over issues not fundamental to U.S. national security.

Under Eisenhower, U.S. leaders looked more sympathetically on Nation-alist aspirations to return to the mainland (even while preparing a legal basis for Taiwan's separation from China). Several factors underlaid more posi-tive appraisal of liberation: ideological sympathy for liberation and antipa-thy toward containment; a desire to seize the initiative in the struggle against the Sino-Soviet bloc, and a desire to make greater use of indigenous forces. A radical and effective reorganization of Nationalist military forces during the early 1950s also played a role, making it more plausible that Nationalist forces might, after all, become an effective fighting force.

In his first state-of-the-union message on 2 February 1953, just two weeks after taking office, Eisenhower announced that he was ordering the Seventh Fleet to no longer prevent Nationalist operations against the main-land. Eisenhower tied this move to the war in Korea: earlier U.S. policy had "permitted [the Chinese] Communists, with greater impunity, to kill our soldiers . . . in Korea." "We certainly have no obligation to protect a nation fighting us in Korea," Eisenhower added.[1] Eisenhower was using the Na-tionalist threat to signal Chinese leaders that the ongoing hot war would be expanded if peace was not soon reached in Korea. Shortly before Eisen-hower made this statement, U.S. minister Karl Rankin informed Chiang

Kai-shek of its content, and sought and received from Chiang assurances that the Nationalists would consult the United States before undertaking significant attacks on Communist-held territory.[2]

In May 1953 Chiang seized the opportunity of U.S. planning for an expanded Sino-U.S. war in the eventuality of a collapse of the Korean peace talks. Chiang proposed an invasion of the mainland by sixty Nationalist divisions, to be raised and trained within three years. This was a force nearly three times as large as deemed appropriate for Nationalist China by U.S. strategic planners. The objective of the proposed landing was nothing less than the overthrow of the Chinese Communist regime. The Free World should strike swiftly, Chiang urged, before the military and economic plans of Communist China were completed. Once those plans were completed, the resources of China and Russia would be pooled for a combined offensive against the United States. Chinese Communist military forces had suffered immense casualties in Korea and were still in the process of rearming and reorganizing. If the Free World struck now, it could topple the CCP regime without risking a war with the Soviet Union. In a few years, however, when those countries were economically and militarily prepared, this would be impossible, Chiang warned.[3]

In June 1953, during the final tense weeks of the Korean armistice negotiations, JCS Chairman Arthur Radford proceeded to Taiwan for talks on the Asian situation. During those talks, Chiang laid on the table a detailed plan for his proposed return. Radford declined to discuss the plan but did propose that in the event of a U.S.-supported Nationalist amphibious landing on the mainland, the commander of the U.S. naval forces would have overall command. In the event that U.S. ground forces participated "temporarily" in the landing, the U.S. commander would have command of all ROC forces until such time as U.S. forces were withdrawn.[4] Chiang immediately agreed to both proposals. He was pessimistic about the efforts to reach a truce in Korea, and he strongly urged that the United States respond to collapse of the talks with a blockade of the China coast and with the bombing of bases in Manchuria.[5]

As part of the effort to signal Beijing that the United States would expand the war rather than accept indefinite stalemate, Washington authorized a major Nationalist offensive against the mainland. On the night of 15 July 1953, a Nationalist force of 10,000 set out from Jinmen for Dongshan Island, a relatively large island (165 square kilometers, with three-quarters of a million inhabitants) just off the southern Fujian coast. The force landed early the next morning. Two detachments of paratroopers were dropped on the north side of the island to prevent reinforcement across the 500-meter channel separating Dongshan from the mainland. The People's Liberation

Army (PLA) nonetheless succeeded in pushing in reinforcements. After a 7½–hour battle, the Communists prevailed. Three thousand Nationalist soldiers were killed. The remainder withdrew to Jinmen.[6]

The Korean truce was signed on 27 July. The Eisenhower Administration accordingly shelved Chiang's proposals for a large-scale invasion of China. This decision was conveyed to Chiang by Vice-President Richard Nixon during an October 1953 visit to Taipei.[7] U.S. interest in and support for small-scale Nationalist offensive operations continued, however. NSC 146/2, the Eisenhower administration's first definitive statement of policy toward Nationalist China, signed by the president on 6 November 1953, committed the United States to support *limited offensive operations* by the Nationalists. It provided that "without committing U.S. forces, unless Formosa or the Pescadores are attacked, [the United States would] encourage and assist the Chinese National Government to defend the Nationalist-held offshore islands against Communist attack *and to raid Chinese Communist territory and commerce*" (emphasis added). But it also limited the U.S. commitment by providing that the United States would avoid "any implication of U.S. obligation to underwrite the Government or to guarantee its return to power on the mainland."[8]

Six months later, the NSC reported that this provision had been implemented by "discrete expression of attitudes on the part of Embassy Taipei, important Defense visitors to Taipei, and the MAAG [Military Assistance Advisory Group], rather than by public exhortations or rebukes which have generally proven to be counterproductive in the Chinese scene." "It has been made clear that the GRC [Government Republic of China] cannot assume that the United States is going to put [it] back on the mainland." The progress report also identified the "divergence" of U.S. and Nationalist perspectives as an "emerging problem." It continued, "The limited U.S. objectives are in increasing contrast to the larger objectives sought by the GRC (e.g., return to the mainland)[sic], which must depend on the United States to develop its capacity to reach its objectives. It may be expected that the GRC will become progressively more dissatisfied with the absence of U.S. agreement to support with U.S. forces the GRC's attempt to overthrow the Chinese Communist regime."[9]

Early in 1954, Taipei again proposed preparations for an invasion of the mainland. This proposal came in the form of a plan for a major expansion of Nationalist armed forces submitted in February 1954 to MAAG Commander General Samuel Chase. The plan called for an expansion of the Nationalist army by 46,700, to a total of 341,700 men. This proposal was advanced in the context of U.S.-ROC discussions over reorganization of GRC military forces and the U.S. formulation of a new two-year (1955–56)

Mutual Defense Assistance Program (MDAP). It was also submitted at a time when the French position in Indochina was rapidly deteriorating and President Eisenhower was considering a plan to land Nationalist forces on Hainan Island as a diversionary move to support the French position at Dien Bien Phu.[10] In August the Joint Staff Planning Committee (JSPC) reported to the JCS that the force levels proposed in Taipei's plan considerably exceeded the force levels considered necessary for the accomplishment of the defensive and limited offensive missions outlined in NSC 146/2. It would also, the JSPC reported, require an additional $1.3 billion in military assistance. In line with this, in September the JCS rejected Taipei's proposal and ruled out U.S. support for any expansion of GRC military forces through 1956.[11] By that time, of course, the United States had already acceded to the Communist takeover of North Vietnam.

The Utility of Nationalist Pressure

Although the Eisenhower administration repeatedly gave active and serious consideration to the large-scale use of Nationalist forces against Communist China, it ultimately concluded that unless war were imposed by the actions of the PRC itself, the United States would seek to avoid a general Sino-American war. Several broad considerations underlay Eisenhower's rejection of support for a Nationalist return to the mainland. First of all, U.S. officials were not sanguine about the military capabilities of the Nationalist regime. An NSC staff study of 6 April 1953 analyzing U.S. Far Eastern policy found that:

> The disparity in military potential between the Chinese Communist regime and the Chinese Government is so great that it is safe to assume that as long as the former remains intact and maintains its hold on the mainland (and there is no evidence that it will not do so in the foreseeable future) it will never view the Chinese National Government as a serious military threat. It constitutes a threat to Peiping (other than of a local nature) only in so far as it is an adjunct of U.S. power in the Far East.[12]

Given this estimate of the military balance between the Communists and the Nationalists, approval of a major Nationalist offensive against the mainland unsupported by U.S. forces would have resulted in Nationalist defeat, eviscerating the Nationalist ability to defend Taiwan itself.

U.S. leaders also discounted prospects for popular anti-Communist uprisings in response to a Nationalist invasion. As CIA Director Allen Dulles told Eisenhower at a NSC meeting on 18 June 1953, the prospect for an anti-Communist uprising in China on the order of the uprising then under way in East Germany "was the most remote of all the current possibilities."[13] Regarding the Nationalist claim in early 1953 of contact with 650,000 anti-Communist guerrillas on the mainland, Taiwan MAAG G-2 estimated that 70,000 was a more realistic number.[14] Again the U.S. estimate of the actual military balance between Taiwan and the mainland led America to discredit Chiang's repeated claims that a Nationalist return could succeed without large-scale U.S. participation. A successful Nationalist return would require a major war between the PRC and the United States. If, however, the U.S. government led the American people to war with China other than in direct and clear response to Chinese aggression, the American people, and their European allies, would not support such a war. Secretary John Foster Dulles succinctly made this point during a 19 August 1954 NSC review of U.S. policy toward China: "World public opinion," Dulles said, "was a tremendous force which must be reckoned with."[15]

Still another U.S. fear was that a major U.S.-PRC war would greatly enhance the USSR's relative global position by diverting U.S. resources from Europe while alienating America's European allies. Europe was the central theater of the Cold War, U.S. leaders felt. To counter Soviet pressure there, the United States needed to strengthen the North Atlantic alliance. A major war with China would run counter to this, forcing the United States to shift resources and attention to Asia. If, as most U.S. leaders deemed likely, the Soviet Union remained nonbelligerent in a U.S.-PRC war, it would be able to concentrate its resources on Europe while the United States was bogged down in Asia. West European capitals might also disassociate themselves from a Sino-American war they perceived as ill-conceived and far removed from their own vital interests. A Sino-American war might, in other words, undermine efforts to build a North Atlantic security community. A Chinese-American war would thus be a great boon to the Soviet Union in Europe. As Secretary of Defense George Wilson pointed out at an October 1954 NSC discussion of the possibility of a Sino-American war: "Nothing would be so good for Russia as to get the United States involved in a war with Communist China."[16]

The Eisenhower administration also rejected Nationalist proposals for an attack on the PRC because it remained hopeful that the Sino-Soviet alliance would pull apart, and wanted to do nothing to hinder that process. The NSC staff paper of 6 April 1953, for instance, said that disrupting the Sino-Soviet alignment and detaching China from the Soviet orbit was a priority in dealing with the threat posed by Chinese Communist aggression. The paper postulated two ways that a Sino-Soviet split might be achieved: either by defection of the Beijing government or by the overthrow of the Beijing regime. It then proceeded to argue that there was no immediate need to make a choice between these two options since both would be facilitated, at least in the short term, by a U.S. policy of pressure against China. Support for the Nationalist regime was one important way in which the United States could exert such pressure.[17]

Pressure by a militarily potent and U.S.-backed Nationalist China would help induce a Sino-Soviet split. The basic strategic aim of the Eisenhower Administration was the same as that of the Truman Administration: splitting the Sino-Soviet alliance. The means, however, were exactly opposite. Whereas the Truman Administration sought to foster Chinese "Titoism" by disengaging from Nationalist China or, after June 1950, by signaling its willingness to re-disengage following the restoration of peace in Korea, the Eisenhower Administration sought to achieve the same end by engaging the Nationalists and using them to pressure Communist China. Both administrations understood that a major war between the United States and the PRC would solidify the Sino-Soviet alliance.

The issue of the durability of the Sino-Soviet alliance was discussed foursquarely at an NSC meeting on 18 August 1954. Army Chief of Staff Matthew Ridgway (who did not attend the meeting but whose opinions were conveyed to it) took the most forceful position regarding the possibility of a Sino-Soviet split. Such a split was quite possible, and encouragement of it should be the "basic principle" of U.S. China policy, Ridgway said. To this end he favored a conciliatory approach toward China. At the other extreme were Radford and Eisenhower. Radford felt that the Sino-Soviet bond was of a "religious" nature and that there was little possibility of breaking it. Eisenhower seconded Radford's view and opined that it was hopeless for the United States to imagine that it could break China away from the Soviets short of a general war. The middle ground was occupied by Secretary of State Dulles and Vice-President Nixon who argued that over a long period of time, perhaps twenty-five years, Chinese pride and Russian arrogance would combine with conflicts of national interests to produce a rupture. Such a break would not be fostered, however, by a "soft" conciliatory U.S. policy toward China, but by a "tough coexistence" policy midway between appeasement and war.[18] The Dulles-Nixon view precluded war with Communist China if that could be avoided. That is, it ruled out U.S. support for a Nationalist invasion. The *threat* of such an invasion, however, along with Nationalist harassment and subversive operations against the mainland, were useful in keeping the Sino-Soviet alliance under pressure and thereby facilitating its disintegration.

The Taiwan Strait crisis of 1954–55 and the tighter U.S.-ROC association deriving from the mutual security treaty of December 1954 prompted the United States to modify its support for Nationalist limited offensive operations. As tension in the strait mounted with the beginning of PLA artillery bombardment of Jinmen and Mazu, Washington withdrew its authorization for Nationalist limited offensive operations *against the mainland.* On 24 September Eisenhower accepted a proposal by Secretary of Defense Wilson to stop encouraging Chinese Nationalist offensive operations against the mainland. Such a move would allow Nationalist forces to "cool off," minimizing prospects for their "intentionally or accidentally provoking increased hostilities with the Chinese Communists." Secretary of State Dulles concurred in this decision, but successfully insisted that Nationalist operations against maritime traffic to and from Communist China (as opposed to targets on land) be allowed to continue.[19] This allowed Nationalist maritime harassment of PRC commerce to continue—a topic considered in chapter 7. Finally, the exchange of notes following the mutual security treaty also ruled out an independent Nationalist decision to launch a return to the mainland. As Secretary Dulles subsequently explained to the U.S. Senate during the ratification debate, those notes meant that "offensive military operations by either party from the territories held by the Republic of China would be undertaken only as a matter of joint agreement."[20]

Although administration officials rejected the idea of U.S. support for a Nationalist invasion, they did not rule out such an invasion per se. While publicly disassociating the United States from a Nationalist return, the administration was careful to keep alive Nationalist hopes that such support might, someday, be forthcoming. During 1955 Dulles privately outlined to ROC leaders U.S. views about when a Nationalist return to the mainland might be permissible. The first contingency involved a split between Chinese Communist Party (CCP) leaders comparable to the Trotsky-Stalin split of the 1920s. The second was a widespread uprising against CCP rule. The third was a general war against Communist China in which it would be advisable to attack China from all directions. If any of these eventualities materialized, Dulles told Foreign Minister George Yeh, then the Nationalists might return with U.S. support. Moreover, such eventualities were bound to arise, and when they did, "the importance of having a free China ready to move into such a situation is tremendous." But while holding out hope of eventual U.S. support for a Nationalist return, Dulles also told Yeh that these conditions could not be created by the Nationalists. Nor could the Nationalists act alone; U.S. consent would be necessary. Nationalist Taiwan should, therefore, bide its time and build its strength until the moment to strike arrived. Until that time, Dulles said, it would be better for Taipei to talk less about return to the mainland, since continued talk in lieu of action would expose the Nationalists to ridicule abroad and would eventually lead to disillusionment and a decline in morale at home. For his part, Chiang Kai-shek assured the Americans that Taipei would undertake no large-scale operations against the mainland without full consultation with the United States.[21]

Early in 1956 Chiang attempted to persuade Washington that the conditions for liberation outlined by Secretary Dulles a year earlier had now materialized. During talks with Dulles and Assistant Secretary of State Walter Robertson in March, Chiang urged U.S. support for wars of national unification and liberation by South Korea and Nationalist China. The Free World should adopt aggressive new tactics to create "confusion and trouble in Communist territory," preventing consolidation of Communist rule and countering Communist subversion in the Free World, Chiang said.[22] Robertson replied that while the United States was determined to oppose Communist aggression, it would not launch an offensive anywhere for any purpose. But Robertson was also careful to hold out hope of eventual U.S. support of a Nationalist return. An uprising against Communist rule was certain to occur, Robertson said, and when it did, Free China was certain to play an important role.

Chiang presented his ideas directly to Eisenhower in a letter the next month, calling on the United States to support "sustained action by the forces of free China" to induce revolution in China. The great majority of Asia's people were "ardent friends" of the United States, and the U.S. philosophy of freedom was having a profound impact on Asia, Chiang told Eisenhower. China was the crux of the great contest between freedom and Communism then under way in Asia: "Whether or not freedom in Asia [is] made secure depends to a very large extent on the success or failure of China's efforts to regain her freedom by overthrowing the Communist regime." The Free World, Chiang argued, should seize the initiative and induce revolution in Communist countries. Free China, Chiang said, "must be given the opportunity to achieve a breakthrough of the Iron Curtain at the earliest possible moment." The Chinese Communist regime was undergoing "extreme social and economic difficulties" and was ripe for revolt, Chiang asserted. "Once the forces of Free China . . . [have] established beachheads on the coast . . . there is every possibility that the population throughout the country will rise in revolt." Addressing American fears that such action would lead to world war, Chiang assured Eisenhower that the Soviets were too weak to intervene. The Soviet Union would avoid world war unless directly attacked, Chiang told Eisenhower. If Moscow did intervene, Chiang said, such intervention would be confined to the area north of the Yellow River. Nor would "direct participation in actual combat" by U.S. forces be necessary, Chiang promised. American "logistics support" would be sufficient. Such bold action would eliminate the Communist menace to Korea and Vietnam, prevent the Soviet bloc from accumulating the strength necessary to launch a new world war, and greatly reduce the Communist threat to Southeast Asia and the Middle East.[23]

Washington rejected Chiang's proposal. Admiral Radford conveyed the American response during an August 1956 visit to Taipei. The United States would not accept Chiang's proposal, Radford said, since to do so would initiate a war. If war with China occurred, Radford said, the Communists must clearly bear responsibility for starting it. Otherwise the American people and their allies would not support the war effort. Chiang responded that since no U.S. forces would be involved in his invasion, America's allies would have no basis for accusing the United States. Moreover, he was not pushing for immediate action, Chiang asserted, but merely for an agreement in principle that the purpose of U.S.–Nationalist China alliance was the ultimate recovery of the mainland. "We shall certainly ask for your concurrence when the moment comes for us to implement any plan," Chiang told Radford. "But you must first agree to the principle ... of counter-attacking the mainland. Indefinite waiting with no plan will seriously affect the morale of our troops and people."[24]

The uprising in Hungary in October and Eisenhower's election to his second term in November 1956 prompted Chiang to push once again for U.S. consent to a Nationalist return. On 11 December Chiang sent Eisenhower a letter congratulating him on his reelection and urging him to shoulder the Lincoln-like task of leading the "emancipation of the captive peoples in Europe as well as in Asia." Recalling Eisenhower's 1952 election campaign calls for the liberation of captive peoples, Chiang said that his reelection would "make it possible for you to lead the Free World to undertake this historic task, upon the outcome of which hinges the fate of mankind and human civilization." At the end of his letter, after calling for what amounted to a third world war, Chiang wished the Eisenhowers a merry Christmas.[25]

Eisenhower replied to Chiang on 26 December. He "agreed" that a continuation of the "present firm policy" toward China would lead to a "growing rebelliousness among the captive peoples ... which the Communist rulers will, in the end, be unable to contain." Nationalist China and the United States should calmly and steadfastly await that moment, Eisenhower said, and prepare to take advantage of it in an "appropriate manner when the time arrives."[26] Again the U.S. message was, "Yes, but not now."

JOHN MOORES UNIVERSITY LRC
AVRIL ROBARTS
TEL. 0151 231 4022

Alliance Bargaining: The Threat of
Nationalist Defection

One important reason the United States did not explicitly rule out support for a Nationalist return was a fear that this would lead to extreme Nationalist dissatisfaction with American policy, perhaps even resulting in Nationalist defection from the alliance. Chiang Kai-shek was not interested in mere containment of Communist China. Nor was he interested in splitting China from the Soviet Union, an unlikely development, he felt, which in any case was likely to lead to some sort of PRC-U.S. modus vivendi. Chiang's maximal objective was nothing less than destruction of Communist rule over the mainland. He realized, however, that this could be achieved only with all-out U.S. support. This translated into continual efforts to persuade Washington to adopt a policy of liberation and to maneuver Beijing and Washington into collision.

Chiang had several levers of influence over U.S. policy. One important instrument of leverage, exercised directly on the highest level of the U.S. decision-making elite, was the threat of collapse of Nationalist morale. Threat of defection is one of the major bargaining dynamics of alliances. By threatening to defect from an alliance, one partner seeks to modify the behavior of its alliance partner. In the case of Chiang Kai-shek and the U.S.-ROC alliance, the threat of defection took a subtle and indirect form—the threatened collapse of Nationalist morale. Chiang and other Nationalist leaders repeatedly told U.S. leaders that abandonment of the mission of recovery of the mainland, failure to defend the offshore islands, admission of Communist China to the United Nations, and so on, would lead to a collapse of Nationalist morale. The consequences of this collapse of morale could be, U.S. leaders feared, the loss of Taiwan as a link in the western Pacific defense perimeter.

U.S. fear of Nationalist demoralization involved several interrelated concerns.[27] One was a belief that if the Nationalists lost hope of returning to power on the mainland, they would come to terms with the CCP. Nationalist leaders were Chinese patriots committed to the establishment of China as a leading world power. They had no interest in becoming instruments of the permanent alienation of Taiwan from the Chinese nation, a role that would condemn them to being recorded by future Chinese historians as traitors to the Han race. If Nationalist leaders were confronted with the reality that their great mission of overthrowing the Communists could simply not be fulfilled, in part because of lack of U.S. support, Nationalist leaders might decide to strike a deal with the CCP. If Nationalist leaders had been willing to break with the United States and to help bring about the incorporation of

Taiwan into the PRC, CCP leaders would certainly have been willing to reward them with prominent, if honorific, positions. Some might even have been incorporated into the CCP's ruling structure. For all Nationalists, a deal with the Communists would have permitted them to return to their ancestral homes.

Another path to loss of Taiwan via Nationalist demoralization was through increased vulnerability to Communist subversion and pressure. The CCP was unremitting in its efforts to build up a clandestine infrastructure in Taiwan, to persuade Nationalists to cooperate with CCP efforts, and to foment revolt among native Taiwanese. These efforts were ultimately unsuccessful, in part because of effective Nationalist counterespionage efforts, as well as because of the rapid and equitable growth of Taiwan's economy during the 1950s and 1960s.[28] Another factor contributing to the failure of Communist subversion was high Nationalist morale. This in turn required, or at least so Nationalist leaders believed, active combat operations against the Communists and ideological mobilization—hatred of the Communist enemy and belief in the inevitability of his destruction. Compromise, negotiation, and a pacifist policy toward the enemy would lead, the Nationalists argued, to ideological disarmament, to a desire to reach an accommodation with the Communists. Once this slippery path was embarked upon, Communist subversion of the anti-Communist forces would follow. A militant, confrontational approach to the Communists—the drawing of clear demarcation lines between enemies and friends, between Communist and anti-Communist forces—was essential to foil Communist subversion, the Nationalists argued. Militant policies toward the mainland were a corollary of this.

Even during the heyday of militant anti-Communism in the 1950s, U.S. leaders did not accept the Nationalist proposition that negotiations and peaceful coexistence with Communism necessarily opened the door to Communist subversion. Yet they did take seriously the argument that dissipation of the Nationalists' militant anti-Communist spirit could open the door to subversion. This question was discussed, for example, on 9 April 1952 by the Department of State and the Joint Chiefs of Staff, which met to consider whether or not to redefine the mission of the Seventh Fleet to allow Nationalist attacks against the mainland. CIA deputy director Allen Dulles was especially concerned that if Nationalist soldiers lost hope of fighting their way back to their mainland homes they would "go back as individuals." Therefore, Dulles argued, the mission of the Seventh Fleet should be altered to "assure that Formosa is an asset" in the event of a general U.S.-China war. Although fear of enabling Chiang to precipitate an expanded Sino-U.S. war overrode this consideration, State Department

Counselor Charles E. Bohlen summarized the consensus of the meeting thusly: "We want to have a [Nationalist] capability ready for use in case of certain eventualities. We want to be ready to use it if and when certain circumstances arise. The question this raises is whether we can keep Formosa as an asset with our present policy [of demoralizing the Nationalists by not allowing them to strike at the mainland]."[29]

As Bohlen's words indicate, "demoralization" would also lead to erosion of Nationalist military capabilities. U.S. leaders recognized that military effectiveness depended not primarily on weapons and technical proficiency, but on psychological factors including belief in a transcendent objective and the attainability of that objective, an aggressive state of mind, and a willingness to sacrifice. Offensive military operations against the mainland fostered these psychological attributes. Offensive operations also constituted training under actual combat conditions that enhanced Nationalist military effectiveness. U.S. leaders valued this military effectiveness because, in the first instance, it was essential to the defense of Taiwan. Conversely, a weaker Taiwan was more susceptible to Communist pressure. More effective Nationalist forces could also make a greater contribution to the collective effort in the event of a general war in East Asia. Military effectiveness pointed toward acceptance of limited Nationalist offensive operations predicated on return to the mainland.

From Chiang Kai-shek's perspective, threatening collapse of Nationalist morale provided him effective leverage with the *mainstream* of the U.S. elite that believed in containment, not merely with the small minority that embraced the doctrine of liberation. There were some true believers in liberation in the Eisenhower Administration—Assistant Secretary of State Walter Robertson and JCS Chairman Admiral Arthur Radford being the two most prominent. But these men represented a minority view. Containment was the mainstream. To influence U.S. policy, Chiang had to appeal to this mainstream. The doctrine of collapse of Nationalist morale allowed him to do this. Because mainstream Republican leaders valued Nationalist Taiwan as an asset in containing Communist China, they feared that the loss of Taiwan would dangerously weaken containment. By asserting that particular U.S. actions would lead to the collapse of Nationalist morale, Chiang was thus able to threaten to deny Taiwan to Washington.

Chiang's ploy of threatening defection qua collapse of morale significantly influenced U.S. policy. Fear of undermining Nationalist morale was a major consideration in U.S. decisions to support Nationalist retention of Jinmen and Mazu. The desire to maintain Nationalist morale was also a key reason for the United States' refusal to explicitly reject Chiang's policy of return to the mainland. Administration officials generally believed that if the

Nationalists were confronted with outright U.S. rejection of a Nationalist return, their morale would collapse. As a National Intelligence Estimate (NIE) of September 1954 said, "Nationalist leaders feel that to renounce this objective [of return] would be to accept as final and absolute the destruction of Chinese society and culture by alien and barbarian forces. This objective underlie[s] all of Nationalist China's policy considerations and behavior."[30]

U.S. concern about a possible collapse of Nationalist morale appeared again and again during the 1950s. A NIE of April 1955, for example, investigated the impact of the loss of Jinmen and Mazu on Nationalist morale and concluded that their loss would have a substantial adverse effect on Nationalist morale.[31] A 1957 decision to deploy atomic-capable Matador missiles to Taiwan was motivated in part by the impact this move was expected to have on Nationalist morale.[32]

As the United States moved to "neutralize" the Taiwan Strait in 1954–55, consideration was given to flatly telling the Nationalists that, short of a general U.S.-PRC war, the United States would not support a Nationalist return. This would open the way, so the argument ran, to consolidation of the status quo in the Taiwan Strait. A NIE of August 1957, for example, noted that "However important it may be for Nationalist morale to hold out the promise of return, continued emphasis on this theme constitutes a major vulnerability in the Nationalist position," since it was certain to produce frustration. The NIE continued, "The staying power of the Republic of China will be determined by the ability of Nationalist leaders to adjust to life on Taiwan." The implicit conclusion was that the Nationalists should be pressured to drop their policy of return. This was challenged at some length by Assistant Secretary Robertson. Robertson argued that hope of "return" was "a key part of the very rationale" of Nationalist China, and rejected the "dubious proposition" that Nationalist acceptance of Communist control of the mainland would improve Nationalist morale.[33]

Robertson's view prevailed in a series of NSC meetings in September and October 1957, in which it was debated whether the United States should drop its support for Chiang's claim to the mainland. Again the maintenance of Nationalist morale proved decisive. The debate was framed in terms of whether the military mission assigned to Nationalist forces should be purely defensive (the defense of Taiwan, the Pescadores, Jinmen, and Mazu) or whether it also should include an offensive component. Secretary of State Dulles argued strongly in favor of allowing an aggressive component. According to Dulles, to deprive the Nationalists of hope of eventually overthrowing the CCP would destroy morale on Taiwan, make defense of that island impossible, and lead to its loss to the Communists. If

Nationalist hopes of returning to the mainland were "destroyed," Dulles said, the United States "would lose the whole show in the Far East." Eisenhower strongly seconded Dulles, arguing that only the hope of ultimately returning to the mainland sustained Nationalist morale. The president pointed out, however, that the United States need not actually work for such a return, but only allow the Nationalists to believe that it did.[34] U.S. policy toward a Nationalist return involved calculated ambiguity. U.S. leaders had decided that short of a major U.S.-PRC war, the United States would not support a Nationalist return. They could not say this, however, since to do so would critically undermine Nationalist morale. Moreover, to encourage Nationalist hopes, and to maintain Nationalist morale and military effectiveness, the United States had to agree to limited Nationalist offensive operations predicated on return. Moreover, these limited offensive operations were not without utility, especially in the area of intelligence collection.

U.S. policy required careful management of the contradiction between maintaining Nationalist morale and checking Nationalist actions that might entangle the United States in a war with China. To fulfill its assigned role in containing Communist China, Nationalist China had to be strong and confident. Yet the stronger and more confident the Nationalists became, the more able they were to draw the United States into confrontations with Communist China. If the United States supported Nationalist forces in attacking China, it risked war with Communist China over peripheral issues. Yet if it did not support Nationalist offensive operations, Chiang threatened, elliptically, to throw himself out the window ("defenestration" in the vernacular of the day), taking Nationalist China with him and thereby severely weakening the structure of power containing Communist China.

The PRC's "Three Hard Years" and the Nationalist Return

By 1959, the CCP's Great Leap Forward was collapsing into one of the most severe famines of modern history. By the time the situation began to ease in 1962, perhaps as many as twenty million people had died, many of them children.[35] Signs of widespread popular discontent were abundant. By May 1962, for example, 5,000 refugees per day were pouring into Hong Kong.[36] In the words of one Nationalist official, "The Mainland is a powder keg on the verge of explosion."[37]

Chiang Kai-shek seized on the collapse of the mainland economy to push, yet again, for U.S. support for a return. In October 1959 Chiang submitted to Washington a plan of action. In its evaluation of Chiang's proposal, JCS G-2 agreed that there was indeed "widespread dissatisfaction and suffering" on the mainland. There was, however, "no evidence to indicate any weakening of the absolute control exercised by the regime, whose forces are loyal to it and are capable of suppressing any popular movement to overthrow it." JCS G-2 believed that Chiang's proposal was mainly a "trial balloon" to see if the United States was now ready to support a return. JCS G-2 was also concerned with prospects for an unauthorized Nationalist attack on the mainland. This was not likely, the report concluded, since an invasion launched without U.S. support would "easily" be repulsed by the Chinese Communists, who were called "Chicoms." But there was still an "outside chance" that Chiang would launch such an attack on the assumption that the United States would support him after the fact:

> He is getting no younger and the ChiComs are solidifying their control. He may truly feel that this is the last and best chance to attempt retaking the mainland. The risk of creating a general war is not likely to worry the Generalissimo very much; the risk of failure—which he realizes as inevitable without U.S. support—will be his major concern.[38]

When the Kennedy Administration took office in January 1961 it promptly confronted Nationalist proposals for a return to the mainland. Dealing with such proposals became almost a rite of passage for new U.S. administrations during the first two decades of the Cold War. As with the newly installed Eisenhower Administration eight years earlier, certain factors inclined the new U.S. leaders toward a favorable response to Nationalist proposals. John F. Kennedy came into the White House convinced that the United States faced a critical test in its history, and indeed in the history of the human struggle for freedom. Colonialism was collapsing. The Communist camp had targeted the newly independent countries for revolution. If this new Communist offensive succeeded, freedom would perish throughout much of the Third World, and these newly emerging nations would develop along totalitarian lines rather than along pluralistic, democratic lines. This was an epic contest, the outcome of which would determine the fate of mankind for "ten thousand years."[39] America could not, Kennedy believed, meet this challenge passively. It should "move forward to meet Communism, rather than waiting for it to come to us and then reacting to it."[40]

This bold approach translated into the strategy of "flexible response," a stress on counterinsurgency warfare, and a growing concern with the Communist-led revolution in South Vietnam. The challenge in Vietnam was, the New Frontiersmen believed, a "test case" which had to be met boldly and aggressively. Thus, in mid-1961, Kennedy decided to substantially expand the U.S. commitment to South Vietnam. Among the measures he approved was a program of CIA-coordinated covert operations (code-named "Operation Farmhand") against the Ho Chi Minh trail in Laos and against North Vietnam.[41]

Kennedy also believed it was necessary to "fight fire with fire" by supporting subversive and guerrilla warfare within Communist countries which were supporting revolution abroad.[42] On the other hand, the Kennedy Administration also showed signs of moving toward some sort of understanding with Communist China. The United States' commitment to defend Jinmen had emerged as something of a litmus test in the Kennedy-Nixon campaign debates, and Kennedy had questioned the wisdom of such a commitment. Underlying this position was a recognition that Communist rule in China was not a passing phase and that the United States should begin looking toward some change in the U.S. policy of regarding the Nationalist government as the true government of all of China.[43] There were, in short, contradictory urges in the Kennedy Administration and indeed within Kennedy himself.

In the context of countering China's global revolutionism and punishing its support for Hanoi's expanding revolutionary effort in Indochina, support for a Nationalist invasion of the mainland had much in its favor. What better way to counter China's support for subversion and revolution in South Vietnam than by supporting comparable activities in China? What better way to exploit the paradox of a Communist power itself tottering on the verge of collapse while fostering revolution in other countries? Why not act to destabilize the power itself, thus encouraging destabilization—that is, why not fight fire with fire? Some influential people, such as CIA director John McCone, felt that this should be done.[44]

In March 1962, Chiang Ching-kuo carried to Washington a detailed plan for a Nationalist return. It involved a "covert" but large-scale Nationalist landing disguised to look like a spontaneous uprising, a sort of giant-sized Bay of Pigs operation. The Kennedy Administration considered Chiang's proposal throughout the spring of 1962.[45]

While Washington was considering Taipei's plan, Chiang intensified preparations for war. Draft calls were increased. The period of military service was extended indefinitely. The Counter-Attack Action Committee was set up, and the Nationalist cadre school outside of Taipei began training cadre to reestablish GRC institutions in areas of the mainland liberated by invading ROC armies. The government instituted a special war tax to raise U.S. $60 million. There were major purchases of foreign weapons. Surveillance activities along the mainland coast increased. Beijing took the Nationalist threat quite seriously. Mao Zedong ordered emergency preparations to counter an invasion. Naval units were deployed from the northern to the eastern fleet.[46]

Taipei's efforts were not successful. At a meeting at the White House on 20 June 1962, it was decided to disassociate the United States from any Nationalist invasion effort and to so inform Beijing. This was done at a special meeting of the Warsaw talks on 23 June 1962.[47] Once again the U.S. government had decided in favor of a cautious path which avoided provoking China. By late 1963, Nationalist propaganda had begun to stress that time was on the Nationalist side and that the Nationalists should, therefore, bide their time.[48]

Notes

1. *Department of State Bulletin,* 9 February 1953, p. 209.
2. Chiang to Rankin, 1 February 1953, *FRUS,* 1952–54, vol. XIV, part 1, pp. 35–36.
3. Jones to State Department, 27 May 1953, *FRUS,* 1952–54, vol. XIV, part 1, pp. 197–98.
4. Memoir of Chiang-Radford conversation, 18 June 1953, *FRUS,* 1952–54, vol. XIV, part I, pp. 205–10.
5. Jones to Department of State, 22 July 1952, *FRUS,* 1952–54, vol. XIV, pp. 76–77.
6. *Zhongguo xiandai zhanzheng zhanlue jiexi cidian* (Analytical dictionary of modern Chinese wars and strategy), Beijing: Guofang daxue chubanshe, 1991, p. 696.
7. Richard M. Nixon, *Memoirs,* vol. I, New York: Warner Books, 1978, p. 154.
8. NSC Progress Report on NSC 146/2, 16 July 1954.
9. Ibid.
10. Nixon, *Memoirs,* vol. I, p. 185.
11. MAAG, Formosa to CINCPAC, 30 October 1954, and JSPC report to JCS, 5 August 1954, in National Archives, RG 218, JCS, Geographic File 1954–56, 381 Formosa, box 18, sec. 15.
12. *FRUS,* 1952–54, vol. XIV, part 1, p. 178.
13. Ibid., p. 204.
14. Ibid., p. 209.
15. Ibid., p. 531.
16. Ibid., p. 698.
17. Ibid., pp. 175–79.
18. Ibid., pp. 534–36.
19. Ibid., p. 651.
20. Statement before Senate Foreign Relations Committee, 7 February 1955, in *State Department Bulletin,* 21 February 1955, p. 289.
21. Dulles to Yeh, 10 February 1955, *FRUS,* 1955–57, vol. II, p. 256.
22. Memoir of Chiang-Dulles discussions, 15 March and 16 March 1956, *FRUS,* 1955–57, vol. III, pp. 326–29, 331–32.
23. Chiang to Eisenhower, 16 April 1956, *FRUS,* 1955–57, vol. II, pp. 343–48.
24. *FRUS,* 1955–57, vol. II, p. 413.
25. Ibid., pp. 447–48.
26. Eisenhower to Chiang, 26 December 1956, *FRUS,* 1955–57, vol. II, pp. 462–63.
27. Thomas E. Stolper, *China, Taiwan, and the Offshore Islands,* Armonk, NY: M.E. Sharpe, 1985, pp. 83, 88, 93.

28. See Ralph Clough, "Taiwan Under Nationalist Rule, 1949–1982," in *Cambridge History of China,* Roderick MacFarquhar and John K. Fairbank, eds., vol. 15, part 2, New York: Cambridge University Press, 1991, p. 838.

29. *FRUS,* 1952–54, vol. XIV, pp. 31–43.

30. Ibid., part 1, p. 631.

31. *FRUS,* 1955–57, vol. II, pp. 479–89.

32. Ibid., vol. III, p. 284.

33. Ibid., pp. 585–87.

34. Memos of NSC meetings of 23 September and 2 October 1957, in ibid., pp. 612–17.

35. Jonathan D. Spence, *The Search for Modern China,* New York: W.W. Norton, 1990, p. 583.

36. Roger Hilsman, *To Move a Nation: The Politics of Foreign Policy in the Administration of John F. Kennedy,* New York: Delta, 1967, p. 312. Hilsman was director of intelligence and research in Kennedy's State Department.

37. Cited in Melvin Gurtov and Byong-Moo Hwang, *China Under Threat, the Politics of Strategy and Diplomacy,* Baltimore: Johns Hopkins University Press, 1980, p. 127.

38. Report dated 22 October 1959, National Archives, RG 218, JCS, Central File 1959, 9142/5420.

39. See Louise Fitz-Simmons, *The Kennedy Doctrine,* New York: Random House, 1972.

40. Quoted in Henry Fairlie, *The Kennedy Promise,* Garden City, NY: Doubleday, 1973, p. 72.

41. See National Security Action Memorandum (NSAM) 52, 11 May 1961, in *United States–Vietnam Relations, 1945–1967,* Book Eleven, pp. 150–52.

42. Fitz-Simmons, *Kennedy Doctrine,* pp. 179–87.

43. Hilsman, *To Move a Nation,* p. 303.

44. Ibid., p. 318.

45. Ibid., pp. 312–19.

46. *Dangdai Zhongguo haijun* (Contemporary China's navy), Beijing: Zhongguo shehui kexueyuan, 1987, p. 369. In this PLA account, Chinese preparations for war were deemed responsible for deterring a U.S.-supported Nationalist invasion at this juncture.

47. Kenneth Y. Young, *Negotiating with the Chinese Communists: The United States Experience, 1953–1967,* New York: McGraw Hill, 1968, p. 250. Regarding the White House meeting, see Hilsman, *To Move a Nation,* pp. 318–19.

48. Hilsman, *To Move a Nation,* pp. 319–20.

6

Covert Operations Against the Mainland

The Decision to Wage Covert War

Nationalist China was important to the United States as an instrument for the conduct of covert operations against the mainland. These operations were an important component of U.S. strategy, intended to confuse, demoralize, and weaken the enemy. These operations involved close cooperation between the clandestine services of the United States and Nationalist China, and are partially explained by the strong institutional interests of the newly established Central Intelligence Agency (CIA). The CIA had strong organizational interests impelling it to favor cooperation with the Nationalists. For historic reasons, the U.S. intelligence apparatus in Asia was quite weak circa 1950, in sharp contrast to the robust state of that apparatus in Europe. During World War II, the Office of Strategic Services (OSS), the CIA's predecessor, developed very substantial assets in Nazi-occupied Europe. Upon Germany's surrender it also became heir to the very impressive intelligence apparatus built up in Eastern Europe by German intelligence under its eastern section chief, Reinhard Gehlen.[1] In Europe, the OSS and its successor, the CIA, found few cultural, social, and linguistic barriers to effective operations. Asia was different. In the Southwest Pacific theater during World War II, Douglas MacArthur flatly prohibited OSS operations, relying instead on the intelligence capabilities of his own staff.[2] In the China theater, the OSS became destructively entangled in China's factional struggles. First, the OSS found itself confronted with a rival organization run by U.S. Navy Captain Milton Miles, with the patronage of Dai Li, Chiang Kai-shek's immensely powerful head of secret police. Deep enmity developed between the OSS and Miles' organization in China. The OSS further antagonized Chiang's cortege when it became one of the prime movers behind the dispatch of a U.S. mission to the CCP capitol at Yennan in northwest China in 1944. While this move made excellent sense from many perspectives, one consequence was deepened hostility from Chiang and Dai Li. The OSS suspected, though it was never able to prove, that Dai Li's agents were murdering Chinese OSS agents. In any case, the OSS infrastructure in China remained very weak. This apparatus was then hit by the intense antispy campaigns of the CCP as the PLA swept across China in 1948–49. The result of all this was that, by 1950, the CIA had virtually no base of operations in China, or indeed, in the Far East more generally.

In the new global conflict that was emerging, the CIA was critically weak in the Far Eastern theater. To deal with the new global threat, and to remain a player in U.S. Far Eastern policy, the CIA needed to expand its Far Eastern infrastructure rapidly. Cooperation with Nationalist intelligence provided a way to do this. By cooperating with the Nationalists to wage covert war against Communist China, the CIA could contribute to the containment of Communist China, securing for itself a piece of the policy action in the Far East. In the process, it could build an infrastructure of operational and intelligence assets in East Asia, thereby making itself even more useful to U.S. leaders.

U.S. leaders thought of covert operations against the People's Republic of China (PRC) in terms of "psychological warfare." During World War II the United States had relied heavily on psychological warfare—"psywar"—defined as efforts to influence the opinions and behavior of enemy groups in certain desirable ways. The U.S. psywar apparatus was disbanded following 1945, but was reassembled, with NSC 68, when U.S. leaders concluded that the Free World was under sustained political, psychological, and clandestine attack and should "fight back with the same weapons."[3] In April 1951, the National Psychological Strategy Board was established.[4]

The United States soon began to resort to strategies of psychological warfare developed during World War II. Modern technology, ranging from long-distance aircraft to powerful radio transmitters, was once more harnessed for activities designed to demoralize the populace and undermine the governments and military forces of enemy countries. CIA Director Bedell Smith was dismayed by the scope of psychological warfare operations he found at the CIA when he took over the agency late in 1950. Fearing that these operations would interfere with the CIA's intelligence collection function, which he regarded as primary, Smith sought unsuccessfully to have the Defense Department assigned responsibility for guerrilla operations. The need for deniability, however, dictated that the CIA continue to assume primary responsibility.[5]

The first definitive reformulation of Asian policy following the outbreak of the Korean War, NSC 48/5 of May 1951, contained several provisions outlining the objectives of U.S. psychological warfare against Communist China. The United States was to:

—Expand and intensify, by all available means, efforts to develop non-Communist leadership and to influence the leaders and people in China to oppose the present Peiping regime and to seek its reorientation or replacement.

—Foster and support anti-Communist Chinese elements both outside and within China with a view to developing and expanding resistance in China to the Peiping regime's control, particularly in south China.[6]

Cooperation with the Nationalists in pursuit of these two objectives was implicit. Planning for the implementation of these two points had begun early in 1951. In February, about two months after China's entry into the Korean War, the Joint Chiefs of Staff (JCS) considered a plan drafted by its Joint Intelligence Committee (JIC) and proposing large-scale U.S. support for an estimated 600,000 dissidents within the PRC. About half of these "dissidents" professed allegiance to the Nationalist government. The other half were "traditionally dissident bandit and war lord groups." "It appears to be true," the JIC report said, "that many ex-Nationalist officers command guerrilla groups and that the Nationalist government maintains an extensive spy and courier system" on the mainland, but that "actual [Nationalist] control and direction of operations is almost non-existent." "Communications are so poor and the real loyalty of the personnel is so questionable that the word 'control' is largely a euphemism," the report concluded.[7]

The JIC report identified several key weaknesses of the "dissident forces" that might be overcome with external support. There was a virtual absence of command and control among dissident units. This might be remedied by the supply of radios and by putting dissident forces with a command center in Taiwan. Weapons and other supplies were in short supply, limiting dissident effectiveness and appeal to the populace. These shortages could be ameliorated by sea or air deliveries of weapons, equipment, gold, and cash. If an external power helped the anti-Communist forces overcome their weaknesses, prospects for their success were good, the report concluded.

JOHN MOORES UNIVERSITY
AVRIL ROBARTS LRC
TEL. 0151 231 4022

The purpose of the proposed operation was to cause "disruption of civil control, promoting general dissension and weakening the capability of the Chinese Communist forces to engage in external operations, and, later, to assist in such further actions as may be taken to insure the destruction of the Chinese Communist regime." "Large scale guerrilla action in southern and central China could eventually tie down very large numbers of Communist armed forces," while eliminating "the physical aspects of Chinese Communist support in Indo-China." This apparently meant that the guerrillas would hinder or prevent the movement of material from Communist China to Ho Chi Minh's Viet Minh. More broadly, said the report, successful guerrilla action in China would "do much to counter the psychological impact of belief in Communist invincibility throughout the world." "Very considerable restrictions [would be] placed on both the extent and effectiveness of Communist propaganda. At the same time, any such successful challenge of the myth of Communist invincibility might importantly strengthen the will to resist among the peoples of Western Europe."

The JIC report concluded with a list of recommendations about the implementation of the plan. It also recommended the authorization of munitions worth $34 million to arm 200,000 guerrillas with 80,000 rifles, 7,000 machine guns and submachine guns, 6,000 radios, and 1,320,000 pounds of TNT. This was equipment for a very sizable operation. In August 1951, the JCS reported to Secretary of Defense George C. Marshall that the "importance and potential effectiveness" of the program justified a supply priority "immediately below that of operations in Korea."[8]

Covert operations against the mainland grew rapidly. Proposals for further expansion of covert operations in early 1952 were successfully opposed by the JCS, however, on the grounds that they would increase the risk of overt U.S. participation or of disclosing U.S. support.[9] The strongest opposition to the program of covert war against the PRC came from the British and the U.S. State Department. British leaders got wind of U.S. planning early in 1951 and warned against a "campaign of subversion or guerrilla warfare" involving the use of Chiang Kai-shek's forces. Such a move would "certainly" "provoke China to extend hostilities beyond Korea."[10] President Harry S. Truman turned aside Prime Minister Clement Attlee's warning, while Secretary of Defense Marshall wondered to the NSC "when we would do something to Communist China," asking rhetorically if it were not perhaps paying "too big a price for Hong Kong."[11] Within the U.S. government, Dean Acheson led the opposition to covert operations in association with the Nationalists. Acheson explained in his memoir that, in his view, "A policy of harassment of the [Chinese Communist] regime and seizure of every opportunity to weaken and if possible overthrow it offered little hope of success, short of massive military intervention and not much even if that extreme measure were to be included."[12] Under the impact of Chinese entry into the Korean War, Acheson himself was compelled to accept covert operations against China.

It is significant that the U.S. government adopted the program of covert operations against China as a wartime measure, in response to China's massive intervention in the Korean conflict. In the first instance, covert operations were wartime measures designed to weaken, divert, and demoralize a hostile nation deploying large armies against American forces in Korea. Yet, once adopted, covert operations assumed a life independent of their original hot-war context, becoming an important instrument of the protracted political war the United States waged, off and on, until 1969. NSC 146/2 of November 1953, the first definitive, post–Korean War statement, entitled "U.S. Objectives and Courses of Action with Respect to the Chinese National Government," stated that the United States would "encourage and covertly assist the Chinese National government to develop and extend logistical support of anti-Communist guerrillas on the mainland of China, for purposes of resistance and intelligence." Formosa was also to be developed as "an effective base for psychological operations against the mainland."[13]

The link with Nationalist China provided the United States with important instruments for the conduct of this war. The alliance with Nationalist China also provided an important legal basis for the U.S. conduct of clandestine operations against China. Since the Republic of China (ROC) government claimed sovereignty over all of China, including continental China, and since the United States recognized that government, U.S.-Nationalist actions directed against the mainland were strictly speaking legal. Only after Washington recognized Beijing's sovereignty over the mainland and rejected Taipei's comparable claim would U.S. activities be strictly illegal. This legal fiction was important to creating and sustaining a political base in the United States and other Western democracies for covert warfare against China.

Civil Air Transport and Air America

A key element in the conduct of covert operations against the PRC, and in U.S.-ROC cooperation in that regard, was the Civil Air Transport (CAT) company and its successor, Air America. During the post-1945 Civil War in China, CAT became a virtual adjunct of the Chinese Nationalist air force, ferrying troops to and from battle, evacuating the wounded, air-dropping supplies to isolated garrisons, and evacuating valuable personnel from besieged cities. When the Nationalist armies fled to Taiwan at the end of 1949, CAT withdrew with them.

In June 1950, the CIA acquired CAT through a front company. The CIA needed a reliable and ostensibly private source of transportation to move personnel, to air-drop supplies and agents, and otherwise to support clandestine operations against the Communist countries of Asia. If U.S. military aircraft were used for such operations, public attention would be attracted, and, if the operation was disclosed, its connection with the U.S. government would be obvious. The activities of an ostensibly private airline, however, could be disassociated from the U.S. government. With its record of proven paramilitary service, CAT was a promising asset.[14]

While CAT aircraft operated from facilities around virtually the entire periphery of China—from South Korea, Japan, Okinawa, the Philippines, Hong Kong, French Indochina, Thailand, Malaya, and India—Taiwan was its main base of operations. CAT aircraft were registered in Taiwan under ROC law and flew under the ROC flag. Taipei's main airfield, Songshan Airport, provided the headquarters for CAT flight operations. Extensive CAT repair facilities were based at Gaoxiong and Tainan. By mid-1954, CAT had 2,000 employees on Taiwan, half of whom worked for CAT's maintenance division. CAT facilities not only kept CAT aircraft in top shape, but also serviced U.S. military planes on a contract basis.

CAT aircraft undertaking "black" or covert operations against China were usually sent from Taiwan to bases in third countries—Japan, French Indochina, or Thailand—rather than operating directly out of Taiwan. There were both geographic and political reasons for this. It made more geographic sense for aircraft operating over Manchuria, for example, to begin their missions from forward bases in Japan. Aircraft operating over Yunnan or Tibet debarked from bases in Southeast Asia, usually Thailand. With shorter ranges, the C-46 and C-119s that were the mainstay of CAT's fleet in the 1950s could carry less fuel and therefore greater payloads. Politically, involvement of Taiwan in various conflicts, for example those in Indochina and Korea in the early 1950s, could be inexpedient—for the United States, though not necessarily for the ROC—enhancing the likelihood of greater PRC involvement.

From mid-1952 until late 1954 there was sharp dispute between U.S. and Nationalist agencies over CAT's continuing operation in Taiwan. One source of this crisis was the CIA's desire to regularize and institutionalize CAT's status in Taiwan. Until 1955 CAT operated on the basis of arrangements worked out between General Claire Chennault and the ROC Ministry of Communications. The CIA found such ad hoc arrangements unsatisfactory, and sought instead an ongoing arrangement institutionalized under ROC law. By 1955, the dispute had been resolved, and by the next year, CAT was functioning on a legally institutionalized basis in the ROC, with regular and rigorous administrative controls, and under tighter supervision from CIA headquarters in Langley. It was ready to undertake new operations further afield. By 1959, CAT had a registered fleet of twenty-eight aircraft of C-46s and C-47s, and two Catalina flying boats. This was a small fleet compared to major airlines such as British Overseas Air Company, Air France, American Airlines, and so on. It was, however, comparable to the national airlines of many small countries.[15]

CAT and its subsidiaries worked closely with U.S. covert operations throughout East Asia. As Brigadier General Edward G. Lansdale, then Special Assistant for Special Operations at the Pentagon, explained to President John F. Kennedy's national security adviser, General Maxwell Taylor, in July 1961, CAT provided air logistic support under commercial cover to the CIA and other agencies of the U.S. government. In the decade preceding 1961, Lansdale said, CAT had flown more than 200 overflights of mainland China and Tibet.[16] In 1951 CAT ferried arms to Nationalist remnant forces in northern Burma that were being reorganized and readied for operations in southern Yunnan. In 1954 it conducted extensive air drops of supplies to the besieged French forces at Dienbienphu. Beginning in 1959, a subsidiary of CAT, Air Asia, began operations in support of CIA-supported Meo and Hmong tribesmen in Laos fighting the Communist Pathet Lao. It also reportedly supported Nationalist remnant forces operating in Laos during the early 1960s.[17]

Although definitive documentation is lacking, it seems safe to assume that Chiang Kai-shek was fully aware of and condoned CAT's close relation with the CIA and its extensive involvement with U.S. covert operations. U.S. and ROC covert action agencies probably worked together closely, through CAT and its subsidiaries and with the full knowledge of the highest authorities of their respective governments, to support various anti-Communist struggles inside the PRC and in countries around its periphery.

Operations Against the Mainland

On Taiwan the CIA developed an extensive infrastructure to support its mainland operations. In the words of one CIA officer, the range of CIA activities on Taiwan in 1951 was "rather spectacular."[18] The CIA then had over 600 people in Taiwan, who were involved in providing guerrilla training, logistical support, overflight capabilities, and the distribution of propaganda to the mainland by radio and leaflet balloon. Commercial cover was provided for these operations by fictional enterprises. Command over CIA training on Taiwan was exercised by Colonel Raymond W. Peers, who had commanded an OSS detachment in Burma during World War II.[19] On the ROC side, mainland operations were conducted (at least in 1954) by the Continental Operations Department (COD), directly under Chief of the General Staff Chou Chih-jou. Although nominally part of the Ministry of National Defense (MND), the MND and the General Staff were in fact usually not informed about COD operations. On the Nationalist offshore islands, the local commander wore two hats, one as commander of the regular forces, and another as commander of COD forces. There were parallel but separate command structures for regular and COD forces upward to the Chief of General Staff. COD forces included various sorts of ships and boats, units of ROC marines, and unconventional guerrilla forces. The COD worked closely with the CIA.[20]

The earliest U.S. operations to insert agents into Communist China targeted Jilin and Liaoning provinces, beginning in March 1952. Long-range penetration missions from Taiwan into "Western China" soon followed. Later that year the U.S. Air Force turned over to CAT a B-17 bomber and a C-54 that were thereafter used extensively for deep penetration operations.[21] The C-54 had a maximum range of 3,100 miles when fully loaded with cargo.

Drops of leaflets along coastal areas were fairly routine and casual operations. Drops of agents or supplies followed more meticulous security procedures: Pilots were given detailed briefings on PLA air defenses, designated coastal penetration points, specified approach corridors to drop zones, and checkpoints for breaking radio silence. Most overflights were conducted on nights with a full moon to enable use of ground features for navigation. Aircraft avoided large cities where PLA air defenses were concentrated. In spite of these precautions, drops often missed their designated zones by as much as twenty miles. A small group of volunteer CAT pilots and crew were used for the most dangerous missions. Volunteers were never lacking, however, with CAT pilots motivated by a combination of patriotism, belief in the anti-Communist cause, love of adventure, and money. Nationalist Chinese copilots, radio operators, and "kickers" who pushed the cargo out of the hold were not volunteers.[22]

Between 1951 and 1953, a total of 212 Chinese agents were apparently parachuted, in small teams of two or three, into mainland China. They carried with them a substantial number of guns, ammunition, radio sets, gold bars, fake PRC documents, invisible ink, and other tools of the trade. Some agents were supposed to link up with local anti-Communist elements, providing the leadership, organizational and military skills, and external liaison necessary to turn those forces into effective guerrillas. Rescue, escape, and evasion of downed U.S. pilots were other missions which were especially important in the operations along the North Korean border during the Korean War. Collection and transmission of intelligence was another mission.[23]

Little practical benefit seems to have resulted from these operations—with the significant exception of intelligence collection and the Tibetan operation, both of which are discussed below. Most of the air-dropped Nationalist Chinese agents surrendered shortly after landing. CIA officers running these operations assumed that if a team established contact with base after its insertion, it had been infiltrated or turned. This assumption proved correct on one occasion in November 1952, when a CAT C-47 was called in to withdraw a team previously inserted into Jilin Province. During the final approach, the aircraft was downed by Chinese antiaircraft fire. Two CAT pilots were killed and two CIA employees, John Downey and Richard Fecteau, were captured.[24]

U.S. Air Force and U.S. Navy craft also occasionally delivered infiltrators into the mainland. While the CIA was the U.S. agency with primary responsibility for these operations, it was assisted by the Air Force and the Navy. On at least one occasion, the PLA shot down an Air Force B-29 engaged in covert operations over the mainland. But reliance on CAT was advantageous, since it permitted plausible denial of official U.S. involvement in actions that went awry. When CAT planes were downed, the U.S. government adamantly denied Chinese accusations that its aircraft and personnel were dropping people and supplies into China. The U.S. media of that era generally did not question this.

Mainland Operations and the Contingency of General War

During the late 1950s, Taiwan and its operational assets vis-à-vis the mainland were integrated into U.S. planning for general war with the Sino-Soviet bloc. Here the U.S. Army's Special Forces, established in 1952 to wage unconventional warfare behind enemy lines, played a key role. The U.S. Army viewed unconventional warfare as a relatively cheap way of tying down enemy forces, thereby limiting the enemy offensive while the United States rushed to mobilize its manpower and industry for a strategic counteroffensive after the nuclear exchange that, it was assumed, would begin a general war. To this end, the Special Forces were charged with preparing for extensive guerrilla operations against Sino-Soviet forces. Special Forces cadre were to join with indigenous anti-Communist forces, providing the leadership and technical skills necessary for the conduct of guerrilla operations to disrupt the rear areas of Sino-Soviet forces while the United States built up its forces for a more effective counterattack.[25]

Okinawa was the headquarters of Pacific-based Special Forces. This island's geographic situation made it difficult for Sino-Soviet forces to seize without a major effort. From Okinawa, mobile Special Forces training teams fanned out to other countries: South Korea, the Philippines, South Vietnam, and Taiwan. Special Forces efforts focused on China, whose armies, it was assumed, would play the major role in any bloc offensive in the initial stage of a general war in Asia. In April 1956 a small Special Forces Operational Detachment was secretly activated, with the mission of training and leading Asian resistance against the armies of the Sino-Soviet bloc in the event of a general war.

Over the next eighteen months, Special Force Operational Detachments were established in Hawaii and East Asia. The first Special Forces training team arrived on Taiwan in February 1957 to conduct intensive training of Chinese cadre for six months before returning to Okinawa. The Chinese cadre then proceeded to train the ROC's own Special Forces at a training center fifty miles south of Taipei, with U.S. Special Forces returning periodically for advanced training. The first exercise combining U.S. and ROC Special Forces was carried out in May 1959 and involved U.S. and ROC troopers simulating unconventional warfare on the Chinese mainland. Further combined exercises were held again during May–June 1960, with the exercise area covering one-third of Taiwan. In the fall of 1960, a Special Forces detachment was permanently transferred to Taiwan.[26]

The intended strategic role of Taiwan in the event of a major war with China was apparent in U.S.-ROC military maneuvers during the late 1950s and the 1960s. Beginning in 1959 and continuing through 1968, military forces of the two sides practiced unconventional warfare operations virtually every year (1962 was an exception). These ranged in duration from three weeks to five months, covered a large part of the island, and frequently involved air and naval as well as special forces, marine, and regular infantry elements. Typically U.S. and Nationalist special forces conducted guerrilla and counterguerrilla operations with tactical air support and air resupply. ROC regular forces often played the enemy role, learning antiguerrilla tactics in the process. Attention was paid to the utilization of psychological and political warfare in unconventional warfare, especially as regards mobilization of popular support for guerrilla operations. By 1965 a reinforced Nationalist parachute battalion was dropped behind hypothetical enemy lines; it carried out guerrilla operations with tactical air support. Efforts were made to mobilize local political support for these guerrilla operations. The next year, paratroops joined up with hypothetical friendly guerrillas to wage unconventional warfare against enemy regular forces. In 1967 a reinforced battalion conducted an amphibious landing in association with an air drop by a reinforced battalion. The two units then linked up and faced the conventional forces of the enemy.[27] Joint U.S.-ROC unconventional warfare exercises are listed in Table 6.1.

The role of Taiwan in U.S. preparations for expanded unconventional operations against China in the context of a general war should not be exaggerated. Taiwan was only one element of the U.S. military system in East Asia. Thailand, South Korea, the Philippines, and South Vietnam were also important elements of that system, while Japan and Okinawa provided the key logistic bases for the entire region. Yet Taiwan made an extremely important contribution, providing large numbers of highly trained Chinese-speaking and acculturated cadre inspired by intense anti-Communist conviction.

Covert Operations in the 1960s

After petering off in the late 1950s, Nationalist offensive operations against the mainland resumed in the early 1960s. This occurred in the context of U.S. awareness of the rapidly deepening Sino-Soviet split. According to historian Gordon Chang, early in 1962 the Kennedy Administration began thinking through the policy implications for the United States of the effective collapse of the Sino-Soviet alliance. U.S. leaders were gratified that the differentiated policy toward the PRC and the USSR had finally succeeded in driving a wedge between those two countries. They were surprised, however, that it was Moscow rather than Beijing that showed interest in cooperating with the United States. When the "wedge" policy had been adopted in the early 1950s, U.S. leaders had imagined that a Sino-Soviet split would lead to Chinese rapprochement with the United States. In 1962, however, U.S. leaders concluded that China, with its militant anti-imperialism and its encouragement of insurgency in South Vietnam, posed the greater threat to the United States.[28] Consequently, U.S. policy began working toward an understanding with Moscow regarding cooperation in dealing with the Chinese threat. Kennedy continued a differentiated policy toward the two Communist powers, relaxing pressure toward the USSR while continuing it toward the PRC.[29]

The administration also saw covert operations as an important component of the U.S. response to the mounting Chinese-supported North Vietnamese challenge in Indochina. On 11 May 1961, for instance, the National Security Council (NSC) adopted a program of covert actions against North Vietnam as part of the U.S. response to Hanoi's initiation of armed struggle to take over South Vietnam.[30] China was North Vietnam's

Table 6.1

U.S.-ROC Unconventional Warfare Exercises

Date	Code Name	Description
1–29 May 1959	Xianfeng	Testing of unconventional war command, doctrine, tactics, and equipment.
15 May– 21 June 1960	Kunlun	Special Forces, air, and naval units of the two countries sought remedies to defects observed in Xianfeng and developed strategy appropriate for use on mainland.
18 June– 15 July 1962	Emei 1	Guerrilla and counterguerrilla operations by Special Forces.
4 March– 28 June 1963	Emei 2	Special Forces practiced guerrilla, counterguerrilla, and psychological warfare, and escape and evasion, over an area covering half of Taiwan.
25 March– 29 May 1964	Emei 3	Political warfare in context of guerrilla and counterguerrilla operations. Test of ability of Special Forces to operate behind enemy lines with air resupply and telecommunications equipment. Central mountain range of Taiwan.
5 January– 31 May 1965	Emei 4	Simulated dropping of reinforced parachute battalion behind enemy lines, and test of ability to resist, with air support and resupply, enemy conventional forces. Central mountain range of Taiwan.
6 January– 30 May 1966	Liming	Simulated linkup of reinforced parachute battalion with Special Forces and guerrillas under air support. Psywar and political war in support of unconventional war. Covered most of Taiwan.
4 January– 30 April 1967	Tongzhou	Air drop of reinforced parachute battalion, and linkup with Special Forces battalion landing by sea. Under tactical air support, force then confronted conventional forces of enemy. Use of political war in support of unconventional war.
4 January– 15 May 1968	Yongshi	Political war under conditions of nuclear, unconventional, and pacification war. Linkup of parachute-dropped reinforced battalion with battalion landed by sea. Infantry division then carried out pacification with tactical air support.

Source: Meijun zaiHua gongzuo jishi (lujun guwen bu) [Record of U.S. Military Activities on Taiwan (Army Advisory Section)], Taipei: Historical Bureau, Ministry of National Defense, 1981, pp. 273–77.

major foreign backer at that junction, and it may have been because of the escalating conflict in Indochina that covert pressures were extended to Hanoi's Chinese supporter. In any case, in March 1962 President Kennedy sent a letter to Chiang Kai-shek outlining seven points of agreement regarding U.S.-ROC cooperation on activities to be carried out on the Chinese mainland.[31] The contents of this letter have yet to be declassified. Circumstantial evidence suggests that the letter provided the basis for a resumption of Nationalist offensive operations against the PRC as a way of placing further strains on the Beijing-Moscow relation. The Dulles-Yeh notes of 10 December 1954 had provided that "use of force will be a matter of joint agreement." The scale and duration of Nationalist offensive operations in the early 1960s strongly suggest that those operations were conducted with U.S. approval and support. According to official PLA histories, U.S. military advisers on Taiwan helped plan and actively participated in Nationalist offensive operations in the early 1960s.[32] This assertion was presumably based on interrogation of captured Nationalist "guerrillas."

Nationalist offensive operations against the mainland from 1960 through the first half of 1962 remained very occasional. Then, in mid-1962, the tempo of Nationalist operations began to pick up substantially. According to Nationalist sources, 873 personnel were dispatched to carry out anti-Communist operations on the mainland from March through December 1962.[33] Table 6.2 lists Nationalist limited offensive operations for 1960–65.

According to an official history of the People's Liberation Army-Navy (PLA-N), in 1962 Chiang Kai-shek began dispatching large numbers of small armed units to the continent. The units landed by boat, usually in remote, scarcely settled areas with mountains nearby, destroyed signs of their landing, and then infiltrated inland to designated areas where they attempted to set up "guerrilla bases." The infiltrators were often disguised as PLA soldiers or local cadre and carried fake travel documents and other papers.[34] Between October 1962 and September 1965, the PLA intercepted forty-three batches of Nationalist agents infiltrated by sea or air.[35]

Most Nationalist infiltrators did not last long. Communist control was too tight and efficient. In spite of these setbacks, however, the operations continued for some time. According to the PLA account of these activities, Chiang Kai-shek's view was that multiple losses and failures did not matter, as long as the operations produced even one success. Chiang's objective, according to the PLA, was to influence U.S. policy.

According to PLA histories, early in 1963 the focus of Nationalist operations shifted from attempted establishment of guerrilla bases in the interior to commando raids against installations along the coast. The zone of operations also expanded from the Guangdong coast to encompass Fujian,

Table 6.2

Nationalist Limited Offensive Operations, 1960–65*

Date	Location	Nature of activity
1960		
19 Feb.	At sea east of Dongshan Island	Downing of MiG-17
2 Mar.	Vicinity of Beilin Island	Sea clash; Nationalist gunboat sunk
1961		
1st half of year	Beijing, Tianjin, Nanjing	Air drop of 60,000 bags of rice
5 Feb.	Vicinity of Mazu	Sea clash
July	Vicinity of Penghu Island	Detention of 2 fishing boats
1962		
17–24 Nov.	Island in Xianwei harbor	Commando raid killing 10
19 Nov.	Qingdao, Shandong	Sabotage of railway and steamship
19 Dec.	Hwangpo harbor, Guangzhou	Commando raid destroying ammo dump
July–Dec.	Guangdong coast	9 commando raids
23 Dec.	Guangdong	Sabotage of Guangzhou-Shenzhen railway
1963		
18 Jan.	Guangzhou, Guangdong	Guerrilla bombing of rail line
3 Feb.	Northwest of Mazu Island	Sea clash
25 Mar.	Zhongshan county, Guangdong	Bombing of locomotive
13 June	Zhejiang, Jiangxi provinces	Bombing of rail line
20 June	Kaiping county, Guangdong	Attack killing 10 CCP cadre
27 June	Zhejiang, Fujian, Guangdong	Landing of 12 guerrilla groups
27 June	Yunnan	Guerrilla attack kills 10 PLA
July	Fujian, Guangdong	Landing of 5 guerrilla groups
May–July	China coast	Landing of 15 guerrilla groups
Aug.	Fujian, Guangdong, Zhejiang	Landing of 6 guerrilla groups
1 Oct.	Guangdong coast	Bombing of factory; 20 killed
9 Oct.	Island in mouth of Min River	Raising of ROC flag
Oct.	Central China coast	Landing of 11 guerrilla groups
24 Oct.	Fujian coast	Commando raid
June–Oct.	Shandong, Jiangsu, Guangdong, Guangxi, Fuyjian, Zhejiang	Landing of 32 guerrilla groups
11 Nov.	Mainland	204 air drops by Air Force
Mar. 1962–Nov. 1963	From Hebei to Guangdong	Landing of 1,785 guerrillas
18 Nov.	Langqi Island, mouth of Min River	Attack killing 10 people
22 Nov.	Nanri Island, Fujian	Attack killing 10 people

Table 6.2 *(continued)*

1964

1 Jan.	Shandong	Guerrilla attack killing 30
2 Jan.	Zhejiang military harbor	Guerrillas destroy warehouse and dock
17 Feb.	Guangzhou-Shanghai Railroad	Explosion
4 Mar.	Lianjiang county, Fujian	Guerrilla attack killing 15
Jan.	Mekong River, Yunnan	Bridge destroyed
15 May		Destruction of rail station
20 June	Guangdong	Guerrilla attack killing 20
26 June	Guangdong	Guerrilla attack killing 28
16 Nov.	Guangzhou	Destruction of coal depot
26 Nov.	Fujian	Psywar team lands

1965

13 Mar.	Fujian	Bombing of military troop train; more than 100 killed
24 Mar.	Shenzhen, Guangzhou	Bombing of police station
7 May	Yunnan	Guerrilla attack killing 30 on train
May	Yongan, Fujian	Guerrillas support insurrection by local militia
1 May	Vicinity of Mazu	Sea clash; 4 PLA gunboats and 1 ROC gunboat sunk
6 Aug.	South of Jinmen	Sea clash; 5 PLA and 2 ROC gunboats sunk
1 Oct.	Yunnan	Guerrilla attacks
13 Oct.	Guangzhou, Guandong	Bombing of rail line
Oct.	Guangzhou, Guandong	Bombing of shipyard
13 Nov.	Wuzhou Island	Naval clash; 4 PLA and 1 ROC, gunboats sunk

*Exclusive of incidents involving U-2s or in Tibet.
Source: Zhongyang ribao (Central Daily), Taipei, Taiwan.

Zhejiang, Jiangsu, and Shandong. Often, islands under the jurisdiction of South Korea or South Vietnam were used as jumping-off points for the operation—a fact that Beijing saw as further indication of U.S. support for the operations. In one operation in October 1963, for instance, boats set out from Taiwan to South Korea's west coast. After resupplying off South Korea, the Nationalist commandos then transferred to a fake "Japanese fishing boat" and proceeded to the Shandong coast. Nationalist raiders also began to use fast, highly maneuverable speed boats with hulls made of plastic or bamboo. Because of their nonmetallic construction, small size, and low profile, these boats were difficult for PLA-N radar to pick up. At other times, commandos would row ashore in rubber boats. The Nationalist commandos still favored remote areas lacking PLA-N radar coverage, or having reefs and other barriers that made surprise by the PLA-N difficult. The object of the raids was typically to attack some isolated unit, to take a few prisoners, to seize documents, and to destroy a few facilities. By PLA count, fifty-four groups of Nationalists landed during 1964. Half were commandos, half were infiltrators. Some of the commando groups had as many as fifty or even eighty people.

Nationalist vessels also began conducting psychological warfare operations among mainland fishermen detained on the high seas. During the spring and fall fishing seasons, two large, specially equipped landing ship tanks (LSTs) set out from Taiwan, escorted by Nationalist warships. Usually they headed for the Fujian coast, but sometimes they ranged as far afield as Shandong. After any PLA-N warships protecting the fishing fleet had been driven away, the mainland fishing boats were collected, and their crews and officers were invited aboard the LSTs. There they were shown movies, treated to banquets and anti-Communist propaganda, and given presents for themselves and their families. They were then returned to their boats and allowed to continue their fishing. By August 1964, such psywar operations had been conducted 24 times, involving 370 PRC fishing boats. The peak came in 1964 when the occupants of 210 boats were subjected to indoctrination.[36]

During 1965 Nationalist fast boats began to lay mines in mainland coastal waters. The mines were simple, impact-contact types that carried between 20 and 25 kilograms of TNT and were kept afloat by inner tubes. The PLA-N used increasingly aggressive tactics against Nationalist vessels conducting special operations in coastal waters. On 6 August 1964 (four days after the first Gulf of Tonkin incident), six PLA-N corvettes attacked a 1,250-ton ROC mine sweeper and a 450-ton submarine chaser operating off Dongshan Island in southern Fujian. In a nighttime attack, the PLA-N warships closed with the Nationalist vessels, sinking both of them. In the words of the PLA-N history, this was "the most beautiful naval battle of the 1960s."[37] A little over a year later, in November 1965, six PLA-N corvettes and six patrol torpedo (PT) boats attacked a 600-ton ROC submarine chaser and a 650-ton gunboat engaged in mine-laying operations off Fujian. Again the PLA-N attacked at night, sinking one ship and heavily damaging the other. When Nationalist unconventional warfare operations against the mainland ended in 1966, the PLA had engaged thirty-five Nationalist ships during the previous four years, sinking fifteen and capturing another twenty-six.

The reason for the termination of Nationalist unconventional warfare operations is unclear. Most probably it was related to the escalation of the Vietnam conflict. As the war in Vietnam escalated, Washington moved cautiously to avoid triggering another Sino-American war along the lines of Korea. In such highly sensitive circumstances, Washington probably did not want Taiwan to undertake actions that might anger, confuse, or provoke Beijing. It seems most likely that Washington demanded that Taipei cease these activities, and Taipei complied.

What was the value of these covert operations? They did not succeed in sparking the widespread rebellions and guerrilla war against CCP rule that had initially inspired them. It also seems that they were not successful in diverting PLA forces from either the Korean Theater or the Indochinese Theater. They probably did stimulate the CCP's fears of a possible U.S.-supported Nationalist invasion, and by doing this, they encouraged stepped-up military spending, tighter internal control, and intensified repression. This militarization arguably retarded economic growth and improvement of quality of life for the masses, thereby intensifying the internal contradictions of China's Stalinist system. One U.S. objective was to diminish the political appeal of the Chinese Communist revolution and state, and this could have been served by the intensified Stalinization resulting from U.S.-Nationalist covert operations.

Intelligence collection was a modest gain from covert operations. Information provided by local Communist cadre or peasants interrogated by Nationalist raiders was probably of questionable value. One can imagine the methods used and the quality of information provided under extreme duress. Documentary materials seized were more reliable and probably provided important insight into an extremely closed society.

What did joint covert operations contribute to the overall balance of power? U.S. leaders and analysts of that era believed that they kept alive the fighting morale of Nationalist forces—honed their combat skills and kept alive their martial spirit. Would Nationalist forces have been useful in the conduct of unconventional war against Sino-Soviet bloc and (after 1960) Chinese forces in the event of a general East-West or Sino-U.S. war? Perhaps the most that can be said with confidence is that U.S. planners *thought* they would be useful. Nationalist forces played a significant role in U.S. planning for such contingencies.

Notes

1. See Richard Deacon, *Spyclopedia, The Comprehensive Handbook of Espionage,* New York: William Morrow, 1987, pp. 296–97.
2. R. Harris Smith, *OSS, The Secret History of America's First Central Intelligence*

Agency, Berkeley: University of California Press, 1972, pp. 250–51. Also Major General John K. Singlaub, *Hazardous Duty: An American Soldier in the Twentieth Century,* New York: Summit Books, 1991, pp. 156–59. Singlaub was the China officer for the CIA in 1949. Much of his career was spent in intelligence and special operations in the Far East.

3. Paul M. A. Linebarger, *Psychological Warfare,* New York: Arno Press, 1972, pp. 269–77. Ludwell Lee Montague, *General Walter Bedell Smith as Director of Central Intelligence, October 1950–February 1953,* University Park: Pennsylvania State University Press, 1992, p. 203. This book is a declassified CIA history. The American world view underlying the covert war against Communist China was perhaps best expressed by CIA Director Allen Dulles in his memoir, *The Craft of Intelligence,* New York: Harper and Row, 1963, pp. 220–36.

4. Montague, *Bedell Smith,* p. 204.

5. Ibid.

6. NSC 48/5, 17 May 1951.

7. Joint Chiefs of Staff, Decision on JCS 2118/19, "A Report by the Joint Intelligence Committee on Estimate of the Effectiveness of Anti-Communist Guerrilla Operations in China," Records of the Joint Chiefs of Staff, part 2, 1946–53, "The Far East," JCS Historical Office, The Pentagon.

8. Walter J. Poole, *JCS and National Policy, 1950–1952,* Historical Division, Joint Secretariat, JCS, December 1979, p. 399.

9. Poole, *JCS and National Policy,* p. 408.

10. *FRUS,* 1951, vol. VII, pp. 37–39.

11. Ibid., pp. 93–94.

12. Dean Acheson, *Present at the Creation: My Years in the Department of State,* New York: W.W. Norton, 1969, p. 344.

13. *FRUS,* 1952–54, vol. XIV, part 2, p. 308.

14. William M. Leary, *Perilous Missions: Civil Air Transport and CIA Covert Operations in Asia,* University, AL: University of Alabama Press, 1984, p. 173.

15. *Air World Transport Statistics, 1959,* Montreal: International Air Transport Association, 1960, p. 18.

16. *The Pentagon Papers,* New York: Bantam, 1971, p. 137.

17. Peter Dale Scott, *The War Conspiracy: The Secret Road to the Second Indochina War,* New York: Bobbs Merrill, 1972, pp. 6–11, 195–98.

18. Leary, *Perilous Missions,* p. 133.

19. Ibid.

20. CTF 74 [sic] Taipei to CINCPAC, 26 May 1954, National Archives, RG 218, JCS, Geographical File 1954–56, 381 Formosa, box 18, sec. 14. MAAG, Formosa to CINCPAC, 27 November 1954, sec. 16.

21. Leary, *Perilous Missions,* p. 136.

22. Ibid., pp. 135–36.

23. Ibid., p. 141.

24. Ibid., p. 140. Both Fecteau and Downey were sentenced to twenty years imprisonment. Fecteau, who had been with the CIA for only five months at the time of his capture, was released in December 1971, two months before President Nixon's scheduled trip to Beijing. Downey was released in March 1973, one year before his sentence was up and after President Richard Nixon acknowledged at a press conference that he had been a CIA employee.

25. Shelby L. Stanton, *Green Berets at War, U.S. Army Special Forces in Southeast Asia, 1956–1975,* Novato, CA: Presidio Press, 1985, pp. 1–5.

26. Stanton, *Green Berets,* pp. 7–9.

27. "Zhong mei lianmeng lujun tezhong budui zuozhan yanxi zhongda chengxiao" (Major results of the unconventional warfare exercises by allied land forces), in *Mei jun zaiHua gongzuo jishi (xiefang zhi bu)* (Record of work of American forces in China, joint defense), Taipei: Guofangbu shizheng bianyizhu, October 1981, pp. 273–77.

28. Gordon H. Chang, *Friends and Enemies: The United States, China, and the Soviet Union, 1948–1972,* Stanford, CA: Stanford University Press, 1990, pp. 217–27.

29. Alan P. Dobson, "The Kennedy Administration and Economic Warfare Against Communism," *International Affairs,* vol. 64, no. 4 (Autumn 1988), pp. 599–616.

30. NSAM No. 52, *United States-Vietnam Relations, 1945–1967* ("Pentagon Papers"), Washington: Government Printing Office, 1971, pp. 151–52.

31. This agreement is mentioned in a memo of a 16 April 1964 discussion between Dean Rusk and Chiang Kai-shek, in the ROC Foreign Ministry archives, files no. 412.2, 22, 300, bei mei ci (Office of North American Affairs) 77.

32. *Dangdai Zhongguo haijun* (Contemporary China's navy), (hereafter cited as *Dangdai haijun),* Beijing: Zhongguo shehui kexueyuan, 1987, pp. 370–91.

33. *Zhongyang ribao* (Central News), Taipei, 9 February 1963.

34. Unless otherwise noted, this account of post-1962 mainland operations is drawn largely from *Dangdai haijun,* pp. 370–91.

35. Mao Shi and Wang Gongan, *Guo Gong liangdang guanxishi* (History of KMT-CCP relations), Wuhan: Wuhan chubanshe, 1988, p. 624.

36. Major General John K. Singlaub, who was in charge of special warfare operations in Vietnam in the late 1960s and early 1970s, recounts in his memoir a similar operation involving North Vietnamese fishermen. Groups of fishermen were rounded up at sea and taken to an island off the coast of South Vietnam. There a Potemkin "liberated village within North Vietnam" had been set up to convince the fishermen of the beauty of life without the Communists. Before being returned to their boats, the fishermen were fattened for several days on good food and anti-Communist education. See Singlaub, *Hazardous Duty.*

37. *Dangdai haijun,* p. 386.

7

The Offshore Islands

The Management of Intra-Alliance Conflict

As discussed in chapters 5 and 6, there was a contradiction within the
U.S.-ROC alliance regarding the aims of the two partners. Chiang Kai-
shek's ultimate objective was to draw on U.S. strength to return to the
mainland, defeating the Communists and restoring ROC rule on the mainland. Chiang, of course, had lesser objectives as well, including using U.S.
power to protect Taiwan and securing U.S. largesse for the Kuomintang and
for its followers and its Taiwan base. Chiang took quite seriously, however,
the objective of return to the mainland. U.S. strategists found the Nationalist
belief in return to the mainland useful in certain regards. That faith increased Nationalist morale and therefore the usefulness of Chinat assets
against the PRC. It increased the threat facing the PRC and therefore the
consequences should Beijing decide on war against the United States or its
allies. In other words, the Nationalist creed of return to the mainland enhanced the utility of Nationalist China as an instrument for pressuring Communist China. But U.S. strategic interests would not be served by war with
the PRC. The United States' interest, at least during the 1950s, was to split
apart the Sino-Soviet alliance.

This contradiction between Nationalist and American perspectives came
into focus over the issue of Nationalist possession of small islands scattered along China's central coast. Nationalist control and utilization of
those islands was useful for the psychological warfare and covert operations discussed in chapter 6. Yet the close engagement of the two sides

also gave Chiang Kai-shek an ability the enmesh the United States in conflict with Communist China. Most important, a clear territorial break between the ROC as Taiwan and the Chinese mainland would facilitate the creation in the United States of a political base for ongoing support for Taiwan, even after a possible settlement between the United States and China.

The optimal strategic outcome for the United States would be to split the Sino-Soviet alliance and then keep denying Taiwan to the PRC or to the USSR. Once China broke from the USSR, a new Sino-American relation would be worked out, *and* Taiwan would remain beyond the PRC's grasp. Throughout the first half of the 1950s, John Foster Dulles worked to create a legal basis for such an eventual outcome. As discussed in chapter 4, Dulles' main effort in this regard was to prepare a legal basis for an eventual "two-Chinas" solution by restricting the ROC's jurisdiction to Taiwan and the Pescadores. During the negotiations for a peace treaty with Japan, during negotiation of the U.S.-ROC mutual security treaty, and through actions at the United Nations, Dulles sought to create a legal basis for confining ROC jurisdiction to Taiwan and the Pescadores. Dulles apparently hoped that, once the Sino-Soviet alliance unraveled and a new Sino-American relation could be built, these actions could confront Beijing with a fait accompli, compelling it to acquiesce to Taiwan's indefinite separation from Communist China.

Chiang Kai-shek understood the ultimate two-Chinas objective underlying various U.S. actions during the mid-1950s. So too did Mao Zedong. Both agreed that Taiwan should not be separated indefinitely from the political entity embracing the mainland of China, and the two leaders in effect worked together to create the two Taiwan Strait crises of the 1950s. Both hoped these crises would abort the United States' two-Chinas project, though they had very different ideals about how that would happen. Ironically, they agreed that a confrontation over the small offshore islands was a good way to spoil the United States' two-Chinas policy.

This raised the question of who held the initiative in the U.S.-ROC-PRC triangle. Perhaps the key tactic used by the United States to manage the contradiction between its strategy of "all means short of war" and the Nationalist strategy of war with Communist China was to keep the initiative in American hands. U.S. leaders would decide, they hoped, whether, when, and where U.S. military forces would engage PRC forces. Nationalist occupation of the offshores gave both Chiang Kai-shek and Mao Zedong a way to precipitate engagement of U.S. and PRC military forces via the intermediary of the Nationalists. The lever Chiang used to prod the Americans into engagement with the Communists was threatened Nationalist defection to the Communists.

A key dimension of the U.S.-Nationalist alliance of the 1950s was a deep U.S. belief that Chiang Kai-shek wanted to enmesh the United States in war with the PRC as a way of returning to the mainland. After initialing the draft of the 1954 mutual security treaty, Secretary of State John Foster Dulles reported to President Dwight Eisenhower that the negotiations had been tough but that the result "stakes out unqualifiedly our interests in Formosa and the Pescadores and does so on a basis which will not enable the Chinese Nationalists to involve us in a war with Communist China."[1] The Nationalists believed, Dulles told the NSC, that they had no real future, in the absence of a general war with China.[2] U.S. military circles shared this belief. A JCS report of September 1958 on the Taiwan Strait situation reported that the United States hoped to assist the Nationalists in the defense of the offshores "without . . . inviting the GRC to create a situation which will cause our immediate involvement."[3] This perception of Nationalist efforts at entrapment would have a deep impact on the psychological dynamics of the U.S.-Nationalist alliance.

The Offshores as an Instrument of Pressure

An analysis of U.S. policy toward the Nationalist-held offshores must begin with an understanding of the utility of those islands as an instrument for pressuring Communist China.

As the victorious Communist forces swept across the China mainland in 1949, Nationalist forces managed to hold several dozen islands scattered along the central and southeastern Chinese coast.[4] The PLA was in the process of wresting these islands from the Nationalists when Truman ordered U.S. forces to protect Taiwan on 27 June 1950. At that point the Nationalists still held two dozen small islands. The largest and most important of these was Jinmen, situated in Xiamen harbor. Ten days after Truman's volte-face on Taiwan, the ROC foreign ministry passed an aide-mémoire to the U.S. embassy, calling the attention of the U.S. government to the fact that "considerable" Nationalist forces were "maintaining positions" on offshore islands, and asking for its views regarding this situation.[5] Two problems thus confronted the United States. First, should the Nationalist-held offshores be included in the area of U.S. defense responsibility deriving from Truman's 27 June statement, and if so, should U.S. forces be used to assist in those islands defense? Second, what was the attitude of the United States toward Nationalist use of the offshores to launch raids against the mainland?[6]

One consideration shaping U.S. policy toward the offshores was the absence of a legal basis for U.S. involvement with the offshore islands. The legal basis for U.S. relations with Taiwan and the Pescadores after 25 June 1950 was the "undetermined" status of those islands which rested, in turn, on the fact that those islands had been transferred from Chinese to Japanese sovereignty in 1895 and then promised again to China with the Cairo declaration of 1943. The smaller offshore islands, however, had never been under Japanese sovereignty. They had never been anything other than part of China. This situation, combined with the Truman Administration's desire to keep the Nationalists at arm's length, led the administration to rule out engagement on behalf of the offshores. Thus, on 22 July 1950, Secretary of State Dean Acheson informed Taipei that the United States would not help defend the Nationalist offshores, but neither would it stand in the way of Nationalist defense of those islands.[7] U.S. support for Nationalist offensive operations from the offshores was implicitly ruled out.

The Eisenhower Administration's more positive estimate of the Nationalists was reflected in its policy toward the offshores. Washington now began supporting Nationalist efforts to hold the offshores, and began utilizing the offshores for offensive operations designed to pressure Communist China. NSC 146/2, approved by Eisenhower on 6 November 1953, provided that, "without committing U.S. forces" unless Formosa or the Pescadores was attacked, the United States would "encourage and assist the Chinese National Government to defend the Nationalist-held offshore islands against Communist attack and to raid Chinese Communist territory and commerce." Shortly thereafter, elements of the Seventh Fleet were authorized to pay occasional visits to the Dachen Islands 200 miles north of Taiwan "in order to make a show of strength that might deter the Chinese Communists from attacking these islands."[8] U.S. air and naval craft also began conducting surveillance in the vicinity of the offshores. U.S. military advisers were also stationed on the Nationalist offshores for the first time. Previously only CIA personnel had been based there. About the same time, Chief of Naval Operations (CNO) Admiral Robert E. Carney pointed out the useful role the offshores played in the more assertive policy of the Eisenhower Administration toward Communist China. The offshores were useful, Carney said, for conducting psychological warfare, commando raids, intelligence-gathering operations, sabotage, and escape and evasion for pilots downed over enemy territory. They were also useful for what Carney called "maritime resistance" operations,[9] which were Nationalist efforts to disrupt the maritime and coastal commerce of Communist China.

NSC 146/2 also provided that the United States would support the development of "a small [Nationalist] navy capable of conducting limited coastal patrols, anti-shipping, and commando operations." Such forces "would be able to undertake more effective raids against the Communist mainland and seaborne commerce with Communist China."[10] In 1954, ROC naval strength was substantially augmented when two large landing ships, two destroyers, and ten submarine chasers were transferred to the Nationalists. Previously, only two medium-sized landing ships had been transferred to the Nationalists since their retreat to Taiwan.[11]

The operations against mainland Chinese shipping were ostensibly *Nationalist* actions. In fact, U.S. support and encouragement of proxy maritime warfare was an important U.S. policy instrument. Maritime trade played an extremely important role in the PRC's development efforts in the early 1950s. Most of the foodstuffs, raw materials, and capital goods that China imported, and most of its exports, traveled by sea. Overseas trade played a vital role in the PRC's development strategy.[12] The new PRC government quickly recognized the importance of maritime commerce and pressed into service every available vessel, while encouraging the vessels of other countries, including the United States and Britain, to come to Chinese ports to pick up or deliver cargoes.

Following their loss of northern China in early 1949, Nationalist naval forces had attempted to hamper the maritime trade of Communist-controlled areas. On 20 June 1949 the Nationalist government announced the "closure" to foreign commerce of all Chinese ports under Communist control. The Nationalists did not declare a "blockade," since under international law this would have conferred protected status on the ships of neutral states while recognizing the CCP as something more than mere insurgents. After their retreat to Taiwan, the Nationalists continued their effort to constrict the maritime commerce of Communist China.[13]

Prior to the Korean War, the U.S. government did not support Nationalist attempts to interfere with PRC seaborne commerce. When the Nationalist government issued its 20 June 1949 "port closure" order, Washington protested the action as illegal. On 16 September 1949 the State Department announced that the United States would not recognize the Nationalist government's proposed blockade of mainland ports.[14]

U.S. policy shifted in late 1949, when Washington decided to "ignore the strictly legalistic approach" and "permit the Nationalists to take the kind of action that would make the running of the [Nationalist] blockade unprofitable for those engaged in it." Truman directed U.S. agencies to do nothing to reduce the effectiveness of Nationalist blockading actions. The motivation for doing this was to avoid right-wing charges that Truman had given the coup de grâce to the Nationalist regime. The JCS proposed U.S. "recognition" of the Nationalist blockade, but this was blocked by Acheson.[15]

U.S. policy shifted fundamentally with the outbreak of the Korean War. In July 1950 the State Department informed Taipei that "The United States

Government would not stand in the way of air and naval reconnaissance by the Chinese Government, provided such reconnaissance did not involve armed offensive actions *against the mainland*" (emphasis added).[16] Actions against Communist Chinese maritime commerce were thus implicitly approved. Support for Nationalist disruption of PRC maritime commerce offered the United States a way of weakening Communist China by means short of war.

The State Department and the JCS disagreed about whether the Nationalists should be empowered to "visit and search" only Chinese Communist vessels or third-country ships as well. The State Department objected to the search of third-country vessels, while the JCS favored such a course. This difference was in line with the State Department's desire to avoid difficulties with friendly countries (such as Britain), whose ships might be seized, and with the Pentagon's desire to minimize the flow of military supplies to hostile ports while U.S. forces were at war. The Pentagon conceded that stopping third-country ships could create political difficulties, but argued that the U.S. government could intercede with Taipei in cases of "undue detention and diversion of vessels found to be innocent."[17] As of June 1956, no official decision had been rendered resolving this issue.[18] Meanwhile, Nationalist seizures of European, Soviet, and Chinese Communist shipping continued. Between September 1949 and October 1954, Nationalist warships and planes interdicted sixty-seven foreign vessels trading with China. Half of those vessels were British.[19] According to British sources, Nationalist forces interfered with British shipping 141 times during roughly the same period.[20]

U.S. support for Nationalist maritime interdiction activities were linked to a desire to plug loopholes in the U.N.-imposed embargo of China during the Korean War. In May 1951, the General Assembly called on states to embargo the shipment to the PRC and North Korea of all material of any strategic or military value. One major weakness of this embargo, however, was the noncooperation of the Soviet Union and its Eastern European satellites. By encouraging Nationalist interdiction, Washington helped to raise the disincentives for Soviet and Eastern European leaders to risk ships by carrying cargoes to Chinese ports. Since the PRC's own merchant marine was then minuscule, discouragement of Soviet-bloc traffic constricted Communist China's maritime trade.

Soviet bloc ships were not Washington's only concern. Western European ships, especially British, also carried cargoes to the PRC. Indeed, as the frequency of visits by Soviet-bloc ships fell off in 1952, visits by British ships increased.[21] U.S. military leaders suspected that British ships were delivering strategic goods to the PRC. When U.S. officials raised this issue with their British counterparts, they were told that British ships entering Chinese ports carried virtually no cargo, while those leaving carried such innocuous cargoes as tea, silk, rugs, and tung oil. U.S. leaders did not entirely believe this explanation. U.S. Navy planes photographed almost all large ships bound into or out of Chinese ports, showing the name, nationality, and degree of draft of each ship. Photos of incoming British ships showed many carrying near maximum loads. CIA requests to review the manifests of suspect ships were also refused. U.S. efforts to raise this issue during Prime Minister Winston Churchill's January 1952 visit to Washington caused considerable friction. Strong U.S. State Department pressure forced the Pentagon to drop the issue, but the feeling persisted that the British were "not playing fair" by trading with Communist China while American soldiers were fighting Chinese armies in Korea.[22] In this context, Nationalist "visit and search" of third-country ships provided accurate first-hand information about ship cargoes. This was welcome to U.S. authorities.

Nationalist warships also interdicted PRC coastal traffic. According to a PLA-N history, Nationalist occupation of the offshore islands virtually severed the sea lines of communication off Zhejiang in 1950. PRC fishing activity was also seriously disrupted. The Yangzte River estuary and the Zhejiang coast were especially important in this regard, providing some of China's finest fishing fields, yet within range of the Nationalist-held offshores. By mid-1950, Nationalist sea raiders were so active off Zhejiang that local fisherman were afraid to put out to sea. Nationalist maritime raiding reached its peak during 1951. During the first half of that year, the PLA-N recorded 137 incidents of Nationalist "piracy." The PLA-N responded to Nationalist maritime raiding by stepped-up patrol activity. Clashes were frequent.[23]

Intensified PLA-N patrolling forced the Nationalists to abandon large-scale attacks in mid-1951, adopting instead small-scale raids using more deceptive methods. Nationalist raiders increasingly operated as disguised fishing boats and attacked at night. They would mingle with ordinary fishing or commercial boats, then suddenly open fire on unsuspecting PLA-N patrol boats. Sometimes they would fly the PRC flag before opening fire when approached by PLA-N boats. The PLA-N found it difficult to deal with Nationalist raiders because they often included local seamen possessing an intimate knowledge of the weather, current, and geography of the region in which they operated. There was a long history of piracy along the Zhejiang and Jiangsu coasts, and the Nationalists recruited many individuals traditionally engaged in this line of work. Nationalist raiders maintained liaison with anti-Communists ashore, and were frequently forewarned of the PLA-N's approach. In many cases, Communist naval commanders were also new to the sea.

Constriction of coastal traffic between northern and southern China imposed substantial burdens and costs on Beijing. Large amounts of foodstuffs, produced in China's warm southern regions, had to move north, while large volumes of coal, China's primary fuel, had to move from mines in the north to cities in the south. Moreover, China's road and rail network was extremely underdeveloped in the early 1950s, and a very large portion of this traffic moved by junks or barges along the coast. Disruption of this movement created transportation bottlenecks and retarded the pace of Chinese development. In the June 1956 estimate of CINCPAC (Commander in Chief, Pacific) Felix B. Stump:

> I consider the Chinese Nationalist Navy with its limited resources and assistance from the Nationalist Air Force has had far reaching effects, greater than the majority of people realize, on the interruption of sea traffic to and from Communist China. As a result of the Nationalists' efforts a negligible amount of foreign shipping transits the Taiwan Straits. Except for a certain amount of junk traffic, the bulk of commerce and goods flowing north or south on the mainland of China must be carried inefficiently by costly overland means, thus extending an already overburdened transportation system. I expect the disruption of trade is considerable.[24]

Maritime interdiction also worked to increase Chinese depending on Moscow, thereby fostering tensions in the Sino-Soviet alliance. By restricting PRC trade with third countries and by retarding PRC economic development, it increased the level of Soviet assistance required by the PRC. It also increased the costs assumed by Moscow in assisting its Chinese ally and encouraged Chinese demands for Soviet action to protect the PRC's maritime commerce.

As with covert operations, the policy of maritime interdiction continued after the end of the Korean War. Once begun, operations assumed an inertia of their own. Shortly after the Korean truce, the Commander in Chief, Pacific (CINCPAC) prohibited Nationalist attacks on vessels in mainland ports and obviously nonmilitary targets such as passenger ferries and fishing sampans.[25] In other regards, however, the interdiction campaign was expanded. Nationalist actions against Soviet and East European shipping were now authorized.

In October 1953, an 8,000-ton Polish ship, the *Praca,* was seized by Nationalist ships on the basis of information supplied by U.S. aircraft. Seven months later, in May 1954, another Polish ship, the *Gottwald,* a 5,000-ton tanker, was seized. Poland charged the United States with responsibility for both seizures. The United States denied any connection with the incidents.[26] In June 1954 an 8,800-ton Soviet tanker, the *Tuapse,* was seized by Nationalist warships on the high seas midway between the

Philippines' Luzon Island and Taiwan. The *Tuapse* was bound for the PRC, loaded with kerosene usable as jet fuel. It was taken to Gaoxiong, where the cargo was unloaded and confiscated, and the crew of forty-nine were encouraged to defect.[27]

Nationalist apprehension of these ships was made possible by the U.S. supply of aerial surveillance intelligence. The Nationalists took the U.S. supply of such intelligence as tacit approval of such actions—as did U.S. authorities themselves. In a telephone conversation with President Eisenhower on 16 June 1954, seven days before the seizure of the *Tuapse,* Secretary of State Dulles explained that "Our plane flies high, spots these boats, tells Chiang where they are, and he picks them up. He himself has insufficient reconnaissance, and can't have effective blockade. . . . They treat our notification to them as being acquiescence, or invitation to action."[28] The question before Eisenhower during his discussion with Dulles on 16 June was whether intelligence regarding the location and bearing of the *Tuapse* should be passed on to Chiang. Dulles explained to Eisenhower that he was:

> . . . rather disposed to let them go ahead on these boats. Our own hand won't be shown. Don't think it critical, one way or another. As to our moral position, and whether we're acting in good faith, [Dulles] said it isn't the kind of thing we would do openly. [But] We're not sending American boat or plane to round up and stop this traffic. We do encourage the Chinese Nationalists, who are theoretically in state of civil war. They do it in exercise of their own belligerent rights.[29]

Eisenhower said the he didn't "know of any reason why they [the Nationalists] should not be told." The Nationalists might "get themselves in a fix," but Eisenhower was "quite certain this would not be something for which the Soviet [sic] would try to declare war." If the Nationalist seizure developed into an incident, the United States would be in a position to make a "straight forward statement" that "we had no part" in the "detention of these ships." If the question of aerial reconnaissance came up, Eisenhower said, the United States could say that it gave this information to the Nationalists "as a matter of habit," as part of the U.S. mission to defend Formosa. In line with these considerations, the "President gave permission to give them the information."[30]

As soon as the *Tuapse* was seized, the Soviet government ordered all Soviet ships on the high seas to proceed to the nearest port, apparently fearing that the Nationalist seizure was the first step in a U.S. move to seize all Communist shipping.[31] Moscow delivered two strong protests to the U.S. government, holding the United States responsible and demanding immediate release of the ship, the crew, and the cargo, along with compensation for losses. The United States denied responsibility. Since Moscow had no diplomatic relations with the ROC, it was not in a position to talk with Taipei about securing the release of the ship, its cargo and crew. Moscow therefore asked the United States to intercede with Taipei on its behalf. American diplomats in Taipei conveyed Soviet demands to the Nationalists, but in a sometimes lighthearted manner. Nationalist authorities refused to release the ships and their personnel. As it became apparent that the Nationalists intended to hold to the *Tuapse* and its crew for some time, the State Department shifted position and began pushing more earnestly for their release. Taipei still resisted. In the view of Ambassador Karl Rankin, State Department pressure was ineffective because Chiang Kai-shek was not convinced that this represented the wishes of President Eisenhower himself. U.S. representations regarding the *Tuapse* were purely formal, conveyed with the mere purposes of publicly disassociating the United States from the seizure and assuaging Soviet anger, Chiang believed, rather than being intended to secure the release of the *Tuapse*. In the words of a 29 October 1954 cable from Rankin to Assistant Secretary of State Everett Drumright:

> As in the case of the troops in Burma for so long, it . . . is taken for granted by the Chinese that representations made by the Embassy about the Tuapse are for the record only and do not represent the true wishes of the United States Government. I should not be surprised if a personal message from President Eisenhower to President Chiang would be required eventually in the present instance.[32]

Rankin also suspected that U.S. military representatives were giving Chiang advice at variance with that of the State Department. In this, Rankin was probably correct. As noted earlier, the U.S. government was divided over the wisdom of countenancing Nationalist seizures of non-PRC shipping; as of mid-1956, this dispute had not been resolved by presidential decision. Regarding the seizure of the *Tuapse*, CINCPAC Admiral Felix Stump believed it "probably did more good than harm." Nonetheless, Stump concluded that "considering all the trouble the United States has taken to persuade the Chinats [Chinese Nationalists] [to] release [the *Tuapse*] without success, we should attempt to discourage further seizures of this kind unless directed by higher authority." Stump saw no need, however, to push Taipei for a statement of policy on this issue. Such a statement "would serve no useful purpose" and would "embarrass the Chinats and at the same time restrict our flexibility."[33]

On 24 September 1954, as the first Taiwan Strait crisis escalated, Eisenhower reconsidered his 1953 decision encouraging Nationalist raids against Chinese Communist territory *and* seaborne commerce. The purpose of this move was to "cool off" the Nationalists, preventing them from "intentionally or accidentally provoking war with Communist China."[34] Eisenhower's approval was contingent upon Secretary of State Dulles' agreement, however, and this was not forthcoming. While not challenging the new ban on actions *against the mainland,* Dulles argued against banning Nationalist actions against Communist China's seaborne commerce. Such a ban, Dulles told the NSC on 21 November, would deprive the United States of "flexibility." The CIA should continue conducting liaison with these operations, Dulles said, with higher guidance being given by the State Department and the Pentagon on a case-by-case basis.[35] Dulles prevailed. A clause ruling out U.S. assistance to Nationalist actions against "seaborne commerce with Communist China" was dropped from a new statement of Far Eastern policy, NSC 5429/5 dated 22 December 1954.[36] Nationalist maritime interdiction operations continued with quiet U.S. support and tacit authorization.

The Communist Campaign to Break the "Nationalist Blockade"

The Nationalist offshore islands were linked to Nationalist maritime interdiction efforts. As a Special National Intelligence Estimate (SNIE) of 4 September 1954 explained, "Although the capture of the offshore islands would not, by itself, relieve the blockade of ocean shipping, it would afford a greater degree of security to coastal traffic."[37] PRC economic development thus required clearing the Nationalists from the offshores.

In 1952, as the fighting in Korea continued in a stalemate, and as Soviet assistance to the modernization of PLA naval and air forces began to take effect, Beijing launched a campaign to clear the offshores of Nationalist forces. By early 1953, the PLA was beginning to bring superior weight to bear against Nationalist offshores along the Zhejiang coast. With an armistice in Korea in July, the PLA began using its recently acquired MiG-15 jet aircraft in the campaign against the offshores. Piloted by Korean War veterans and operating out of a new naval air base at Ningpo, the MiG-15s quickly won air superiority over the offshore battle zone. MiG-15s were vastly superior to the piston-powered F-47s and P-51s flown by Nationalist pilots. Throughout 1953 the battle raged with fifty-two clashes between Communist and Nationalist vessels. The PLA sank sixteen Nationalist ships and captured twenty-six more. Increasing Communist pressure forced the Nationalists to abandon smaller islands, concentrating their forces on the larger ones.[38]

As long as Nationalist forces were able to defend the offshores with only indirect U.S. support and without direct U.S. military intervention, the United States could avoid the drawbacks associated with their defense while enjoying the benefits deriving from their utilization by the Nationalists. The rapid development of PLA military power, however, made such a policy increasingly untenable. Washington was forced to decide whether to directly use U.S. power to support Nationalist efforts to hold the offshores. U.S. endorsement of Nationalist "limited offensive operations" against PRC maritime commerce had been predicated on noninvolvement by the United States. While building up Nationalist military strength and providing critical intelligence essential to successful maritime interdiction operations, U.S. leaders calculated that the United States would not itself become directly and openly involved. The steady unraveling of the Nationalist offshore position made such an approach untenable.

The First Taiwan Strait Crisis

U.S. leaders were forced to reconsider policy toward the offshores in mid-1954 when the PRC launched a press campaign stressing the liberation of Taiwan and then began heavy artillery bombardment of Jinmen and Mazu beginning on 3 September 1954. Prior to the beginning of the artillery bombardment, Washington attempted to deter Chinese moves against the offshores by ordering a U.S. naval demonstration in the vicinity of the offshores. On 19 August 1954, destroyers of the Seventh Fleet visited the Nationalist-held Dachens off the Zhejiang coast, with major units of the fleet hovering nearby.[39] Secretary Dulles also found occasion to tell a press conference, in response to a question about whether the United States was obligated to help the Nationalists defend the offshores, that in view of the fact that some of the offshores were related to the defense of Formosa, the United States would be justified in concluding that the defense of Formosa "comprehended" the defense of the offshores.[40] U.S. moves failed to deter Beijing. On 26 August the PLA raided Jinmen. A week later, heavy bombardment of that island began.

The question for U.S. leaders posed by the initiation of a large-scale PLA offensive against the offshores was whether the United States should alter its policy and use U.S. military forces to support the Nationalist defense of those islands. There was a consensus that without direct support by U.S. air and naval forces the Nationalists would not be able to defend the offshores against the all-out Communist assault that seemed to be building. There was also a consensus that intervention by U.S. forces would require U.S. air strikes against PLA artillery emplacements, airfields, and troop concentrations on the mainland. There was no way of knowing how Beijing would respond to such U.S. air attacks, but it could well decide to escalate the conflict further.

In such an eventuality, the United States would have to resort to atomic weapons, since these were the only weapons that would allow the United States to prevail in a large-scale conflict with Communist China without committing land forces. Eisenhower and Dulles believed that China probably would not back down after U.S. strikes against mainland positions, and that general war with China could well be the result.[41] The NSC should get one thing clear, Eisenhower told that body on 12 September 1954: they were talking about war, and not about a limited war with Communist China as in Korea. If the United States was forced to attack Communist China, Eisenhower said, he was firmly opposed "to any holding back" as in Korea.[42] A general war with China over the offshores, Dulles said, "would probably lead to our initiating the use of atomic weapons."[43] Moreover, a general war with China would also mean a general war with the USSR, Eisenhower told the NSC on 2 November, because if Moscow failed to fulfill its obligations to China under the 1950 treaty, "the Soviet empire would quickly fall to pieces."[44] On other occasions, however, Dulles suggested and Eisenhower concurred that Moscow might remain nonbelligerent in the event of a general U.S.-PRC war while supplying China with munitions and other support. Such a war would give Moscow an excellent opportunity to undermine the U.S. position in Europe and elsewhere around the globe. Whichever course Moscow selected would be extremely costly for the United States.

Eisenhower and Dulles were especially concerned that a general Sino-U.S. war triggered by the offshores would lack American and international support. The NSC would do well to remember, Eisenhower told that body on 2 November 1954, that the American people would not go to war for capricious reasons.[45] The NSC should recognize that Jinmen "is not our ship," Eisenhower said, and that war with China would have to be justified "by a terrific case" to enlist the support of the American people. "The West coast might agree" to a war with China, Eisenhower said, but his letters "from the farm areas constantly say don't send our boys to war. It will be a big job to explain to the American people the importance of these [offshore] islands to U.S. security."[46] It was also important, Eisenhower stressed, to keep in step with the European allies, especially Britain, which simply would not go along with a war over the offshores. Dulles fully shared these concerns. His main objection to "getting sucked into the offshore islands," Dulles told the NSC, was that war over this issue would put the United States in an isolated position, with its enemy enjoying the backing of world opinion.[47]

Another overriding U.S. concern was that flat refusal to assist Nationalists defense of the offshores, if that was what Chiang insisted on doing, would lead to Nationalist defection from the alliance. The only importance of the offshores was psychological, Eisenhower told the NSC, but that *was* important.[48] For Eisenhower and Dulles, the political and psychological implications—especially of possible Nationalist defection in the wake of U.S. refusal to support a defense of the offshores—far outweighed the narrowly military implications of possible loss of these islands. U.S. policy arose out of contradictory interests in avoiding war without adequate political support and in avoiding Nationalist defection.

Largely because of such considerations, Eisenhower and the NSC decided at meetings on 12 September and 2 November 1954 not to commit U.S. forces to the defense of the offshores.[49] Yet because such a decision would demoralize the Nationalists and further encourage Beijing, it was also decided that this decision *would not be made public.* Instead, U.S. leaders decided on what Dulles called a "fuzzy policy." The United States would not commit itself to help defend the offshores, but would avoid words or actions publicly suggesting this. In this way, Beijing would be kept guessing about U.S. intentions, and this uncertainty might help deter further Communist offensive operations against the offshores. Difficulties with the European allies would be avoided. To foster uncertainty in the minds of Communist leaders, the United States would move forward with the mutual defense treaty with the ROC, while not explicitly limiting the application of that treaty to Formosa and the Pescadores. Rather, some ambiguous language (i.e., the elastic clause of Article VI) would be included in the treaty, leaving open to U.S. determination the issue of whether or not the United States would assist in resisting an attack on the offshores as an attack on Formosa itself.[50]

Eisenhower's first preference was for voluntary Nationalist evacuation of the offshores. If the Nationalists could be persuaded to evacuate the offshores, the danger of embittering them by leaving them standing alone before a PLA assault would not arise. The abandonment of the offshores would not, in itself, critically affect the defense of Taiwan. The PLA would gain open access from Xiamen and Fuzhou, the two major ports it would use for a large-scale assault on Taiwan, and Taiwan would lose forward radar facilities useful for early warning. Against these losses were the major gains derived from drawing the defense perimeter down the middle of the Taiwan Strait, where U.S. air and naval superiority could be brought fully into play. Most important, while the U.S. people would not support a war sparked by the offshores, Eisenhower and Dulles were confident that they would support a war waged in defense of Taiwan itself. Reluctant European allies might also be brought along if a war was clearly over Taiwan.

U.S. diplomacy thus first sought voluntary Nationalist evacuation of the offshores. Chiang adamantly rejected this and insisted that Nationalist forces would defend those islands alone if necessary. This placed U.S. leaders in a quandary. If Chiang stood by his pledge and the Communists assaulted the offshores, Nationalist forces there would be overwhelmed while the Americans stood idly by. If Chiang backed down from his pledge to defend the offshores alone, that too would cause considerable resentment against the United States. Either way, Chiang Kai-shek might be so embittered that he would break with the Americans and strike a deal with the Communists.

U.S. leaders discussed the problem of possible defection in terms of Nationalist "morale." Fear of undermining Nationalist morale was a main factor underlying the U.S. decision not to call Chiang's bluff and leave the Nationalists to defend the offshores alone. In an August 1954 memo to the Pentagon, Dulles said that the State Department was also of the opinion that loss of the offshores would be a "severe political and psychological blow to [the] Chinese [Nationalist] government."[51] Shortly afterward, when the JCS formally submitted their recommendations regarding the offshores, they too stressed the psychological impact on the Nationalists of the loss of the offshores. This, together with the large number of Nationalist soldiers stationed on Jinmen, was "perhaps the overriding" consideration, the JCS said.[52] At a September 1954 White House discussion of the offshores, for example, "All but one [of the participants] recognized the overriding fact that the islands' loss would have bad, possibly disastrous, psychological effects. Therefore, they believed, we should defend them."[53] Finally, at a decisive NSC meeting on 2 November 1954, when Dulles suggested that although loss of the offshores would have an adverse effect on Nationalist morale, this might not be "fatal" since the true defense of Taiwan depended on U.S. and not on Nationalist forces, Eisenhower countered by saying that if the United States pushed Chiang Kai-shek too far, Chiang could "quit us cold" and "renounce Formosa itself."[54] Undermining Nationalist morale was dangerous because it might lead Chiang to strike a deal with the Communists. Eisenhower and Dulles agreed that Defense Secretary Charles E. Wilson, an outspoken opponent of U.S. commitment to the offshores, was right when he told the NSC that one thing was sure: it made no sense to risk general war with China over those "darn little islands."[55] Eisenhower and Dulles differed with Wilson in that they felt what was at stake was retention of Formosa itself as part of the western Pacific perimeter.

Was this belief in the possibility of Nationalist defection via "demoralization" a misperception? The pattern of Chiang's pre-1949 diplomacy toward the powers clearly demonstrates that he regularly used *threats* of defection to influence his allies.[56] But was he prepared to actually follow through on these threats in the mid-1950s? This is a key question which cannot be answered with certainty until Chiang Kai-shek's archives are opened. One eminent scholar long ago provided what is still the best answer available: If U.S. policy threatened continued Nationalist rule over Taiwan, the possibility of a deal between the Nationalists and the Communists was very real.[57] The CCP was quite willing to cooperate with the KMT if it served their interests. The best terms they could offer, however, were the continuation of KMT control over Taiwan within the general framework of PRC sovereignty. If the United States adopted policies that undermined the power of Chiang Kai-shek and the KMT, there would be a strong incentive for the KMT to go over to the CCP, since that party would now offer what the United States was trying to take away—continued KMT rule over Taiwan. Would U.S. abandonment of the Nationalist garrisons on the offshores undermine Chiang's and the KMT's control over Taiwan? U.S. leaders of the mid-1950s concluded it would.

There was also a strong perceptual and emotional aspect to Nationalist reactions to U.S. policy. Here it is necessary to appreciate how Chiang saw the issue. Chiang's raison d'être was to unify China and turn it into a great power. He wanted absolutely nothing to do with policies leading to the permanent alienation of Formosa from China. From Chiang Kai-shek's perspective, the offshores were "springboards" for offensive operations against the mainland, including, ultimately, its recovery. Both symbolically and materially, Nationalist retention of at least several of the offshores was vital for the return. Symbolically, Nationalist possession of the offshores kept alive the hope of eventual liberation from Communist rule among people of the mainland. With Nationalist forces only a few miles from the Communist-held mainland, the people of the mainland could still hope for the eventual Nationalist return. This hope kept alive the spark of resistance to Communism. Materially, the offshores served as essential staging areas for offensive operations by Nationalist forces—operations that honed the combat skills of China's anti-Communist forces and that prepared conditions within China for the return.

Another dimension of the Nationalist perception of U.S. policy was the belief that U.S. policy had been largely responsible for the CCP victory over the KMT during the 1944–49 period. As erroneous as this belief may be, it was nonetheless held with some conviction by many Nationalist leaders. According to this belief, the United States had imposed policies on the KMT during Yalta and the Marshall mediation that brought the Communists to power. Now they insisted on policies accepting the continued existence of Communist rule in China *and* stripping China of Taiwan! To hell with such arrogant Americans, Chinese Nationalists might conclude. It would be better to work out an understanding with the CCP in secret and then invite the Americans to leave Taiwan. In the past the CCP had shown itself flexible and generous enough in dealing with Nationalist leaders willing to help the CCP reach its goals.

The credibility of the United States as an ally was also at stake, U.S. leaders believed. Although the United States had no legal obligation to defend the offshores or to assist a Nationalist defense, this fine point might be lost on the international audiences that would witness American passivity in the face of a PLA overwhelming of Nationalist garrisons there. U.S. credibility went to the heart of the Eisenhower Administration's doctrine of massive retaliation. Under the Eisenhower Administration's "New Look," U.S. conventional forces were reduced, while forward-deployed U.S. troop levels were drawn down. Increased reliance on nuclear weapons was to substitute for diminished conventional forces. There was concern, however, that the strong taboo against the use of nuclear weapons had made use of such weapons virtually unthinkable. Reduced levels of conventional strength, combined with nonusable nuclear strength, would sap U.S. policy of its vital credibility—or so U.S. leaders feared. From this perspective, the offshores were a test of the strategy of massive retaliation. If the United States failed the test, if it capitulated to enemy demands rather than standing firm with confidence in its superior military power, friends of the United States around the world would be filled with doubt about American resolve. The political consequences of such doubt were incalculable.[58]

Sacrifice of the offshores would be detrimental to U.S. policy interests for still another reason: Such a sacrifice was tantamount to a fundamental change in U.S. policy toward China, while the Sino-Soviet alliance was still firm. Abandonment of the Nationalists on the offshores would have involved a very substantial racheting down of U.S. pressure on Beijing, well before the key objective of splitting the Sino-Soviet alliance had been achieved. The offshores were linked to Nationalist raids against the mainland, to covert and psychological operations, and to maritime interdiction operations. Retention of the offshores was also linked to the possibility of a Nationalist return to the mainland and to the standing political-military threat to Communist China which that possibility presented. In this context, a U.S. decision to sacrifice the offshores meant a major shift in policy, a fundamental diminution of hostile actions directed against Communist China. Most important, this basic modification of the policy of weakening China by all means short of war would have been made in response to Communist military pressure and while the Sino-Soviet alliance was still strong.

Rather than drawing back from confrontation with the United States, as U.S. leaders had hoped, Mao Zedong further intensified the confrontation in the straits. On 13 December 1954, ten days after the United States and the ROC signed their mutual security treaty, the PLA's high command ordered the launching of an offensive to liberate the Dachens.[59] Again U.S. deterrence had failed. On 17 January 1955, elements of the Seventh Fleet took up position off the Dachens. Beijing was again undeterred by U.S. demonstrations. The next day the PLA landed in force on Yijiang, overwhelming a thousand Nationalist soldiers who defended the island from well-prepared fortifications. U.S. warships stood by as Yijiang was overrun. Yijiang, which was only 7.5 miles from the Dachens, provided an artillery platform for PLA bombardment of those islands.

The force and boldness of the PLA attack on Yijiang, and the fact that the Communists had not been deterred by U.S. threats, precipitated a reappraisal of U.S. policy toward the offshores and the scrapping of the "fuzzy" policy of calculated ambiguity. Keeping the Communists guessing about U.S. intentions had obviously failed to deter Communist action against the offshores, and might damage U.S. prestige in the region. Since the United States had not said publicly that it would not defend the offshores, Eisenhower and Dulles feared that it was assumed in "many quarters" that the United States intended to defend those islands. When it then failed to do this, as during the assault on Yijiang, those people concluded that the United States had "run away" when danger appeared. The time had therefore come, Eisenhower and Dulles concluded the day after Yijiang's fall, to make U.S. intentions clear and to stick to them. Since abandonment of all the offshores was "not practical" "because this would be such a shock to the ROC that they might turn against us," the United States should press the Nationalists to evacuate the Dachens, in exchange for which the United States would state its intention to hold Jinmen.[60] Mazu Island would be defended if an attack on it was deemed to be a prelude to an attack on Formosa or the Pescadores.[61] An NSC meeting on 20 January 1955 gave its imprimatur to this new policy. At the meeting, Defense Secretary Wilson, supported by Treasury Secretary George Humphrey, renewed his proposal to abandon all the offshores, defending only Formosa and the Pescadores. The United States should not risk being drawn into war with China over territory of little value, they said. Dulles agreed with this objective "over the long period," but rejected it for the present because it would have "a catastrophic effect on Chinese Nationalist morale."[62]

A corollary of the decision to assist in the defense of Jinmen and Mazu was a move to secure congressional support in the event of conflict. Since Eisenhower believed support would be forthcoming only if the issue in question was the defense of Taiwan itself, the defense of the offshores had to be tied to Taiwan. The resolution forwarded by the administration to

Congress on 24 January 1955 provided that the president was authorized "to use U.S. armed forces if necessary for the purpose of securing Formosa and the Pescadores against armed attack, this authority to include the securing and protection of such related positions now in friendly hands, and the taking of such other measures as the President might judge to be appropriate for the security and defense of Formosa and the Pescadores." The resolution passed the House by a vote of 409 to 3, and the Senate vote was 85 to 3 in favor.

While the Taiwan Strait Resolution provided a basis for U.S. assistance in the defense of Jinmen and Mazu, it was a unilateral U.S. policy, subject to the determination of the U.S. president, that an attack on those islands was part of an attack on Taiwan and the Pescadores. Moreover, although Dulles had repeatedly spoken to Yeh in early January of a U.S. "announcement" of its intention to assist in defense of Jinmen and Mazu, by the end of that month U.S. representatives made it clear that no such public declaration would be forthcoming.[63] In terms of a public commitment to defend the offshores, the conditional and unilateral declaration of the Formosa Resolution was the best that Taipei could hope for. Chiang was livid when he discovered American backtracking from what he took to be a promise of an explicit and public commitment to the defense of Jinmen and Mazu.[64] By keeping the U.S. commitment strictly unilateral, Washington sought to avoid an automatic obligation which Chiang could call upon regardless of the circumstances through which a confrontation had developed. By retaining flexibility, Washington hoped to reduce Chiang's ability to involve the United States in a conflict with China which he had provoked.

Another reason for U.S. backtracking from a public commitment to help defend Jinmen was that Britain had just agreed to support the push for U.N. neutralization of the Taiwan Strait only on condition that the United States *not* make a public statement committing itself to defense of the offshores. The United States accepted this, while telling London that it would confidentially inform the Nationalists of the U.S. intention to help defend Jinmen. From Eisenhower's perspective, NATO was absolutely essential to the U.S. global defense against Communism, and nothing should be allowed to undermine its unity. The U.S. struggle was global. It was essential to keep this in mind when considering policy toward the offshore islands, Eisenhower felt.[65]

Chiang Kai-shek attempted to force Washington to make a public statement by refusing to ask for assistance in evacuating the Dachens until such a statement was made.[66] Washington did not budge. When Foreign Minister Yeh threatened that Taipei might be compelled to make a public statement of its own, intended to demonstrate a U.S. commitment to Jinmen, Dulles warned that, in such a situation, the United States might be forced to deny the Chinese statement. The U.S. commitment to Jinmen was to be strictly "voluntary and unilateral," Dulles said.[67] Taipei backed down and requested U.S. assistance in evacuating the Dachens. By the end of February 1955, the only major offshore islands remaining in Nationalist hands were Jinmen and Mazu.

While pressuring Taipei to abandon the Dachens, U.S. leaders began preparing public opinion for the use of atomic weapons should that become necessary to defend Jinmen. In a speech on 8 March 1955, Dulles warned that the administration considered atomic weapons "interchangeable with conventional weapons."[68] This was not bluff. U.S. leaders were aware of the political costs of using atomic weapons against China. On the other hand, many officials, including Eisenhower, felt that the strong taboo that had developed against the use of atomic weapons was undermining the credibility of U.S. power, which under the "New Look" stressed nuclear over conventional forces. If it became necessary to use atomic weapons to hold Jinmen, at least the political costs of that use would be partially offset by increased credibility of U.S. power.[69]

The first Taiwan Strait crisis eased with a series of PRC diplomatic moves in February and March 1955.[70] As the crisis passed, the U.S. government renewed its effort to persuade Taipei to withdraw from Jinmen and Mazu. Eisenhower now urged Chiang Kai-shek to adopt an "outpost" approach to the defense of those islands. According to this approach, only modest Nationalist forces—perhaps about 5,000 men on Jinmen—would be committed to the defense of those islands. Eisenhower hoped that this would meet Chiang's objections to abandonment of further territory to the Communists without a struggle, and satisfy Chiang's desire for early warning of a major Communist effort against Taiwan. Adoption of an "outpost" approach would change Jinmen and Mazu from symbols of Nationalist prestige into expendable outposts, conserving the bulk of Nationalist forces for the defense of Taiwan itself. Were Chiang to agree to an "outpost" approach, Eisenhower indicated, he was prepared to meet Chiang in Honolulu; station a division of U.S. Marines and an additional Air Force wing on Taiwan; further strengthen Government Republic of China (GRC) military forces for use on the mainland when the appropriate opportunity arose; and, most significant of all, initiate joint U.S.-ROC "naval interdiction" of war materials being carried over sea lanes between Shantou in northern Guangdong and Wenzhou in southern Zhejiang. Since there were then no railroads and only a few roads into Fujian, the U.S. envoys explained, such a move would greatly limit Communist ability to build up stockpiles of war materials on the coast opposite Taiwan, thereby constituting a more effective barrier to an attempted invasion of Taiwan than a few scattered island barriers.[71] Admiral Arthur Radford and Assistant Secretary Walter Robertson carried these proposals to Chiang in late April.

Some analysts have been sharply critical of the U.S. offer of "naval interdiction" of the central China coast in exchange for withdrawal from the offshores. Such a move by U.S. naval forces would almost certainly have involved the United States in war with Communist China, it is argued. Had only Chiang Kai-shek been shrewd enough to recognize this, he could have achieved his objective—or at least the objective imputed to him by most American analysts—of a general Sino-American war. It was lucky for the United States that Chiang failed to seize the U.S. offer of a blockade.[72] This criticism assumes, of course, that the United States would actually have followed through on its proposed blockade. Given the direction of U.S. policy in 1955—using all means short of war to pressure China—it seems very unlikely that Eisenhower and Dulles would have moved forward the proposed joint blockade. More likely would have been greater U.S. support for *Nationalist* interdiction efforts: the supplying of more and better warships to the ROC navy, fuller intelligence, authorization of extended Nationalist use of mines, and so on. Once Nationalist forces withdrew from Jinmen and Mazu, they could not easily return. The United States could, however, easily alter its policy toward use of U.S. naval forces in the Taiwan Strait. After all, what precipitated the offer of joint naval interdiction was a U.S. decision to drop an earlier promise of a public commitment to defend Jinmen and Mazu. Distrust of the United States was one reason Chiang rejected the U.S. offer of blockade. As long as his troops sat on the offshores, he held the initiative. Abandonment of those islands in exchange for particular naval moves would have passed the initiative to Washington.

Chiang was utterly dismayed with the American volte-face on defense of Jinmen. Only weeks after Dulles' apparently solemn commitments in exchange for Nationalist agreement to withdraw from the Dachens, the United States was going back on its word and demanding that the Nationalists withdraw their forces from Jinmen and Mazu as well. Robertson did not deny Chiang's assertion that the position now being advanced by the United States was at variance with that stated some weeks earlier. "Circumstances change," Robertson told Chiang. President Eisenhower had simply changed his mind regarding the wisdom of risking a war over the offshores. Chiang replied that he now understood the situation. Free China would not withdraw from Jinmen and Mazu, he insisted. It would defend them with or without U.S. help.[73] Robertson and Radford did not press the "outpost" option, but presented the issue instead as a simple choice of withdrawal or defense. Eisenhower later criticized them for this failure, telling Dulles that

"It is, of course, possible that no presentation could have brought Chiang to recognize the wisdom of some arrangement as this. . . . But it is clear that as long as Radford and Robertson themselves could not grasp the concept [of outpost defense], we simply were not going to get anywhere."[74]

The United States tried again in October 1955 to persuade Chiang to evacuate Jinmen and Mazu, this time offering to break off the ambassadorial talks with the PRC at Geneva in exchange for such a move. Again Chiang refused. The United States then made clear to Chiang that it considered itself under no treaty obligation to defend the offshores. Chiang again said he understood and was prepared to defend the offshores without U.S. assistance.[75]

Washington and Taipei were playing "chicken."[76] Washington said U.S. forces would not help defend the offshores, and urged the Nationalists to withdraw, while Taipei insisted it would defend the offshores and concentrated more and more troops there. Each side refused to modify its policies and insisted that it would adhere to its own course, even though the consequences would be heavy losses for both sides. Eventually it was the American side that "swerved." Failure to intervene on the Nationalist behalf, U.S. leaders concluded, would lead not only to very heavy Nationalist casualties, which would, ipso facto, weaken the defense of Taiwan, but also to Nationalist "demoralization" and to resentment of the United States.

The United States may well have blundered by not making Nationalist withdrawal from Jinmen and Mazu the quid pro quo for conclusion of the mutual security treaty.[77] The main reason the United States backed away from such an approach was fear it would lead to Nationalist defection via "demoralization."

The 1958 Crisis: Chiang's Efforts at Entrapment

Control over the stationing of Nationalist forces on the offshores was tied to defense of Taiwan. If Chiang Kai-shek was able to concentrate a large percentage of Nationalist forces on Jinmen and Mazu, Secretary Dulles told the NSC on 2 November 1954, he could "gut" Formosa's defenses, thereby placing on U.S. forces the burden of defense of that island were it attacked. Concentration of substantial Nationalist forces on the offshores therefore created pressure for the United States to help defend those islands, since to do otherwise would risk the sacrifice of the substantial Nationalist forces stationed there, and would ipso facto weaken the Nationalist ability to defend Taiwan.

During the treaty negotiations in late 1954, the United States insisted on U.S. control over the deployment of Nationalist forces. Nationalist representatives resisted strongly. Eventually a compromise was reached. Notes exchanged by Dulles and Yeh on 10 December provided that "Military elements which are a product of joint effort and contribution by the two Parties" "would not be removed" "without mutual agreement" from Taiwan and the Pescadores "to a degree which would substantially diminish the defensibility of such territories."[78] This meant, Secretary Dulles told the U.S. Senate during debate over ratification of the treaty, that "if the United States has granted supplies and equipment for the forces on Formosa or has aided in the training, support, and equipment of armed forces, the resultant strength will not be removed from Formosa to other areas without our consent."[79]

The notes of 10 December left the Nationalists a number of loopholes, however. Nationalist representatives subsequently advanced four reasons why the buildup on the offshores did not violate those notes. First, the Nationalists insisted that mutual agreement to such unit deployments was required only when those deployments diminished the defensibility of Taiwan and the Pescadores. Since Jinmen and Mazu were, in the Nationalist view, Taiwan's front line of defense, deployments there strengthened rather than diminished Taiwan's defense. Second, the units being posted to the offshores, they said, were not "a product of joint effort and contribution by the two Parties" as specified by the note. Forces being assigned to the offshores were not the primary GRC recipients of U.S. equipment and training under the Military Assistance program (MAP). Nor were they a part of the joint U.S.-ROC command structure. Thus, the units being stationed on the offshores were not covered by the December 1954 note. Third, the 1954 note had recognized that the ROC "possesses with respect to all territory now or hereafter under its control the inherent right of self-defense." A sovereign state could not designate to another the power to determine whether or not, or how, to defend itself. Fourth, the elastic clause of Article VI of the mutual security treaty recognized that the two sides could agree to defend "other territories" by "mutual consent," and the United States had "consented" to the defense of Jinmen and Mazu when the Dachens were evacuated.[80] U.S. representatives refuted these arguments and insisted that the United States would help defend the offshores only if Eisenhower deemed a Communist attack on them part of an assault on Taiwan and the Pescadores.

Chiang upped the ante. Throughout 1956 and 1957, Chiang steadily deployed more of his best troops to the offshores. In September 1954, there were 30,000 Nationalist soldiers there. By April 1956, the offshore island garrisons totaled nearly 100,000 men, along with more than a third of the major items of military equipment available to Nationalist ground forces.[81]

U.S. leaders believed these deployments were an effort by Chiang to embroil the United States in war with the PRC. Was this U.S. perception accurate? Because Chiang Kai-shek's archives have not yet been opened for the post-1949 period, we cannot be sure about the motives underlying these moves. The best guess is that Chiang hoped to create a situation in which a Communist attack on Jinmen and Mazu would, ipso facto, become a threat to Taiwan's security. In the words of Tang Tsou, "Putting one-third of his combat effectives" on the offshore islands was "one of Chiang's boldest political gambles in his adventurous career."[82] Chiang had a U.S. commitment to help defend Jinmen if an attack on it substantially reduced the defensibility of Taiwan. Loss of the men and equipment on Jinmen would certainly have done that. Chiang also knew that U.S. leaders had assumed during the 1954–55 crisis that strikes against mainland bases, quite possibly followed by the use of atomic weapons, would be required in the event of U.S. intervention. All the ingredients for the making of a general U.S.-PRC war seemed to be present.

There is, however, another aspect which must be kept in mind when considering the questions of American culpability and Nationalist entrapment of the United States during the 1958 Strait crisis. This is the matter of U.S. authorization of Nationalist maritime operations against the PRC. As in the case of the first crisis, these operations contributed substantially to the development of tension culminating in the crisis. If such operations were carried out without U.S. authorization, they could be seen as part of a Nationalist effort to manipulate the United States. If those operations had U.S. authorization, Nationalist intentions might still have been the same (to embroil the United States and the PRC), but the culpability of the United States would be considerably greater: The United States was not an innocent party being drawn unwillingly into a conflict created essentially by Taipei and Beijing.

In this regard, a memorandum from CINCPAC to the Taiwan Defense Command (TDC) in January 1958 (shortly before the second Strait crisis), consolidating various directives dealing with what sorts of Nationalist military operations did and did not require U.S. endorsement, is germane.[83] Nondefensive actions *not* requiring U.S. authorization were: small-scale intelligence raids against the mainland and naval covering fire for raid withdrawal, reconnaissance operations of company size or less, naval reconnaissance and patrol operations, air reconnaissance operations "to the limit of capabilities," and "air to air action consistent with other operations requiring no U.S. endorsement, and consistent with the United States policy regarding the undesirability of provoking CHICOM attack against Taiwan and the Pescadores." Actions requiring U.S. endorsement included: combat raids, reconnaissance operations of greater than company size, sea mining, raids on mainland harbors, air attacks against ships alongside mainland wharves or targets on the mainland, and naval gunfire against mainland targets except when covering the withdrawal of reconnaissance patrols. Even assuming that U.S. authorities did not give an explicit green light to the type of actions specified in the second category, this memo makes clear that there was standing, implicit U.S. authorization for a wide range of Nationalist limited-offensive actions. Thus, while Nationalist deployment of large numbers of troops to the offshores was done against U.S. wishes, the same cannot be said for the low-intensity war under way between Nationalist and Communist forces along the central China coast.

The second Strait crisis was precipitated by Mao Zedong's decision to begin bombarding Jinmen and Mazu in August 1958. As tension mounted in the Strait, Chiang rejected renewed U.S. calls to withdraw some of the forces, and warned that Nationalist morale would collapse if Washington forced him to withdraw. Chiang also "hounded" Eisenhower (Eisenhower's word) to give local commanders independent authority to respond to attacks from the mainland. As the Communist bombardment intensified, Chiang sent Eisenhower "a frantic letter" (again, Eisenhower's words) saying that, unless Nationalist forces were permitted to take aggressive action on an extensive scale, Jinmen, along with one-third of Taiwan's army, would be lost.[84] During the 1958 crisis, unlike the first Strait crisis, U.S. leaders refused to authorize Nationalist air attacks on PLA positions. Rather than trying to suppress the PLA bombardment as Chiang demanded, U.S. leaders developed a plan to assist in a Nationalist resupply, under fire, of the besieged Nationalist garrisons.

As Communist pressure on the offshores intensified, Eisenhower and his advisers concluded that the United States could not stand idly by while the large Nationalist garrisons there were cut off and forced into submission. They were acutely aware that the utility of the islands in harassing the PRC paled in comparison to the immense political and material costs of a war with China sparked by those islands. During the second Strait crisis, Eisenhower and Dulles felt even more strongly than during the first that congressional and European allied opposition would leave the U.S. government isolated in the event of a war with China over the offshores. Yet they also concluded that for the United States to acquiesce to PLA subordination of the Nationalist offshores garrisons would so demoralize the Nationalist regime that it would become vulnerable to Communist subversion. As in 1954–55, administration leaders feared that this could breach the offshore defense perimeter, rendering vulnerable other elements of that chain to the north and south of Taiwan. Eisenhower also believed that the spectacle of

U.S. passivity in the face of PLA subjugation of the offshores would persuade small countries around China's periphery that the United States could not or would not protect them reliably against China, and that prudence required a timely accommodation with Beijing. Failure to back the Nationalist defense of Jinmen, in other words, would lead to an unraveling of the structure containing Communist China.

U.S. leaders responded with a massive display of force. A huge armada of six aircraft carriers, three heavy cruisers, forty destroyers, several submarines, and twenty support ships quickly assembled in the Taiwan Strait region. Shipment of artillery, aircraft, and advanced weapons, such as highly accurate Sidewinder air-to-air missiles, was expedited. Large numbers of additional warplanes, including special units configured to wage atomic warfare, were deployed to the Far East. To ensure that Beijing got the message, these deployments were not kept secret. Eight-inch-caliber howitzers capable of delivering atomic warheads were also conspicuously deployed to Jinmen. One way the 1958 crisis was unlike the first Strait crisis, however, is that this time Eisenhower was wary about the actual use of atomic weapons. During the several intervening years, he had become more appreciative of the strong domestic and international backlash that would follow any use of atomic weapons. Thus, while he was conspicuously preparing for nuclear war with China, Eisenhower rejected Pentagon requests for discretionary authority to use these weapons, and he told the JCS that atomic weapons would not be used even in the event of an attack on Taiwan itself. Military planners felt this departure from plans established during the first Strait crisis endangered U.S. ability to defend against China's superior numbers, and demanded corresponding increases in conventional forces. Eisenhower agreed, and large amounts of conventional munitions were airlifted to the Taiwan area. From Beijing's perspective, it looked like the United States was preparing for large-scale nuclear and conventional war against China.[85]

The immediate threat to Nationalist forces on the offshores during the crisis came not from actual assault by the PLA but from an effective blockade created by the intensity of PLA bombardment. Given the size of the Nationalist force on the offshores, logistic requirements were substantial. Further logistical constraints emerged in the first days of the blockade, when a Nationalist ship sank in Jinmen's harbor, blocking entry. Until that ship could be removed, resupply would have to be by amphibious means, and since the Nationalist navy had limited amphibious capabilities, this pointed toward resupply by the U.S. Navy. The United States quickly supplied substantial numbers of amphibious ships and trained Nationalist personnel in techniques for conducting amphibious landings under heavy enemy fire. U.S. warships were then to convoy Nationalist resupply ships to the three-mile limit of international waters off Jinmen and Mazu, and stand by protectively while the cargoes of those ships were transferred to smaller amphibious vessels, which would then proceed to the beaches of the off-shores. U.S. warships were authorized to retaliate if fired upon by PLA shore batteries. U.S. leaders calculated that the PRC would seek to avoid conflict with American forces, and this calculation proved correct. Nationalist forces were also given the ability to maintain air superiority by the transfer of advanced fighters and sophisticated Sidewinder air-to-air missiles to the Nationalists. Maintenance of Nationalist air superiority was a prerequisite for success of amphibious operations.

Chiang was strongly opposed to the U.S. plan and demanded, instead, effective suppression of Communist artillery batteries via air strikes. He insisted that Nationalist planes could do the job. U.S. military leaders doubted this, however, and suspected that U.S. aircraft would have to be called in to finish the job begun by the Nationalists. Once U.S. planes bombed China, Beijing might feel compelled to retaliate and the conflict could escalate. This was exactly what Chiang wanted, American leaders suspected. This belief found confirmation in the fact that, as the U.S.-Nationalist resupply effort gained in effectiveness, Chiang's threats to bomb Communist shore batteries became still stronger.[86] Again U.S. leaders took this as indication that Chiang's real objective was to enmesh the United States in war with the PRC. They likewise suspected there were ulterior motives for Nationalist incompetence in the U.S.-designed resupply effort. During the last several days of August and early September 1958, Nationalist-manned landing ship tanks (LSTs) attempted five voyages to the off-shores, but failed to land. The "inability or unwillingness on part of ChiNat navy to utilize resources they have is major cause for failure to get necessary ammo and other supplies" to Jinmen, CINCPAC reported to the JCS on 5 September.[87] The Nationalists "could resupply islands if they would use resources available," CINCPAC informed Washington. CINCPAC tried to determine the exact reason for repeated Nationalist failures to implement the U.S. plan, but were confronted by a wall of Nationalist secrecy "on operational matters." Finally, after a week of repeated failures, Nationalist forces completed their first successful large-scale resupply operation on 14 September.

Mao Zedong was surprised by the strength of U.S. mobilization in response to the bombardment. "I simply did not calculate that the world would become so disturbed and turbulent," he confessed to his comrades.[88] On 6 September 1958, Zhou Enlai proposed that the Warsaw talks be resumed. The United States quickly agreed. No progress was made and the talks remained stymied over the Taiwan issue, but tension in the Strait began to subside.

After Beijing and Washington defused the crisis, the United States distanced itself from Nationalist actions and militancy. At a press conference in Taipei on 30 September, after talks with Chiang Kai-shek, Dulles termed a Nationalist return to the Mainland "a highly hypothetical matter." Any revolt on the mainland, he said, would probably be primarily under local auspices and local leadership.[89] A joint communiqué issued on 23 October, at the conclusion of Dulles' visit, underscored the GRC's intention to recover the mainland principally by *political* rather than by military means. Dulles also persuaded Chiang to make several statements to the effect that nonviolent means would be the principal ones employed to liberate the mainland. Such statements, Dulles told Chiang, would refute Communist propaganda, which "had convinced many people and nations" that Chiang sought to involve the United States in a war with Communist China in order to regain the Mainland.[90] Subsequently Taipei asserted that the joint communiqué did not preclude GRC use of force in the event of a large-scale uprising on the mainland, and the United States expressed concurrence with this view.[91] Taipei also defined "political means" to include paramilitary operations designed to foment revolt. It acknowledged, however, that, under the terms of the notes exchanged in December 1954, it was obligated to consult with the United States prior to initiating such operations.[92]

U.S. leaders were extremely bitter about what they perceived as Nationalist efforts to embroil the United States in war with the PRC. Eisenhower told Undersecretary of State Christian Herter that he was "just about ready to tell Chiang Kai-shek where to get off," and Defense Secretary Neil McElroy proposed sponsoring a coup d'état against Chiang to bring to power someone willing to evacuate the offshores.[93]

Some analysts have suggested that U.S. exasperation over manipulation by a small and vulnerable ally "alienated" U.S. leaders.[94] This may well be, but it should also be noted that the U.S.-Nationalist alliance held together in spite of such tensions for over a decade after the 1958 crisis—until Beijing abandoned its alliance with Moscow and Washington abandoned its containment of the PRC. There was bitterness on both sides of the U.S.-Nationalist alliance: The Nationalists were bitter because of U.S. pursuit of a two-Chinas policy and willingness to come to terms with the PRC. The Americans were bitter because of Nationalist efforts at enmeshment and refusal to adopt liberal political reforms internally. In spite of these cleavages, mutual need held the alliance together. The U.S.-Nationalist alliance, like many others, was based not on mutual love, but on common hatred.

Costs and Gains

Virtually all writings on the two Strait crises of the 1950s have stressed the risks and costs of those episodes: alienation of European and Asian allies; division between the legislative and executive branches of the U.S. government; the risk of an unpopular war with China that might escalate to the nuclear level, and the possibility of activating the Sino-Soviet treaty, thereby precipitating a global nuclear war. Without question, these were real and substantial dangers. What has perhaps not been adequately appreciated is that U.S. willingness to assume these risks was testament to the perceived utility of Nationalist China as an instrument of U.S. policy. Moreover, the firm position of the United States during the two crises helped achieve a major U.S. objective: splitting the USSR-PRC alliance.

From the perspective of U.S. leaders, what was at stake during the two Strait crises of the 1950s was the retention of Taiwan in the western Pacific defense perimeter and of Nationalist China as an element in the U.S.-supported balance of power in that region. For this, U.S. leaders were willing to accept war with the PRC. Were U.S. elite beliefs about loss of the offshores leading to Nationalist demoralization and the loss of Taiwan wrong? It can be argued that had the United States stood firm and refused to assist in the defense of the offshores, Chiang would eventually have agreed to the evacuation of those islands, or that, even if the 100,000-man army there was forced to surrender while the United States stood idly by, Chiang would not have reached a settlement with Beijing inviting the Americans to leave Taiwan. Against such speculation must be weighed Chiang's deep bitterness toward America's China policy (as he perceived it), beginning with the Europe First strategy of World War II, followed by the Yalta–Marshall Mission period of 1945–46, and continuing through the move toward a two-Chinas policy in the mid-1950s. What would have been involved, from Chiang's point of view, if the United States had acquiesced to PLA subordination of the offshores would have been the sacrifice of 100,000 Nationalist soldiers to impose on China a two-Chinas arrangement utterly unacceptable to Chiang. CCP leaders, by mid-1958, were increasingly aware of the advantages of a strategy of courting rather than pressuring the Nationalists. Shortly after the declination of the 1958 crisis, PRC Defense Minister Peng Dehuai called for CCP-KMT reconciliation and cooperation in the great project of national unification. If extreme Nationalist bitterness at American betrayal over the offshores had been combined with CCP promises of high honors and generous stipends for Nationalist leaders who helped bring Taiwan back to the motherland, what would have been the outcome? It takes hubris to conclude that the United States could have imposed on Taiwan whatever arrangement it found desirable. In any case, U.S. leaders of the era believed the risk of Nationalist defection was too great.

The tough U.S. stand during the two Strait crises exacerbated Sino-Soviet tensions. By supporting Nationalist harassment from bases on the off-shores, Washington, in effect, goaded Beijing into action against those outposts. Then when Beijing struck, by threatening all-out war with China while cultivating détente with Moscow during the 1958 crises, Washington precipitated deep Chinese suspicions of Moscow as well as Soviet suspicions about Beijing.[95]

Throughout the 1950s, Beijing was intensely dissatisfied with the fact that U.S. power prevented the incorporation of Taiwan into the PRC. Late in 1957, Chinese leaders concluded that a favorable shift in the global correlation of forces made desirable a militant, confrontational approach by the entire socialist camp, led by the USSR, against U.S. imperialism. Soviet leaders were deeply skeptical about this Chinese approach. Beijing, in turn, feared that Moscow's policy of peaceful coexistence with the United States would diminish the prospects for Taiwan's recovery. In fact, Beijing suspected Moscow of trying to signal Washington and Beijing that Taiwan was not a high priority and should be laid aside.[96]

The initiation of the PLA bombardment on Jinmen and Mazu in August 1958 was a challenge to Moscow's policy of peaceful coexistence. Soviet leaders felt compelled to support their Chinese allies, and at the height of the crisis threatened the United States with retaliation should it attack China. Yet Moscow and Beijing emerged from the 1958 crisis with deepened misgivings about one another. Soviet leaders suspected that Chinese actions might draw the USSR into war with the United States. Beijing concluded that Moscow was not prepared to give China the support it desired on an issue China deemed fundamental to its national interest.

Once the second Strait crisis passed, Soviet leaders concluded that their interests would not be served by facilitating China's efforts to acquire nuclear weapons. Khrushchev also sought a way to remove the Taiwan issue as a cause of war. During talks with Mao in October 1959 (just after Khrushchev's Camp David talks with Eisenhower), Khrushchev proposed that China handle Taiwan in the same way as Lenin had handled the Far Eastern Republic. Lenin had recognized that Republic as an independent country prior to its annexation in 1921.[97] In effect, Khrushchev was proposing that Mao acquiesce to Washington's two-Chinas proposal. Mao bitterly refused. Khrushchev's refusal to support Mao's efforts to take Taiwan, and his proposal that Mao accept the indefinite separation of Taiwan from China, contributed substantially to Mao's conclusion that Khrushchev valued détente with the United States above solidarity with China and, at bottom, wanted China to remain weak.

Would the breakdown of the Sino-Soviet alliance have occurred without the 1958 Strait crisis? Almost certainly. It is doubtful, however, whether that breakdown would have occurred as soon as it did if the United States had not kept that alliance under intense pressure. By denying Beijing some of the key goals it sought through its alliance with Moscow, while simultaneously forcing it into greater dependence on Moscow, U.S. strategy exacerbated Sino-Soviet contradictions. Without the intensification of intra-alliance conflicts by U.S. pressure, the Sino-Soviet alliance would probably have endured longer than it did. If Beijing had gotten what it wanted from its alliance with Moscow—U.S. sacrifice of the Nationalist garrison on Jinmen and Mazu out of fear of *global* war and the consequent estrangement of U.S.-Nationalist relations—it would have had far less reason to be discontented with its Soviet alliance.

Had Taiwan not been the catalyst that precipitated Sino-Soviet tensions in 1958–59, some other issue would undoubtedly have served as well. Yet the historical record indicates that it *was* the Taiwan issue upon which that alliance first foundered. Moreover, it was Washington's tough approach to that issue that produced this contradiction, both by persuading Mao that forceful means were necessary and then by convincing Khrushchev that Mao's measures were unacceptably reckless. Had Mao's measures succeeded in driving a wedge between Washington and Taipei, had Washington stood aside while the PLA mopped up Jinmen and Mazu, Moscow would have had less reason to deem Mao's moves reckless, and Mao would have had less reason to be unhappy with Moscow's support.

U.S. leaders were not so prescient as to foresee the precise sequence of events that unfolded in 1958–59. The very logic of the pressure-cooker strategy, however, was that if U.S. pressure against the PRC was met by Chinese counterpressure, the Chinese countermoves would be contained by superior power. Only if pressure was maintained would Beijing make demands on Moscow which the latter could not or would not satisfy. The sequence of events that actually transpired in Sino-Soviet-U.S. relations in the 1950s roughly approximated this conceptualization.

Gordon Chang makes the important point that the exacerbation of Sino-Soviet tensions was as much the result of the U.S. policy of détente with Moscow as it was of a hard line toward Beijing. He also notes that the hard line toward Beijing was intended to serve objectives other than undermining the Sino-Soviet alliance. Concern for the credibility of the United States as an ally and for the general climate of political opinion in Asia were at least as important by 1958.[98] Yet, as Chang masterfully demonstrates, undermining the Sino-Soviet alliance remained an important U.S. objective which executive branch leaders believed would be served by a tough policy toward Beijing. Stated somewhat differently, the U.S. decision not to sacrifice the Nationalist garrisons on Jinmen and Mazu partially arose out of and effectively served the overriding interest in breaking apart the Sino-Soviet alliance. The very real costs and risks of the Strait crises must be weighted against these gains.

Divergent Goals and Conflict over Alliance Policy

Both Taipei and Washington sought multiple objectives through their alliance. Some of those objectives were similar, others diverged. Chiang Kai-shek's minimal goal was to defend Taiwan against the PLA. Washington shared this objective, although for somewhat different reasons than Nationalist leaders. The overriding, maximal Nationalist objective was to build Taiwan as a base for recovering the mainland, and then engage U.S. power in an effort to overthrow Communist rule. From Washington's perspective, retaining Nationalist control over Taiwan was part of the utilization of Nationalist China as an instrument of pressure on the Sino-Soviet alliance. But U.S. strategists were apparently already thinking beyond this period and preparing for some future order in which the United States might find it expedient to improve relations with the People's Republic of China. Under such conditions, the continued denial of Taiwan to Beijing (or Moscow) would make an important contribution to the maintenance of U.S. supremacy in the western Pacific region. The United States thus sought to create conditions—legal, political, and geographic—for the protracted denial of Taiwan to the PRC. Primary among these conditions was restriction of ROC jurisdiction to Taiwan and the Pescadores.

Chiang Kai-shek and his comrades wanted nothing to do with America's two-Chinas maneuvers. From their perspective, U.S. suggestions that Taiwan might be something other than merely a province of China was completely unacceptable. This proposition touched on core Nationalist beliefs. If the United States insisted on imposing noxious two-Chinas arrangements on Taipei—or at least went too far in imposing such arrangements—Chiang indicated he was prepared to defect from the alliance with the United States via "demoralization."

The offshores brought these disputes into focus. From the standpoint of maximizing the comparative advantage of U.S. naval and air power so that denial of Taiwan to Communist China might be sustainable over a long period of time, drawing the defense perimeter down the middle of the 100-mile-wide Strait made excellent sense. U.S. planners also realized that in terms of creating a political base in the United States for ongoing support of Taiwan's denial to Communist China, a clear break between the island and the continent was important.

Chiang Kai-shek divined U.S. purposes, refused to withdraw from the offshores, and then concentrated large forces on Jinmen, as a way of thwarting U.S. two-Chinas efforts. For Chiang, the offshores were leverage to influence U.S. policy. By 1955, Washington understood what Chiang was doing. It refused to impose a U.S. solution on him, for fear that it would prompt Nationalist defection. In effect, Washington sacrificed an element that would have been useful to long-term objectives, rather than imposing a solution that put at risk the alliance with the Nationalists.

Chiang Kai-shek won the contest with Washington, but the Americans emerged from the 1958 crisis deeply embittered. A small ally, deeply dependent on the United States, had not only rejected U.S. advice on a fundamental issue, but had maneuvered the United States into a near-war confrontation with a major power. For a generation of Americans, the 1958 Strait crisis became the quintessence of a small power's willful entrapment of a great power in a major war. That memory became an important part of the U.S. belief system about Taiwan: too close an embrace might give Taipei too much leverage over American policy.

Notes

1. *FRUS,* 1952–54, vol. XIV, p. 923.
2. Ibid., p. 833.
3. "The Taiwan Straits Situation," 3 September 1958, National Archives, RG 218, GF 1958, CCS 381, Box 147, sec. 38.
4. By PLA count, Nationalist forces controlled thirty-six offshore islands of varying sizes at the start of 1950. *Dangdai Zhongguo haijun* (Modern China's navy) (hereafter cited as *Dangdai haijun*), Beijing: Zhongguo shehui kexueyuan chubanshe, 1987, p. 181.
5. *FRUS,* 1950, vol. VI, p. 371.
6. Ibid., pp. 379–80.
7. Ibid., p. 387.
8. Progress report on NSC 146/2, 16 July 1954.
9. *FRUS,* 1952–54, vol. XIV, p. 603.
10. NSC Progress Report on NSC 146/2, 16 July 1954, National Archives.
11. See Table 4.4 on page 69.
12. Regarding the role of trade in China's industrialization, see Alexander Eckstein, *Communist China's Economic Growth and Foreign Trade,* New York: McGraw Hill, 1966.
13. Edward J. Marolda, *The U.S. Navy and the Chinese Civil War, 1945–1952,* Ph.D. dissertation, Department of History, George Washington University, 1990, pp. 94–95.
14. "Review of CHINAT Interception of Russian and other ships," Annex to Appen-

dix A of a memo by the Chief of Naval Operations for the Joint Chiefs of Staff, dated 29 June 1956, National Archives, RG 218 JCS, Geographic File 1957, 381 Formosa, as box 9, sec. 33. (Hereafter cited as "Annex to Appendix A.")

15. Marolda, *U.S. Navy,* p. 95.

16. *FRUS,* 1950, vol. VI, p. 404.

17. Ibid., p. 406.

18. "Annex to Appendix A."

19. *New York Times,* 14 October 1954, p. 11.

20. *New York Times,* 23 November 1954, p. 16. This compared with twenty-seven instances of interference by Communist warships and planes.

21. *FRUS,* 1952–54, vol. XV, pp. 532–38.

22. Arthur R. Radford, *From Pearl Harbor to Vietnam: The Memoir of Admiral Arthur R. Radford,* Stephen Jurikia, ed., Stanford, CA: Hoover Institution Press, 1980, pp. 276–77.

23. *Dangdai haijun,* pp. 181–88.

24. "Annex to Appendix A."

25. *FRUS,* 1952–54, vol. XIV, pp. 655–58.

26. *New York Times,* 23 November 1954, p. 16; 9 December 1954, p. 3.

27. *FRUS,* 1952–54, vol. XIV, China and Japan, part 1, pp. 480–81, 483; 1955–57, vol. III, p. 1972.

28. *FRUS,* 1952–54, vol. XIV, part 1, pp. 472–74. This is a memorandum of the conversation prepared by Dulles secretary.

29. Ibid.

30. Ibid.

31. Ibid., vol. I, pp. 543–44.

32. Ibid., vol. XIV, part 1, p. 813.

33. "Annex to Appendix A."

34. *FRUS,* 1952–54, vol. XIV, part I, pp. 661–62.

35. Not until July 1955, over a year after the *Tuapse*'s seizure, were twenty-two of the crewmen allowed to return to the USSR. The *Tuapse* itself was apparently never released. Nor did Moscow receive compensation for the ship's cargo. While under Nationalist detention, the crew was subjected to intense and sustained "education" to encourage them to defect. A number of the crew resisted indoctrination, and "diligent" effort was necessary to persuade them to defect. A representative of an émigré Russian anti-Communist organization based in the United States traveled to Taiwan to assist in the reeducation process. Moscow protested to the United States the "spiritual and mental coercion" being applied to the crew, and the U.S. ambassador to Taipei passed these protests on to the GRC foreign ministry. Within four months, twenty-one of the crew of forty-nine had been persuaded to request political asylum. Of the twenty-two who defected, nine returned to the USSR via the United States, another four via Brazil. Seven remained indefinitely in Taiwan. In 1966 they applied for admission to the United States, but this was refused. *Tuapse* file, June 1954–November 1966, no. 143/7.73, Ministry of Foreign Affairs, Taipei.

36. *FRUS,* 1952–54, vol. XIV, part 1, pp. 1044–47.

37. Ibid., p. 567.

38. *Dangdai haijun,* pp. 184–209.

39. Edwin B. Hoope, Dean C. Allard, and Oscar P. Fitzgerald, *The United States Navy and the Vietnam Conflict,* vol. I, *The Setting of the State to 1961,* Navy History Division, Washington: Department of the Navy, 1976, pp. 347–50.

40. *FRUS,* 1952–54, vol. XIV, p. 562.

41. Ibid., pp. 611–23, 831.

42. Ibid., pp. 613–23.

43. Ibid., pp. 611–13.

44. Ibid., p. 831.

45. Ibid., p. 828.

46. Ibid., p. 612.

47. This was the general tenor of discussion at the 12 September 1954 meeting, but no explicit decision was made on the key issue of U.S. use of force. By the time of the 2 November meeting, however, views had solidified sufficiently to produce a consensus that the 12 September meeting had, in fact, decided not to use U.S. forces.

48. *FRUS, 1952–54*, vol. XIV, p. 621.

49. Ibid., p. 835.

50. Ibid., p. 828.

51. Ibid., pp. 244–45.

52. Ibid., pp. 556–57.

53. Dwight D. Eisenhower, *The White House Years,* vol. II, *Mandate for Change,* Garden City, NY: Doubleday, 1963, pp. 463, 467.

54. *FRUS, 1952–54*, vol. XIV, pp. 833–35.

55. NSC meeting of 2 November 1954, in ibid., p. 831.

56. My own work deals with this pattern during the 1937–45 period. John W. Garver, *Chinese-Soviet Relations, 1937–1945: The Diplomacy of Chinese Nationalism,* New York: Oxford University Press, 1988.

57. Tang Tsou, "The Quemoy Imbroglio: Chiang Kai-shek and the United States," *Western Political Quarterly,* vol. 12 (1959), p. 1088.

58. H.W. Brands, Jr., "Testing Massive Retaliation, Credibility and Crisis Management in the Taiwan Strait," *International Security,* vol. 12, no. 4 (Spring 1988), pp. 124–51.

59. *Dangdai haijun,* pp. 214–16.

60. *FRUS, 1955–57,* vol. II, pp. 41–43.

61. Ibid., pp. 46–50, 95–96.

62. Ibid., pp. 69–83.

63. Kenneth W. Condit, *The Joint Chiefs of Staff and National Policy, 1955–1956, History of the Joint Chiefs of Staff,* vol. VI, Washington: Historical Office Joint Staff, 1992, pp. 200–201.

64. *FRUS, 1955–57,* vol. II, pp. 46–48, 106–10.

65. Ibid., pp. 173–77.

66. Ibid.

67. Ibid., p. 156.

68. Gordon H. Chang, "To the Nuclear Brink: Eisenhower, Dulles and the Quemoy-Matzu Crisis," *International Security,* vol. 12, no. 4 (Spring 1988), p. 106.

69. H.W. Barnds, "Testing Massive Retaliation."

70. Regarding Beijing's shift in approach, see Thomas E. Stopler, *China, Taiwan, and the Offshore Islands,* Armonk, NY: M.E. Sharpe, 1985, pp. 95–103.

71. Condit, *JCS and National Policy, 1955–1956,* p. 206. *FRUS, 1955–57,* vol. II, pp. 511–17.

72. Chang, "To the Nuclear Brink," pp. 96–123.

73. *FRUS, 1955–57,* vol. II, pp. 511–17, 524.

74. Cited in Condit, *JCS and National Policy, 1955–1956,* p. 206.

75. Dulles to Yeh, 4 October 1955, *FRUS, 1955–57,* vol. III, pp. 110–12.

76. "Chicken" is a pattern of bilateral interaction modeled on a "game" played by U.S. male adolescents in the 1950s. Two youths would careen down a highway in their autos straight toward one another at high speeds. Unless one swerved out of the way, the

two cars would collide, killing both drivers. The driver that swerved was "chicken," a coward, that is, he feared death and thus "lost" the encounter.

77. This is argued by Tang Tsou in "The Quemoy Imbroglio," in *The Embroilment Over Quemoy; Mao, Chiang, and Dulles,* Institute of International Studies, Salt Lake City: University of Utah, 1959.

78. *United States Treaties and Other International Agreements,* vol. 6, part 1, Washington: Government Printing Office, 1956, p. 454.

79. Statement before Senate Foreign Relations Committee, 7 February 1955, in *State Department Bulletin,* 21 February 1955, p. 289.

80. Shao Yu-ming, *Zhong Mei guanxi yanjiu wenji* (Collected research on Sino-American relations), Taipei: Chuanji wenxue chubanshe, 1980, pp. 111–16. Shao Yu-ming, *Zong menhu kaifang dao Zhong Mei duanjiao* (From the open door policy to the severing of Sino-American relations), Taipei: Danjiang daxue chubanshe, 1983, pp. 25–28.

81. Condit, *JCS and National Policy, 1955–1956,* p. 208.

82. Tang Tsou, "The Quemoy Imbroglio," pp. 1075–91.

83. Enclosure to memo by CNO for JCS, 23 August 1958, National Archives, RG 218 JCS GF 1958 CCS 381, sec. 37, box 147.

84. Dwight D. Eisenhower, *Waging Peace, 1956–1961,* Garden City: Doubleday, 1965, pp. 298–99.

85. Gordon H. Chang, *Friends and Enemies, The United States, China, and the Soviet Union, 1948–1972,* Stanford, CA: Stanford University Press, 1990, pp. 188–90.

86. Tang Tsou, "The Quemoy Imbroglio," p. 1085.

87. CINCPAC to JCS, 5 September 1958, National Archives, RG 218, GF, LCS 381, sec. 41, box 148.

88. Allen S. Whiting, "New Light on Mao; Quemoy 1958: Mao's Miscalculations," *China Quarterly,* no. 62 (June 1975), p. 265.

89. *New York Times,* 1 October 1958, p. 8. Cited in Tang Tsou, "The Quemoy Imbroglio," p. 1087.

90. Eisenhower, *Waging Peace,* p. 304.

91. NSC OCB Report on NSC 5723, 15 April 1959, National Archives.

92. NSC OCB Report on 5725, 18 May 1960, National Archives.

93. Chang, *Friends and Enemies,* pp. 194, 198.

94. Nancy B. Tucker, *Taiwan, Hong Kong, and the United States, 1945–1992: Uncertain Friends,* New York: Twayne, 1994, p. 38.

95. Chang, *Friends and Enemies,* p. 187. A. Doak Barnett, *China and the Major Powers in East Asia,* Washington: Brookings Institution, 1977, p. 189.

96. Barnett, *China and the Major Powers,* pp. 33–35.

97. Tracy B. Strong and Helene Heyssar, "Anna Louise Strong: Three Interviews with Chairman Mao," *China Quarterly,* no. 103, September 1985, p. 504. Strong's account has been confirmed to me by senior Chinese scholars with access to Mao Zedong's archives.

98. Chang, *Friends and Enemies.*

8

The Burma Campaign: Operation Paper and Its Aftermath

The Korean War Burma Operation

One of the main U.S.-Nationalist operations of the 1950s was in Burma. It involved efforts to use the remnants of Nationalist armies in southern Yunan Province and northern Burma to spark anti-Communist guerrilla war in China's southwest. From the Nationalist perspective, the operation was an attempt to begin the return to the mainland. From the American perspective, the operation was primarily a way of diverting Chinese energies away from the Korean War theater. The operation was an unmitigated failure. Its political costs were high and it produced few advantages for the United States. "Operation Paper," as the Burma operation was called, must be placed firmly in the debit column in an appraisal of the value of the Nationalist alliance to the United States.

Chinese entry into the Korean War in November 1950 placed U.S. forces in a dire situation. It was uncertain whether a foothold on the peninsula could be held. In this situation, U.S. leaders looked for moves that might divert Chinese forces from Korea. One seemingly promising opportunity presented itself in China's Southwest. There were some 45,000 Nationalist troops in Yunnan Province in early 1950.[1] Late in 1949, a KMT organizer had traveled to southern Yunnan from Taiwan and attempted to organize an anti-Communist base area there.[2] This effort failed when the PLA directed large-scale "anti-bandit" operations against the Nationalist "remnant" forces in Yunnan early in 1950 in order to secure the PLA's flanks for its planned advance into Tibet later that year. By October, most Nationalist "remnants" had either laid down their arms or fled into Burma.[3] The largest group that fled to Burma was a contingent of about 4,000 men commanded by Nationalist General Li Mi. Li Mi's force settled at Monghsat in northeastern Burma. They were, however, poorly equipped.[4]

Burma at this juncture had a very weak central government. Several months after Burma's independence in January 1948, the Burma Communist Party (BCP) mounted an insurrection. The BCP formed a united front with another Communist group that had taken up arms, two years earlier, with rural militias and politicians unhappy with the new government in Rangoon, and with a separatist movement among the Karen people in Burma. By 1950 this coalition of anti-Rangoon forces dominated central and southern Burma, and the Rangoon government was struggling for survival.[5] The CCP's policy toward the Burmese revolutionary movement was a critical variable. The BCP's line on foreign affairs was indistinguishable from that of the CCP, and the CCP's commentaries on Burmese developments clearly indicated its sympathies for Burma's Communist forces. The CCP began providing large-scale assistance to the Indochinese revolutionary movement in late 1949 and early 1950. Were the CCP to decide to give comparable assistance to the Burmese revolution, this support could have made a crucial difference. As it was, the CCP decided not to give material support to the BCP. By 1954, the Burmese army was gradually reasserting its authority over Burma's central Irrawaddy valley. In this context, both the presence of Nationalist remnant forces in northern Burma and the links of U.S. and Nationalists with those forces were especially risky. Not only did they further complicate Rangoon's situation, more dangerously, they tempted CCP support for Burma's revolutionary movement.

Sometime in late 1950 or early 1951, President Harry S. Truman approved a plan for the CIA to supply arms and other assistance to Li Mi's forces as a way of diverting Chinese forces from Korea. The plan projected that Li Mi's forces would become a catalyst for resistance to the new Communist regime in a region with a long and strong tradition of independence from China's central government. Truman approved the plan over the objection of CIA Director W. Bedell Smith, who felt that the PLA had more than enough troops and that any activities in Burma would not divert forces otherwise destined for Korea.[6]

Operation Paper, as the Burma operation was dubbed, began in February 1951. CAT aircraft ferried to Chiang Mai and Chiang Rai in northwestern

Thailand loads of ammunition and small arms from stockpiles of World War II weapons maintained by the CIA on Okinawa. The munitions were then turned over to the Thai border police who arranged deliveries to Li Mi. U.S. Army engineers were also sent to Monghsat via Thailand to upgrade the tiny airfield there into a base capable of handling large cargo aircraft. By February 1951, C-46 and C-47 aircraft were carrying arms and ammunition directly to Monghsat. In April, Li Mi's forces left Monghsat and marched 175 miles north to Mongmao. CAT planes air-dropped supplies along the route.[7]

Chinese Nationalist agencies worked with the United States to transform Li Mi's ragtag force into an army that, it was hoped, would be capable of challenging the PLA. Li Mi began receiving a monthly subsidy worth $9,000 from Taipei. Radio operators and technicians were also sent from Taiwan to join Li Mi's forces.[8]

In May 1951, Li Mi's force of about 10,000 moved back into Yunnan. It advanced about sixty miles, was joined by local guerrillas, and threatened the airfield at Menglian.[9] The objective of the offensive was to set up an anti-Communist base area in five southwestern counties of Yunnan along the Burma border south of the old Burma Road. The PLA responded with "bandit suppression" operations. According to PRC sources, fighting was heavy, with the Nationalist forces demonstrating "definite combat ability."[10] The geographic parameters of Nationalist operations in Yunnan and their bases in north Burma are illustrated in Figure 8.1.

By the end of June 1951, most Nationalist forces had been pushed back into Burma, although some still hid in the primeval forests north of Menglian. The next month, 3,100 Nationalist forces reentered Yunnan. Again CAT supplied Li's forces for the offensive. The invasion force again headed for Menglian. It succeeded in occupying several county seats in that region before the PLA counterattacked and, within a week, pushed the force back into Burma.[11]

Li Mi's forces then retreated to the relative safety of Monghsat. New troops were again recruited. In February 1952 Taipei airlifted 700 military and special operations "core cadre" into Monghsat to bolster Li Mi's force.[12] By mid-1952, Li Mi's force had again expanded to 8,000 men.[13] Offensive operations into Yunnan were resumed in the form of raids by smaller forces. During the first half of 1952, Li Mi's forces entered Yunnan sixty times, killing over a hundred CCP cadre. The largest incursion came in August 1952, when 2,000 men forayed into Yunnan. They were forced back within a week.[14] Small-unit hit-and-run attacks were much more common, and more difficult for the PLA to counter.[15]

Nationalist forces in Burma grew through the incorporation of many local bandit groups, reaching an overall strength of 18,500 by January

Figure 8.1 **Nationalist Operations in Burma-Yunnan, 1951–53**

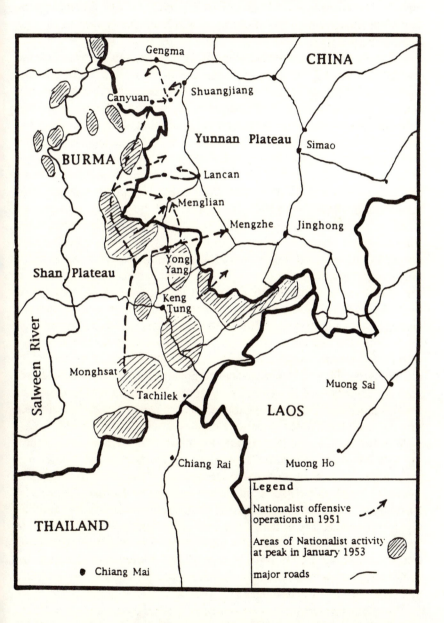

Source: Liu Kaizheng, Zhu Danggui, *Zhongguo zeng sanjia yichang zui mimi zhanzheng* (China's most secret war). Beijing: Hongqi chubanshe, 1994, pp. 25, 102.

1953. Equipment and supplies came from the CIA. From early 1952 to early 1953, twenty-one CAT aircraft landed every couple of weeks at the airfield at Monghsat, delivering many tons of communications equipment and medical supplies.[16]

For our purposes, the exact nature of the U.S.-Nationalist role in these operations is crucial. While the evidence is still unclear, it is probable that the U.S. and Chinese Nationalist intelligence agencies worked together to conduct the operation in north Burma with authorization by the highest levels in both governments—at least during the Korean War. Following that war's end, the relationship probably changed, with the Nationalists carrying on the operations without the support or approval of U.S. authorities.

The United States paid a high price for the operations, in terms of damage to U.S.-Burmese relations. The government of Burma repeatedly protested to the United States about the presence of the Nationalist forces on Burmese territory. Rangoon felt that the presence of these forces, aside from being a violation of Burma's sovereignty, was a gross burden on the people of the affected areas; made the government's efforts to achieve effective national unification more difficult; and tempted Chinese Communist military action, infiltration, or support for various secessionist minorities. Rangoon thus proposed to the United States, in August 1951, that the United States should persuade Taipei to issue orders to Nationalist forces to leave Burmese territory or accept internment by the government of Burma.[17] Rangoon repeated these demands with increasing urgency over the next several years. Concern about Nationalist forces was a major headache for the besieged government of Burma. In March 1953, after U.S. actions failed to satisfy Rangoon, Burma terminated the U.S. assistance program and appealed to the United Nations for help.[18]

Washington issued orders to its diplomats in Taipei, apparently complying with Rangoon's demands. The U.S. chargé d'affaires, Karl Rankin, met with the director of the East Asian Department, Wang Xiaoxi, in October 1951 to convey the requests of the government of Burma. (Taipei and Rangoon at that time had no diplomatic relations. Burma had established diplomatic relations with the PRC on 8 June 1950.[19]) Wang presented to Rankin a number of reasons why the ROC government could not issue orders to Li Mi's troops to leave Burma. Rankin conveyed these arguments to Washington, along with Wang's comment that "public discussion of this affair [would] not be in best interest of U.S."[20]

U.S. diplomats repeatedly told Burmese officials that there was no direct or indirect U.S. involvement with Nationalist forces in north Burma. These denials had little positive effect on Rangoon. Following the defeat of the Nationalist invasion of Yunnan in June 1951, the Burmese government delivered a strong protest to American Ambassador David M. Key. "Participation by Americans in these KMT operations" was well known to the government of Burma and constituted a "serious impediment" to U.S.-Burmese relations, Key reported to Washington. "Denial of official U.S. connections with these operations" was meaningless, Key said, "in face of reports they [are] constantly receiving from their officials in border areas that KMT troops are accompanied by Americans and receiving steady supply of American equipment, some of which [is] dropped from American planes, and of reports from their Bangkok Embassy of American support [of] activities going on in Siam, which is an open secret there." "Whatever the original justification may have been for these operations," Key continued, "it now seems obvious . . . that they have failed to achieve useful results commensurate with the harm they have done to our interests in Burma. For this reason I feel strongly that the time has come to call a halt to any further American participation in these operations."[21]

Secretary of State Dean Acheson ordered Key to keep lying on behalf of his country. On the basis of an "exhaustive investigation" of rumors of American connections with Li Mi's forces, Acheson told Key, the latter was to "categorically deny to GOB that there is or could be in [the] future any official or unofficial U.S. Government connection whatsoever with this force." The United States had "for months" exerted its influence to ensure that Li Mi's forces "confined their operations to Yunnan province."[22]

In spite of these repeated denials, there was substantial physical evidence of U.S. involvement. Burmese troops found equipment of American manufacture in the hands of Nationalist soldiers captured in northern Burma. Captured Nationalist officers told their Burmese interrogators that "America" was helping them. In the year prior to November 1951, there were at least two instances of Americans "in uniform" seen with Nationalist units in Burma. Several dead Caucasians were found among the Nationalist casualties recovered by Burmese forces. Personal materials on the corpses indicated they were Americans.[23] U.S. diplomats did their duty and denied that this evidence indicated American involvement.

The evidence strongly suggests U.S. participation in a covert operation to strengthen and organize the Nationalist forces in north Burma in conjunction with the ROC special services.[24] The disclaimers of U.S. diplomats were part of a calculated effort to camouflage the U.S. effort in north Burma and to contain the adverse political fallout of that effort. Most immediately, Rangoon might be dissuaded from resorting to the United Nations and condemning the ROC and the United States for "aggression" and "interference" in north Burma. Presumably, U.S. diplomats had no need to know about U.S. covert activities in north Burma. Yet a number of them knew enough to understand that they were being used as instruments of disinformation, an awareness that apparently caused them some discomfort. Ambassador David Key in Rangoon resigned in disgust over U.S. support for Li Mi's forces.[25] But while those required to lie for their country might protest, top-level U.S. leaders felt the benefits outweighed the costs. They were also presumably confident that various pro forma requests made by U.S. diplomats in Taipei or Bangkok, in line with Rangoon's demands, would not interfere with operations in north Burma. Those requests would be sidetracked by top-level Nationalist or Thai leaders who were au courant with and had given their assent to the covert operation.

The Purpose of Operation Paper

According to recent PRC accounts of the Burma imbroglio, the plan for the U.S.-ROC north Burma operation called for Nationalist forces to establish a durable base of operations inside Yunnan Province. This information is presumably based on Chinese interrogation of Nationalist prisoners at the time. It is also implied by confidential statements of American officials to Burmese, British, and other representatives. When confronted with complaints about the Nationalist presence in north Burma, U.S. diplomats often agreed and replied that those forces should be in Yunnan, not Burma.[26]

It must be kept in mind that during Operation Paper the United States was at war with China in Korea, though it was not a war formally declared by the U.S. Congress. Moreover, the war strained U.S. infantry capabilities. Although the United States began rebuilding its land forces after the North Korean invasion in June 1950, constraints were still tight in early 1951. The growing militarization of the Cold War in Europe also intensified demands for more U.S. troops there. This created strong incentives to utilize whatever means seemed promising to minimize Beijing's ability to concentrate forces in Korea. Thus a memorandum from the Joint Chief of Staffs to the Secretary of Defense in March 1952 called for covert operations in support of anti-Communist forces in the Far East, noting in this regard "the military potential inherent in the Chinese Nationalist forces along the northern frontier of Burma."[27] If several tens of thousands of Nationalist guerrillas could be established in Yunnan, they might tie down a substantial number of PLA forces. Forcing the PLA to undertake a protracted pacification effort in this remote region would also impose substantial costs on Beijing. Should the Sino-American conflict become general, anti-Communist armies and liberated areas in Yunnan might also provide a beachhead for operations—perhaps in conjunction with a Nationalist landing on the Guangdong coast.

The Termination of American Participation
in the North Burma Operation

The presence of Nationalist forces in north Burma quickly became a major factor in Burma's foreign relations, souring Burmese-U.S. relations and fostering Sino-Burmese cooperation. Beijing was sympathetic toward Rangoon's problems with Nationalist remnants, while Rangoon was increasingly angry with American duplicity. By 1953 Rangoon was pressing ahead with a formal complaint to the United Nations—something that U.S. diplomacy had prevented during 1951 and 1952. The United Nations passed a watered-down resolution condemning the presence of unspecified "foreign troops" in Burma and accepted a U.S. proposal to establish a quadripartite military committee (with representatives from Burma, the United States, Thailand, and the ROC) to investigate the situation. Washington was increasingly interested in wooing Burma, and felt that continued support for the Nationalist remnant forces would interfere with this. As importantly, the Nationalist forces had not been able to establish themselves permanently inside Yunnan.

Ten days after Eisenhower took office on 20 January 1953, a cable went out from Acting Secretary of State Dulles to the U.S. Embassy in Taipei saying that, after consultations with the Department of Defense, the State Department had become convinced that the U.S. government should make a vigorous attempt to eliminate the explosive situation resulting from the presence of Chinese Nationalist forces in Burma. The U.S. chargé d'affaires in Taipei, Karl Rankin, was to convey to Chiang Kai-shek the "strong view of the United States government" that the activities of Nationalist troops in Burma constituted a "serious threat to the security and a disruptive influence in Burma and throughout Southeast Asia." While the U.S. government understood and sympathized with the Chinese government's desire to support the Chinese people's resistance to Communist oppression, Dulles said, "it cannot condone activities [of Chinese] troops in Burma which are being carried out at [the] expense [of] security of [a] free nation and which in any event are not contributing tangibly to such resistance."[28]

Rankin's negotiations with Chiang Kai-shek and other top ROC officials over this issue began on 30 January 1953 and continued over a period of "several weeks."[29] U.S. diplomats had raised this issue with ROC officials several times before "during the previous year," according to Rankin, but "now we were insistent." Chiang and his advisers "were genuinely surprised" at the American request, Rankin recalled, and the ensuing negotiations were "among the least pleasant of my China experiences." From Chiang Kai-shek's perspective, what was at stake in the continuation of the north Burma operation was nothing less than the viability of "return to the Mainland." When Rankin conveyed to Chiang the U.S. decision to shut down the Burma operation, Chiang protested that a "retreat" of this type was contrary both to ROC policy and to that of the new U.S. administration. Washington should seize the initiative rather than retreating, Chiang said.[30] Dulles replied that, although the United States indeed sought to seize the initiative, it did not envision undermining the authority of friendly, non-Communist governments such as Burma. The U.S. government had concluded, Dulles said, that "these troops have not accomplished this objective but have succeeded only in seriously threatening stability [of] Burma. Thus whatever original merits of Chinese troops mission, [the] seriously deteriorating situation [in] Burma now calls for immediate remedial action." Chiang asked Rankin to put the U.S. request in writing.[31]

By late January 1953, U.S. officials were pressing for a clear, unequivocal ROC acceptance of the principle of complete withdrawal of all Nationalist forces from Burma to Taiwan, and for adoption of effective measures to achieve this to the best of Taipei's ability. They encountered strong resistance from Taipei. ROC officials raised a number of difficulties with the U.S. proposal. The United States wanted the ROC to make an explicit commitment to withdrawal, prior to determining whether such a withdrawal was feasible. It made more sense, Taipei argued, to first determine whether Rangoon and Bangkok were willing to cooperate in accomplishing such a withdrawal. The major problem, however, according to Nationalist officials, was that Taipei had very limited influence with the Nationalist forces in North Burma. If Taipei issued a flat, explicit order such as that demanded by the Americans, it simply would not be obeyed. Most of the soldiers in Burma were Yunnanese. North Burma was at least similar to their homes, while Taiwan was a distant and strange land. Moreover, many of them had already found employment in Burma, or acquired land and begun farming, or married local women and begun families. For these reasons, most of the troops would simply ignore orders to evacuate to Taiwan. Moreover, the nonexecution of orders from Taipei would entail a major loss of face for Chiang Kai-shek, or so Nationalist officials told their American counterparts.

One important reason for Chiang's reluctance to comply with the State Department's demand was, apparently, a suspicion that the State Department's views did not represent the "U.S. Government as a whole."[32] To eliminate such illusions, Rankin told Chiang Kai-shek, on 21 March 1953, that the "U.S. position is the result [of a] high-level inter-agency decision." When Chiang asked why the United States was unwilling to support Li Mi when it was supporting anti-Communist guerrillas elsewhere,

Rankin replied that Li Mi's activities were weakening the position of the government of Burma, which the United States believed should be saved from Communism. Rankin also indirectly raised the possibility that U.S. aid to Taiwan might be affected by ROC rejection of U.S. demands.[33]

Finally, on 27 March 1953, the ROC government authorized the U.S. government to inform the government of Burma of its readiness to cooperate in the withdrawal of Nationalist forces operating in Burma.[34] Taipei's statement included the caveat, however, that since it did not fully control the troops concerned, it "could not be held responsible for accomplishing more than [was] reasonable."[35] Taipei would stall for another eight months.

Washington and Taipei remained at loggerheads over this issue until mid-December 1953. In April Secretary Dulles directed Rankin to block ROC efforts to use CAT aircraft to "reinforce" Li Mi's forces. Rankin should seek assurances that no clearance would be given for any further flights from Taiwan to forces in Burma, Dulles said. "You may state that if such flights take place, we could only conclude that [the] Chinese Government has no intention of cooperating with [the] U.S. Government on this matter and that such flights could not but have most serious consequences for the maintenance of that mutual confidence so important between two governments."[36]

On 22 April the Political and Security Committee of the UN General Assembly voted 58 to 0 for a resolution asking Nationalist forces in Burma to leave that country. The quadripartite military commission soon began meeting in Bangkok to hammer out a withdrawal agreement. The recently appointed U.S. ambassador to Thailand, William J. Donovan, former OSS director, supervised the negotiations and played a key role in keeping the talks moving toward a resolution.[37] Taipei stalled the Bangkok commission's work, and Washington repeatedly exerted pressure to overcome this obstruction.[38] On 28 July, for example, Secretary Dulles directed Rankin to tell Chiang Kai-shek that it was imperative to end the "confusion" surrounding the ROC's participation in the Bangkok quadripartite commission. Rankin should tell Chiang that "continued dilatory and inconclusive Chinese Government action" would jeopardize the ROC's "United Nations position."[39] This was an implicit threat of weakened U.S. support for the ROC in the United Nations.

Taipei tried to placate Washington by offering to withdraw a few thousand men out of Li Mi's much larger force, and then disclaiming concern for any Chinese irregular forces remaining in Burma. The numbers were too small and the pledges regarding future support were too equivocal for Washington. Finally, on 28 September 1953, President Dwight Eisenhower intervened in the difficult U.S.-ROC negotiations with a "personal and confidential" letter to Chiang Kai-shek. Eisenhower told Chiang that he had personally been following the "international efforts" to resolve the question of the "Chinese irregular forces" in Burma and was confident that Chiang shared his concerns regarding this issue. "I am now writing to you personally regarding this matter because I feel that the time has come when concrete results must be produced if this problem is to be resolved at all," Eisenhower said. The American president recognized the limits on the influence of the ROC government on the situation in Burma, but felt that "this fact should not deter you from utilizing your influence to the maximum to bring about immediately the evacuation of as many of the irregular forces as possible and to make clear that those who remain will not have your sympathy or support." "Unless such concrete results can be achieved," Eisenhower said, "I fear that a situation will be created which the Communists will not fail to exploit . . . to the detriment of both your Government and the Burmese Government." "In the light of the close and cordial relationships which exist between our two Governments," Eisenhower concluded, "I am confident that I can count on your full cooperation in this matter."[40] When Eisenhower met the next day with Chiang's son, Lieutenant General Chiang Ching-kuo (then director of the Political Department of the ROC Ministry of Defense), who was on a visit to the United States, he again expressed his concern with the Burma problem and "strongly urged [the] Chinese Government [to] get troops out at earliest date."[41] Chiang Ching-kuo replied that his government was doing everything possible to accomplish this objective. Chiang Kai-shek replied on 8 October to Eisenhower's letter. Chiang's message restated the earlier Nationalist offer to withdraw a few thousand men from north Burma.[42]

As the evacuation got under way in October and November, problems and tensions proliferated. Taipei had pushed throughout 1953 for Burma to stop its air bombardment of Nationalist forces during the process of evacuation. Such attacks were a major obstacle to evacuation, Taipei argued, making difficult movement and concentration of troops for evacuation, and angering the besieged Nationalist troops, perhaps leading them to decide to refuse evacuation and stay to fight the Rangoon government which had ordered the bombing. Because of such objections, Washington urged Rangoon to suspend military operations against Nationalist forces. On 13 October, Ambassador William J. Sebald in Rangoon informed the State Department that the Burmese government had promised to take no military action over the next month.[43] Two weeks into the cease-fire, the commanders of the Nationalist forces in Burma cabled Taipei that Burmese planes were bombing Monghsat, and asked for U.S. intervention to secure the suspension of Burmese bombing. Rankin passed this message on to Washington and received the reply that the "alleged bombings had been declared a fabrication by the Burmese government." The "jungle generals," Acting Secretary of State Walter Bedell Smith said, were seeking a "pretext" to suspend evacuation after the first token withdrawal. As the "jungle generals evidently enjoyed excellent communications with Formosa," Smith told Rankin, the Chinese government should use this channel to "reiterate importance of prompt evacuation 2000 [men] to China's position before UN and world." The State Department was "confident this unwarranted gambit will not cause [the] Chinese Government [to] weaken its determination [to] continue, as will [the] U.S. government, [the] joint effort to achieve maximum evacuation."[44]

The first group of Nationalist irregulars assembled at Tachilek and crossed the border into Thailand on 8 November 1953 for evacuation by CAT airplanes to Taiwan. The initial contingent of evacuees were not able-bodied men, suggesting that Li Mi was culling his ranks for his less fit men. Nor did the evacuees bring many weapons or equipment with them. Many of the guns they did bring were antiques, not the modern types recently supplied from CIA arsenals on Saipan. Burmese leaders were livid with Chinese Nationalist duplicity. Assistant Secretary of State Walter Robertson strongly protested Taipei's half-hearted compliance with the evacuation agreement. On 24 November Robertson warned Taipei of the "serious consequences" its noncompliance would have for Taipei's position in the United Nations.[45]

American pressure finally prompted Chiang Kai-shek to act. On 5 December, Chiang sent a "strongly worded" telegram to the commander of the Chinese irregular forces in Burma, insisting that all soldiers who could should evacuate. On 19 December, the ROC foreign ministry delivered an aide-mémoire to the U.S. embassy in Taipei, saying that the Chinese government had persuaded the leaders of the guerrilla forces to evacuate another 2,000 men. It laid out a detailed timetable for the evacuation and stated that the evacuees would bring their arms with them to the evacuation point. The ROC note also asked Washington to secure a further extension of the Burmese cease-fire and conveyed a request by the "guerrillas" for $250,000 to settle their debts in Burma.[46] Washington agreed to provide the $250,000 and secured a Burmese extension of the cease-fire.

A second airlift began in February 1954 and continued until late March. Smaller groups were subsequently evacuated. By October 1954, a total of 5,742 had been evacuated to Taiwan.[47] In May 1954, Li Mi announced the liquidation of the Anti-Communist and National Salvation Army of Yunnan Province. On 28 September 1954, the quadripartite military committee submitted its final report to the U.N. General Assembly, and on 14 October

1954 the ROC representative told the U.N. General Assembly's Special Political Committee that it would "make no objections" if Burma did "whatever it sees fit" with former Nationalist forces remaining in Burma. It had done its utmost to get those troops to accept evacuation to Taiwan and had no control over those who had refused.[48]

A top-secret report by the U.S. Embassy in Taipei in April 1954 traced the shift in ROC policy in December 1953 to a major reevaluation at the highest level. According to the report, the ROC government had "at one time" adopted a plan providing for only token compliance with the U.N. resolution calling for evacuation of foreign forces. The bulk of Nationalist forces were to be left intact for "future operations against the Communist rear." This plan was abandoned in December 1953 in favor of a complete withdrawal. Chinese officials responsible for forcing this reversal reportedly had to overcome powerful elements "within the several branches" of the ROC government.[49]

Round Two

Following the evacuation of 1953–54, the Nationalist Chinese irregular forces remaining in north Burma continued to soldier on. Though their interests turned increasingly to the opium trade, they continued to conduct some operations in Yunnan. Agricultural collectivization in the PRC between 1955 and 1957 hurt the Chinese irregular forces by increasing the CCP's control over life in China's villages. This reduced the ability of the Nationalist irregulars to garner intelligence or new recruits from within Yunnan. Steady expansion of the PLA's communication and transportation infrastructure in the border regions also made operations inside Yunnan increasingly dangerous for the irregulars. Thousands of Nationalist soldiers surrendered to Yunnan authorities during this period. As irregular forces declined in military effectiveness, the Kunming Military Region was able to begin using smaller, squad-size patrols to deal with irregular penetrations of the border. In August 1958, as the crisis in the Taiwan Strait escalated, Taipei ordered its Burma forces, now under the command of Liu Yuanlin, to resume operations in Yunnan; 1,400 troops duly advanced into Yunnan.[50]

With the Lhasa uprising of March 1959, Mao Zedong became concerned with the growing disturbances in Yunnan. Responding to a report of the Central Military Commission (CMC) on these disorders, Mao ordered the CMC to adopt immediate and effective measures against Nationalist activities. The next day the CMC sent Vice Chief of Staff Yang Chengwu to Yunnan to investigate.[51]

In 1960, as China's economy collapsed and insurgency flared in Tibet, Taipei strengthened its Burma forces. In July, 400 Nationalist cadre and a large shipment of weapons were ferried by aircraft into Liu Yuanlin's base. By November 1960, Nationalist forces there numbered 9,400. Attempts to move into Yunnan were not very successful, however, because of PLA vigilance and preparations. The Nationalist forces were successful, however, in disrupting the work of the Sino-Burma Joint Boundary Commission, which was then attempting to demarcate the boundary. Determined not to let Nationalist activities thwart progress toward settlement of their disputed border, Beijing and Rangoon decided on joint military operations against Nationalist forces. Between 22 November 1960 and 9 February 1961, the PLA carried out two large-scale incursions into Burmese territory, with the permission of the Burmese government. Fighting was heavy. PLA casualties numbered 230, including 79 killed. Out of deference to Burma's nonaligned position, the Chinese incursion was not publicized. Simultaneously with the PLA incursions, the Burmese army launched offensive operations against the Nationalist forces. Following the February 1961 operations, some 5,000 Nationalist troops remained scattered along the border region of Burma, Thailand, and Laos.[52]

When John F. Kennedy took office in January 1961, his administration began looking for ways to reduce tensions with the PRC. One measure it decided upon was to, once again, pressure Chiang Kai-shek to withdraw the irregular Nationalist forces from Burma. Chiang agreed to withdraw all Nationalist soldiers who wished to go to Taiwan—a so-called "voluntary withdrawal." Some 4,000 troops were airlifted to Taiwan during 1961.[53]

As the PRC's Cultural Revolution gained steam during 1966, the irregulars in Burma once again ventured into Yunnan. During the first nine months of that year, they launched eight raids into Yunnan, resulting in four clashes with the PLA. Each clash cost Nationalist forces dearly. According to PLA sources, after these raids the irregular forces ceased armed incursions into Yunnan.[54]

The Calculus of Costs and Benefits for the United States

It seems fair to conclude that Operation Paper not only did not serve U.S. interests, but was, in fact, counterproductive. The constraints it imposed on PLA capabilities in Korea were minimal. The scope of the Chinese irregular force's challenge to the PLA in Yunnan never became substantial enough, the war in northeast Asia remained limited enough, and the human and material resources of the PLA were robust enough that the fighting in Yunnan never forced the PLA to divert from Korea resources that would otherwise have been sent to that theater. Even if one considers, as U.S. leaders of course did, the possibility of an expanded U.S.-PRC war arising out of the Korean conflict, the Chinese irregular forces were too weak to have been of much use. In this regard, it is instructive that the Eisenhower Administration pushed vigorously for Nationalist withdrawal of the irregulars throughout the first half of 1953, just as it was planning for a major escalation of the war should the Pyongyang talks continue to be barren. Eisenhower's letter to Chiang came only on 28 September 1953, two months after the Korean armistice. But throughout the previous nine months, State Department officials from Secretary Dulles down lobbied intensively to secure evacuation of the irregulars. American planners had concluded that the proper utilization of Nationalist forces in the contingency of an expanded U.S.-PRC war was in a theater where U.S. air-naval power could be more decisive, perhaps Hainan Island, not in the interior of Asia.

The one clear benefit to the United States from U.S. operations in north Burma seems to have been the intelligence garnered from them. As we shall see in chapter 10, U.S. intelligence agencies developed extensive and valuable assets in Yunnan through cooperation with Nationalist remnants in north Burma. It remains an open question, however, whether these strictly intelligence activities were facilitated by Operation Paper. It may well be that the effort to seize towns, establish liberated base areas, and so on led to greater PLA vigilance, which made conventional spying operations more difficult.

Against these rather modest and problematic gains must be balanced clear and substantial losses. First of all, Operation Paper had an adverse impact on U.S. policy interests toward Burma. The government of the Union of Burma that emerged from British India in 1948 was extremely weak and tenuous. Rebellions by various nationalist, Communist, and ethnic groups proliferated. Only disunity among the various rebel forces plus the leadership skills of U Nu enabled the government to build a new army and save the nascent Union.[55] The U.S.-supported Nationalist remnants were one important ingredient in the destabilization of the Union of Burma. As Ambassador Key and other U.S. diplomats opposed to Operation Paper at the time pointed out—and as NSC decision memoranda of the time indicated—the United States had an interest in stabilizing the Union of Burma government; in preventing fragmentation, Communist insurgency, or Chinese Communist infiltration, and in foiling PRC diplomatic offensives. Operation Paper worked counter to these objectives. It was, of course, primarily because of this that Operation Paper was scrapped by the U.S. government in 1953. Yet substantial damage had already been done. In terms of the policy interests of the United States, U.S.-ROC activities in

Burma were one factor underlying the cordial Burma-PRC relations that emerged in the 1950s—a development counter to the containment of PRC influence.

One must also include in the debit column of Operation Paper the ill will toward the United States among friendly governments caused by duplicity, deriving inevitably from that operation. Leaders and diplomats from Britain, Thailand, and Burma who sympathized with the objectives of U.S. policy were alienated by being lied to by U.S. diplomats. Some probably felt their intelligence was insulted when such transparent falsehoods were repeatedly peddled to them. If this fraying of American credibility were offset by substantial gains in other areas, that would be one matter. Without such compensation, the moral costs must weigh heavily.

The most egregious injury to U.S. interests associated with Operation Paper was unforeseen at the time: the emergence of the northern Burma-Thailand-Laos region as a major source of heroin for international markets. The area of north Burma into which the Nationalist remnants withdrew in 1950 happened to already be a major opium-producing region. During the 1860s, British authorities had encouraged the tribal chieftains of that region to produce opium for export to China. Opium quickly became the most important cash crop of the region. When Nationalist forces entered the area, they soon realized the economic potential of opium. They quickly took over administration of the opium business, imposing stiff opium taxes on the various tribal villages under their control; they pressed the villages to double and then quadruple production. The Nationalist remnant leaders developed export channels by establishing links with the ethnic Chinese criminal syndicates of Thailand. The involvement of the Nationalist remnants in the narcotics industry was gradual, paralleling their military setbacks at the hands of the PLA. During the early 1950s, the major focus of remnant force activities was apparently on preparing for military operations in Yunnan. As defeats by the PLA mounted, however, the Nationalist forces devoted themselves increasingly to the infinitely more lucrative and less dangerous narcotics industry. Operations of this industry also became increasingly internationalized, involving not only northeastern Burma, but northwestern Laos, northwestern Thailand, southwestern Yunnan, and even northwestern North Vietnam. Some of the Nationalist remnant probes into Yunnan may have been in conjunction with these business operations.[56]

As might be expected, the nature of the relationship between official circles in Taipei and Washington, on the one hand, and the narcotics industry run by Nationalist Chinese irregular forces, on the other hand, is extremely murky. A good starting point for analysis is recognition that there was not a clear dividing line between involvement in the narcotics industry and anti-Communist activities. As General Tuan Shiwen, then commander of Nationalist remnants on the Burma-Thai border, told a British journalist in 1966: "Necessity knows no law. That is why we deal with opium. We have to continue to fight the evil of communism, and to fight you must have an army, and any army must have guns, and to buy guns you must have money. In these mountains, the only money is opium."[57] There were elements of both self-justification and truth in this statement. While money and arms from Taipei and/or Washington could strengthen the anti-PLA capabilities of these forces, so too could money and arms deriving from the narcotics industry. From the standpoint of the tough-minded decision makers in Taipei and Washington, the imperative of fighting and defeating the Chinese Communist threat meant that one could not be supercilious about moral scruple. Dirty methods and moral compromise were required in war. If the anti-Communist side worked only with entirely pure people and forces, its coalition would not be very large. On the other hand, cooperation with the Nationalist remnant forces, even though they were involved in narcotics, could be a significant asset to the Free World in its intense struggle with international Communism—or so the reasoning of Taipei and Washington probably ran. No one foresaw that the spread of narcotics might one day become a major threat to U.S. society and national security.

Notes

1. *Zhongguo 9 ci da fabing* (Nine cases of China's dispatch of troops), Chengdu: Sichuan wenyi chubanshe, 1992, pp. 125–26.
2. Bertil Lintner, "The CIA's First Secret War," *Far Eastern Economic Review,* 16 September 1993, pp. 56–58.
3. *Zhongguo 9 ci da fabing,* pp. 125–26.
4. William Leary, *Perilous Missions: Civil Air Transport and CIA Covert Operations in Asia,* Tuscaloosa: University of Alabama Press, 1984, p. 129.
5. John H. Badgley, "The Communist Parties of Burma," in *The Communist Revolution in Asia,* Robert Scalapino, ed., Englewood Cliffs, NJ: Prentice Hall, 1969, pp. 309–28.
6. Leary, *Perilous Missions,* p. 129.
7. Ibid., pp. 129–30.
8. Chargé d'affaires in the Republic of China (Karl Rankin) to Department of State, 3 March 1953, in *FRUS,* 1952–54, vol. XII, East Asia and Pacific, part 2, pp. 671–72.
9. Leary, *Perilous Missions,* p. 130. Leary names the threatened city as Mengra. I found no such name on maps and concluded that this must be the same city as Menglian.
10. *Zhongguo 9 ci da fabing,* p. 128.
11. Ibid., pp. 129–32. Leary, *Perilous Missions,* p. 131.
12. *Zhongguo 9 ci da fabing,* p. 132.
13. Leary, *Perilous Missions,* p. 195.
14. Ibid.
15. *Zhongguo 9 ci da fabing,* p. 132.

16. Chargé d'affaires in the Republic of China (Karl Rankin) to Department of State, 3 March 1953, *FRUS,* 1952–54, vol. XII, part 2, pp. 61–62.

17. Ambassador in Burma to Secretary of State, 24 September 1951, in *FRUS,* 1951, vol. VI, part 1, pp. 296–97.

18. Leary, *Perilous Missions,* p. 195.

19. Liang Liangxing, ed. of English edition, *China's Foreign Relations, A Chronology of Events, 1949–1988,* Beijing: Foreign Languages Press, 1989, p. 207.

20. ROC Director East Asian Department, Ministry of Foreign Affairs, Wang Xiaoxi, to U.S. chargé d'affaires, 3 October 1951, in *FRUS,* 1951, vol. VI, part 1, p. 300.

21. Ambassador in Burma to Secretary of State, 15 August 1951, in *FRUS,* 1951, vol. VI, Asia and Pacific, part 1, pp. 288–89.

22. Secretary of State to U.S. Embassy in Burma, *FRUS,* 1951, vol. VI, part 1, pp. 289–90.

23. Chargé d'affaires in Burma (Henry B. Day) to Secretary of State, 28 November 1951, *FRUS 1951,* vol. VI, part 1, pp. 313–16. Also Bertil Lintner, "The CIA's First Secret War," *Far Eastern Economic Review,* 16 September 1994, p. 58.

24. In addition to sources cited above, see *FRUS,* 1951, vol. VI, part 1, pp. 287–88, 298. U.S. Ambassador to India (George V. Allen) to Department of State, 30 November 1953, in *FRUS,* 1952–54, vol. XII, part 2, pp. 178–79. The Ambassador in the Republic of China (Karl Rankin) to Department of State, 2 December 1953, in *FRUS,* 1952–54, vol. XII, part 2, pp. 179–80. Chargé d'affaires in Thailand to Secretary of State, 28 September 1951, in *FRUS,* 1951, vol. VI, Asia and Pacific, part 1, p. 298. Memorandum by the Special Assistant for Mutual Security Affairs, 28 November 1951, in *FRUS,* 1951, vol. VI, Asia and Pacific, part 1, pp. 316–17.

25. Lintner, "The CIA's First Secret War," p. 58.

26. See Deputy Assistant Secretary of State for East Asian Affairs Livingston T. Merchant to the Counselor of the British Embassy, August 1951, in *FRUS,* 1951, vol. VI, part 1, pp. 287–88. U.S. deputy representative to the United Nations to ROC U.N. representative Jiang Tingfu, October 1951, in *FRUS,* 1951, vol. VI, part 1, p. 301.

27. Memorandum of Joint Chiefs of Staff to Secretary of Defense, 4 March 1952, in *FRUS,* 1952–54, vol. XIV, China and Japan, part 1, pp. 15–19.

28. Acting Secretary of State to the Embassy in the Republic of China, 30 January 1953, in *FRUS,* 1952–54, vol. XII, part 2, p. 489.

29. Karl L. Rankin, *China Assignment,* Seattle: University of Washington Press, 1964, pp. 157–58. According to *FRUS,* the negotiations continued for eleven months.

30. Chargé d'affaires in the Republic of China (Karl Rankin) to U.S. Department of State, 22 February 1953, in *FRUS,* 1952–54, vol. XII, part 2, pp. 56–57.

31. *FRUS,* 1952–54, vol. XII, part 2, pp. 58–59, 82.

32. The phrase was used by Karl Rankin in a cable to the State Department on 16 March 1954, in *FRUS,* 1952–54, vol. XII, part 2, pp. 79–80.

33. *FRUS,* 1952–54, vol. XII, part 2, pp. 79–80. There are striking parallels between U.S. calculations at this juncture and Chinese Communist calculations during the 1950s and 1960s regarding whether or not to support various left-wing revolutionary movements. Support for such movements might drive governments thus targeted for revolution toward U.S. imperialism, Beijing realized, while nonsupport for revolution, or even active Chinese participation in preventing a revolutionary movement (e.g., Pakistan), might draw the country into the "united front" against U.S. imperialism. Perhaps all governments undertaking covert operations go through a similar matrix of calculations balancing projected gains to be derived from the accomplishments of the insurgent forces against projected loses deriving from the negative reaction of various governments affected by the revolutionaries.

34. Rankin, *China Assignment,* p. 158.

35. *FRUS,* 1952–54, vol. XII, part 2, pp. 85–86.

36. Secretary of State to Embassy in the Republic of China, 4 April 1953, in ibid., pp. 92–93.

37. Leary, *Perilous Missions,* p. 195.

38. See, for example, the 1 May and 1 July 1953 talks between Karl Rankin and Chiang Kai-shek, in *FRUS* 1952–54, vol. XIV, part 2, pp. 101–2, part 1, p. 224.

39. John Foster Dulles to Karl Rankin, 28 July 1953, in *FRUS,* 1952–54, vol. XII, part 2, pp. 121–22.

40. *FRUS,* 1952–54, vol. XII, pp. 2, p. 152–53.

41. Ibid., pp. 154–55.

42. Ibid., p. 158.

43. Ibid., p. 159. The U.S. request for this action was dated 3 October 1953 and is on pages 155–57 of the same volume.

44. Acting Secretary of State to Embassy in the Republic of China, 5 November 1953, in *FRUS,* 1952–54, vol. XII, part 2, pp. 170–71.

45. Secretary of State to Embassy in the Republic of China, 25 November 1953, in *FRUS,* 1952–54, vol. XII, part 2, p. 174.

46. *FRUS,* 1952–54, vol. XII, part 2, p. 190.

47. *Facts on File 1954,* New York: Facts on File Inc., 1954, p. 337. Leary puts the total at 5,583, in *Perilous Missions,* p. 196.

48. *Facts on File 1954,* p. 346.

49. Ambassador in Burma (William J. Seabald) to Director of the Office of Philippine and Southeast Asian Affairs (Philip W. Bonsal), 29 April 1954, in *FRUS,* 1952–54, vol. XII, part 2, pp. 220–21.

50. *Zhongguo, 9 ci da fabing,* p. 135.

51. Ibid.

52. Ibid., pp. 138, 141.

53. Roger Hilsman, *To Move a Nation,* New York: Delta Books, 1964, pp. 304–5. *Facts on File* put the number at 5,000. *Facts on File 1961,* p. 122.

54. *Zhongguo, 9 ci da fabing,* p. 141.

55. Joseph Silverstain, *Burma, Military Rule and the Politics of Stagnation,* Ithaca: Cornell University Press, 1977, pp. 26–27.

56. Fenton Bresler, *The Chinese Mafia,* New York: Stein and Day, 1989, pp. 66–69.

57. Quoted in Bresler, *The Chinese Mafia,* pp. 68–69.

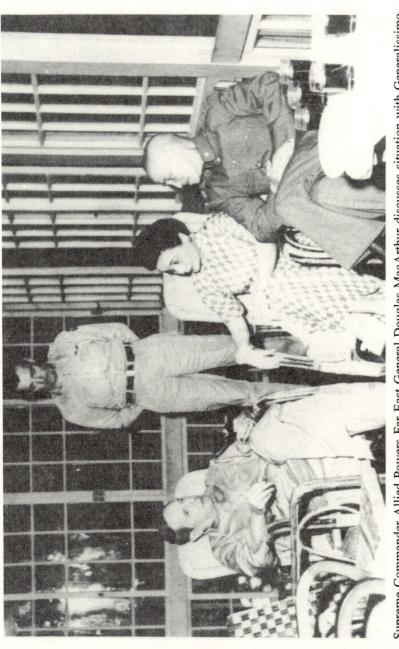

Supreme Commander Allied Powers Far East General Douglas MacArthur discusses situation with Generalissimo and Madame Chiang Kai-shek, 31 July 1950. Courtesy *Zhongyang ribao*, Taipei.

U.S. 7th Fleet commander and wife visit Taiwan, 1952. From right: General Chou Jih-jou, Howard Jones, Assistant to U.S. Ambassador, Admiral Joseph J. Clark, Wu Kuo-chen, Wang Chi-ming. Courtesy KMT Committee on Party History, Taipei.

Roman Catholic priest with Polish crew of *Praca* at press conference at Taibei, 18 March 1954. Courtesy KMT Committee on Party History, Taipei.

Escort Carrier U.S.S. Strait of Baodeng in Keelung Harbor, 25 June 1955. Courtesy KMT Committee on Party History, Taipei.

Minister of Defense Yu Ta-wei presenting calligraphy scroll to MAAG commander Major General William C. Chase upon his rotation from Taiwan. Chief of Staff Chou Chi-jou on right. Courtesy KMT Committee on Party History, Taipei.

U.S. Secretary of Defense Neil H. McElroy (left) and ROC Minister of Defense Yu Ta-wei (center), at Taipei's Songshan airport, 30 September 1959. Chief of Staff Peng Meng-chi on right. Behind with dark glasses, U.S. Ambassador Everett Drumright. Courtesy KMT Committee on Party History, Taipei.

South Vietnamese President Ngo Dieh Diem meets with ROC Vice President Chen Cheng, Taibei, 16 January 1960. Courtesy KMT Committee on Party History, Taipei.

Ngo Dieh Diem being briefed on the Shi Men Reservoir project, Taiwan, 16 January 1960. Courtesy KMT Committee on Party History, Taipei.

President Dwight D. Eisenhower makes the only visit to Taiwan by an incumbent U.S. President, September 1960. Generalissimo and Madame Chiang to Eisenhower's left. Courtesy KMT Committee on Party History, Taipei.

Press conference during U.S. Secretary of State Dean Rusk's visit to Taipei, 16 April 1964. ROC Foreign Minister Shen Chang-huan and U.S. Ambassador Jerauld Wright to Rusk's left. Courtesy *Zhongyang ribao*, Taipei.

Private citizen Richard M. Nixon arriving in Taipei, November 1964, to deliver a lecture to the 10th meeting of the Asian People's Anti-Communist League. Courtesy KMT Committee on Party History, Taipei.

U.S. Secretary of Defense Robert McNamara and ROC Minister of Defense Chiang Ching-kuo at the Pentagon, 23 September 1965 for discussions of strategy in Vietnam. Courtesy *Zhongyang ribao*, Taipei.

Chiang Ching-kuo visits Chinese Agricultural Technical Mission in South Vietnam circa 1967. Courtesy JCRR, Taipei.

9

The Tibetan Operation: Joint Support for the Tibetan Resistance

The Tibetan Insurgency

The most extensive U.S.-Nationalist covert operation against the PRC was very probably in Tibet. There the secret services of the two countries helped sustain an eighteen-year-long Tibetan struggle against CCP rule. From the standpoint of utility to U.S. strategic interests, the Tibetan operation is more ambiguous than the Burma operation (clearly a debit) or the joint intelligence operations discussed in chapter 10 (overall, on the credit side of the ledger). The scope of the Tibetan rebellion became quite substantial. Indeed, it developed into a full-blown rebellion and became a major difficulty for the CCP regime. CCP repression of that rebellion helped undermine PRC moral standing among the developing countries and especially within the Indian-led nonaligned movement. It may also be that U.S.-Nationalist support for the Tibetan resistance helped undermine the warm Indian-Chinese relations of the 1950s. Documentation is not currently available to allow us to determine whether or not this was a U.S. objective, but if it was, a strong argument can be made that it was achieved. On the other hand, there are troubling moral questions which cannot be avoided and which call into question the American contribution to the modern tragedy of the Tibetan people.

Before detailing U.S. and Nationalist involvement with the Tibetan insurgency, I should note that that involvement was probably peripheral to the course of the insurgency itself. The roots of Tibetan resistance to Chinese rule in the 1950s and 1960s were deep, and it should not be thought that United States and Taiwanese involvement was the major cause of the Tibetan rebellion. Tibetan resentment against China's attempt to impose its rule over Tibet is rooted in a century of interaction, during which modern Chinese nationalists reconceived the concept of the Chinese nation and worked to transform China's medieval protectorate of Tibet into an integral part of the modern Chinese state. Tibetan resentment against Communist Chinese rule was also rooted in the efforts of an alien revolutionary elite to modernize a truly medieval society that had survived into the middle of the twentieth century. It is not necessary to go into the origins of the Tibetan rebellion here.[1] For our purposes, it is adequate to recognize that virtually all national independence movements have foreign support. This was the case with the Tibetan insurgency.

The first ethnically Tibetan region occupied by the PLA in 1949 was Xikang (now the western part of Sichuan Province). Xikang had been a part of Tibet until the 1750s, and its population remained overwhelmingly Tibetan into the 1950s. It is an extremely rugged region inhabited by Tibetan nomadic tribes, the Khambas, renowned for their banditry, martial skills, fearlessness, arrogance, and cruelty. When the PLA entered Xikang, they found local Khamban leaders plotting a revolt, together with various Amdoan (Qinghai) leaders, against the Lhasa government. CCP representatives urged that the projected revolt proceed, but in association with the CCP and the PLA. Deeply suspicious of Chinese aims, the Khamban leaders—two brothers, Rapga and Topygay Pangdatshang—stalled for time; retreated into the mountainous regions beyond the PLA's reach; and then dispatched an emissary to India to solicit foreign support for armed resistance to the Chinese military occupation of Kham, Amdo, and Tibet proper. The emissary was a Scottish missionary named George Patterson, who had lived for many years in Kham and spoke the Kham dialect of Tibetan. Patterson later wrote an account of the early stages of the Tibetan insurgency.[2] Patterson proceeded to India, where he met with British, Indian, and U.S. officials to convey the Khamban request for support. According to Patterson, these appeals came to naught.[3] He continued to act, he says, as an intermediary between Khamban leaders and Western intelligence services. His subsequent accounts provide one of the few detailed descriptions of those interactions. While there is to date no independent verification of Patterson's account, the substantial evidence of links between Khamban rebels and the CIA suggest that there must have been links through someone such as Patterson with good language skills and area expertise. Patterson's account has a strong ring of plausibility and fits very well with an array of known facts.

Initial contacts between Taiwan's covert services and Tibetan leaders were apparently made by the Dalai Lama's second brother, Gyalo Thondup, who had been educated in pre-1949 China and was married to the daughter of a top KMT official. Thondup fled Lhasa in 1950 and traveled to Taiwan before returning to India and settling in Kalimpong.[4] According to another source with good contacts in the Tibetan refugee community, Thondup reached an intelligence-gathering arrangement with the CIA in 1951, an agreement that was later upgraded to include covert support for guerrilla activities within Tibet.[5] Another of the Dalai Lama's brothers, Thubten Norbu, conducted discussions with U.S. officials in Calcutta in June 1951. Although an agreement between the Dalai Lama and China's new government providing for the "peaceful liberation of Tibet" by the Chinese PLA had just been concluded, the Dalai Lama was still in Yadong, just across the border from India, contemplating whether to return to Lhasa or to flee abroad. According to Patterson, Thubten Norbu reached a tentative agreement with his American friends in Calcutta according to which the Dalai Lama was to repudiate the recent agreement with Beijing, go into exile, and appeal to the United Nations for help. The United States would then provide finance for "whatever was required in Tibet's fight for freedom."[6]

During 1952, there was increased fighting between the PLA and Tibetans in Kham and Amdo. Some 14,000 Nationalist soldiers formerly under the command of the Muslim warlords Ma Bufang and Ma Honggui were scattered around Amdo and apparently continued their resistance to the Communists. According to Patterson, these forces were supplied with arms by "KMT planes" operating from Taiwan.[7] As noted in chapter 6, CAT was conducting "black flights" into "western China" by 1952. According to Patterson, early in 1953 the son of another top Amdoan leader arrived in Kalimpong seeking foreign assistance for revolt against Communist authorities. Patterson, who was then living in Kalimpong and acting as an intermediary and an interpreter between Khamban leaders and the Western powers, arranged passage for this man to the United States so he could present his case to top U.S. officials, only to have the U.S. government intervene and tell him he should go instead to Taiwan, and that the United States would use its influence to secure him a visa for that purpose.[8]

The Tibetan rebellion entered a new phase in 1954, with the first widespread uprisings against Chinese Communist authority in the Kanding region of Xikang. Xikang, like Qinghai, was not part of "Tibet" proper. This meant that, although populated largely by ethnic Tibetans, those provinces were not covered by the pledge of autonomy included in the agreement of May 1951 between the Dalai Lama and Beijing. (That agreement had recognized Chinese authority over Tibet and accepted occupation of Tibet by the PLA.) Antireligious agitation, "struggle" against the old local elite and imposition of a Leninist apparatus thus began in Xikang and Qinghai as soon as they came under effective PLA occupation. The result was broad discontent, which flared into open revolt in 1954. It spread quickly, and by the end of 1955 there was widespread guerrilla resistance to China throughout Kham and Amdo. In the same year, Xikang was incorporated into Sichuan Province.

According to an authoritative PRC history of Tibet, influential members of the Tibetan regional government had used the Dalai Lama's passage through western Sichuan and Xikang in 1954, when he was on the way back to Lhasa after attending a meeting of the Nationalist People's Congress in Beijing, to establish a network of secessionists. The Tibetan government was Tibet's traditional Lamist government, which was headed by the Dalai Lama and which had signed the May 1951 agreement with Beijing. According to the PRC history, officials of the Tibetan government were covertly plotting resistance and rebellion from 1956 on, while feigning loyalty to Beijing. The recent transfer of the ethnically Tibetan area of Xikang to Sichuan Province in 1955 had accelerated "democratic reforms" in that region, and members of the Dalai Lama's entourage used this to mobilize anti-Beijing sentiment among the local elite. A secret communications network was established to maintain contact with anti-Chinese groups in the coming armed struggle. Other Tibetan officials took a more northerly route back to Lhasa, performing the same duties along the way. Once back in Lhasa, the secessionists in the Tibetan government sent lamas to Qinghai and to the Tibetan regions of Gansu, to establish communication with anti-China groups there.[9]

In March 1955, the Khamban leader Rapga Pangdatshang arrived in Kalimpong, seeking broad foreign support for a large-scale Tibetan war against China. Following the collapse of his 1950 bid for foreign support, Rapga Pangdatshang had served as a major figure in the local Xikang government under CCP authority. Clandestinely, however, he had worked with other Khamban and Amdoan leaders to build an anti-Chinese network and to restrain local anti-Chinese rebellions until the ground could be laid for a unified rising against Chinese authority. By 1955, this network counted 100,000 armed men prepared for revolt, or so Pangdatshang claimed. Chinese authorities had consented to Pangdatshang's 1955 visit to India as a quid pro quo for his agreeing to serve on the Political Consultative Committee, which was being set up by Beijing.[10]

In Kalimpong, Pangdatshang met with an American "representative," with Patterson reportedly serving as interpreter. When presented with the Tibetan request for support, the U.S. representative responded by laying out a comprehensive and well-thought-out ten-year plan for revolution against China. The political objective of the revolution was to be the overthrowing of the feudal-collaborationist government of Tibet and the establishment of a new, progressive government. The movement's program was not to be simple anti-Communism or anti-Chinese sentiment; instead, it was to be pro–land reform, and it called for an end to forced labor and deportations from Tibet, along with an end to the coerced sale of products. In addition, the Tibetan people were to be involved in the administration of the new, revolutionary government. The initial focus of the movement was to be on political organization with a Tibet-wide organization being the objective. The American representative stressed that his proposal was a "tentative outline" which, should Pangdatshang agree to the plan, would have to be submitted to the appropriate officials. The American also said that he would recommend the appointment of a special agent who would have no contact with the U.S. embassy in India, but who would be officially appointed to handle Tibetan affairs. This special agent would channel U.S. financial assistance and would advise on political and economic questions that might arise. He would also help out with problems of printing and radio broadcast of propaganda.

The American representative also urged Pangdatshang to secure Indian support. (Tibetan sentiment was generally hostile to India at that time, due to a feeling that India had betrayed Tibet by recognizing, in 1954, that Tibet was an autonomous region of China.) Not only could India provide territorial sanctuary, the American representative pointed out, but eventual Indian diplomatic support would be essential in securing UN recognition of Tibet. In the event that the new Tibetan government appealed to the United Nations for recognition, support from the West would be automatic, but success would require broader support. In this regard, India's influence with the Afro-Asian and Middle Eastern countries could be decisive. Pangdatshang promised to consider these arguments.[11] This discussion of UN recognition of an independent Tibetan state foreshadowed later U.S.-ROC disagreements over the political orientation of the Tibetan insurgency. It is obvious that the March 1955 plan, integrating as it did economic, political, organizational, and military aspects, involved considerable staff work. The diverse evidence of U.S. involvement with the Tibetan insurgents at about this time suggests that Patterson's account of this episode is truthful. The U.S. representative was probably from the CIA.

Tibet blossomed into full-blown insurgency in 1956. According to the

PRC history of Tibet, armed rebellion began in July 1956, with an attack on the Sichuan-Tibet road in the vicinity of Amdo. By the end of August, twenty-one sections of that road had been destroyed. Attacks on PLA units also began in August, with a motor detachment being ambushed. Thereafter there were continuous attacks along these roads. The rebel objective was to cut transportation and communication in and out of the Ningjing area.[12]

U.S.-Nationalist support apparently began as soon as the Tibetan insurgency erupted. By 1956, it seemed to Taipei that one of the contingencies outlined by Dulles in early 1955 had in fact been realized and that the time to strike had arrived. Armed resistance to Beijing's rule began among the Khamba people of eastern Tibet in 1955 and expanded rapidly over the next year. In the fall of 1955, the Khamba rebels approached the Nationalists for assistance, and early in 1956, Taiwan began supporting the Tibetan rebellion.[13]

U.S. and Nationalist clandestine services cooperated to support the insurgency. Out-of-country military training was provided for Tibetan fighters. Initially, such training was organized out of Kalimpong by Gyalo Thondup. When the training program began, recruits were sent individually and on foot out of Kalimpong, then picked up by vehicle some distance outside the city, and driven to Silurgi in West Bengal. There they were given compasses and told to walk south toward East Pakistan, a few hours walk away. At the Pakistani border they were met by a Chinese-speaking American, two Pakistani officers, and a Tibetan interpreter. They were given Punjabi pajamas and turbans, and told to walk to Dacca. There they were put on an airplane for a five-hour flight to Taiwan.[14] An alternate route for trainees was a nighttime truck ride from Silurgi to Calcutta, where they were smuggled aboard specially chartered aircraft and flown to Taiwan.[15]

Once in Taiwan, Tibetan rebels were put through a four-month training program of map reading, radio operation, parachuting, and use of various types of weapons and explosives. After completing training, the Tibetans were broken into three groups. Most were sent back to Calcutta and then overland to Kham, where they became leaders of guerrilla groups. A second group remained in Taiwan for further training and insertion by parachute. Another, smaller group was flown to the United States for additional training.[16] According to one source, the first batch of trainees parachuted back into Tibet in autumn 1957, carrying with them bazookas, mortars, machine guns, antitank rockets, and hand grenades.[17] Some of the Tibetans, who were selected to stay in Taiwan for a longer period, received training in Chinese language and in the political theories of Sun Yat-sen.[18]

So as to better plan the air drops into Tibet, the CIA dug up World War II files of Kham. Aerial photographs of this region were abundant, as it had been the "hump" over which supplies were ferried from Assam to Nationalist China from 1942 to 1945. A number of U.S. aircraft had gone down in this area during World War II, and topographic data had been collected to facilitate search-and-rescue operations. Khampas in Taiwan helped the CIA to identify specific rivers, mountains, and villages on the aerial photos, and to select sites for airdrops. CIA air drops of arms to insurgent forces began in late 1958. The first load included a hundred British-made rifles, twenty submachine guns, and two 55-millimeter mortars, along with 300 rounds of ammunition for each weapon and sixty hand grenades.[19] Several C-130s were especially modified to operate at high altitudes. The air supply operations apparently functioned out of forward bases in Thailand. Drop zones were marked, either with flares or with large cloth panels, by Khampas especially trained for such tasks.

There is very little hard information about the respective roles of U.S. and Taiwanese intelligence services in these operations. It seems safe to assume, however, that the two sides worked closely. Many of the aircraft involved in Tibetan operations were CAT planes based on Taiwan. The Nationalists helped train and inspire the Tibetan rebels. These activities imply the full knowledge and support of the top Nationalist leadership, and close coordination with the Americans.

The Khampan rebels organized themselves into the National Volunteer Defense Army (NVDA), which Michel Peissel estimated had to have 80,000 "well organized guerrillas" under arms by 1957.[20] The Tibetan guerrillas did not operate under central control, but consisted of approximately thirty-nine rebel bands organized largely along tribal lines. Most of the rebel fighters were Khampan and Amdoan tribesmen, skilled horsemen and marksmen used to a rugged life. These guerrillas had three great advantages over the PLA: first, being completely acclimated, they were capable of strenuous activity at elevations as high as 20,000 feet. Second, they were able to move speedily across roadless country either on foot or on horseback.[21] Third, they had a good knowledge of the rugged terrain. PLA troops massed for river crossings were machine gunned from adjacent heights. Convoys were subjected to mine and machine gun attacks. Isolated units of the PLA were subjected to swift assaults and were sometimes overrun.[22]

The PLA faced several disadvantages in dealing with the insurgency. One was its dependence on long, vulnerable logistic lines. Although the PLA could and did levy or purchase food from the local economy, this had the effect of creating inflation, shortages for the local population, and resentment. Most foods and almost all other supplies had, therefore, to come by truck over the roads across Qinghai or western Sichuan. These roads passed through extremely rugged territory and were quite vulnerable to sabotage and ambush. PLA supply convoys became favorite targets for

Tibetan guerrillas. The second disadvantage faced by the PLA was hostility from the local populace. As a result of this hostility, the Tibetan rebel bands often enjoyed very good intelligence about PLA positions and activities.[23]

By mid-1958, insurgent leaders began developing a base area in the Loka region in southeastern Tibet, the heavily wooded region south of the Brahmaputra and east of Lhasa. Pack trains were bringing supplies into Loka over the many high passes of Bhutan and India's North Eastern Frontier Agency (NEFA).[24] The insurgency expanded rapidly. By May 1958, according to the PRC account, the army of the Tibetan government began to "openly participate" in the rebellion, sending teams to the Loka region to train rebel soldiers. By October, the Tibetan army as a whole (then numbering perhaps 3,000) had joined the rebellion. Also in October, 700 rebels besieged a PLA unit at Zedong (the main city in the Loka area, which was only thirty miles southeast of Lhasa) for seventy-four days, eventually forcing the PLA to withdraw, along with all Chinese cadre. In January 1959, 3,000 rebels kept another large town, Dingqing, under siege for three months. That assault, however, was eventually repulsed.[25]

According to evidence collected by the International Commission of Jurists, Chinese counterinsurgency methods were brutal. Torture and the forced separation of children from their parents were frequently used in an attempt to cow the populace. Many people were sent to prison camps outside Tibet. The extremism of the Great Leap Forward also sharpened the antireligious aspects of Chinese policy in Tibet. Heavy fighting in Kham and Loka, and mounting Chinese repression in response to the insurgency, led to a flight of refugees to Lhasa. By the end of 1958, perhaps 15,000 families lived in tents around Lhasa's main market.[26]

Chinese repression did not diminish the effectiveness of the Tibetan resistance forces, at least not in the short term. Men who had seen their families killed and property destroyed by the Communists, and who desired nothing more than revenge against the Chinese Communists, swelled insurgent ranks. The fighting was brutal. Neither side took prisoners. Tibetans too seriously wounded for flight were killed by their comrades rather than being left for the PLA to torture for information. The Tibetans also adopted a scorched-earth policy, burning crops and killing herds in hopes that the Chinese would be driven out of Tibet by lack of food. This, of course, increased the hardships of the people. Casualties were high on both sides. According to Patterson, between 1956 and mid-1958, Chinese casualties numbered 40,000, while the insurgents lost 15,000.[27] In spite of casualties and repression, the scope of insurgent activity expanded steadily.[28]

The Lhasa Uprising

In March 1959 there was a large-scale uprising in Lhasa. This uprising was underlain by the deep cleavages between Chinese and Tibetans, exacerbated by the transformation of the relation between China and Tibet in the 1950s, and fueled by the dislocation and resentment caused by the cycle of rebellion and repression that began in 1951. It was sparked by a seemingly trivial incident—the insistence of the Chinese command in Lhasa that the Dalai Lama attend, without his usual bodyguard, a cultural performance to be held at a PLA camp. On 10 March a hastily assembled Tibetan People's Congress formally declared independence and began raising an army of national defense. Within about a week, an army of 7,000 had been formed. Orders also went out to insurgent units in outlying regions to destroy all roads, bridges, and telecommunications lines to hinder Chinese countermobilization activities. There were continuous attacks on traffic moving into Tibet over the Qinghai road. On 16 March the Lhasa rebels sent a radio message to Kalimpong, via the Indian consul in Lhasa, announcing the 10 March declaration of independence and asking that it be communicated to India, the United Nations, the World Buddhist Association, and other international bodies.[29]

The PLA responded to the uprising in Lhasa with a general assault on the Norbulinka, the Dalai Lama's palace. A sweep of the entire city then followed. By the morning of 22 March, Lhasa was once again under Chinese control. Fighting, destruction, and casualties were heavy.

The CIA-Nationalist role, if any, in the Lhasa uprising is still unclear. Beijing placed the blame on Washington and Taipei, saying they were operating through Tibetan agents based in Kalimpong. This may be, but solid evidence is lacking. It seems more likely that the uprising was genuinely spontaneous. Once the popular movement began, however, Tibetan resistance forces in contact with the CIA and the Nationalists certainly joined in the movement, giving it form and direction.

If the CIA was not involved in instigating the Lhasa uprising, however, it played a central role in rescuing the Dalai Lama from the Chinese repression that followed. As the PLA surrounded the Norbulinka, the Dalai Lama and his advisers decided that he should flee Lhasa for India. Once the decision to flee had been made, the CIA provided extensive assistance in its execution. U.S.-trained Khampas joined the Dalai Lama's entourage and maintained radio contact with the CIA station in Dacca. The CIA planned the escape route using its now-excellent maps of southern Tibet. CIA aircraft also air-dropped food and fodder, guns and ammunition, for the Dalai

Lama's entourage. Once again, documentation is lacking regarding the rationale for CIA assistance to the Dalai Lama's flight from Tibet. Presumably, U.S. strategists planned to use the Dalai Lama as a rallying point for the Tibetan resistance to Chinese rule. The Dalai Lama's abandonment of collaboration with Chinese authority would substantially delegitimize that authority in the eyes of many Tibetans. If the Dalai Lama cast his lot with the resistance, new support for the armed struggle would be mobilized, while the forces of ethnic and regional factionalism that were sapping effectiveness of the National Volunteer Defense Army (NVDA, as the rebel forces were formally called) could be better contained. Both the Dalai Lama's new ability to travel overseas without restriction by Beijing and his personal prominence would also raise the Tibetan issue in international forums in a way that had not previously been possible. In short, the safe flight of the Dalai Lama was probably seen as making an important contribution to the anti-CCP struggle in Tibet.

Chiang Kai-shek wanted to go much further than Washington in responding to the Lhasa uprising. Chiang urged the United States to undertake *large-scale* airdrops of supplies to the Tibetan insurgent forces. In Taipei, Chiang summoned U.S. Ambassador Everett Drumright to his villa on Grass Mountain and placed such a proposal before him. According to James Shen, who was present at the meeting as interpreter and who would later become ROC ambassador to the United States, the U.S. side "stalled, pleading logistic difficulties." After discussions went nowhere, Chiang abruptly rose and left the room. During ten years of translating for Chiang Kai-shek in his dealings with five U.S. ambassadors, this was the one occasion when Shen saw Chiang lose patience with a U.S. representative.[30] Chiang Kai-shek also broadcast a message to Tibet, urging people there to intensify their struggle against the Communists and telling them that his government was "making every possible effort to give you continuous and effective aid."[31]

Following the Lhasa uprising and the Dalai Lama's flight to India, the United States undertook new operations deep inside Tibet. In May 1959 a top-level conference convened in Washington to consider establishment of a Tibetan guerrilla base deep inside Tibet in the mountains near Lake Koko Nor (Qinghai Lake). This would place the guerrillas in a position to keep the northern Chinese supply road into Tibet, running southwest of Lanzhou over the Qinghai plateau, under surveillance and to sabotage it. This route into Tibet, the most convenient route for the PLA, was immune to disruption, at least in its northern stretches. Guerrillas operating out of the Koko Nor region, however, could destroy bridges, cause landslides, and otherwise close the road. U.S. planners estimated that the PLA had to send out twenty-two truckloads of fuel and supplies in order to deliver successfully one truckload of supplies to troops near the border with India. Disruption of the PLA's vital but tenuous road network would increase these costs further, confronting Beijing with the choice of withdrawing its forces from Tibet or spending huge sums of money to keep them there. The more southerly roads into Tibet via western Sichuan were already subject to guerrilla interdiction. Establishment of a base near Koko Nor would bring the Qinghai route under attack. The plan received White House approval and went into operation.[32]

Advanced training was necessary for such a deep penetration operation. Khamba tribesmen and other Tibetans were recruited and sent secretly to Camp Hale in the high country of Colorado for training. The first group of trainees arrived at Camp Hale in August 1959. After the training was completed, C-130 aircraft especially modified to carry extra fuel inserted guerrilla teams to the Koko Nor area. Further flights brought reinforcements and supplies. The program was just getting into full swing when President Eisenhower ordered the suspension of all overflights of Communist countries following the downing of Francis Gary Powers in his U-2 in May 1960. The CIA and the Pentagon petitioned for a waiver of Eisenhower's order for the Koko Nor program, but their effort failed.[33]

The Koko Nor program was supported by Nationalist China. The U-2 aircraft whose aerial photography scouted and mapped the Koko Nor terrain for the guerrillas were initially piloted by Americans rather than Nationalists. After Eisenhower ordered the suspension of such flights by U.S. pilots, however, two U-2s were sold to the Nationalists (in July 1960) and Nationalist pilots soon took over surveillance flights into western China. The C-130 aircraft used for the Koko Nor program were CAT-operated.

The PLA's Counterinsurgency War

Following the Lhasa revolt the PLA launched an "all-out war" against the Tibetan rebellion.[34] After crushing opposition in Lhasa, in April 1959 the PLA launched a large, two-pronged offensive to retake Loka. The PLA fought forty-seven engagements within two weeks and inflicted 2,000 casualties on the Tibetan rebels.[35] By August 1959, the PLA was in control of the Bhutan border. Once the border was sealed, the PLA began an extensive counterinsurgency campaign to pacify the interior of the Loka region; 100,000 troops were devoted to this campaign. Many miles of new road were built with forced labor brought from China. The PLA also utilized political tactics to "disintegrate the rebels from within." By mid-1960, the main forces of the rebels had been destroyed, and by the end of 1961, Loka was "basically pacified."[36]

The establishment of effective Chinese control over the Bhutan border, along with increasing Indian vigilance against Tibetan movement over the NEFA border, led to a decision in late 1959 to shift the Tibetan resistance's main base into central Loka. U.S. and Taiwanese aircraft soon began dropping supplies to the insurgent forces in the new base area. China protested to India about 300 violations of Tibetan airspace between 1960 and 1962.

India was increasingly drawn into the Tibetan imbroglio after the Lhasa uprising. Chinese repression produced increasing immigration to India. Welcomed by the Indian government and provided with basic subsistence by India on humanitarian grounds, these refugees tended to settle in camps in northern India and Nepal near the Tibetan frontier. These camps soon became bases for recruitment for insurgent forces operating inside Tibet. The Tibetan insurrection also increased the importance of the PLA's westerly lines of communication, running from Xinjiang to central Tibet across the Aksai Chin plateau. The plateau, which China controlled but India demanded, was the crux of the Sino-Indian territorial dispute. The Xinjiang-Lhasa road over that plateau was also a key target of attack by Tibetan resistance forces.

Early in 1961, the Tibetan resistance decided to shift the focus of its operations from Loka westward to the Tsang region of Tibet north of Nepal. The Tibetan border in this region was still largely unguarded by the PLA, unlike the borders with Bhutan and India's NEFA. It was also within easy striking distance of the strategic Xinjiang-Lhasa road. The PLA was slow to react to the shift to Tsang, and in 1961 the insurgency apparently reached a new peak, at least in terms of the scope of fighting. NVDA forces were very active in the Tsang region, frequently cutting the Xinjiang-Lhasa road. New recruits flowed into Tsang from Kham and from training camps in Taiwan and the United States. The famine conditions then general in China in the aftermath of the Great Leap Forward were also common in Tibet, and this helped produce a steady stream of new recruits for the rebel cause. Operations continued in Loka as well, though at a much reduced level. Fighting also flared again in Amdo and Kham.[37]

Again the superior weight of the PLA began to tell. Insurgent forces were gradually worn down. Toward the end of 1961, the Tibetan resistance, with the advice of the CIA, decided to shift its main base of operations still further west to the Mustang region of Nepal.[38] This was an extremely isolated region, located on the north side of the Himalaya Mountains, with an average elevation of 12,000 feet. Although it had been a part of Nepal for over a hundred years, Mustang was populated by 10,000 or so ethnic Tibetans, mostly subsistence farmers. The central Nepali government had no presence in Mustang, which was ruled by a local raja. The region was a thirteen-day mule ride from Pokhara, the closest paved road and airfield in central Nepal. It was approachable from the south only through an extremely narrow gorge. When defended, this gorge was virtually impassable. To the north, the Mustang plateau opened onto the Tibetan plateau. Historically this route along the Kali Gandaki River had been a trade route between Tibet and central Nepal.[39]

According to John Avedon, Tibetan resistance forces began arriving in Mustang in late 1960.[40] They were spearheaded by men who had retreated from Loka, passed through India's northeast territories and the then-dense jungles of southern Nepal, and finally traveled up the Kali Gandaki gorge. There they set up a series of interlocking bases. Soon after construction began, the CIA began to air-drop supplies. The first load included rifles, light artillery, and forty recent graduates of the Camp Hale training program.[41] By mid-1962, there were 6,000 Khampa fighters in Mustang, a force level that was maintained at least through 1964.[42]

From the Mustang base, Tibetan guerrillas attacked PLA convoys moving along the Xinjiang-Lhasa road. The usual raiding group, consisting of several dozen men, would operate inside Tibet for up to a month. The most successful ambush came in 1966, when an entire Chinese convoy carrying the head of the PLA's western Tibetan command was annihilated. A cache of documents relating to the Cultural Revolution, then beginning to unfold, was also captured and was of great use to the CIA. Espionage was a second focus of the Mustang operations. The guerrillas recruited a fairly large network of informants from among ethnic Tibetan CCP cadre inside Tibet. The CCP cultivated Tibetan cadre in an effort to bridge the gap between Han and Tibetan, but frequently these cadre were secretly sympathetic to the Tibetan resistance.[43]

Following the 1962 India-China war, Indian policy toward the Tibetan insurgency changed dramatically. The United States thereby gained a new partner in supporting the Tibetan resistance, creating new complications for the U.S.-Nationalist cooperation in Tibet. Previously, India had adopted a hands-off policy toward the Tibetan rebellion. Following the 1962 war, however, the Research and Analysis Wing (RAW) of the Indian Intelligence Board began active cooperation with the CIA and the Tibetan insurgents. RAW set up a special communications base in a radio-signal sparse area of Orissa state, where two large receivers and transmitters hooked up to special antennas maintained regular radio contact with Tibetan insurgent forces operating in even the most remote regions of the country. RAW, CIA, and Tibetan rebel officers met weekly to review activities inside Tibet and to issue directives for future operations.[44]

While RAW apparently continued to maintain links with the Tibetan rebels until their final demise in 1974, Indian interest shifted increasingly to another instrument, the Special Frontier Force (SFF). Founded in November 1962 under RAW, the SFF operated out of a military base at Chakrata. Except for a very few top-level officers temporarily transferred from the Indian army, the SFF was an entirely Tibetan force, ultimately numbering 10,000, designed to guard India's borders with Tibet against Chinese infiltration and to serve as commando forces operating behind PLA lines in Tibet in the event of a Sino-Indian war. The SFF was initially trained by U.S. personnel, but a dispute over "procedures" led to U.S. disengagement from the project and to Indian assumption of sole responsibility for the SFF. The Tibetans serving in the SFF were recruited with promises of fighting for Tibetan independence from China. Unlike the Tibetan resistance forces, which operated as lightly armed guerrillas, the SFF were trained as high-altitude commandos. According to John Avedon, Indian contingency planning called for a bold move to wrest Tibet from China in the event of another Sino-Indian war. The SFF were to be parachuted behind Chinese lines throughout Tibet. There they would sever PLA transportation and communications links, rally the populace, and disrupt the PLA's flank and rear areas. Meanwhile, the Indian army would advance into Tibet, meeting the PLA head-on. India's planned objective in the event of a war, according to Avedon, was nothing less than the independence of Tibet.[45]

India's alleged contingency plan to reestablish Tibet as a buffer state between itself and China antagonized Nationalist Chinese leaders. While India never openly endorsed the objective of an independent Tibet, the projected use of the SFF outlined above suggests that Indian planners envisioned seeking such a goal should a second Sino-Indian war occur. Taipei, however, was strongly opposed to such a course. Taipei's objective was greater Tibetan autonomy and freedom within the context of a restoration of the Republic of China on the mainland of Asia.

Following the 1962 Sino-Indian war, Taipei began using its influence to direct the Tibetan insurgency away from advocacy of independence from China and toward advocacy of Tibetan autonomy within a non-Communist China. Propaganda produced by Nationalist-supported groups began to speak more openly and forcefully against Tibetan independence and about Tibet's being a part of China.[46] Taiwan also intensified its links with the Amdoan leaders within the Tibetan resistance, and then urged them to attempt to take over general leadership of that organization. The Amdoans were more Sinicized than the Khampas. Most spoke Chinese and, unlike the Khampas and the Dalai Lama, did not claim full independence from China.[47] Tribalism was strong among the Tibetans, and the Nationalist Chinese-supported Amdoan bid for leadership and endorsement of Chinese sovereignty over Tibet was enough to turn Amdoan-Khampa tension into a blood feud. Armed clashes occurred between the Amdoan and the Khampas in Mustang in the fall of 1963. The Amdoans were forced to flee from Mustang.[48] When the Khampas gained the upper hand, Taiwan cut much of its aid and withdrew its agents still with the Amdo group. The Dalai Lama intervened to call for unity, and dispatched his brother to Taiwan to seek a solution to the conflict. By 1964, a compromise arrangement had been worked out.[49] The fratricidal infighting had already weakened the insurgency, however.

While disagreements among the foreign powers supporting its cause created problems for the Tibetan rebels, the gradual attrition of the rebels by the PLA was the major factor in the insurgency's demise. Because of its superior forces and its mobility, the PLA was able to commit fresh troops to track down the insurgents. The same small bands of rebels found themselves constantly hounded by fresh enemy troops. PLA control over the roads and their relatively abundant trucks also allowed the Chinese to move new troops into position to outflank or encircle rebel groups. PLA airplanes were also able to track and attack rebel bands. Gradually the guerrillas were killed, wounded, exhausted, or discouraged. By the mid-1960s at the latest, the insurgency was no more than a nuisance for China.

The insurgency sputtered on throughout the 1960s. Gradually the United States disengaged from this insurgency, concentrating its energies and interests on the war in Indochina. Fully engaged with a counterinsurgency of its own, the United States gradually lost interest in imposing a counterinsurgent war on China. Final U.S. disengagement came in 1971 following Kissinger's visit to Beijing in July.[50] As part of the U.S.-PRC rapprochement, American money, arms, and intelligence no longer flowed to the Tibetan rebels.

Goals and Costs

While the broad contours of U.S. and Nationalist involvement in Tibet are clear, the exact nature of Taipei's and Washington's objectives, and of their degree of cooperation in carrying them out, is not. Taipei's objective seems relatively easy to infer: to foment rebellion as a way of creating the conditions for a Nationalist return to the mainland. ROC Premier General Chen Cheng provided some insight into Nationalist hopes for future developments in March 1959 when he expressed the hope that the Tibetan revolt would lead to the merger of all anti-Communist forces in northwest and southwest China and that this movement would then spread into central China.[51]

American motivations seem to have been more complex. As we have seen, after several years of large-scale but ultimately fruitless efforts to foment rebellion, U.S. leaders concluded that prospects for widespread rebellion against CCP rule were not good, and henceforth nixed Nationalist proposals for large-scale operations against the mainland. Why was Tibet different? The answer may simply be that prospects seemed better in Tibet. There was seething popular discontent against Chinese Communist overlordship. The geography was also different. PLA logistic lines into Tibet were tenuous. The PLA was much better able to move men and materials around China proper than to move them into Tibet, where its supply lines were long and vulnerable. Because of these differences, U.S. leaders may have concluded that a Tibetan rebellion had a fair chance of succeeding. Of course, even if the rebellion ultimately failed, repressing it would impose heavy fiscal, military, and political costs on Beijing.

The costs to Beijing of repressing the Tibetan resistance were great. For nearly a decade, the PLA waged a counterinsurgency war against a determined enemy. The fiscal burden imposed by Beijing by such a war *may* have been heavy, but data allowing us to reach a sound judgment on this are simply not available. The political costs of Beijing's Tibetan repression are more calculable. Despite Beijing's efforts at secrecy, word of the scope of resistance and brutality of repression got out. This information substantially tarnished Beijing's reputation among Western and Third World publics. The antireligious zealotry of Beijing's repression of Tibet was especially damaging to Beijing's reputation among the attentive elites of the newly independent, developing countries.

The cost in terms of Sino-Indian relations was especially heavy. India and China had reached a modus vivendi in 1954 on the basis of Indian recognition that Tibet was part of China and Chinese granting of a substantial degree of autonomy to Tibet. From New Delhi's perspective, China's repression of the late 1950s violated that understanding. From Beijing's perspective, the rebellion in Tibet greatly increased the sensitivity of the unresolved border dispute with India. By the early 1960s, Chinese leaders increasingly suspected that India's territorial-border claims were linked to the Tibetan rebellion—part of a vast international conspiracy to split Tibet from China. After all, acceptance of India's claim to the Aksai Chin plateau in southern Xinjiang would have denied the PLA its main western access corridor into Tibet. In short, the Tibetan rebellion played a major role in the deterioration of Sino-Indian relations, while U.S.-Nationalist activities played an important role in sustaining that rebellion.

Was spoiling the cozy Sino-Indian relation of the mid-1950s a U.S. objective in supporting the Tibetan resistance? Scholars cannot yet answer this question. Decision-making memorandums for the Tibetan operation which would permit us to answer this question have yet to be declassified. All we can presently say is that it *may* have been a U.S. objective.

Many U.S. leaders—though *not* President Eisenhower—were dismayed by what they took to be India's pro-Communist nonalignment of the early and mid-1950s.[52] Given these perceptions, a spiraling anti-Communist insurgency in Tibet, especially one that was met by PLA repression, could be expected to sour Indian-Chinese relations in various ways. It is possible to find statements by U.S. diplomats indicating an awareness of this relationship.[53] It is a big leap, however, to go from such statements to the proposition that spoiling Sino-Indian amity was a U.S. objective. It *may* be that U.S. leaders viewed support for Tibetan rebellion as a win-win situation. If PLA repression was ineffective, Tibet might throw off CCP rule. If it was effective, China's standing with India and other nonaligned countries would plummet. To repeat, however, there is no direct evidence for this hypothesis, and a firm conclusion one way or the other must wait until the records on the Tibetan operation are declassified. If it ultimately turns out that this was a U.S. objective, then the Tibetan operation was clearly a success, at least in this regard.

Before we leave the topic of U.S. objectives in Tibet, several additional points should be placed on the table. First, U.S. assistance went to the Tibetan people in their struggle to free themselves from Communist rule. As noted at the beginning of this chapter, the fundamental causes of the Tibetan rebellion of the 1950s and 1960s lie in the history of the relations between China and Tibet. The Tibetans rebelled for reasons of their own and welcomed foreign assistance. If the United States was manipulating the Tibetan rebels, then equally those rebels were manipulating the United States to further their own ends. Yet it cannot be denied that U.S. activities led Tibetans to expect support for Tibetan independence and that this was not forthcoming. Moreover, when rapprochement with Beijing beckoned in 1971, Washington dropped the Tibetan struggle flat. The Tibetan people were pawns in the vast political war being waged by Washington and Beijing. One is reminded of the Allied call for the French Resistance to rise on D-Day in June 1944, not in expectation that those risings would escape Nazi repression, but rather in expectation that they would divert German forces at a crucial moment. War carries its own moral logic. From a strictly legal point of view, U.S. activities in Tibet were less problematic. While U.S. activities involved violations of the sovereignty of the People's Republic of China, the United States had not recognized the PRC, and indeed, it recognized the ROC government as the legal government of all China, including Tibet. From a purely legal perspective, therefore, U.S. activities in Tibet had the full sanction of China's sovereign government, or at least of the government recognized by the United States as exercising sovereignty over Tibet. Politically, U.S. support for insurgency in Tibet can be seen as the counterpart of PRC support for insurgency in Indochina and elsewhere in Southeast Asia. Neither Beijing nor Washington felt constrained by boundaries or legal niceties in the struggle they were waging against one another.

Notes

1. Regarding the establishment of the Chinese protectorate over Tibet in the eighteenth century, see Luciano Petech, *China and Tibet in the Early XVIIIth Century: A History of the Establishment of the Chinese Protectorate in Tibet,* Leiden: E.J. Brill, 1972. Regarding modern Tibetan-Chinese relations, see A. Thomas Grunfeld, *The Making of Modern Tibet,* rev. ed., Armonk, NY: M.E. Sharpe, 1996.

2. George N. Patterson, *Tragic Destiny,* London: Faber and Faber, 1969, pp. 17–28.

3. Another firsthand account, however, says that Khamban forces at Qamdo received a shipment of automatic weapons sometime in 1950. Robert Ford, *Wind Between the Worlds,* New York: McKay, 1957, p. 36. Ford, a former Royal Air Force sergeant, was serving, under contract with the Tibetan government, as a radio operator based at Qamdo when that city was seized by the PLA in October 1950.

4. George N. Patterson, *A Fool at Forty,* Waco, TX, and London: World Books, 1970, pp. 9–10. Cited in Grunfeld, *Modern Tibet,* p. 148.

5. John F. Avedon, *In Exile from the Land of Snows,* New York: Knopf, 1984, p. 84. Avedon's account is based largely on information supplied to him by Tibetans associated with the resistance movement.

6. Patterson, *Tragic Destiny,* pp. 85, 88–89.

7. Ibid., pp. 108–9.

8. Ibid., pp. 107–9.

9. *Dangdai Zhongguo de Xizang* (Modern China's Tibet), vol. I, Beijing: Dangdai Zhongguo chubanshe, 1991, p. 245. Deng Lifeng, *Jianguohou junshi xingdong quanlu* (Complete record of military activities since the founding of the nation), Taiyuan and Shanxi: Renmin chubanshe, 1994, p. 185.

10. Patterson, *Tragic Destiny,* pp. 130–34.

11. Ibid., pp. 136–38.

12. *Dangdai Zhongguo de Xizang,* p. 246.

13. Michel Peissel, *The Secret War in Tibet,* Boston: Little, Brown, 1973, pp. 61, 105. Peissel was a graduate student conducting field research for his doctoral dissertation in the Mustang region of Nepal in the mid-1960s. His information, like Avedon's, comes largely from Tibetan refugees and insurgent leaders.

14. Grunfeld, *Modern Tibet,* p. 149.

15. Peissel, *Secret War,* pp. 79–80. See also Michael Morrow, "CIA's Spy Team Inside Red China," *San Francisco Chronicle,* 4 September 1970, pp. 1, 24.

16. Peissel, *Secret War,* pp. 80–81.

17. Grunfeld, *Modern Tibet,* p. 149.

18. Uncle Sam, "Taiwan and Tibet," *Tibetan Review,* vol. 11, no. 1–2, 1976, p. 19.

19. Chris Mullen, "The CIA: Tibetan Conspiracy," *Far Eastern Economic Review,* vol. 89, no. 31 (1975), pp. 1–31.

20. Peissel, *Secret War,* p. 105.

21. George Patterson, "The 'Fish' in the 'Sea' of Tibet," *Current Scene,* vol. III, no. 23 (15 July 1965), p. 6.

22. Patterson, *Tragic Destiny,* p. 178.

23. Patterson, "The 'Fish' in the 'Sea'," pp. 7–8.

24. Peissel, *Secret War,* pp. 105, 108.

25. *Dangdai Zhongguo de Xizang,* pp. 247–48. *Jiangouhou junshi xingdong quanlu,* p. 187.

26. Peissel, *Secret War,* p. 11. Regarding the harshness of Chinese repression in Tibet, see International Commission of Jurists, *The Question of Tibet and the Rule Of Law,* Geneva, 1959.

27. Patterson, *Tragic Destiny,* p. 178.

28. *Dangdai Zhongguo de Xizang,* p. 250.

29. Ibid., pp. 252–55.

30. James C.H. Shen, *The U.S. and Free China: How the U.S. Sold Out Its Ally,* Washington: Acropolis Books, 1983, pp. 31–32.

31. "Chiang Promises Freedom to Tibet," *New York Times,* 27 March 1959, pp. 1, 4.

32. L. Fletcher Prouty, Colonel in U.S. Air Force (Retired), "Colorado to Koko Nor," *Denver Post,* Empire Magazine Section, 6 February 1972, pp. 11–17. Prouty was a U.S. Air Force officer serving as liaison with the CIA in the Koko Nor program.

33. L. Fletcher Prouty, *The Secret Team, The CIA and Its Allies in Control of the United States and the World,* Englewood Cliffs, NJ: Prentice Hall, 1973, pp. 381–82.

34. Chinese People's Liberation Army, *Zhongguo renmin jiefangjun liushinian da shiji (1927–1987)* (Record of 60 years of major events), Beijing: Junshi kexue chubanshe, 1988, pp. 579–80.

35. Peissel, *Secret War,* pp. 163, 166.

36. *Zhongguo xiandai zhanzheng zhanlie jiekan zidian* (Explanatory dictionary of wars and strategy of modern China), Wang Yingjian and Qian Shifu, eds., Beijing: Guofang da xue chubanshe, 1991, pp. 701–2. *Zhongguo renmin jiefanjun liushinian da shiji (1927–1987),* pp. 579–80.

37. Peissel, *Secret War,* p. 175.

38. Ibid., p. 184. Avedon says this decision was made in the "middle of 1960," in *Exile,* p. 122.

39. Michel Peissel, *Mustang, The Forbidden Kingdom,* New York: E.P. Dutton, 1967, pp. 32–34.

40. Avedon, *Exile,* p. 123.

41. Ibid.

42. Peissel, *Secret War,* pp. 191, 219.

43. Avedon, *Exile,* p. 124.

44. Ibid., pp. 121–30.

45. Avedon, *Exile,* p. 130.

46. Uncle Sam, "Taiwan and Tibet," p. 19.

47. Peissel, *Mustang,* pp. 38–39.

48. Ibid., pp. 38–39.

49. Peissel, *Secret War,* p. 207.

50. Avedon, *Exile,* p. 125.

51. "Chiang Promises Freedom to Tibet."

52. Dennis Kux, *India and the United States: Estranged Democracies,* Washington: National Defense University Press, 1992, pp. 139–60.

53. *FRUS,* 1952–54, vol. XIV, part 1, p. 51.

10

Joint Intelligence Operations
Against the Mainland

Joint U.S.-ROC Intelligence Efforts

During the 1950s and 1960s, the United States derived a substantial portion of its information about PRC affairs from Chinese Nationalist intelligence or from cooperative activities with Nationalist intelligence agencies. U.S. dependence on ROC sources was probably very great during the early 1950s and declined progressively thereafter. But to the very end of the U.S.-ROC alliance, Taiwan's intelligence agencies were an important and valued source of intelligence about the PRC.

The value of cooperation with the Nationalists on intelligence matters was demonstrated in the fall of 1950. As war flared in Korea and United Nations troops advanced northward across the thirty-eighth parallel, the CIA needed information about PLA activities in Manchuria, especially in areas adjacent to North Korea, in order to estimate the probability of Chinese entry into the war. They recruited a former high-ranking Nationalist officer who was born and raised in Shanghai and later served with Nationalist forces in several provinces. Many of this officer's former colleagues were serving with the PLA in 1950. After training by the CIA, the man was sent to the mainland, where he made his way to Manchuria and got in touch with many of his former associates. Subsequently, the man was able to report to the CIA with detail and precision about the PLA buildup that was under way north of the Yalu River. Other ROC intelligence sources provided similar information in late 1950 about Beijing's preparations to enter the conflict.[1] President Harry S. Truman apparently read the CIA reports based on this intelligence, but this did not decisively influence U.S. policy. Once Chinese forces entered the conflict in mass, however, the quality of the product provided by Nationalist intelligence (at least in this instance) was apparent.

Collection of intelligence about the PRC was an important objective of Nationalist "limited offensive operations" against the mainland authorized by the United States throughout the 1950s. Several months after President Dwight Eisenhower ordered the suspension in September 1954 of authorization of Nationalist raids against Chinese Communist territory, for example, he granted a waiver for small-scale raids for intelligence purposes.[2] The U.S. MAAG on Taiwan urged the Nationalists to use current aerial photographic intelligence in designing their raiding operations, and helped to set up a photo-processing center at the Taoyuan air base. Equipment and training for the center were provided by the Pentagon.[3] Documents, weapons, and other items useful for intelligence purposes were seized whenever possible by Nationalist raiders.[4] Local PRC officials were also important targets for capture and interrogation. Usually they were interrogated by cadre from the political department after their return to one of the Nationalist offshore islands. Nationalist maritime infiltration also entailed occasional efforts to plant long-term "sleepers" within the PRC. These people were intended to lie low, gradually work their way into responsible or otherwise useful positions, and then become active. Between 1962 and 1966, the PLA caught thirty such "sleepers" dispatched by Taiwan's Intelligence Bureau to the mainland. All were shot.[5] There is no way for scholars limited to declassified information to know how many Nationalist "sleepers" went undetected by PRC counterintelligence.

While U.S. leaders were impressed by the quality of intelligence provided by the Nationalists, they were less enamored by the ROC intelligence organization itself. According to CIA director Allen Dulles, until a major reorganization began in October 1954, Nationalist intelligence organization was characterized by "confusion" and "inefficiency." Through reorganization, however, a completely new intelligence organization was set up and then fleshed out with personnel "from the many components of the previous organization."[6] Presumably, U.S. intelligence organizations advised in this reorganization, just as the U.S. military was then assisting the reorganization of the armed services. The result of this intelligence reorganization was apparently satisfactory. A report by Chief of Naval Operations (CNO) Admiral Robert Carney, following a visit to Taiwan in March 1955, concluded that "The intelligence available in Taipei is better than had been apparent in

Washington and there can be immediate improvement in the distribution process."[7] Carney also recommended further assistance by the Department of Defense in improving Nationalist collection, evaluation, and distribution of intelligence.

U.S.-ROC cooperation in the collection of intelligence via sophisticated technological means began in March 1955 with an agreement between Taiwan's Bureau of State Security and the U.S. Navy. This was shortly after the conclusion of the U.S.-ROC mutual security treaty. Four months later, in July 1955, the CIA signed an agreement with the State Security Bureau. Under these agreements, the U.S. side agreed to supply equipment, technological assistance, and financial support, as well as "other support for personnel stationed overseas." The ROC side agreed to share completely with the United States all electronic intelligence and codes gathered. Regular intelligence and cooperation meetings were instituted, and the first such meeting took place in August 1955. Agreements regarding joint mapping operations were also concluded in March 1955. This led to the exchange of survey data for the construction of accurate maps (with a scale of 1: 250,000) of China and its vicinity. The United States also provided the ROC with instruments for accurate surveying and mapmaking.[8] It is perhaps well to remember that this was before the days of satellite photography and cartography.

Extensive telecommunications monitoring facilities were set up on and about Taiwan, including, probably, on the Nationalist-held offshore islands. Because of the primitive state of China's telecommunications system, most People's Liberation Army (PLA) units then communicated with one another by radio (rather than by more secure "hard wiring"), making monitoring relatively easy. Facilities on and about Taiwan and aboard U.S. warships cruising off the China coast monitored and recorded these transmissions. PLA deployments and maneuvers, communications between PLA headquarters in Beijing, the Military Regions and Field Armies, and the PLA's order of battle were thus determined. So too was the pace of development of PRC electronics capabilities. People's Liberation Army-Navy (PLA-N) movements all along the China coast were monitored, as were aircraft deployments. PRC postal telecommunications and shore-to-ship communications were monitored, and the information garnered was used to estimate the PRC's political-economic situation. Transmissions between Beijing and its overseas embassies were also monitored. All such monitoring activity was, of course, extremely secret.[9]

During the twenty-year confrontation between the United States and the PRC, the sort of hard intelligence derived from joint U.S.-ROC operations proved useful to U.S. planners and decision makers. It allowed them to piece together a picture of enemy military locations and strengths, and provided a basis for estimating enemy intentions. Was this information of a high quality? Were U.S.-Nationalist efforts genuinely able to penetrate Chinese counterespionage and ferret out accurate information? Were the results of U.S.-Nationalist collection operations tainted by Nationalist ideology and interest in exacerbating U.S.-PRC conflict? Was the information collected worth the costs in lost and ruined lives? Was it better, or worse, than information culled from public sources—Chinese newspapers, radio broadcasts, and so on? These are questions which continuing government secrecy (in Beijing, in Washington, and in Taipei) make it impossible to answer. Discussions with Americans involved in these operations at the time, however, indicated that some of them now doubt the value of those operations. Perhaps the most that can be said for these operations is that they provided one source of information on a powerful and extremely closed adversary. As such, that information was valued by the American leaders who received it.

Collection of solid order-of-battle intelligence was probably one reason for the U.S. endorsement of intensified Nationalist raids in the early 1960s that was discussed in an earlier chapter. North Burma provided an important operational base for intelligence-gathering activities. The former Nationalist First Independent Unit there operated 1,500 specially trained troops who maintained an impressive espionage network in the border region. Commanded by General Ma Ching-ko and reporting to the Intelligence Mainland Operation Bureau of the Ministry of National Defense (MND) in Taipei, as well as to the CIA's base at Nam Yu in northwestern Laos, General Ma's troops detailed troop movements in southern China.[10]

As Chinese foreign policy became increasingly militant in the early 1960s, and as tension between the United States and China mounted over Laos, U.S. military planners became increasingly concerned with PLA deployments. U.S. intelligence had extensive data regarding the radio transmissions of various PLA units, or at least supposed PLA units in south China. U.S. analysts were trying to determine whether these deployments indicated that Beijing was planning a move against Laos or into Vietnam, another offensive against India, or a move against Taiwan. All scenarios had their advocates within the U.S. military, and hard evidence was needed to resolve the debates.[11] Monitoring of radio transmissions among PLA unit commands provided the basis for such assessments. From the analysis of these transmissions, U.S. intelligence had compiled a fairly comprehensive picture of the PLA order of battle, what units were deployed where, and what their respective chains of commands were. U.S. analysts did not necessarily know the content of all the messages—some were deeply encoded—but even so, they knew that unit X reported to unit Y, thereby helping compile a complete picture of the PLA chain of command.

National Security Agency (NSA, the agency responsible for monitoring these transmissions) analysts faced a serious problem of deliberate PLA disinformation, however. Chinese leaders were aware of U.S. monitoring of PLA radio transmissions and took countermeasures. One countermeasure was to set up ghost PLA units around the country, units consisting of only a radio unit simulating a unit headquarters by sending out transmissions to other units. These ghost units would move around the country, simulating the movements and the consequent radio transmissions of substantial armies. Thus, NSA analysts were sometimes in the position of trying to determine whether an apparent deployment of perhaps several PLA armies into some region was genuine or a hoax.

One of the ways of doing this was to insert small clandestine teams into the China mainland. These teams would then proceed to the area whence some unit's transmission had come and look for physical evidence of that unit's presence. Such teams were inserted from several points around China's periphery. One jumping-off point was the Nationalist-held offshores. However, even there, at least some of the operations were conducted without the approval or even the full knowledge of Nationalist authorities, since the CIA feared that information provided to Nationalist authorities might end up in Communist hands. This suspicion was reciprocated by Nationalist intelligence officials. U.S. intelligence operatives were frequently tailed by apparent Nationalist intelligence people. On several occasions in the early 1960s, U.S. intelligence operatives were beaten up under circumstances that led American officials to suspect that Nationalist intelligence agencies were responsible and were using these crude means to convey a warning to the arrogant Americans.

Joint Aerial Reconnaissance Efforts

Beginning in the early 1950s and continuing into the early 1970s, the United States and the ROC cooperated to conduct large-scale aerial reconnaissance flights over the PRC. The United States provided the advanced aircraft that generally maintained a substantial lead over the PLA's air defense capabilities, trained the pilots to operate these sophisticated aircraft, and probably designated the targets for these surveillance flights. ROC pilots flew the aircraft, and the ROC assumed political responsibility for the flights. This arrangement was mutually advantageous. Both sides gained valuable intelligence about such matters as PRC military deployments and weapons development programs—matters of deep interest to the leaders of both countries. The ROC gained familiarity with state-of-the-art aircraft and their capabilities. Through cooperation with Taiwan, U.S. personnel avoided risk of death or capture by Communist China and, more importantly perhaps, the United States was absolved of formal responsibility for the operations. The United States maintained plausible deniability and could formally and plausibly disassociate itself from the aircraft criss-crossing the PRC's airspace. U.S. disassociation from the overflights denied Beijing opportunities to "prove" its frequent charges of American aggression against the PRC. For its part, the ROC was fully willing to assume full responsibility for overflights of the China mainland. Nor was Taipei embarrassed, domestically or internationally, by losses of aircraft and pilots. As the sovereign power over the entire China mainland, so it claimed, Taipei had the full legal rights to order aircraft to fly wherever and whenever it desired.

U.S.-ROC cooperation in this field apparently began during the Korean War. According to PLA histories, during the Korean War about 100 Nationalist aircraft per year, or one every three to four days, penetrated mainland airspace. B-17 aircraft flying at night were used for many of the flights. Because the PLA had few pilots trained in night operations, and because of the primitive nature of PLA antiaircraft and radar systems, the Nationalist aircraft met little obstruction. The rapid progress of the PLA's Soviet-assisted modernization changed this, however, and began to create difficulties for piston-powered ROC aircraft by 1955–56.[12] Table 10.1 lists U.S. deliveries of specialized reconnaissance aircraft to Nationalist Taiwan.

Prior to 1955, it took three to four weeks to process and evaluate aerial reconnaissance film and pass it on to top levels in Washington, D.C. This was too long. Early in 1955, the procedure was reworked to shorten the time to six days.[13] As tension built in the Taiwan Strait during the crisis of 1955, the Office of Naval Operations requested and received authorization from the State Department for a series of Nationalist photoreconnaissance missions over the mainland to determine the extent of PLA military activities. Three ROC RF-86s (F-86 Saber fighters modified for photoreconnaissance operations) were to make several passes, one plane at a time, over "enemy territory," each pass of less than twenty minutes duration. If the planes were detected or intercepted, they were to break off their flight and return to their base.[14] Such cautious tactics were necessary because of the rapid modernization of PLA air defenses. By mid-1956, PLA air defenses were proving their effectiveness. Many Chinese pilots were now night-qualified, and a ground radar net had been established that could guide interceptor aircraft to the vicinity of intruders allowing visual contact by moon light. The PLA also began using jet inceptors. On 23 June 1956, a MiG-17 shot down a Nationalist B-17 over Jiangxi Province. Two months later, an

Table 10.1

U.S. Deliveries of Reconnaissance Aircraft to Taiwan

Type of Aircraft	Number of aircraft												
	1953	1954	1955	1956	1957	1958	1959	1960	1961	1962	1963	1964	1965
RF-51D	15												
RT-33A		2	7										
RF-86F			5	2									
RF-84F				18	2	5							
RB-57D						2							
RF-100A							4		2				2
RF-101A							4		2				2
RF-104G											8		
U-2								2		1	1	3	

Source: Meijun zaiHua gongzuo jishi (Record of U.S. military activities on Taiwan), Taipei: Air Force Headquarters, 1981.
Note: Regarding U-2 deliveries, see Dick Vander Aart, *Aerial Espionage Secret Intelligence Flights by East and West*, New York: Prentice Hall, 1986, pp. 33–54. Also see Jay Miller, *Lockheed U-2*, Austin, TX: Aerofax, 1983, p. 3.

ROC electronics reconnaissance aircraft was downed over Zhejiang. The next month, an ROC C-46 was shot down near Shaoshan.[15]

As PLA air defenses improved, it became apparent that continuation of Nationalist photoreconnaissance operations over the mainland would be dependent on rapid upgrading of ROC air capabilities. There was strong resistance within the U.S. government to provision to the GRC of the most advanced, most sophisticated U.S. reconnaissance aircraft, probably because of fear that the PRC and its Soviet ally might get access to vital aeronautical technology should the aircraft be downed. One of the earliest proposals to supply Taiwan with very advanced aircraft came in July 1956, when JCS Chairman Arthur Radford proposed to Secretary of State John Foster Dulles that RB-57 aircraft be supplied to Taipei in order to meet the increased demand for photoreconnaissance intelligence "of the inland Chinese mainland in order to determine the Chinese Communist intentions." The RB-57D was developed in the mid-1950s as a stopgap high-performance reconnaissance aircraft to meet U.S. needs until the more revolutionary U-2 came on stream. Only twenty RB-57Ds were produced. The first squadron became operational at Yokota Air Force Base in Japan in mid-1956, and began flying missions over China and the Soviet Union.[16] In his July 1956 cable to Dulles, Radford urged that RB-57s be supplied to Taiwan because the "limited range and performance" of aircraft currently available to Taiwan prevented "adequate coverage of inland targets and the distant strategic areas of military concentration on the Chinese mainland." The JCS recognized, Radford said, "that a considerable degree of direct U.S. maintenance and logistic support" would be required in the event that RB-57 aircraft or other high-performance aircraft were delivered to the Nationalists. However, the JCS felt that "this support is necessary if the United States is to receive the desired photo intelligence of the mainland of China on a continuing basis."[17] Early in 1959, Nationalist pilots began operating RB-57Ds over the mainland.

The steadily increasing demand for ROC-supplied photo reconnaissance intelligence combined with U.S. reluctance to provide its most advanced aircraft to Taiwan to produce mounting Nationalist discontent. Nationalist leaders bridled at the arrogance they saw in U.S. insistence that ROC pilots undertake dangerous missions to secure intelligence primarily for the United States but with aircraft less capable than those employed by the United States for similar missions by its own pilots. As the U.S. Pacific Command explained to Washington in July 1958:

> Chinats extremely unhappy because of inability successfully reconnoiter inland bases. RF-84 and RB-57A [aircraft] have been intercepted and shot

down. Chinats have openly expressed feelings to COMTDC/MAAG [Commander, Taiwan Defense Command/Military Assistance Advisory Group] personnel that U.S. attempting obtain results from Chinat recco [sic] effort without providing equip suitable for requirements and evidence Chinat reluctance continue recco [sic] with current [equipment] is now widespread.[18]

Given the importance of this intelligence and mounting Nationalist reluctance to continue operating with second-class equipment, CINCPAC recommended that the "seriousness of situation, particularly from Chinat point of view makes evident fact that U.S. should provide latest types high speed, high performance ACFT [aircraft] as soon as possible." Four RF-100 aircraft had been offered to the ROC, even though more advanced RF-101 aircraft were available. CINCPAC urged that RF-101 aircraft be provided to Taiwan during late 1959 or early 1960. Or, "If the United States possesses other high performance [reconnaissance aircraft] with characteristics similar to the RF-101 they should be considered. However, time is of the essence to keep the show on the road." The memo added: "Desire reiterate this is not routine MAP [Military Assistance Program] problem but rather a situation wherein U.S. would benefit directly from successful recon missions. Believe the future success of Chinat recon effort depends on type of equipment offered at this time."

Late in 1959, four RF-101 aircraft were delivered to Taiwan. The intelligence supplied by Nationalist overflights was too valuable to risk continued cooperation. Early in 1960, Nationalist-piloted RF-101 photoreconnaissance aircraft began ultra-low-altitude penetration operations over the mainland. Many Nationalist missions were successful, but ultimately the PLA devised ways to counter the intruders. In August 1961, after nearly a year and a half of overflights of the mainland by Nationalist RF-101s, one was downed by PLA antiaircraft in the vicinity of Fuzhou.[19]

The success of the Nationalist-piloted RB-57Ds and RF-101 overflights led to a U.S. decision to transfer two U-2s to Taiwan; the U-2 was America's most sophisticated spy plane. Again there was strong opposition to this move from within the U.S. government, out of fear of compromising America's most advanced spy technology. A number of alternatives were tried before the radical solution of making America's most advanced, most sophisticated spy aircraft available to foreign powers was adopted. Moscow was aware of the U-2 (which had been overflying the USSR since July 1956) and was working to develop a comparable plane of its own.[20] Beijing was a close ally of the USSR, and U.S. leaders assumed that any U.S. aircraft technology picked up by China would make its way to Moscow. A number of Nationalist pilots had defected to the Communists, and it could be assumed that Beijing would solicit defection. If China and the Soviet

Union obtained U-2 technology, it could be a serious loss to the United States. That these objections were eventually overcome was a testament to the value of the intelligence the U.S. government received from Nationalist overflights. As it turned out, Beijing offered a reward of a quarter of a million dollars in gold to any Nationalist U-2 pilot who defected with his aircraft. None did.

The decision to supply U-2s to Nationalist China was made in 1959. Flight training for the first batch of six ROC pilots had begun in March of that year.[21] Eisenhower's May 1960 suspension of U.S. U-2 overflights of the USSR following the downing of Francis Gary Powers strengthened the rationale for supplying U-2s to Taiwan. Although Eisenhower's ban of overflights did not apply to China, the increased sensitivity of overflights led the U.S. intelligence community to reduce the number of U.S. "black" overflights of China for a while. The need for intelligence regarding the PRC continued, however. In July 1960, two U-2s were sold to Taiwan and overflights of the mainland by Nationalist U-2s began soon afterward.[22] Nationalist willingness and ability to pilot U.S.-supplied aircraft, and to share fully with the United States all information collected, allowed a way for the United States to continue flights over China suspended over the USSR in 1960.

The Nationalist U-2s operated for two years with impunity. Flying out of Taoyuan, operations focused on the Chinese uranium gaseous diffusion plant near Lanzhou, and nuclear weapons and ballistic missile development centers at Lop Nor in Xinjiang. The turnaround point for most flights was Yumen in Qinghai Province—1,800 miles from Taiwan. Nationalist U-2s completed many missions without incident, but in September 1962, one was finally brought down over central Jiangxi Province by a newly devised PLA method of attack in which multiple missiles were fired at one target. Another Nationalist U-2 was downed in November 1963.[23] The United States replaced the downed U-2s and trained additional pilots.

Following the first downing and confronted with physical evidence of the U-2 presented to world media by Beijing, the State Department announced that Lockheed Corporation had sold two U-2s to the Nationalist government in 1960, and thereafter the United States had nothing to do with the aircraft. The State Department representative admitted that Nationalist pilots had been trained in the United States to operate the high-performance aircraft and that it "could be assumed" that Taiwan exchanged with the United States any information gathered.[24] The official cover story was that these aircraft were engaged in weather data collection.

Nationalist U-2 overflights also produced intelligence regarding the reality of the Sino-Soviet split. The CIA had substantial assets in the Communist Parties of non-Communist countries at that juncture, and these individuals had reported on the intensifying polemics between the CCP and the CPSU during 1959 and early 1960. The mainstream of the CIA had concluded by late 1959 that the split was real; simply too many people were involved for the conflict to be a charade. The chief of counterintelligence, James Angleton, believed quite strongly, however, that the "split" was an elaborate hoax designed to mislead the United States. A special committee was established to look into the "hoax" hypothesis; eventually the committee rejected the hypothesis. Some of the most convincing evidence against the hoax hypothesis came from Nationalist U-2 flights. The photos taken on these flights made clear the abrupt halt of work at PRC nuclear facilities and at missile and nuclear test sites following the departure of Soviet specialists from China in mid-1960. No progress was made at these facilities for a considerable time after the Soviet withdrawal. This was regarded by the CIA as conclusive evidence of the reality and depth of the Sino-Soviet split.[25]

As Beijing's nuclear weapons program gradually resumed, following the Soviet withdrawal, so did U.S.-Nationalist efforts to monitor that program. In 1962, twelve more Nationalist pilots began U-2 training in the United States. Nationalist-piloted U-2s were regularly shot down in the course of providing Washington and Taipei with information about the PRC. One was downed by a missile in November 1963. Another three U-2s were shot down in 1964. Altogether, about twelve ROC pilots died on U-2 missions over the mainland.[26] None ever defected, in spite of Beijing's offer of a generous gold bounty.

In October 1968, a more powerful version of the U-2 became available. This was the U-2R, and it could fly higher and farther, and could carry considerably heavier reconnaissance equipment. Its new long-range oblique photography camera could take detailed photographs at oblique angles from a distance of ninety-three miles. The first U-2Rs available went to Taiwan.[27]

When the United States began moving toward rapprochement with the PRC during Nixon's first administration, it no longer cooperated with Nationalist China in conducting aerial surveillance of mainland China. That had been made unnecessary by further technological advances. Late in 1966, the United States began using another ultra-high-performance aircraft, the SR-71, which flew at speeds of over 2,000 miles per hour and at altitudes of up to 80,000 feet. SR-71s flew over China, but they operated not out of Taiwan, but out of Okinawa and Thailand, and later directly out of California. The SR-71, and its capabilities and technologies, were *not* shared with Taiwan. By the late 1960s, all U.S. overflights of China were conducted by SR-71s. None were ever shot down—over China or elsewhere. U.S. spy flights were suspended in late 1971 as part of the process of

Sino-U.S. rapprochement. ROC flights continued as usual. U.S. leaders believed that PRC radar was good enough to distinguish between a U.S. SR-71 and a Nationalist U-2.[28]

A major advantage to the United States of relying on Taiwan to conduct photoreconnaissance operations over China was that U.S. personnel were not put at risk. If U.S. personnel had been captured in the course of operations over the mainland, they could have been used by Beijing to create propaganda against the United States. Securing their release also would have become an object of U.S. policy attention, would have occupied the time of U.S. leaders, and could have constrained U.S. actions. Indeed, securing the release of U.S. civilians held in China after 1949 was a major U.S. objective at the ambassadorial talks with the PRC in 1955.[29] Richard Fecteau, captured when his plane crashed in China during the Korean War, was not released until December 1971. John Downey, a CIA employee shot down over China in 1952, was not released until March 1973, when two other U.S. military pilots shot down over China in 1965 and 1967 were also released.[30]

A final type of U.S.-ROC cooperation in aerial reconnaissance of the mainland involved unmanned drones. Beginning shortly after the Gulf of Tonkin incident in August 1964, Ryan 147 B "lightning-bug" drones were launched from the wing of a DC-130 Hercules aircraft operating from Okinawa. Once dropped, the drones flew over mainland China or North Vietnam before returning to the Taoyuan air base in Taiwan, where their engines cut off and they parachuted to the ground over a 0.5- by 2-mile recovery zone. Three to four U.S. personnel were permanently stationed at Taoyuan to man radar in association with this program. When a mission was scheduled, additional flight controllers would be flown in from Okinawa. After recovery, the drones would be picked up by another C-130 and taken back to Okinawa for reuse. ROC Air Force insignia was painted onto the drones the night before the mission, then covered over with cardboard; the cardboard was removed just prior to takeoff. After recovery, the ROC Air Force insignia was painted over before the drones were shipped back to Okinawa.

Drones had the advantage of being able to operate easily over heavily defended zones, such as the areas of South China used as staging areas for the PLA's support of Hanoi during the Vietnam war. One of the major duties of the drones during the early stages of the Vietnam war was to monitor for indications of Chinese preparations to intervene in that conflict. "Scores" of drones were shot down over China—out of many hundreds, perhaps even thousands, of overflights. The first downing was on 15 November 1964. When Beijing put the downed drones on display, Washington replied with a "no comment." Drone flights too were suspended in July 1971.[31]

The Results of Operations Against the Mainland

Fear of Chinese entry into the Vietnam War was a major factor underlying Lyndon Johnson's strategy of gradual escalation. Those fears were based, in part, on substantial deployment of PLA forces in southern China adjacent to Vietnam and inside North Vietnam. To the extent that this intelligence was derived from lightning-bug drone flights, those flights played an important role in shaping U.S. strategy.

The photoreconnaissance information collected by Nationalist-piloted aircraft was probably critical to the development of bombing target plans by U.S. planners preparing for the contingency of war with China. Accurate targeting information would have been vital for the swift and effective application of superior U.S. airpower in the event of a Sino-U.S. war. If one assumes that the United States should prepare to fight and win the wars in which it might become engaged, the information derived from Nationalist overflights was critical, even though it was never used for its intended purpose.

The importance of intelligence cooperation with the ROC to the United States greatly diminished with U.S.-PRC rapprochement in 1972. Rapprochement quickly reduced the probability of a Sino-American clash and, therefore, the need for timely order-of-battle information about the PLA. The development of more advanced means of overhead surveillance—the SR-71 and more especially photoreconnaissance satellites—also reduced the importance of Nationalist cooperation in this area. The gradual opening of China to the world during the 1970s created new opportunities for the assessment of Chinese developments. Presumably, the CIA was active throughout the post-1949 period, remedying the deficiencies that were so grievous in the early post–World War II era. By the mid-1970s, cooperation with Nationalist intelligence was probably of secondary importance to the United States. Conversely, during the period of U.S.-PRC confrontation, when U.S. intelligence capabilities toward China were relatively underdeveloped, the U.S.-ROC intelligence link was important to U.S. leaders.

The leaders of most countries desire information about the capabilities and intentions of their foreign opponents. The greater the power and the level of hostility, the greater the perceived need for such information. This creates a major problem for liberal democracies locked in rivalry with twentieth-century totalitarian systems. A democracy such as the United States, with its free and muckraking press, its adversarial system of separation of powers, and its relatively open governmental process makes an easy intelligence target. China in the 1950s was extremely closed and tightly controlled. Add to these structural asymmetries the vast cultural differences between China and the United States, and the historical handicaps hobbling U.S. intelligence agencies in China in the 1940s. The conclusion is clear: The intelligence collection activities run in cooperation with Nationalist China in the 1950s and 1960s were valuable to U.S. leaders. Much of the information collected was of poor quality. Much of it was useful. And some of it was apparently crucial. In short, this information, and the operations that provided it, proved useful to the United States at that point in history.

Notes

1. Harry Rositzke, *The CIA's Secret Operations, Espionage, Counterespionage, and Covert Action,* New York: Readers Digest Press, 1977, p. 53. Rositzke was head of the CIA's Soviet Division for a number of years. He does not say whether the former Nationalist officer employed by the CIA in 1950 was still associated with the Nationalist government or its intelligence services at that time. See also *Foreign and Military Intelligence,* Book I, p. 19.

2. *FRUS,* 1955–57, vol. II, p. 25.

3. *Meijun zaiHua gongzuo jishi (guwentuan zhi bu)* [*Record of U.S. military activities on Taiwan (Advisory Group)*] (hereafter cited as *Guwentuan zhi bu*), Taipei: Historical Bureau, Ministry of National Defense, October 1979, p. 23.

4. *Dangdai Zhongguo haijun* (Modern China's navy), Beijing: Zhangguo shehui kexueyuan chubanshe, 1987, p. 375.

5. *Dangdai Zhongguo haijun,* p. 376.

6. Allen Dulles, "Chinese Vulnerability to Subversion," 16 March 1955, in *FRUS,* 1955–57, vol. II, China, p. 383.

7. Robert Carney, "Memorandum of Record and Understanding," 6 March 1955, in *FRUS,* 1955–57, vol. II, China, pp. 335–36.

8. *Guwentuan zhi bu,* pp. 24, 26.

9. Ibid., p. 121.

10. Bertil Lintner, "The CIA's First Secret War," *Far Eastern Economic Review,* 16 September 1994, p. 58.

11. Interview with an anonymous NSA analyst who was personally involved in these activities at the time.

12. *Zhongguo 9 ci da fabing* (Nine cases of Chinese use of military force), Sichuan wenyi chubanshe, 1992, p. 196.

13. *FRUS,* 1955–57, vol. II, p. 398.

14. "Director, Political Military Policy Division, Office of Deputy Chief of Naval Operations (Plans and Policy)," 1 April 1955, in *FRUS,* 1955–57, vol. II, pp. 438–39.

15. *Zhongguo 9 ci da fabing,* p. 196.

16. Jay Miller, *Lockheed U-2,* Austin, TX: Aerofax, 1983, p. 16.

17. Arthur Radford to John Foster Dulles, 18 July 1956, National Archives, RG 218, JCS, Geographic File 1957, 381 Formosa, box 9, sec. 33.

18. 24 July 1958, in National Archives, RG 218, JCS, Geographic File 1958, 381 Formosa, box 147, sec. 37.

19. Wang Liujian and Yu Shifu, eds., *Zhongguo xiandai zhanzheng zhanlie jiesi cidian* (Explanatory dictionary of wars and battles of modern China), Beijing: Guofang daxue chubanshe, 1991, pp. 702–7.

20. Miller, *Lockheed U-2,* p. 118.

21. Ibid., pp. 32–33.

22. Dick Van der Aart, *Aerial Espionage, Secret Intelligence Flights by East and West,* New York: Arco/Prentice Hall, 1986, pp. 33–34.

23. *Zhongguo xiandai zhanzheng,* pp. 702–7.

24. Aart, *Aerial Espionage,* p. 34.

25. Tom Mangold, *Cold Warrior, James Jesus Angleton: The CIA's Master Spy Hunter,* New York: Simon and Schuster, 1991, p. 112.

26. Miller, *Lockheed U-2,* p. 33.

27. Aart, *Aerial Espionage,* p. 35.

28. Ibid.

29. See Kenneth T. Young, *Negotiating with the Chinese Communists: The United States Experience, 1953–1967,* New York: McGraw Hill, 1968, pp. 65–90.

30. *China, U.S. Policy Since 1945,* Washington: Congressional Quarterly, 1980, pp. 203, 209.

31. Aart, *Aerial Espionage,* pp. 72–73. William Wagner, *Lighting Bugs and Other Reconnaissance Drones,* Fallbrook, CA: Aero Publishers, 1982, pp. 56, 65, 74–75.

11

Taiwan and the Vietnam War

The U.S.-ROC Alliance and the War in Vietnam

The United States' decision for war with North Vietnam in 1964–65 was closely related to the containment of the PRC. As Taiwan was *the* major partner of the United States in the containment of the PRC, it was inevitable that Taiwan would play a significant role in U.S. strategy and conduct of the Vietnam War. Nationalist China played a significant role in the U.S. effort to prevent the takeover of South Vietnam by the Vietnamese Workers [Communist] Party. It did this by providing a logistical base for the massive U.S. effort in Indochina, and by assisting the nation-building efforts of the besieged South Vietnamese government. More subtly, but perhaps more importantly, Nationalist China figured into the debates within the U.S. government and between Saigon and Washington about how to deal with the mounting challenge in South Vietnam.

By the early 1960s, Washington viewed Taiwan as an increasingly successful part of the Free World. Washington hoped that all the non-Communist countries of the region would stand together, helping one another resist the onslaught of Communism supported by the PRC and the USSR. In many ways, Washington viewed Taiwan as a model for South Vietnam, demonstrating that a non-Communist state besieged by international Communism could prevail. Moreover, Nationalist China's experience offered a model of how this might be done.

Taipei was strongly supportive of South Vietnam and U.S. efforts there. Relations between the Republic of China (ROC) and the Republic of Vietnam (RVN) became intimate in the late 1950s. In July 1958, relations were elevated to the ambassadorial level. Two months later, a South Vietnamese mission traveled to Taiwan to study Taiwan's successful agricultural reforms. The next month, a Vietnamese commercial delegation visited officials and factories in Taiwan. Subsequently, ten ROC technicians were hired to help set up three sugar-refining factories in South Vietnam. In December of the same year, Taipei set up an economic counselors office in Saigon to promote the development of South Vietnam's agricultural technology. Economic cooperation expanded. Political goals also increasingly converged.[1] This was symbolized by a five-day visit by South Vietnamese President Ngo Dieh Diem to Taiwan in January 1960. Significantly, Diem's entourage included South Vietnam's minister of public construction and the head of the agricultural cooperative association. Diem met *seven* times with Chiang Kai-shek. They had long, wide-ranging, and "extremely cordial" talks. While emphasis on Taiwan's success in development dominated the rhetoric of Diem's visit, there was also a distinct military aspect. After Diem spent several days inspecting military bases, Chiang Kai-shek flew to Gaoxiong for a further meeting with him. Again they engaged in a detailed discussion of the overall anti-Communist situation in Asia. Diem was quite impressed by ROC military capabilities. The ROC, he said, was a "major military power."[2] Deepening ROC-RVN relations mirrored the PRC's expanding support for North Vietnam.

As the Communist insurgency in South Vietnam accelerated in 1961, Diem proposed the use of Chinese Nationalist troops in South Vietnam. Nationalist forces were highly trained by then, were strongly motivated to fight Communism, and were more familiar with Vietnamese customs than were Americans. Perhaps most important, they were racially and ethnically less intrusive in Vietnamese society. Diem felt that Nationalist soldiers and advisers could meet South Vietnam's needs for increased technical expertise without introducing more European and African faces into South Vietnam. By the early 1960s, Diem was increasingly apprehensive about the rapidly increasing Americanization of the war effort, fearing that it might turn patriotic sentiment against his government.[3] When Chairman of the Joint Chiefs of Staff General Lyman Lemnitzer discussed the situation with Diem in May 1961, Lemnitzer asked him what the United States could best do to aid South Vietnam. Diem responded that Washington should encourage other Asian anti-Communists to support South Vietnam—for example, by using the Chinese Nationalists in Southeast Asia, while deploying U.S. air and naval forces *to replace depleted ROC forces in the defense of Taiwan.*[4] In October, South Vietnamese officials again raised the possibility of using Chinese Nationalist manpower in South Vietnam. When General

Maxwell Taylor and State Department official Walt W. Rostow visited Saigon in that month, RVN Chief of Presidential Staff Thuan Nguyen told them that South Vietnam wanted either Chinese Nationalist or South Korean forces, preferably the former, to serve as cadre for the village defense forces.[5] President Diem also told the U.S. envoys that Chiang Kai-shek had said that sending combat units to South Vietnam would be a delicate matter, but that cadre could be sent, even for use in combat. Thuan told Taylor and Rostow that he recognized that use of Chinese Nationalist cadre in South Vietnam would have to be kept secret, but he felt that this could be done, even if thousands of individuals were involved.[6]

Several different methods of clandestine use of Chinese Nationalist forces were discussed within the U.S. government at the end of 1961. In November 1961, the South Vietnamese submitted a proposal to the United States calling for the use of Nationalist Chinese Special Forces to train South Vietnam's village defense forces. Some 3,000 to 5,000 Nationalist veterans between the ages of thirty-five and forty were to enter Vietnam as Vietnamese nationals; were to be given additional cover by brief stays ("sheep-dipped" in the policy vernacular of the day) in Cholon, the Chinese section of Saigon; and then were to be recruited by South Vietnam's services. They would be used in the Mekong delta, where large numbers of ethnic Chinese lived.[7] Another proposal for covert use of Chinese Nationalist forces entailed a logging operation, "human defoliation," in the jungles of the Mekong Delta. Dense jungle vegetation hindered aerial reconnaissance and provided excellent cover for the Communist guerrilla forces. Later, in 1962, this problem would begin to be addressed with chemical defoliants. In 1961 more low-tech methods were used. A logging contract was to be awarded to an ROC firm, which would then bring in Chinese Nationalist veterans, again thirty-five to forty years of age, to conduct the logging operation. The Chinese workers might be accompanied by a Vietnamese team to provide additional cover and conduct liaison. The Chinese logging teams would be armed and would themselves handle small groups of Viet Cong they encountered. Larger contingents of Viet Cong would be reported to and handled by the South Vietnamese army. The logging operation was to be commercially viable, but would have the primary advantage of clearing the jungle.[8] Most proposals for use of Chinese Nationalist personnel in South Vietnam were scotched by the U.S. State Department, out of fear that this would lead to increased Chinese Communist involvement. The United States' objective, explained a State Department memorandum rejecting the proposal to use "sheep-dipped" Chinat Special Forces trainers, was to meet the insurgency within South Vietnam "without attracting substantial ChiCom intervention. The introduction of ChiNats would certainly in some degree increase this hazard."[9] The same concerns led U.S. leaders to rule out proposals in 1964, 1965, and 1967 to use Chinese Nationalist forces in South Vietnam.[10]

Most historians of the U.S. effort in Vietnam agree that one of the major mistakes of the United States was the progressive Americanization of the effort there. The introduction of ever more Americans lent credence to Communist charges that Diem was an American puppet and that the Americans were bent on replacing France in Vietnam. It also bred a sense of resentment and apathy on the part of South Vietnamese soldiers and officials. At some level, Diem sensed these dangers and, in response, sought surrogates to the United States. One can only speculate about the outcome had U.S. leaders decided, say, to combine greater Chinese Nationalist and South Korean involvement *within* South Vietnam with a more forceful U.S. air campaign against North Vietnam. For some time, U.S. advisers had been training Chinese Nationalist and South Korean personnel for just such an eventuality. This did not happen primarily because of U.S. fears of greater PRC involvement. As in Korea fourteen years before, U.S. leaders feared that the presence of ROC combat troops in South Vietnam would either anger Beijing or provide a convenient pretext for Chinese intervention.

The issue of Chinese Nationalist troops in combat in Vietnam came up for the last time in June 1967, when the ROC military attaché in Saigon, acting with the permission of his government, wrote to General William Westmoreland, requesting attachment of ROC officers to U.S. forces serving in Vietnam. Groups of eight to ten officers in the areas of intelligence, artillery, armor, ordnance, and engineering were to be assigned for one-month periods to U.S. units to enhance the combat experience of the ROC officers. General Westmoreland and the U.S. Embassy opposed the request on the grounds that the exposure of Chinese Nationalist officers to combat meant the risk of their death or capture, thus providing a ready-made situation for Chinese Communist charges of Nationalist Chinese military intervention. Moreover, Westmoreland argued, approval of the ROC request would establish a precedent likely to encourage other countries to follow the ROC's example, thereby placing a serious burden on the U.S. military, without any tangible benefits. When the chief of the U.S. MAAG in Taiwan explained the views of the United States to Defense Minister Yu Dawei, Yu withdrew the proposal.[11]

The Chinat Contribution to the Pacification Effort

One area in which the Nationalist Chinese contribution was quite significant was pacification. Pacification, Vietnam's "other war," was (at least in theory), in the U.S. view, a seamless web of economic, military, political, and cultural activities designed to strengthen the Saigon government's control over the population of South Vietnam. It was a war that the United States neglected until late in the game, a failure which many analysts have concluded was one of the major causes of the U.S. defeat.[12] More significant for our purposes, it was an effort in which Taipei played an early and significant role.

In 1958 William H. Fippin, the American Commissioner of the Joint Commission on Rural Reconstruction (JCRR) in Taiwan, was reassigned to South Vietnam. The JCRR was a bilateral U.S.-ROC commission that engineered the very successful development of Taiwan's agriculture during the 1950s and 1960s. Its bold and energetic land reform and rural development programs laid the basis for Taiwan's subsequent rapid economic development and political stability.[13] After his reassignment, Fippin proposed that the JCRR cooperate with South Vietnamese ministries to implement programs similar to those that had proved so successful in Taiwan. Negotiations between the ROC, the RVN, and the U.S. governments soon resulted in an agreement under which U.S. Agency for International Development (AID) would provide financial support, the Chinese Nationalist side of JCRR would recruit qualified Chinese personnel and provide the needed materials, and South Vietnamese ministries would cooperate to implement programs modeled after those already implemented so successfully in Taiwan.[14]

The first eleven ROC agricultural specialists arrived in South Vietnam in December 1959. Their focus was on the establishment of farmers' associations in villages. Modeled after similar organizations in Taiwan, these associations supervised the setting of rents, the cooperative marketing of produce, the organization of villagewide projects, the administration of funds provided under various government programs, and so on. Two more ROC teams, focused on crop improvement and irrigation, arrived in 1960. In July 1964, the various teams were consolidated into the Chinese Agricultural Technical Mission (CATM). More teams soon arrived. CATM soon included eighty-three Chinese specialists.[15]

The establishment of agricultural extension services was a major focus of CATM activity. Cadre from the South Vietnamese Ministry of Agriculture were shown how to conduct regional trial plantings of various crops, put on local demonstrations of crop results and methods, and organize training courses for farmers. Local research centers were established to test the feasibility of new types of crops. A large number of new crops were introduced: okra, cotton, corn, mung beans, sorghum, onions, Irish potatoes, tobacco, and so on. By mid-1965, more than twenty new varieties of vegetables had been successfully introduced into South Vietnam. Importation of onions, Irish potatoes, and garlic by South Vietnam was no longer necessary. In cane-growing regions of central Vietnam, new varieties of sugar cane became dominant within four years. New methods were tested and demonstrated: artificial insemination of hogs, double cropping and crop rotation, pisciculture, the raising of poultry, the vaccination of animals against diseases, the use of chemical fertilizers and pesticides, the cultivation of fruit trees, the use of compost, the advantages and use of various agricultural machinery, and so on. Better strains of crops were developed through hybrid breeding and irradiation programs. Six rice experimentation stations were established, for example, to test 1,000 varieties of rice collected from abroad and within Vietnam.

Development of cottage industry was another thrust of CATM activity. Various sorts of agricultural processing were demonstrated and encouraged. Export possibilities of various items were explored. Agricultural organization was another thrust. CATM personnel assisted the Government of (South) Vietnam (GVN) in drafting regulations establishing a cooperative bank channeling loans to farmers. Regarding irrigation, CATM assisted GVN ministries in surveying and planning large-scale projects designed to carry water from remote mountainous areas to local irrigation systems. They assisted 56 such projects, many of which were in areas controlled, at least initially, by the Viet Cong.

CATM personnel were active in twenty-six of South Vietnam's forty-four provinces. While some senior CATM personnel advised top GVN officials in Saigon, most of them lived in the villages and worked side by side with their Vietnamese counterparts and local farmers. The relative similarities in agricultural environment and rural customs of South Vietnam and Taiwan facilitated understanding and interaction. Altogether, CATM implemented over 300 programs, involving many hundreds of training classes and hundreds of thousands of South Vietnamese farmers. As early as mid-1965, for example, 293 training classes had been conducted, involving 3,679 district cadre and local leaders. A total of 109,267 farmers had received one-day training, and another 122,090 farmers had participated in various sorts of demonstrations.

Chinese Nationalist advisers also counseled Army of the Republic of Vietnam (ARVN) commanders on the conduct of "political warfare" against the Communists. In October 1964, the ROC Military Assistance Advisory Group (MAAG) was established in Saigon. It included the Political Warfare Directorate, with fifteen personnel. Under the ROC MAAG were five political warfare advisers assigned to the Saigon Military District; three to the Political Warfare School at Dalat; and two each to the I Corps Tactical Zone at Danang, the II Corps in Pleiku, the III Corps at Bien Hao, and the IV Corps at Can Tho, making a total of thirty-one political warfare advisers.[16] These political warfare specialists presumably advised ARVN on the use of military force to establish, consolidate, and expand the GVN's pacification programs in the countryside.

As noted earlier, U.S. strategists overlooked for too long the necessity of breaking Viet Cong control and establishing effective GVN control over the rural populace of South Vietnam. Belatedly, however, this was done with substantial effect. There is a near consensus among scholars that by 1971–72 the Viet Cong insurgency (as opposed to North Vietnam's regular army) had been largely destroyed or at least pushed out of the populous areas of South Vietnam. The reasons for this are complex. I would merely suggest that one factor, perhaps a significant one, was the dissemination of JCRR-model reforms, the work of ROC personnel in that dissemination, and the efficacious effects of those reforms on the livelihoods of thousands of South Vietnamese rural families. The role of this factor pales in significance, of course, to the combined effect of the Tet uprising, which exposed the Viet Cong infrastructure, and Operation Phoenix, which targeted that infrastructure, and to the torrent of U.S. dollars that financed South Vietnam's land reform and rural development programs.

Taiwan's Role as a Support Base for the U.S. Effort

Taiwan played a very important role as a support base for the U.S. effort in Vietnam. The great distances involved in the Pacific, the heavy logistic demands imposed by the American style of war, and the rapid expansion of the Vietnam War beginning in 1965 posed great challenges for the U.S. military logistic services.[17] Taiwan became one of the major support bases that enabled the U.S. military to meet those challenges.

In October 1962, a memorandum of understanding was signed providing for expanded use of bases on Taiwan by the U.S. Air Force.[18] Over the next several years, and especially in 1964–65, as the United States confronted the possibility of PRC entry into the Vietnam War, extensive work was done on these bases. Facilities were expanded and hardened to withstand attack. The newly completed air base at Kung Kuan, outside Taizhong in central Taiwan, was a major focus of activity. This base was later renamed Ching Chuan Kang, and was commonly known to Americans as "CCK" air base.

Early in 1966 three squadrons of C-130 transport aircraft were redeployed from Clark Field in the Philippines and Okinawa to CCK. From there, the C-130s rotated through South Vietnam on one- to two-week cycles, returning to Taiwan for maintenance after completion of their tours.

In South Vietnam they provided tactical airlift support for U.S. and South Vietnamese forces. Conditions at CCK were harsh when the U.S. Air Force first moved in, with tents that sometimes collapsed in Taiwan's torrential rains serving as offices. The facilities were gradually improved, however. By 1972, the number of U.S. Air Force C-130 squadrons at CCK had grown to four. One squadron of C-130s operating out of CCK was the Air Force unit most active in overwater airlift; this squadron frequently assisted the movement of U.S. troops between South Vietnam and offshore U.S. bases in the East Asian region. Air America also operated C-130s and other aircraft out of CCK in support of U.S. operations, including clandestine ones, throughout Indochina.[19] Several squadrons of F-100 fighter aircraft, EC-121 electronic warfare aircraft, and KC-135 tankers for air refueling operations also operated out of Taiwan. The five EC-121 aircraft supporting U.S. air operations in Indochina had their main base in Taiwan, but generally operated out of forward bases in South Vietnam.[20] Taiwan, along with the Philippines and Okinawa, provided a base of operations for heavy repair of U.S. aircraft operating in South Vietnam.

In December 1965, the United States approved the phased expansion of CCK. The enlargement of CCK permitted the operation of KC-135 aircraft from that base to refuel B-52s and other U.S. aircraft on their way to and from Vietnam. Work was sufficiently advanced on CCK by September 1967 to permit deployment of KC-135s there from Okinawa. The major problem was design and construction of a fuel supply system that could deliver aviation fuel in amounts adequate to support up to sixteen KC-135 tankers carrying 22,000 gallons of fuel on each sortie. Up to twenty KC-135s could operate out of CCK, and it quickly became the major base for refueling operations for U.S. aircraft in the Southeast Asian theater. Usually, CCK KC-135s would rendezvous with B-52s over the South China Sea. This greatly facilitated the increase in B-52 bombing sorties and the total tonnage of bombs delivered. By being able to refuel en route, B-52s could carry more bombs. CCK also served as typhoon evacuation base for U.S. aircraft stationed elsewhere in the region. Weather was a major problem for U.S. air operations in Southeast Asia.[21]

Secrecy marked U.S. Air Force operations in Taiwan. When the State Department negotiated with Taipei the agreement to use CCK as weather evacuation base, they refrained for political reasons from obtaining outright permission for such use. Air Force Headquarters also ordered that dissemination of all information regarding Taiwan's use as a weather evacuation base for B-52s should be kept to the absolute minimum.[22]

Taiwan also provided major maintenance facilities for U.S. armed services during the Vietnam War. The U.S. Navy, for instance, confronted major logistic difficulties as the war in Vietnam escalated. Most of its ships were old, of World War II vintage. Thin military budgets during the pre–Vietnam War years had meant that maintenance had been kept to a minimum. As the tempo of operations increased in 1965, this, along with the stress of sustained gunfire, resulted in many malfunctions and breakdowns. The size of the U.S. fleet in Southeast Asian waters also grew rapidly, from 115 ships in January 1965 to a peak of 207 in 1969. More ships meant more maintenance work.[23] Much of this was done on Taiwan.

Navy maintenance policy called for maintenance and repair to be conducted at the lowest possible level. To send ships or parts back to the continental United States for repairs required more time than to have the repairs done in Asia. Longer time for repairs meant fewer ships kept in action and operating at full capability. Moreover, repairs in the United States were much more costly. One man-day cost $82 in a shipyard on the West Coast of the United States, whereas on Guam it cost $57, at Subic Bay it was $16, and in Taiwan it was $6. Indirect costs were virtually absent in Asian facilities, but quite substantial in the continental United States.[24] In response to these factors, the U.S. Navy developed a network in the western Pacific to carry out repairs in the theater of operations whenever possible. The most important of these facilities were at Subic Bay in the Philippines, at Guam, and at Sasebo and Yokosuka in Japan. Taiwan was also part of this offshore repair and maintenance network. Equipment and ships were contracted to commercial operators for repair.

Vietnam also placed heavy demands on the U.S. Army's maintenance capabilities. Vietnam's dusty atmosphere, broken road surfaces, rough cross-country terrain, steep grades, and high monthly mileages were particularly hard on Army trucks. Cracked blocks and heads, blown head gaskets, and broken valve stems and connecting rods became common problems. In July 1966, the standard engine replacement rate for the Army's five-ton truck was changed from six per hundred vehicles per year to one per vehicle per year. A shortage of engines led to many trucks being out of commission while waiting for repairs. In response to this crisis, the Army too developed a network of offshore repair facilities. Taiwan was one of the most important of these.[25] By 1969, Taiwan was a major site for the rebuilding of heavy equipment for the U.S. Army in Vietnam. Jeeps, trucks, tractors, electrical generators, armored personnel carriers, and tanks were sent to a complex of base depots and maintenance shops in the vicinity of Taipei and Taizhong for repair or rebuilding under U.S. supervision. Contractors in Taiwan were familiar with the U.S. Army supply system because of their earlier participation in the military assistance program to Taiwan. Direct labor cost in Taiwan was 57 cents per hour, compared to $12 per hour for comparable work in the continental United States. The cost of transport to Taiwan was also far below the cost of transport to the continental United States. Additionally, parts were often available from Taiwan firms at costs substantially below what they cost in the United States. These great cost savings made it possible for U.S. forces to save much money, and to repair and reuse equipment rather than throwing it away and replacing it with new items. During the period of drawdown in South Vietnam during the early 1970s, these cost savings were very important. Increased reuse of damaged equipment also meant that the Army could use new equipment to outfit Reserve units in the United States, and could begin building up the readiness of U.S. units in Germany and elsewhere, after years of depleting these units to serve the effort in Vietnam. In the words of the deputy chief of staff for logistics in the early 1970s, Lieutenant General Joseph M. Heiser, Jr., the Taiwan maintenance operation "turned out to be one of the finest logistic actions taken by the Army" during the Vietnam War. According to another source, the Taiwan maintenance activity was "one of the most successful, largely unknown logistics operations that occurred in the Far East. It should remind us of the importance of recognizing capabilities that exist wherever they happen to be."[26]

The importance of Taiwan as a support base for the U.S. effort in Indochina should not be exaggerated. The Philippines, Thailand, Okinawa, Japan, and Guam also provided important bases for such operations. The point is *not* that bases in Taiwan were more important than bases in other countries. Rather, the U.S. effort in Vietnam depended on a regionwide system of offshore bases, with bases on Taiwan constituting an important part of that system. Figures presented in a 1970 briefing entitled "Depot Maintenance Posture in the Pacific Area" provide a basis for gauging the relative importance of various areas to the U.S. logistic effort. These figures are presented in Table 11.1.

Bases on Taiwan also helped maintain the security of U.S. sea lines of communication in the western Pacific during the Vietnam War. U.S. forces operating out of Taiwan bases monitored the movement of Soviet aircraft, surface vessels, and submarines in the western Pacific. They provided protection for U.S. aircraft carriers operating in the Gulf of Tonkin against North Vietnam, and for all U.S. aircraft carriers moving through the area. They monitored the movements of Soviet, Chinese, and North Vietnamese trawlers used to supply Viet Cong and North Vietnamese units in South Vietnam. They conducted search and rescue operations for U.S. military personnel downed in the area. They conducted electronic intelligence monitoring and visual photography of all "Communist warships," auxiliary ships, mer-

Table 11.1

Taiwan's Relative Importance as a Theater Rebuild Site, FY 1969 and FY 1970 (Number of units rebuilt)

	Taiwan	Okinawa	South Korea	Japan
Generators	100	3,750	0	0
Trucks and tractors	3,544	2,939	0	0
Engines	0	2,456	0	0
Tanks and armored personnel carriers	155	0	193	2,275

Source: Briefing, "Depot Maintenance Posture in the Pacific Area for Army Policy Council," presented by Deputy Chief of Staff for Logistics, 19 March 1969 [sic], Center for Military History, Washington, D.C.

---

chant ships, and fishing vessels moving in the area. They also monitored all trade, Communist and non-Communist, with North Vietnam.[27]

Taipei's Critique of U.S. Strategy During the War

A study of the Chinese Nationalist role in Vietnam would be incomplete without a discussion of the Nationalist critique of the United States' conduct of that war. While supporting South Vietnam and the U.S. effort, ROC officials were critical of particular aspects of U.S. policy. The assassination of Ngo Dinh Diem in November 1963, and more especially the United States' role in that action, dismayed Chinese Nationalist leaders. Although Taipei took no official position on that episode, newspapers more distant from the government were critical. The *Zili wanbao* (*Independence Evening Post*), for example, warned that Diem's assassination was a "tragedy" for Vietnam. While Diem undeniably had shortcomings, the Communists were certain to use the instability resulting from his assassination.[28] Twelve years later, in an editorial giving "earnest advice" to America on the occasion of the Republic of Vietnam's final demise before Hanoi's Ho Chi Minh Offensive, the Nationalist Party paper *Zhongyang ribao* quoted a comment by William Westmoreland: "The greatest mistake the United States made in Vietnam was supporting the overthrow of President Ngo Dinh Diem."[29]

To many Nationalist leaders, U.S. involvement in Diem's overthrow was another tragic manifestation of American arrogance and misunderstanding of Asian cultures. It was indicative of the U.S. tendency to judge Asian leaders by American standards, of the naive American hubris regarding its ability to engineer solutions it desired in Asian countries, and of a profound misunderstanding of the *political* nature of the Communist strategy of warfare. Nationalist leaders were critical of what they felt was an overemphasis on the purely military aspect and a neglect of the political aspect of the struggle against Communist insurgency. One of the *Zhongyang ribao* editorials following Diem's assassination warned:

> The Communist strategy is to use political camouflage to conceal their military struggle, and use political methods to achieve victories they cannot achieve by military methods. Therefore the anti-Communist struggle must have a firm basis on the political arena, must fight well in this area, for only in this fashion will it be possible to defeat the enemy in the military arena. Failure in the area of politics will inevitably lead to defeats on the military battlefield.[30]

During the Vietnam War, as during the Korean War, Nationalist leaders were highly critical of the U.S. strategy of limited war. Rejection of Nationalist proposals to carry the war to China were a significant, and previously little explored, aspect of the United States' conduct of limited war in Indochina. Chiang and other Nationalist leaders repeatedly urged American leaders to carry the war to North Vietnam *and to China,* striking with overwhelming force to reach a decisive conclusion. When Richard Nixon (then a private citizen) visited Taiwan in late 1964, Chiang told him that the United States could never win in Vietnam without invading North Vietnam. Chiang laughed at the Strategic Hamlet Program then being pursued in South Vietnam. "It is the familiar fallacy that economic development will defeat the Communists," Chiang said. In fact, he told Nixon, "Only bullets will really defeat them."[31] This, of course, contradicted *Zhongyang ribao's* earlier criticism of America's neglect of the political aspect and overemphasis on the purely military side of the Vietnam War. Taipei also pushed for Nationalist involvement in the war. In April 1964, Chiang told Secretary of State Dean Rusk that the best way for Nationalist China to aid South Vietnam was to parachute between 5,000 and 10,000 guerrillas into Yunnan Province to encourage and organize anti-Communist revolution there, with the goal of disrupting Chinese Communist supply lines to North Vietnam, Laos, Cambodia, and Burma. The United States should provide the aircraft for this operation, China urged. Rusk and Chiang also discussed the possible U.S. use of nuclear weapons in Southeast Asia. Chiang adamantly opposed such use.[32]

In September 1965, Nationalist proposals about how to deal with the Indochina situation were discussed in some depth during a ten-day visit by Chiang Ching-kuo (then newly appointed Defense Minister) to Washington. In broad-ranging exchanges of views with Defense Secretary Robert McNamara, Secretary of State Dean Rusk, and President Lyndon Johnson over how to respond to the new Communist aggression in Southeast Asia,

Chiang strongly urged U.S. support for an all-out Nationalist invasion of the mainland. As Chiang explained in his report to the Legislative Yuan after his return, "During this visit, I gave clear expression to our position on recovering the mainland." The reason North Vietnam could undertake its war of conquest against South Vietnam and challenge the United States was that Communist China served as its "secure rear area." If the United States was prepared to seek a thorough solution and not merely a partial and temporary solution to the Vietnam problem, Chiang Ching-kuo told ROC legislators, "The only way to do this was to root out the root of aggression—destroy the Chinese Communist regime." While the U.S. policy of containment might attain some results, it ultimately left the Chinese Communists in a position to continue their subversion of other countries, Chiang said.[33]

The rapid progress of Communist China's nuclear weapons program was another reason adduced by Chiang Ching-kuo for U.S. support of a Nationalist return to the mainland. China had tested its first atomic bomb in September 1964, and U.S. and Nationalist leaders knew that work on an H-bomb was well under way. Continuation of mere containment would allow the Chinese Communists time to develop thermonuclear weapons, which would constitute a grave threat not only to Free China, but to all of Asia, to the United States, and indeed to the entire world. The way to prevent this was, once again, to support Nationalist destruction of the Communist regime.

Chiang's overarching argument was that continued existence of the Communist regime in China would impose upon the United States, and upon China, further wars. Twice in fifteen years, first in Korea and then in Vietnam, the United States had found itself involved in wars linked to Chinese Communist encouragement and support. The United States' failure in Korea to carry the war to Communist China had resulted in Beijing's being willing and able to impose another war on the United States a decade later in Vietnam. If the United States repeated the same mistake in Vietnam, regardless of the outcome there, America was certain to face another war, encouraged and supported by Communist China, somewhere else in Asia in the near future. Moreover, that future war would be even more difficult and dangerous because of the greater power of Communist China. It would be better, Chiang argued, to eliminate the source of aggression in Asia now, while the Chinese Communist regime was still relatively weak. Only in this way could true peace and security be established. The way to do this was for the United States to support a Nationalist return to the mainland.

There was a final argument advanced by Chiang Ching-kuo. It is obvious, but deserves mentioning. The ultimate purpose and justification of a joint U.S.-Nationalist effort to destroy the Communist regime in China was to free the Chinese people from the Maoist totalitarianism under which they suffered. The vast majority of the Chinese people hated Communist rule, Chiang told his American listeners, and longed for freedom. U.S.-supported Nationalist destruction of the CCP regime would free the Chinese people from Communism.

U.S. leaders listened to Chiang's arguments in favor of a joint effort to destroy the CCP regime, and said "no." They shared Nationalist concerns about Beijing's nuclear weapons and missile programs, but inclined toward a more modest solution—a limited antiballistic missile defense system to defend against a possible Chinese strike. They also shared Nationalist concerns about Beijing's support for wars of national liberation. Here the U.S. solution was to wage a limited, local war, carefully avoiding a larger war with Communist China. It may also be said that U.S. leaders looked toward the eventual dismantling of totalitarianism in China, but saw this as the result of a long-term process of political evolution within China, not as the result of a renewed large-scale civil war between the Nationalists and the Communists.

The U.S. strategic objective vis-à-vis Taiwan was still to consolidate that island into the western Pacific offshore defense perimeter. This objective would not have been served by sending Nationalist forces into the interior of the continent. Had the Nationalist return failed, as U.S. leaders deemed likely, the United States would have then found itself confronted with the necessity of making major force commitments to the defense of Taiwan, just as it was rapidly expanding its commitment in Vietnam. In effect, the United States would have been opening up a second front and expanding the war beyond Indochina. President Johnson was determined to fight the war in Vietnam without calling up the reserves, a move he felt would undermine domestic support for the war. Given this frame of mind, the Nationalist proposal to open a new front in the Taiwan Strait was distinctly unattractive to top U.S. leaders. A basic premise of U.S. strategy in the Vietnam War was avoidance of a U.S.-China war. To achieve this, the war had to be carefully limited. The last thing top U.S. leaders wanted was an expansion of the war to the Taiwan Strait.

The Vietnam Debacle and Taiwan

The U.S. military disengagement from Vietnam in 1973 cast major uncertainties over the future of U.S. policy in Asia. Simultaneously with the U.S. withdrawal from South Vietnam, U.S. military forces began withdrawing from Taiwan in accord with the U.S.-PRC Shanghai communiqué of February 1972, in which the United States had pledged to withdraw its military forces from Taiwan "as the tension in the area diminishes." By the end of 1973, more than one-third of all U.S. military personnel previously stationed in Taiwan had been withdrawn.[34]

This withdrawal of U.S. forces led to deep unease among the populace of Taiwan. The local media began paying extremely close attention to the activities of U.S. military forces in Taiwan.[35]

Ironically, just as the Vietnam War had vindicated Douglas MacArthur's 1950 predictions about Taiwan's geopolitical importance, the United States began moving back to the pre–June 1950 strategy of wooing Chinese Titoism. During the Vietnam War, Taiwan had proved itself to be an important part of the western strategic perimeter through which U.S. military forces maintained mastery of the seas and airs off the continent of Asia, and which allowed the United States to mass forces at forward positions far removed from its own shores. These were substantial geopolitical advantages. Against them was balanced another factor at least as weighty: the power of the People's Republic of China in the global contest between the USSR and the United States.

The dramatic collapse of South Vietnam in early 1975 and, perhaps more especially, the passive U.S. acceptance of this collapse made an extremely deep impression in Taiwan. South Vietnam had been a "brotherly" anti-Communist partner of the ROC since the late 1950s. Moreover, it had been a close ally of the United States, which had invested considerable political, human, and economic assets in sustaining it. Yet the United States stood by and watched it collapse before a clear Communist invasion. The underlying fear in Taiwan was that, as the United States returned to its pre–June 1950 position of drawing Communist China away from and directing it against the USSR, Washington was, through Nixon's rapprochement with Beijing, disengaging from Nationalist Taiwan.

A final note on the political consequences of geography in the context of South Vietnam and Nationalist China is in order. It is an obvious point, but one which is seldom made. The Nationalist Chinese state inhabited an island fairly distant from the continent of Asia, while the RVN had to defend territory sprawling 900 miles north to south, and contiguous with large and rugged lands to the west. These differing geographic situations had a profound impact on the ability of the two states to prevent infiltration. U.S. military power proved much more cost-effective in the maritime environment than in the continental one. These simple geographic facts had profound consequences for the historical destinies of the two states. One was able to develop toward liberal democracy. The other was subsumed into a Stalinist socialist state.

Notes

1. *Yuenan gongheguo Wu Tingran zongtong fang Hua* (Republic of Vietnam President Ngo Dinh Diem visits China), Taipei: Executive Yuan Information Office, January 1960.

2. *Wu Tingran zongtong fang Hua,* p. 25.

3. See George C. Herring, *America's Longest War, The United States and Vietnam, 1950–1975,* New York: Knopf, 1986, p. 79. Stanley Karnow, *Vietnam: A History,* New York: Penguin, 1984, pp. 250–51.

4. *FRUS,* 1961–63, vol. I, Vietnam, 1961, p. 91.

5. The major significance of the Taylor-Rostow mission, of course, was its recommendation to President Kennedy for an expanded U.S. commitment to South Vietnam to prevent a Communist takeover.

6. Memorandum of Taylor-Rostow talk with Diem and Thuan, 25 October 1961, *FRUS,* 1961–63, vol. I, pp. 431–32.

7. Assistant for Special Operations Lansdale to Presidential Military Representative Taylor, in *FRUS,* 1961–63, vol. I, pp. 435–36, 523–31, 724.

8. *FRUS,* 1961–63, vol. I, pp. 523, 531.

9. Ibid., pp. 435–36.

10. Stanley R. Larsen and James L. Collins, *Allied Participation in Vietnam,* Washington: Department of the Army, 1975, p. 115. "Memorandum of Conversation, U.S. Embassy Saigon," 19 April 1964, *FRUS,* 1964–68, vol. I, p. 252. William C. Westmoreland, *A Soldier Reports,* New York: Dell, 1976, p. 341.

11. Larsen and Collins, *Allied Participation,* pp. 117, 119.

12. Numerous analyses of various perspectives agree on this point. See Andrew Krepenivich, *The U.S. Army and Vietnam,* Baltimore: Johns Hopkins University Press, 1986. Harry Summers, *On Strategy,* New York: Dell Books, 1982. Neil Sheehan, *Bright and Shining Lie: John Paul Vann and America in Viet Nam,* New York: Random House, 1988. William Colby, *Lost Victory,* Chicago: Contemporary Books, 1989.

13. Regarding JCRR, see Joseph A. Yager, *Transforming Agriculture in Taiwan: The Experience of the Joint Commission on Rural Reconstruction,* Ithaca and London: Cornell University Press, 1988. T.H. Shen, *The Sino-American Joint Commission on Rural Reconstruction,* Ithaca and London: Cornell University Press, 1970.

14. Chang Lien-chun, *Shi er nian zai Yuenan* (Twelve years in Vietnam), Taipei: Joint Commission on Rural Reconstruction, 1973. Chang Lien-chun was the head of the Nationalist mission in South Vietnam.

15. *1st Annual Report of the Chinese Agricultural Technical Mission to Vietnam* (for the year ending July 1965), Saigon, 1965. In 1969 the "Mission" was changed to a "Group." Annual reports for years through 1972 are available at the JCRR office in Taipei.

16. Larson and Collins, *Allied Participation,* pp. 116–17.

17. *Arsenal for the Brave: A History of the United States Army Material Command, 1962–1968,* Historical Office, Headquarters, U.S. Army Materials Command, 30 September 1969.

18. "Mei jun Tai ziijian sheshi an" (Archive on U.S. military construction activities on Taiwan), File No. 900,8/8043, Historical Bureau, Ministry of National Defense, Taipei.

19. Ray L. Bowers, *The United States Air Force in Southeast Asia, Tactical Airlift,* Washington: Office of Air Force History, 1983, pp. 182, 380, 448–50, 560, 563.

20. U.S. Air Force, *The United States Air Force in South East Asia, 1961–1973: An Illustrated Account,* Washington: Office of Air Force History, 1984, pp. 185, 205, 226.

21. Charles K. Hopkins, *SAC Tanker Operations in the Southeast Asia War,* Office of the Historian, Headquarters Strategic Air Command, 1979, p. 67.

22. Ibid., pp. 67–68.

23. *Maintenance,* A Report by the Joint Logistics Review Board, Washington: Center for Military History, p. xx. No date, but apparently written in 1969.

24. Ibid.

25. Ibid., pp. 40–41.

26. Lieutenant General Joseph M. Heiser, Jr. (Retired), *A Soldier Supporting Soldiers,* Washington: U.S. Army, 1991, pp. 146–48. Also see "Briefing Depot Maintenance Posture in the Pacific Area for Army Policy Council," presented by Col. John V. Pfeiffer, deputy chief of staff for logistics, 19 March 1969. For official use only; declassified.

27. Commander, Patrol Force Seventh Fleet, *U.S. Taiwan Patrol Force, Fleet Air Wing One, Command History, 1969,* Washington: Naval Historical Center, 1970.

28. "Quanli, yu guo, ren xin" (Power, the nation, and human nature), *Zili wanbao,* 4 November 1963.

29. "Wei Yuenan wajie xiang mengbang Meiguo deng jin zhonggao" (Earnest advice to America and other allies on the occasion of Vietnam's disintegration), *Zhongyang ribao,* 1 May 1975.

30. "Yuan Yuenan guomin gongtong nuli," *Zhongyang ribao,* 4 November 1963.

31. Richard M. Nixon, *Memoirs,* vol. 1, New York: Time Warner, 1978, p. 318.

32. *FRUS,* 1964–68, vol. I, Vietnam, 1964, p. 247.

33. Report dated 15 October 1965, *Jiang buchang fang Mei jiyao* (Record of Minister Chiang's visit to America), Taipei: Political Warfare Office, Ministry of National Defense, 15 December 1965, pp. 58–62.

34. Commander, U.S. Taiwan Defense Command, *Command History, 1 January–31 December 1973,* compiled by the Public Affairs Office, Headquarters USTDC, Taiwan, 1974, Washington: Naval Historical Center, pp. III-13.

35. Ibid.

12

Nationalist China and the Containment of PRC Influence

**Nationalist China as an Instrument
for Isolating Communist China**

Restriction of the political influence of the PRC was an important element of the U.S. strategy of containment during the 1950–71 period. Diplomatic relations between the PRC and other countries were restricted as much as possible. The PRC was to be denied international venues from which to mount political offensives. If denial of such forums was impossible, Beijing's political gains from use of these forums was to be kept to a minimum. Beijing's efforts to build influence among important foreign constituencies, such as the overseas Chinese or the developing countries, were to be countered. Only in 1971 did the United States abandon this policy of imposed isolation as part of the new arrangement worked out between Beijing and Washington.

Nationalist China played a key role in the U.S. effort to isolate Communist China. By supporting the presence of the ROC in international arenas, Washington minimized the influence of the PRC. Because of the refusal of both Taipei and Beijing to sit in international organizations with one another, keeping the ROC in those bodies, or maintaining ROC representation in a foreign capital, was a way of keeping the PRC out. Throughout the twenty years during which the United States supported the claim of the Government Republic of China (GRC) to represent China in the United Nations, critics often charged that U.S. policy was unrealistic. The government residing in Beijing, not the one in Taipei, had effective control over the mainland of China and its hundreds of millions of people. The state in Taipei, despite its grandiose pretensions, controlled only a small island with ten million or so people, it was said. In retrospect, however, we can say that this criticism somewhat missed the point. It was not a question of principle and logic, but of political conflict. Keeping the ROC in the United Nations was a way of keeping the PRC out, and keeping the PRC out of the United Nations was an important element of the policy of containment of Communist China. Exclusion of the PRC from the United Nations denied Beijing an important forum for conducting propaganda and diplomatic initiatives antithetical to U.S. policy interests. It enhanced the ability of the United States to use the United Nations to counter hostile moves and propaganda by Beijing. It denied Beijing the status that it craved and that would have been so useful for internal legitimization of the CCP regime. The PRC's exclusion from the UN also discouraged various countries, especially countries dependent on the United States, from establishing diplomatic relations with the PRC. Finally, exclusion of the PRC from the United Nations increased Beijing's diplomatic and political dependence on the Soviet Union, thereby creating a pressure-cooker effect that U.S. leaders deemed conducive to exacerbation of Sino-Soviet conflicts. In sum, exclusion from the United Nations contributed in a number of substantial ways to the containment of Communist China. While keeping Beijing out of the UN required nominal U.S. support for Taipei's increasingly fantastic claim to represent all of China, support of this myth was an important element of U.S. strategy in the twenty-year political war with China.

This is not to say that U.S. leaders did not believe in the legal and moral arguments they advanced in favor of ROC representation in the United Nations. Many undoubtedly did. Most people need to believe that policies desirable for the sake of political or economic interests are also in accord with deeply felt moral sentiments. People tend to avoid recognition of contradictions between interests and values by reinterpreting inconvenient facts so as to achieve harmony between them. Some portion of the U.S. foreign policy elite undoubtedly *did* understand the moral and political shortcomings of the KMT regime and the high level of popular support that the Communist regime in Beijing enjoyed. Such considerations, after all, had been the reason for the Truman-Marshall-Acheson policy of disengagement from the Nationalists in 1948–49. U.S. leaders such as Acheson and Marshall probably believed that the United States after 1950 was opposing a popular though highly repressive regime and was supporting an unpopular regime for membership in the United Nations. Yet even such realists endorsed on purely pragmatic grounds the policy of excluding the PRC from the United Nations.

The Questions of Diplomatic Recognition and United Nations Representation

Permanent membership on the UN Security Council institutionalized recognition by the world community of a nation's great-power status. It also provided governments thus honored with a forum for expanding and exercising influence. In addition, UN representation was closely tied to diplomatic recognition. While the two could theoretically be separated, and were in fact separated by seven years in the case of U.S.-PRC relations in the 1970s, for most countries acceptance of PRC membership in the UN led quickly and logically to the establishment of diplomatic relations.

The evolution of U.S. policy toward PRC membership in the UN paralleled the evolution of policy toward the PRC generally. The analysis that led to NSC 37/2 of February 1949 (which abandoned the Nationalists while calling for denying Taiwan to the CCP by diplomatic and economic means) explicitly rejected the notion of support of the Nationalist government "or a rump thereof" as the recognized government of China. This would be the worst option for the United States to pursue, according to the document.[1]

As Communist armies swept across southern China in mid-1949, the question of recognition of the new government became more pressing. U.S. allies in Europe, especially Britain, were inclined to recognize the new government rather quickly. Secretary of State Dean Acheson laid out his reasons for feeling such a course imprudent during a meeting with French and British representatives on 17 September 1949. The allied countries should move slowly, deliberately, and in close coordination with one another in recognizing the new Communist government, Acheson said. The United States considered it a matter of "utmost importance" that it not recognize the Communist government until it was in control of all of China. "We do not want to recognize them and thus acknowledge that they have won the war. We want events to dictate this," Acheson said.[2] Acheson wanted to wait until the PLA took over Taiwan, eliminating the Nationalist government and bringing all of China under its control. In this way, increasing vociferous Congressional critics of the administration could not charge that U.S. recognition of the Communists had led to the destruction of the Nationalists and takeover of Taiwan.

The PRC was not itself particularly interested in establishing diplomatic relations with the United States and other Western states during the first year of its existence. Mao Zedong advanced a policy of "cleaning up the house before inviting guests in," and proceeded to move against the imperialist presence in China. This policy was intended to convince Stalin of Mao's loyalty. Desiring Soviet economic and military support, Mao needed to disprove Stalin's suspicions about his "Titoist" tendencies, and thus could not afford to open ties to the imperialist powers until the PRC-USSR alliance was consolidated.[3]

As China moved into alliance with the USSR and proceeded to extirpate the U.S. economic, cultural, and political presence in China, prospects for U.S. recognition of the PRC faded. From the U.S. perspective, many of the PRC's actions were hostile and violations of international law. Given this, and with the rising chorus of domestic criticism of the Truman Administration's "softness" toward Communism, there was little incentive for Harry Truman to extend recognition and UN membership without a quid pro quo. North Korea's invasion of South Korea with Soviet and PRC support further diminished prospects for recognition. Yet, prior to Chinese entry into that war in November 1950, Washington showed flexibility on the question of UN representation. In a long cable to the U.S. Embassy in London two weeks after the North Korean attack, Acheson suggested that the question of Chinese representation in the United Nations might be dealt with once the fighting in Korea stopped.[4]

Once Chinese forces entered the Korean War, the U.S. position hardened. One of the key memoranda leading up to the authoritative NSC 48/5 of 17 May 1951 provided that the United States should continue to recognize the National Government of China "until the situation is further clarified," and that "it is clearly not in the United States interest" to recognize the PRC. Moreover, the United States should continue to explain to friendly governments the dangers of "hasty recognition of the Chinese Communist regime." Recognition and acceptance of PRC entry into the UN was to be withheld until Beijing's actions merited it. But the document also indicated that keeping the PRC out of the UN was *not* a top U.S. priority. The United States should not take a stand, the memo said, which would engage its prestige in an attempt to prevent recognition. It would be inappropriate for the United States to adopt a posture toward China more hostile than toward the USSR.[5] NSC 48/5 itself provided that "an acceptable political solution" to the Korean War was one that did "not jeopardize the U.S. position with respect to the USSR, to Formosa, or to seating Communist China in the U.N."[6]

The end of the Korean War led to greater international resistance to the U.S. policy of isolating the PRC by supporting the ROC. As an NSC report of July 1954 explained:

The United States has been successful in maintaining the position of [Nationalist] China in the UN and subsidiary bodies. However, this position is maintained with growing difficulty and with a larger accretion of resentment against the United States every time that diplomatic pressure to this end must be exerted. In order to maintain the position of the Chinese [Nationalist] Government among the ten large industrial states in the current session of the International Labor Organization [ILO], it was necessary for our Chief of Mission to make direct and forceful appeals to Foreign Offices all over the world. Many of the ILO delegates were critical of our efforts. There appears to be a slow ground swell of opinion against acceptance of the Chinese [Nationalist] Government as the Government of all China, on the grounds that it is unrealistic and not in accordance with the facts of the situation. There is a growing feeling that the Government in Taipei should be considered only as the Government of the Island of Formosa. The passage of time tends to reinforce this view.[7]

The PRC's participation in the Geneva Conference in early 1954 substantially boosted Beijing's international stature and correspondingly degraded that of Taipei. The Geneva Conference was the first direct, high-level contact between U.S. and PRC officials, aside from the armistice talks at Panmunjom. As such, the Geneva Conference came close to de facto U.S. recognition of the PRC. Moreover, by seating the PRC's representative alongside those of France, Britain, the USSR, and the United States to deal with the critical issues of Korea and Indochina, the conference tacitly recognized the PRC as one of the great powers and, by implication, as the rightful occupant of China's permanent seat on the Security Council.

Recognition of these consequences led Taipei to strongly oppose the Geneva Conference. U.S. leaders shared the Nationalist's apprehensions about the Geneva Conference's adverse impact on the ROC. An NSC report issued shortly after the conference confirmed that it had indeed damaged Taipei's standing. Beijing's performance at that conference, together with its broader pattern of moderate diplomatic activity, constituted a "Growth of Chinese Communist prestige [that was] a threat to the position of the GRC." China's participation at Geneva "signaled Communist China's emergence, after a period of relative quiescence, into the arena of international political affairs" with "a marked effort to acquire prestige and international acceptance, which has been pursued with vigor, persistence, flexibility, and considerable success." Among other successes were visits to the PRC by Prime Minister Clement Attlee, Prime Minister Jawaharlal Nehru, Prime Minister U Nu, and UN Secretary-General Dag Hammarskjold. The renegotiation of the terms of China's relation with the USSR in early 1954 also "had the effect of making Communist China appear to be the independent equal of the USSR." The report continued,

The immediate effect of these developments, as regards the GRC, will be to undercut international support for that government, and to make more difficult the maintenance of its position in the UN, seriously complicating the tasks of the US in this area. There is also likely to be increased pressure from our allies and from certain sectors of the American public and official opinion for an attempt to reach a comprehensive settlement with Communist China.[8]

In spite of these difficulties, NSC 5503, which was approved by Dwight Eisenhower in January 1955, provided that the United States would seek "Continued recognition and political support of the GRC as the only government of China and as the representative of China in the United Nations and other international bodies." This was reiterated verbatim in NSC 5723, which superseded NSC 5503 on 4 October 1957.

Maintaining Taipei's position as China's "only government" and representative in the UN raised new challenges during the late 1950s, as a large number of African countries gained independence. In many cases, the nationalism of these newly emerging countries was strongly tinged with anti-Westernism, which translated into sympathy toward the PRC. By 1958, this was becoming a major problem for Washington. The eruption of the Taiwan Strait crisis in August 1958 created further problems. In Western European capitals, Chiang Kai-shek's insistence on risking a major war over two small offshore islands seemed very unreasonable—as indeed it did in Washington. In Europe, however, dislike of Nationalist adventurousness was not balanced by appreciation of the positive contribution of Nationalist China in containing China. In the words of an NSC report, "There is still a disquieting lack of appreciation, even among our closest allies, of the significance of the GRC's role in our efforts to check and counteract the threat posed by Communist China's growing power."[9]

The United States took a number of moves to address this lack of allied understanding. According to an NSC report of 1959, Washington sought increased understanding and support of U.S. policy toward the GRC position by "discussion with Free World ambassadors, by direct approaches to friendly governments through our missions abroad, by periodic briefings of the North Atlantic Council and SEATO, by presentations to Congressional committees and leaders, and by other means."[10] The Dulles-Chiang communiqué of 23 October 1958 underscoring the GRC's determination to use political rather than military means to recover the mainland, was also intended, in part, to reassure and win over Western public and official opinion to the Nationalist cause. The State Department and the United States Information Agency (USIA) began studying ways of assisting the GRC to "establish a record of achievement to support its claim to be the true representative of the Chinese people and their civilization in contrast to Communist tyranny on the mainland," and to "obtain maximum world awareness of this record." The most dramatic demonstration of U.S. support for the GRC's international position came in June 1960 when President Eisenhower made the one and only visit by a serving U.S. president to Taiwan.

Countering Chinese Influence in the Developing Countries

During the latter half of the 1950s, Cold War rivalry in the developing world intensified. One reason for this was a shift in Communist doctrine and strategy toward the Third World. Following Joseph Stalin's death in 1953, Soviet and Chinese theoreticians scrapped their earlier condemnation of the moderate, non-Communist governments that emerged in many of the newly independent countries. Moscow and Beijing now began courting these "bourgeois nationalist" regimes as potentially progressive. This coincided with Soviet and Chinese interests in countering U.S. containment. In line with this, the USSR began extending economic assistance to strategic non-Communist countries in an effort to guide those countries along a "noncapitalist" path of development. The PRC soon followed Moscow's lead, adopting a large-scale foreign aid program of its own and actively courting non-Communist governments of developing countries. For the first couple of years, Beijing followed Moscow's lead. By the early 1960s, however, the CCP was touting a Maoist model of development as an alternative to the course proposed by the Communist Party of the Soviet Union.

U.S. leaders understood the new political awareness coursing through the newly independent countries, and increasingly saw the developing countries as a key battleground of the Cold War. As Eisenhower declared in his second inaugural address, in January 1957, "New forces and new nations were stirring across the earth . . . one-third of all mankind has entered an historic struggle for a new freedom: the freedom from poverty."[11] To counter the Sino-Soviet offensive in the developing world, Eisenhower sought and secured a substantial increase in foreign aid. U.S. foreign aid more than doubled between 1957 and 1960, reaching a record $822 million in 1960.[12] This money was not scattered widely across the Third World, but was concentrated in key countries of strategic political significance that were deemed able to effectively utilize large amounts of assistance. By concentrating U.S. and Western aid in a few target countries, the restricted availability of capital would effectively be removed as a bottleneck to development, allowing those countries to advance very rapidly and demonstrating what a country could do with market-oriented policies and cooperation with the West.

Taiwan and India were two main countries selected to become showcase "islands of development." Desire to counter Chinese Communist influence was one major factor behind this seemingly odd selection.[13] U.S. specialists saw India's success or failure in development as an important test case for development under liberal, democratic political institutions, especially when juxtaposed to the outcome of Communist China's development efforts. The outcome of this "race" would have a wide-ranging impact in the Third World, they believed. India, with its often anti-Western policies of nonalignment and its proclivities for Soviet-style economic planning, was not, however, popular in the U.S. Congress. Undersecretary of State Douglas Dillon persuaded Eisenhower (and by extension Congress) to accept India as a "showcase" country by agreeing to pick a second country more popular with Congressional Republicans. When aid officials selected Taiwan as that country, Eisenhower was delighted.[14]

Both Taiwan and India countered the appeal of the Chinese Communist model of development. In 1957, China began defining a distinctively Maoist development model, which claimed to achieve very rapid economic growth. Moreover, China began spending large sums of money to disseminate its model in Asia, in Africa, and in Latin America. Large quantities of cheap propaganda were turned out in dozens of foreign languages, while Chinese representatives assiduously courted radical nationalists across Asia and Africa. India and Taiwan were designated as showcases to counter Beijing's appeal. India was similar to China in many ways—large, populous, diverse, impoverished—but with a mixed economy and liberal democratic political institutions. Taiwan was of the same tradition of civilization as Communist China, but it too adopted market economics and non-Communist politics. If both India and Taiwan could outperform the PRC, the appeal of the Maoist model of development in the Third World would be substantially reduced.

Shortly after selection of Taiwan as a showcase, Undersecretary of State Dillon explained the significance of U.S. support for Taiwan's struggle for social and economic progress. Taiwan was "a kind of pilot plant where an ancient civilization and Western techniques are blending to produce a new way of life and a new promise," Dillon said. Taiwan's success in combining rapid economic and social advance with nonviolent change and non-Communist institutions was "beginning to exert a beneficial influence elsewhere in Asia by showing how a low-income area can move forward in freedom and, in the process, develop the needed momentum for sustained growth."[15]

While selecting Taiwan as a showcase to be supported by stepped-up aid, the U.S. government encouraged Taipei to propagandize Taiwan's achievements overseas. In April 1959, the USIA and the International Cooperation

Administration (ICA) completed a study of ways of assisting the GRC: "(1) to establish a record of achievement to support its claim to be the true representative of the Chinese people and their civilization in contrast to Communist tyranny on the mainland, and (2) to obtain maximum world awareness of this record."[16] Programs in the "scientific-educational-cultural field" were to be encouraged, and Taipei was informed that "we would give sympathetic consideration to a request for assistance in support of such measures as it may wish to propose in this field." In other words, U.S. government agencies told Taipei that the United States would help finance whatever it chose to do to publicize the achievements of Taiwan's development.

To some extent, U.S. encouragement of Nationalist political competition with the CCP was a U.S. effort to redirect Nationalist energies away from a *military* return to the mainland. The John Foster Dulles–Chiang Kai-shek communiqué of October 1958 underscored the Nationalist intention to recover the mainland principally by political rather than military means. Recognizing the intensity of Nationalist desires to return, and apprehensive of the demoralizing effects of quashing those desires too unequivocally, Washington tried to channel them into what the United States regarded as less dangerous directions.

Africa was a major arena of PRC-ROC rivalry, in which the Taiwan model was especially useful. As PRC foreign policy became more militant in late 1958, Beijing looked to Africa as a region with excellent prospects for revolution. CCP activities in Africa increased dramatically.[17] Taipei countered Beijing's revolutionary activism with anti-Communist activism focusing on agricultural development. In this area, Taiwan had achieved impressive results in the 1950s. Now Taipei began to disseminate its experience to Africa. Between 1962 and 1969, Taipei signed economic and technical cooperation agreements with twenty-three African countries. Eight sub-Saharan heads of state visited the ROC during the same period. Agricultural demonstration teams were dispatched to twenty-two countries beginning with one to Liberia in November 1961. These teams demonstrated methods of land reclamation, new crops, new tools, and new methods of cultivation. They also conducted experiments to test new crops and farming methods. New varieties of rice were introduced into Africa. ROC specialists set up extension services to popularize new methods. Extensive new irrigation works were opened, including 172 pumping stations and over a million miles of irrigation canals by 1971.[18]

U.S. leaders believed that these activities made an important contribution to countering Communist influence in Africa. When Secretary of State Dean Rusk visited Taipei in April 1964 for talks with Chiang Kai-shek and other Nationalist leaders, he lauded ROC agricultural and technical cooperation activities in Africa and Latin America. "I think you should continue this important work," Rusk said. "In fact, I would say, the more the better." "These visits, especially those to African countries, are exceedingly important," Rusk told Chiang, "because officials in most of these newly independent countries are inexperienced in international affairs." "We will do our best," Chiang promised.[19]

The Chinese communities in Southeast Asia were another constituency targeted for Nationalist Chinese attention as a way of undercutting Communist Chinese influence. In the 1950s, there were between eleven and thirteen million ethnic Chinese in Southeast Asia. In several countries, these "overseas Chinese" controlled substantial wealth, which they might use, if they chose, for purposes antithetical to U.S. policy interests. They might, for example, use their wealth to foster the economic development of the PRC, or to support revolutionary movements within their host countries. Ethnic Chinese played a major role in the insurgency in Malaya in the late 1940s and the early 1950s.

As an NSC study of November 1953 noted, while the pre–World War II colonial empires of Southeast Asia had been quite happy to have large minorities of unassimilated Chinese, the newly independent states that replaced those empires found this situation threatening. Meanwhile, according to the NSC study, Beijing was attempting to convert the overseas Chinese into fifth columns against the countries in which they dwell. In such a situation, "The Chinese National Government can play an effective role as a political counter weight to Chinese Communist influence." This would have to be done in a manner that took account of the nationalist sentiments of the Southeast Asian nations, however. Otherwise Nationalist activities might do "considerable harm." If approached in the appropriate manner, "The Chinese National Government can realize substantial benefits by way of political and financial support from these overseas Chinese groups, while simultaneously lessening the Communist capability of utilizing the overseas Chinese for subversive purposes. U.S. objectives would then be fostered by encouraging the Chinese Nationalist Government to take an active, though discreet, interest in overseas Chinese affairs."[20] NSC 146/2 of November 1953 itself provided that the United States would, "To the extent feasible, encourage the Chinese National Government to establish closer contact with the Chinese communities outside mainland China and Formosa and to take steps to win their sympathy and their support to the extent consistent with their obligations and primary allegiance to their local governments."[21] The same formulation was used in NSC 5503 of 1955.

The first report on the implementation of NSC 5503 said that the ICA had helped the GRC plan and implement a program of encouraging overseas Chinese students to go to Taiwan for education. Several years later, another report judged successful a program encouraging overseas Chinese to study in Taiwan. By 1959, about 7,000 overseas Chinese were studying in Taiwan, with 600 expected to graduate that year.[22] The USIA also directed materials at the overseas Chinese designed to promote opposition to Communism and, "where feasible and desirable to facilitate the efforts of the GRC to appeal to overseas Chinese loyalties."[23]

It is impossible to measure the effect of joint U.S.-ROC efforts to counter the appeal of Communism in Africa and Southeast Asia. From one perspective, it is hard to point to a tangible result from what must have been tens of millions of U.S. taxpayers' dollars spent on these programs. On the other hand, it is equally plausible that Taiwan's agricultural demonstration teams helped some African countries avoid the sort of calamity via Marxist takeover that befell Ethiopia, Mozambique, and Angola in the 1970s. It is also likely that the example of Taiwan and the practical development-oriented advice dispensed by Nationalist advisers contributed to the developmental successes and the fading appeal of Communism in the Southeast Asian countries in the 1970s and 1980s. Militant leftism *was* a significant force among the Chinese communities in Southeast Asia in the 1950s and 1960s. The Malaya insurgency was mentioned earlier. Singapore had a strong militant left labor movement aligned with a militant left wing of the People's Action Party (until that party split in 1961). This strong radical movement deeply influenced Singapore politics, including its entry into Malaysia in 1963. In Indonesia, the Communist Party drew wide support from ethnic Chinese. The Party's influence expanded steadily throughout the early 1960s until it was on the verge of taking power. Ultimately, of course, these leftist forces were defeated, and most of the countries of Southeast Asia developed along rather different political-economic lines. Certainly the exercise of U.S. influence was one factor in shaping that outcome. Nationalist China was one instrument of U.S. influence—not, perhaps, a major instrument, but still a significant one.

Notes

1. "Draft Report by the NSC on the Position of the U.S. with Respect to Formosa," 19 January 1949.

2. *FRUS,* 1949, vol. IX, p. 90.

3. Regarding the policy of "cleaning house before inviting guests in" and the impact of Stalin's suspicions of Mao on early PRC policy toward the United States, see Sergei N. Goncharov, John W. Lewis, and Xue Litai, *Uncertain Partners: Stalin, Mao, and the Korean War,* Stanford, CA: Stanford University Press, 1993.

4. Dean Acheson to London Embassy, 10 July 1950, in *FRUS*, 1950, vol. VII, p. 349.

5. NSC 48/2, 30 December 1950. (The National Archives document is dated 1949, but this must be a typo. The correct date is probably 30 December 1950.) Consideration of the NSC 48 series began after the Korean War began and culminated in NSC 48/5, approved by the NSC and Truman on 17 May 1951, National Archives.

6. NSC 48/5, 17 May 1951, National Archives.

7. Progress Report on NSC 146/2, 16 July 1954, National Archives.

8. Progress report on NSC 146/2, 16 February 1955, National Archives.

9. NSC Operations Coordinating Board (OCB) report on implementation of NSC 5723, 15 April 1959, National Archives.

10. Ibid.

11. Quoted in Dennis Kux, *India and the United States: Estranged Democracies, 1941–1991* (hereafter cited as Kux, *Estranged Democracies*), Fort Lesley McNair, Washington: National Defense University Press, 1992, p. 144.

12. Ibid, p. 150.

13. See Robert A. Packenham, *Liberal America and the Third World; Political Development Ideas in Foreign Aid and Social Science,* Princeton, NJ: Princeton University Press, 1973; and W.W. Rostow, *Eisenhower, Kennedy, and Foreign Aid,* Austin, TX: University of Texas Press, 1985.

14. See Kux, *Estranged Democracies,* p. 175, note 41.

15. Douglas Dillon, "Cooperating with Free Asia for Social and Economic Progress," address before the International Social Service Association, 13 November 1959, printed in *Department of State Bulletin,* 30 November 1959, pp. 779–81.

16. OCB report on implementation of NSC 5723, 15 April 1959, National Archives.

17. John W. Garver, *Foreign Relations of the People's Republic of China,* New York: Prentice Hall, 1993, pp. 141–47. Bruce D. Larkin, *China and Africa, 1949–1970,* Berkeley: University of California Press, 1971. Philip Snow, *Star Raft, China's Encounter with Africa,* Ithaca, NY: Cornell University Press, 1988.

18. Wei Liang-Tsai, *Peking Versus Taipei in Africa, 1960–1978,* Asia and World Monograph Series, no. 28 (April 1982), Taipei: Asia and World Institute, 1982, p. 307.

19. Record of meeting, Dean Rusk with Chiang Kai-shek, 16 April 1964, Ministry of Foreign Affairs, Taipei Archive no. 412.2, 22, 300, bei mi ci 77.

20. NSC staff study attached to NSC 146/2, 6 November 1953, in *FRUS,* 1952–54, vol. XIV, part 1, p. 317.

21. *FRUS,* 1952–54, vol. XIV, part 1, p. 309.

22. OCB report on implementation of NSC 5723, 15 April 1959, National Archives.

23. Ibid.

13

U.S. Policy and
the Taiwan Model

Free China as a Model

During the 1950s, Taiwan emerged as a U.S.-extolled model of non-Communist development. U.S. leaders invested considerable resources in making that model successful, in the expectation that the Free China model would play a significant role in the struggle against Communism throughout the developing world. They also hoped that that model would play a role in persuading the Chinese on the mainland to eventually abandon Communism.

While U.S. efforts to reform Taiwan's society began during 1950, indication of appreciation of the political utility of a Taiwan model is *not* found in the top-level decision documents of the Truman Administration. While Truman Administration requests for economic aid for Taiwan were justified, in part, by broad references to promoting freedom and democracy, this justification was not operationalized into policy during the Truman years. The deep skepticism of Harry S. Truman, George C. Marshall, and Dean Acheson about Chiang Kai-shek's regime apparently precluded any calculated effort to shape Taiwan's political economic evolution. Within a short time, however, this idea emerged. An article in the July 1952 issue of *Foreign Affairs,* for instance, elaborated at considerable length on the potential appeal of the Free China Model.[1] The "harsh realities" of CCP rule over the mainland had shattered the illusion of "New Democracy" under which the CCP had seized power. The "essential questions for all Chinese" was now whether Taiwan would be able to combine the positive elements of Chinese civilization with economic development, democracy, and the rule of law. If it was, this would have great appeal to many Chinese, the article maintained.

These ideas were translated into policy during the first year of the administration of President Dwight D. Eisenhower. NSC 146/2 of November 1953 ranked as the second objective of the United States toward Taiwan encouragement of "An increasingly efficient Chinese National Government, evolving toward responsible representative government and capable of attracting growing support and allegiance from the people of mainland China and Formosa."[2] To this end, the United States would "strive to make clear to the Chinese National Government that its future depends primarily upon its own political and economic efforts and upon its ability to command the respect and support of the Chinese people." The United States would also encourage the Nationalists to enhance their government's "political appeal" and "administrative efficiency." Development of an efficient, progressive-minded, and increasingly democratic government on Taiwan would attract "growing support and allegiance from the people of mainland China and Formosa."

NSC 5503 of January 1955 repeated this phraseology and ranking regarding the Taiwan model. It also added a distinctively economic component to the emerging Taiwan model by providing that U.S. policy would "encourage the GRC to adopt policies which will stimulate the investment of Chinese and other private capital and skills for the development of the Formosa economy, under arrangements avoiding 'exploitation' yet acceptable to private interests."[3] Throughout the remainder of the 1950s, the United States encouraged the evolution on Taiwan of a liberal, democratic political system and a prosperous, developed, capitalist economic system. Taiwan was to become "Free China," in the political rhetoric of the day, serving as a model for Chinese in Southeast, Asia, in North America, and in China itself. The appeal of Free China would diminish the support of those communities for Communist China, and would harness that support instead to the anti-Communist effort.

"Free China" then was not free, but a highly repressive authoritarian state. As a National Intelligence Estimate (NIE) of September 1954 reported, Nationalist China was "in essence a one-party state; authority is centralized in the hands of a few, and ultimate political power resides in the hands of Chiang Kai-shek."[4] Although a series of political and economic reforms that ultimately contributed to Taiwan's democratization did begin in the early 1950s, and although progress toward *political* liberalization began in the early 1970s, as late as the mid-1980s Taiwan remained an authoritarian, nondemocratic state. It was not until the late 1980s—well after the end of the U.S.-Nationalist alliance—that Taiwan made the transition to a liberal and democratic political system.

In what sense, then, did U.S. policy contribute to that eventual transition? To what extent did the United States act to further the goals laid out in NSC 146/2 and NSC 5503? To what extent did those formal goals actually guide U.S. behavior, and to what extent was U.S. influence used to push Taiwan in the direction of liberal, democratic, and prosperous capitalism? While a proper answer to this question carries us beyond the period of the U.S.-Nationalist alliance, it is warranted because the reforms implemented under U.S. sponsorship in the 1950s and 1960s came to political fruition only several decades later. The evolution of a country from one political system to another takes decades, and to understand the impact of U.S. policies designed to accomplish such a transition, it is necessary to take a long view.

Rural Reconstruction and U.S. Influence

The United States played a major role in the process of land reform and rural development in Taiwan in the 1950s and the early 1960s—a process that contributed substantially to Taiwan's democratic political evolution. U.S. personnel played direct and important roles in formulation of rural development policy, while U.S. aid funding greatly facilitated implementation of these policies. The Joint Commission on Rural Reconstruction (JCRR) was the major instrument of U.S. influence on Taiwan's rural reconstruction. Set up in 1948 in implementation of the China Aid Act, it was a joint Chinese-American organization, operating under the authority and supervision of both governments, with commissioners appointed by the chief executives of the two countries and a binational staff hired by those commissioners. It transferred its operations to Taiwan in August 1949. Funding for JCRR operations came almost entirely from U.S. aid funds; it had been set up to disperse the agricultural component of those funds. While operating under the control of the ROC and U.S. governments, the JCRR enjoyed considerable autonomy. On the Chinese side, it reported only to the premier. On the American side, the JCRR operated with a high degree of independence of the U.S. aid establishment. In effect, both the U.S. and the ROC governments agreed to give the JCRR a high degree of independence and autonomy, and both held to this agreement.

The JCRR exercised a great, even decisive, influence on ROC rural policy. It crafted policies for submission to the government, which generally viewed the proposals favorably. It played a leading role in organizing and coordinating programs for dispensing U.S. aid funds to rural areas. It reviewed and approved particular project proposals, and supervised their execution. The projects were generally implemented by the Agriculture Department of the Taiwan provincial government.

The JCRR pursued two key objectives: increasing agricultural production, and promoting social justice. Regarding the second goal, the JCRR sought primarily the creation of an agricultural system based on farmer owners, reduction of the gap between rich and poor in the countryside, and active and deep involvement of ordinary farmers in the process of rural reconstruction and development. The JCRR encouraged local initiation and direction over the development process.[5]

During the period 1949–53, the JCRR concentrated on a sweeping land reform. In 1949, half of Taiwan's farm workers were tenant sharecroppers paying up to 60 percent of their crops in rent to landowners. The impact of land reform was far-reaching. The social and economic power of the land-lord class in the countryside was overturned. Most of Taiwan's farmland was now worked by owner operators. This created powerful incentives for farmers to utilize the scientific inputs into agriculture now being proffered by state agencies in cooperation with the JCRR. Land reform combined with a proliferation of small-scale industry in the rural areas promoted by the pro–private enterprise and pro–export promotion policies to lay the basis for rural prosperity. This in turn, helped to minimize the urban-rural gap that plagued other developing societies. Potential agrarian radicalism dissipated. Instead, Taiwan's farmers became closely tied to the goodwill of the regime through the new instruments of government assistance established under JCRR sponsorship. Finally, farmers were given a measure of economic independence and security which encouraged their participation in local self-government.

Overlapping with land reform was the creation of a system of grass-roots self-government in the countryside. Japanese authorities had set up the village Farmers Association to provide an intermediary between farmers and local officials. In 1949 the JCRR proposed, and again Governor Chen Cheng quickly agreed to, a systematic democratization of these associations. At the village level, various institutions were merged with the local Farmers Associations, and the expanded overall association was assigned important roles in managing critical functions such as irrigation, marketing, health, provision of credit (previously supplied by the landlords), operating rice and feed mills, supplying livestock, crop insurance, and so on. At the village level, farmers elected representatives, who in turn named a board of directors and supervisors. Above the village level, representatives and directors were elected by the level immediately below. Two-thirds of repre-

sentatives, directors, and supervisors had to be tenant farmers, owner-opera-
tors, or farm workers—a provision intended to prevent the return to dominance of the former landowners. The number of Farmers Associations
expanded steadily until, by the late 1970s, there were 4,515 village associations encompassing 950,000 households as members.[6]

Again, these reforms had a deep impact on Taiwan's long-term political
evolution. Farm Association elections were generally competitive and hon-
est, and they involved direct participation of ordinary farmers at the village
level. Moreover, these democratically elected representatives of the people
exercised real, if strictly parochial, powers. This had two major political
consequences. First, it gave rise to a tradition of fair, competitive elections
among Taiwan's ordinary people. Through this grass-roots democracy, people who previously had had no experience with government based on popular election gradually became familiar with the workings and logic of
democracy. This contributed, in an important if imperceptible way, to the
popular demand for an expansion of democracy at the county and provincial
levels—a demand that began to grow strong in the 1970s. The practice of
grass-roots democracy also forced the Kuomintang (KMT) to develop electoral skills and find ways of appealing to the people. While failure of
KMT-endorsed representatives to win positions in Farmers Associations in
no way challenged the party's dominance, it did look bad for local party
leaders or, if too many party candidates lost, for the party as a whole. Thus
the party was forced to acquire the requisite electoral skills. This in turn
gave party officials the confidence that they could win elections, as Taiwan
began moving gradually toward a two-party system in the 1970s.[7]

The U.S. role in the process of rural reform should not, of course, be
exaggerated. Since the focus of this book is on U.S.-Nationalist relations,
we have concentrated here on only one aspect of a complicated process.
Certainly the major dynamics of Taiwan's rural reconstruction had to do
with factors largely unrelated to the United States. Having suffered the
trauma of defeat on the mainland, the Nationalist elite understood that a
major reason for that outcome had been their failure to win support at the
village level. They resolved not to repeat this mistake on Taiwan. This
dovetailed with the Nationalist determination to turn Taiwan into a stable,
secure base for return to the mainland. Most important, perhaps, the fact
that the Nationalist elite had few links with Taiwan's landowning class—or
indeed with the Taiwanese populace generally—facilitated that elite's imposition of policies predicated on long-term goals that were antithetical to
the social-economic interests of Taiwanese landowners.[8] While we recognize the primacy of these and other domestic factors, the significant contribution played by U.S. influence should not be overlooked.

The U.S. Economic Assistance Effort

Large-scale economic aid was another instrument used by the United States to nudge Taiwan in the direction of liberal democracy. U.S. economic assistance to Nationalist Formosa began in 1950 and continued through 1965, when Taiwan was deemed developed enough to "graduate" from dependency on U.S. aid. Taiwan was the sixth-largest recipient of U.S. economic assistance to developing countries during the years 1945–65. During those years, a total of $2,236 million was obligated in aid to Taiwan, making a yearly average of $113.15 million.[9] U.S. aid provided 34 percent of Taiwan's total gross investment, and roughly 13 percent of all investment in industry, 18 percent of all investment in human resources, 59 percent of all investment in agriculture, and 74 percent of all investment in infrastructure.[10] Not only was U.S. aid large-scale, it was extended on generous terms. A full 82.5 percent came in the form of nonrepayable grants, 11 percent was in soft loans repayable in Taiwan dollars, and the final 6 percent was in soft loans repayable in U.S. dollars.

There is wide agreement among those who have studied the transitions to democracy in the 1970s and the 1980s, both in Taiwan and elsewhere, that a fairly high level of economic development was a necessary if not a sufficient condition for these transitions.[11] Per capita income in Taiwan increased rapidly, giving people the personal security, confidence, inclination, leisure, and ability to pay increased attention to public affairs. The social structure became increasingly complex with the emergence of a large industrial proletariat, along with a large middle class including autonomous professionals, a Westernized intelligentsia, and a new elite of Taiwanese entrepreneurs. Most people were well educated and healthy. Relative and steadily increasing prosperity, together with the absence of deep social cleavages, plus the external threat from the PRC, combined to foster a nonviolent, incremental, and moderate approach to demands for increased democracy. The relatively moderate and pragmatic nature of the opposition, in turn, encouraged Chiang Ching-kuo to conclude that the KMT could work with, and perhaps even eventually share power with, the oppositionists.[12] Development of transportation and telecommunications brought Taiwan into closer contact with foreign ways, ideas, and public opinion. While these conditions did not lead directly to demands for greater democracy, or to KMT acceptance of those demands, they were important preconditions for democratization.

Was U.S. economic assistance to Taiwan intended to foster the emergence of "responsible representative government"? Neil Jacoby calculated that seven-eighths of all U.S. aid appropriations were justified to the U.S.

Congress on the grounds of *military preparedness*—to allow Taiwan to maintain an agreed-upon level of military forces without adversely affecting Taiwan's economy. Only one-eighth of U.S. aid to Taiwan, Jacoby found, was justified on the basis of the social-economic development, let alone the democratization, of Taiwan. Only in 1958 did Congress establish a fund for loans to capital projects in Taiwan.[13] Since Congress has the power of the purse in the U.S. system, it would thus seem that Congress spent U.S. monies *not* primarily to foster Taiwan's development, economic, social, or political, but to enhance *U.S.* national security and, implicitly, to ease the burden of conscription on the American population. NSC decision-making memoranda cited at the beginning of this chapter indicate, however, that top officials in the *executive branch* indisputably *were* motivated by a desire to direct Taiwan's development along liberal, democratic lines. Moreover, Jacoby argues that U.S. aid officials in Taiwan shared such concerns. While the overwhelming bulk of U.S. aid funds was appropriated for military-related purposes, the U.S. aid mission to Taiwan utilized those funds quite liberally to fund *development* projects. U.S. aid officials in Taiwan were inspired, Jacoby says, by a desire to foster social and economic development.

Jacoby suggests that, since U.S. senators and Congress members were understandably reluctant to spend the dollars of U.S. taxpayers for such altruistic purposes as fostering development in other countries, aid officials relied on more politically marketable arguments of self-interest to secure the requisite aid appropriations. Executive branch aid officials "produced a certain amount of deception by financing development behind a facade of Defense Support," according to Jacoby.[14] Thus, a complex answer is required to answer the question of whether U.S. aid to Taiwan was intended to foster development, liberalization, and ultimate democratization. At the top level of the executive branch, such aid was indisputably meant to foster these goals. From the standpoint of U.S. aid officials in Taiwan, social-economic development was the objective, and democratization was seen as the probable culmination of that process of development. For Congress, however, the primary objective of the aid program seems to have been related to national security considerations—at least in the 1950s.

During the 1950s, the development of modernization theory in the United States provided a new framework for thinking about the relationship between aid, development, and democratization.[15] U.S. aid was increasingly seen within the context of overall modernization of societies. Appropriate amounts and types of aid could provide a critical catalyst for economic development, modernization theorists said. Social and political development would necessarily accompany change in the economic structure. Liberal democracy was *not* seen as the inevitable outcome of modernization; indeed, the modernization reconceptualization of U.S. aid in 1957–58 was, in part, a clarion call for the United States to do more to prevent developing countries from taking the Communist path of development and moving *away* from liberal democracy. There was no simple or automatic relationship between economic development and political democracy, the developmental theorists-critics said. They did maintain, however, that a country focusing its energies, talents, and resources on peaceful development (as opposed to revolution) was likely to maximize prospects for emergence of a government increasingly responsive to the will of the governed. Moreover, the proper sort of economic development could foster the emergence of new elites, prevent polarizing divisions of society, and create self-confidence at the grassroots level—all of which might contribute to the eventual democratization of politics.[16]

Regarding Taiwan, U.S. aid officials played an important role in shaping policies that created the conditions for democratization of Taiwan. The most crucial of the policy choices in which the United States played a pivotal role were the interrelated decisions in the late 1950s to foster the development of Taiwan's private sector and to shift from a strategy of import substitution to export promotion. Throughout the 1950s, the public sector dominated Taiwan's economy. With the Nationalist takeover of Taiwan from Japan in 1945, Japanese-owned properties, which included most large-scale industry, had been nationalized. By 1951, 55 percent of Taiwan's industrial production, along with virtually all infrastructure, was state-owned.[17] Powerful forces within the Nationalist elite favored continued reliance on the public sector, and were hostile to private enterprise for both ideological and institutional reasons.[18] In terms of institutional and personal interests, a large number of the Nationalist elite that fled to Taiwan in 1949–50 had worked in public sector enterprises on the mainland and now occupied similar positions in Taiwan's public sector.[19] Chiang Kai-shek and other military leaders who favored an early return to the mainland also inclined toward reliance on the public sector, since this seemed best suited to mobilizing the economy for war. Finally, but by no means least importantly, the question of fostering the private sector was linked to the emergence of an economic elite among the native Taiwanese. Mainlander Nationalists dominated and ran the public sector. If private investment and enterprise were allowed to flourish, much of it would be in the hands of Taiwanese who might begin to use their newly acquired economic power for political ends. This would draw into question both the "sacred mission" of return to the mainland and undermine Nationalist Party's monopoly on political power. Until 1958, Chiang Kai-shek served as the leader of the pro–state enterprise coalition.[20]

Opposed to the pro–state sector forces was a group of "industrializing reformers," who favored strengthening the private sector. Led politically by Premier Chen Cheng and inspired by a small cortege of pro-development mainlander technocrats, the reformers favored using an array of government incentives to encourage private industry, relying on both former mainlanders and native Taiwanese entrepreneurs.[21]

U.S. aid officials, and U.S. aid itself, were major allies of the industrializing reformers. U.S. aid officials consistently supported encouragement of private investment in a wide range of industries.[22] State enterprises, with their costly subsidies from off-budget funds, were the bête noire of U.S. aid officials.[23] The U.S.-preferred strategy was not to channel aid funds directly to private enterprises, but to use aid funds to develop the infrastructure and the human and agricultural resources that could support private industry. Government would then abstain from expanding into new industries, and would instead provide incentives for private businesses, domestic and foreign, to do so.[24]

Until the late 1950s, the reformers were unable to set overall economic policy. Yet they were able to use access to U.S. aid, preferential loans, and access to foreign exchange to encourage the development of the private industrial sector. Four-fifths of U.S. assistance to capital development projects went into private enterprises.[25]

Conflict between the pro–state enterprise conservatives and the U.S.-supported industrializing reformers became intense during the late 1950s. During the early 1950s, such conflict had been lessened by the reformers' recognition that rehabilitation of existing plant facility and expansion of the transport, communications, and energy infrastructure were top priorities, and that these tasks required heavy investment in the public sector. By the mid-1950s, however, Taiwan's reformers and their U.S. allies believed that these preliminary tasks had been accomplished and that broad encouragement of industrialization was now in order. Earlier efforts to expand Taiwan's private sector were also reaching the limits of their effectiveness. Taxes were too heavy, investment licensing procedures were too complex, and limits on the private acquisition of land for plant sites were too stringent —or so U.S. aid advisers and their reformist allies felt. Domestic markets were also increasingly saturated, resulting in slowing growth and calls by established industry for stricter limitations on further investment.

The well-reasoned support of U.S. aid officials, along with U.S. offers of expanded aid if Taiwan adopted U.S. advice, gave the reformers crucial support. Early in 1958, Chiang Kai-shek switched sides in the debate over state versus private enterprise, and endorsed the reformist program of liberalization of trade and exchange controls. Chiang's shift led to the resignation of several key conservative officials. Strong urging by U.S. aid officials, along with Chiang's understanding of the recent shift in U.S. aid policy, was an important factor in Chiang's realignment.[26]

Taiwan's economic reform process deepened in 1959, with direct, high-level intercession by the United States. In that year, Undersecretary of State C. Douglas Dillon and Deputy Director of the International Cooperation Administration Leonard Saccio traveled separately to Taiwan to convey the message that the United States was willing to consider further increases in aid to Taiwan if the ROC government adopted a program of accelerated private sector–oriented development. In December 1959, the head of the U.S. aid mission to Taiwan, Wesley C. Haraldson, forwarded to the ROC government an appropriate program of accelerated development. Ten days later, Haraldson met with Premier Chen Cheng and his economic advisers to discuss the plan and explain that while U.S. economic assistance was declining globally, Washington had decided to "showcase" a limited number of countries, increasing their growth and demonstrating the superiority of market systems over Communist ones. Taiwan was on the list of possible "showcases," Haraldson explained, because of its good previous performance. To convince the U.S. Congress that tax dollars would be well-spent, however, it would be necessary to adopt a program of liberalizing reform.[27]

Haraldson's reform program encountered strong opposition from Nationalist conservatives. Eventually, Chiang Kai-shek accepted it, largely on the grounds that it would increase Nationalist independence and self-reliance by generating a flow of foreign currency. After Chiang's approval, the reform program was revised and expanded by Taiwan's reformers. It had a wide-ranging and long-term impact, moving Taiwan toward encouragement of private enterprise, both domestic and foreign, and toward export promotion.[28]

With U.S. encouragement and assistance, Taiwan's private sector grew rapidly, jumping from 40.3 percent of total manufacturing value in 1946 to 86.2 percent in 1973.[29] The United States played a key role in this process.

The private enterprise and export promotion orientation of the Taiwan economy was pushed through by a strong transnational coalition of industrializing reformers within the ROC government and U.S. aid officials in Taiwan and Washington.[30] U.S. arguments and data were conveyed by the reformist technocrats into the broader forums of the ROC government. U.S. aid officials sat in on the meetings of key ROC economic planning and policy-making bodies, actively participating in the proceedings both formally and informally. Meetings were often held in English to facilitate participation by U.S. aid officials.[31] The primary instrument of influence by U.S. aid officials was analysis, written and oral, substantiating U.S. policy preferences. Only very occasionally (on such issues as the cuts in the military budget in 1960, which U.S. aid officials favored) did U.S. aid officials threaten to cut aid if U.S. views were not adopted. Far more frequent and far more important were analytical evaluations by the independent consulting firm J.R. White, which marshaled fact and argument in favor of the U.S. position on such issues as currency exchange, taxation, central banking, and housing. There was a broad convergence of views and interests among U.S. aid officials and ROC reformers, and, through a process of sustained personal contact and interaction, the U.S. side gained increased familiarity with Taiwan's economy, while the Chinese side became increasingly familiar with U.S. views about management and enterprise. Mutual understanding and confidence grew. The relation between Taiwan's reformers and U.S. aid officials was extremely close—the closest possible relation between two independent governments, in Neil Jacoby's words.[32]

Another critical aspect of the success of economic reform in Taiwan had to do with the unusual organizational independence the reformers enjoyed within the ROC governmental structure—an independence due, in part, to American support. The reformers were based in and worked through a series of highly autonomous organizations within the GRC state structure. Because the operational and project funds of these organizations came from U.S. aid, those monies were not part of the regular budgetary process of the ROC government and did not require legislative approval. The reformist organizations were also not subject to regular Chinese civil service regulations, a fact related to their financial independence which made it possible for them to pay salaries substantially higher than those received by regular civil servants. This enabled them to recruit and retain top-level staff, and to cultivate a strong sense of esprit de corps. Such organizational autonomy greatly facilitated the politically unpopular private sector development efforts of the reformers. Thus, while the ROC government was not strongly disposed to develop the private sector during the period 1951–57, reformers were able to use U.S. aid funds to help rehabilitate and expand many private industries. Organizational autonomy also facilitated the continuity of personnel and the development of a close relationship between ROC reformers and U.S. aid officials. Most important, perhaps, the organizational autonomy of the reformers made it possible for them to champion long-term development plans, ignoring, to a substantial degree, the demands of various established interests. According to several scholars, this autonomy from societal demands was crucial to the successful course of reform in Taiwan.[33] From the perspective of this study, what is most important is that this autonomy was linked to a steady and large flow of U.S. aid funds. According to Thomas Gold, U.S. involvement was crucial to producing the development-oriented "revolution from above" that transformed and modernized Taiwan.[34]

As Nationalist conservatives had feared, emphasis on the private sector soon gave rise to a native *Taiwanese* elite. By the mid-1960s, 60 percent of the economy was in private hands *and* 80 percent of private entrepreneurs were Taiwanese. Economic interests and social status soon translated into political activity. Taiwanese businessmen necessarily maintained close contact with Nationalist officials, thereby creating a symbiotic relation. A substantial number of Taiwanese businessmen were enticed to join the KMT, beginning the process of Taiwanization of that party. A few stood for election to local offices, sometimes as KMT candidates but more frequently as non–National Party candidates. The most prominent of these was Kao Yu-shu, who was elected major of Taipei in 1964. More frequently than they ran for office, well-to-do Taiwanese businessmen contributed money to support the activities of other, less risk-averse Taiwanese politicians and activists. Political pressure for expanded political freedom began to build.[35]

U.S. Aid and Democracy on Taiwan

The United States did *not* use its massive aid program to pressure the Nationalist government to adopt sweeping political reforms.[36] The period of U.S. aid to Taiwan coincided with that island's period of hard authoritarianism. Only after U.S. aid ended did Taiwan begin moving toward political liberalization. Some scholars have concluded from this that U.S. aid supported, indeed made possible, the hard authoritarianism of the Nationalists. We will consider this proposition below, but first it is necessary to investigate how U.S. officials understood the relationship between U.S. aid and democratization.

One major reason U.S. leaders decided against using aid as political leverage was a belief that attempted exercise of such leverage would backfire; would alienate the Nationalist elite; and would undermine the Nationalist government, possibly encouraging defection to the CCP rather than resulting in the desired political liberalization. The analysis backing up NSC 146/2 of November 1953, for instance, argued that while the United States sought to increase the "appeal" of the Nationalist government, it could not do this by intervention and supervision. The Nationalist government sought independence and self-reliance, the memo said, and "merely tolerates controls and supervision by U.S. advisers as the price of receiving aid." Dependency on a foreign power "is most unpalatable to any people, especially to the Chinese who for centuries have regarded themselves as a superior race," the NSC analysis said. A combination of dependency and the Chinese sense of superiority "cannot help but breed resentment against the aid giver." Thus, "The Chinese become particularly sensitive to any kind of advice or suggestion made on a high level, especially when this becomes public knowledge." Since aid-leveraged pressure for political reform was likely to create resentment, it would probably not produce the desired results: "Presentation of a blanket political reform program would rouse the deep suspicions of the [Nationalist] leadership and could not be implemented without large-scale U.S. intervention; such intervention would tend to nullify the advantages of any reform it might achieve by giving Formosa the appearance of a U.S. colony rather than the seat of a regenerate Chinese government."[37]

While ruling out "presentation of a blanket political reform program," the analysis underlying NSC 146/2 said that progress toward political reform on Taiwan should be approached on an "empirical basis, involving careful selection of individual problems based on an analysis of the importance of the solution of the problem to increasing both the efficiency of the Government and its political appeal to the Chinese people." U.S. officials should persuade Nationalist leaders that their own self-interest required specific reforms, rather than threatening to reduce aid if U.S. advice was not taken.[38]

Several actions by top U.S. officials in 1953 illustrate this "empirical" approach. In June 1953, the newly appointed chairman of the Joint Chiefs of Staff, Admiral Arthur Radford, traveled to Taiwan for talks with Chiang Kai-shek. During those discussions, Radford urged the easing of entry and exit controls for travel to and from Taiwan, along with a reduction of political indoctrination in the military. Radford told Chiang that there was a "widening impression" in the United States that the ROC was a "police state." Chiang replied that entry and exit controls had already been eased, and promised that further liberalization would be forthcoming. He insisted that the threat of Communist infiltration "made it necessary to retain considerable control." The summary of the conversation by the chargé d'affaires of the U.S. Embassy in Taipei concluded that Radford's "frank and forceful review of certain shortcomings of the Chinese administration from the American point of view served notice that police state tendencies would have to be held in check, if not abated, here to retain effective support of even the most ardent friends of Free China."[39]

During his visit, Radford also met with General Chiang Ching-kuo, Chiang Kai-shek's son, who was in charge of the political control system in military and internal security affairs. Radford invited Chiang to undertake an extended visit to the United States "to gain an appreciation of the nature and significance of American public opinion and an understanding of the way in which a strong democratic government solves [internal security] problems similar to those which face Free China."[40] Chiang Ching-kuo accepted Radford's invitation, and later in 1953, he toured the United

States. This visit was itself a U.S. effort to liberalize the thinking of one of the most powerful figures in the Nationalist elite and a possible successor to Chiang Kai-shek.

During Chiang Ching-kuo's visit, Secretary of State John Foster Dulles continued the American effort at political education during a discussion at the State Department. Dulles told Chiang that he had heard from U.S. representatives on Taiwan that Chiang Ching-kuo "was a little rough" in his methods of handling security matters. This was probably an allusion to arbitrary arrest and the use of torture in interrogation. Chiang's interpreter, James Shen, did not translate Dulles' remark, whereupon Dulles repeated and elaborated on it. He hoped, Dulles said, that during his visit to the United States Chiang would come to understand that it was possible to cope with problems of subversion, disloyalty, and security "without infringing on basic human rights and without denial of due process of law to suspects." Chiang "murmured an inaudible acknowledgment," according to the State Department record of the conversation.[41]

In spite of Chiang Ching-kuo's nonencouraging response, U.S. leaders noted some progress. The CIA reported in September 1954:

> With U.S. assistance and advice, there has been some degree of progress in expanding public services, improving educational opportunities, simplifying the governmental structure, expanding local self-government, and lessening corruption. Police actions have grown less arbitrary, and court procedures have slowly improved. The Kuomintang has . . . broadened its popular base, and has become more responsive to public opinion. Some freedom of expression is permitted, provided it is circumspect in its treatment of fundamental policies and key officials.[42]

The limits of U.S. pressure for political reform were indicated by the low-keyed U.S. response to the purge of General Sun Li-jen in 1955. American military and civilian personnel viewed Sun as one of the Nationalist leaders most inclined toward U.S. views on such key issues as utilization of the indigenous Taiwanese populace. He also happened to be among the most professional officers in the Nationalist military—at least in the American view. A graduate of the Virginia Military Institute, Sun had served with distinction first as a division commander and then as an Army commander under General Joseph Stilwell during the Burma campaigns of 1942–45. With the Nationalist flight to Taiwan, Sun became commander of the Taiwan Defense Command, and in March 1950, he became commander of the Nationalist Army. U.S. observers saw Sun's promotions as part of an effort by Chiang Kai-shek to win renewed American support.[43]

For the next several years, Sun pressed for recruitment of native Taiwanese into the army, opposed the expansion of the political control system in the military, and stressed defense of Taiwan over preparations for return to the mainland.[44] Sun was also a major rival of Chiang Ching-kuo for control of the Army. Sun viewed the political control system as diluting his command authority, while Chiang controlled that system. Sun was relieved of his posts and arrested in August 1955, when several young officers under his command broke ranks during a review by visiting U.S. Army Chief General Maxwell D. Taylor and advanced to present a petition calling for reform of the military. Sun was held responsible for these actions, relieved of his command, and charged with "harboring communists." A subsequent court martial absolved Sun of these charges, but found him guilty of culpable neglect of duties. He was relieved of all commands and remained under house arrest until 1988.

Sun's dismissal was a major setback for U.S. efforts to foster reform. The United States did not, however, use its leverage to thwart this move. Sun's removal was "outside its competence," the State Department explained to the Taipei embassy. The embassy monitored Sun's trial closely and directed U.S. personnel to express their support for Sun's innocence when questioned by Chinese acquaintances. In Washington, JCS Chairman Radford discussed Sun's case with Ambassador Wellington Koo, expressing his great respect for Sun and complete confidence in his loyalty. The commission investigating Sun should also look into the "larger problem of political influences in the Chinese Armed Forces," Radford suggested.[45]

In short, the U.S. government *did* actively seek to nudge the Nationalist Formosa in the direction of liberal democracy during the 1950s, but it did so incrementally and with great circumspection. To do otherwise, U.S. leaders had concluded, would be counterproductive. Heavy U.S. pressure for sweeping reform, followed necessarily by U.S. supervision of implementation of these reforms, would breed resentment among the Nationalist elite, while tarring that elite as puppets of the United States in the eyes of the people. This was a formula for disaster, U.S. leaders concluded. A more prudent, if slower, course was to attempt to urge gradual, incremental reform, on a seemingly piecemeal basis but with the clear long-term objective of political liberalization and democratization.

U.S. Power and Taiwan's Democratic Evolution

For three decades the United States exercised its instruments of national power to foster the emergence of a liberal, democratic, capitalist polity on Taiwan. Massive economic assistance fueled rapid growth along private-enterprise, market-oriented lines. American markets were thrown wide open to Taiwan's exports, as were American universities to Taiwan's students. American advisers played a direct and important role in shaping the policies that allowed Taiwan to combine high growth with equity: encouraging land reform and a sustained emphasis on rural development, stressing universal education and heavy investment in human resources, and encouraging the private sector while ensuring that Taiwanese enjoyed equal opportunity in that sector. Overall, U.S. military power protected Taiwan against attacks by the PRC, which could easily have precipitated economic and political crises that would have derailed Taiwan's development and that could have, quite possibly, subjected the Chinese on Taiwan to the same totalitarian policies that were inflicted by the CCP on the Chinese residing on the continent of Asia. In short, Taiwanese democracy gestated with U.S. assistance and under U.S. protection.

U.S. policy was long-term. U.S. leaders did not lay out a specific timetable for the liberalization and democratization of Taiwan, but certainly most of them thought in terms of decades. They were aware of the difficulties associated with modernizing a tradition-bound society and with grafting Western-derived political institutions onto a Chinese tradition that was several thousand years old. U.S. officials spoke of "generations" when describing how political change on Taiwan might come about. Modernization theory, which was emerging in the 1950s and which shaped U.S. elite thinking about democracy, maintained that democracy was associated with the higher, later stages of economic development. These stages spanned decades.

The outcome of Taiwan's political evolution eventually approximated the objectives underlying U.S. policy during the 1950s and 1960s. By the 1990s, Taiwan had become what many analysts called the first democratic state in China's long history. To some significant degree, this was the result of U.S. policy. While the root causes of Taiwan's political evolution, of course, lie within Taiwan, the exercise of U.S. influence was a significant factor.

Notes

1. Albert Ravenhold, "Formosa Today," *Foreign Affairs,* July 1952, pp. 612–24.
2. NSC 146/2, 6 November 1953.
3. NSC 5503, 15 January 1955 in *FRUS,* 1955–57, vol. II, pp. 30–34.
4. NIE, 14 September 1954, *FRUS,* 1952–54, vol. XIV, pp. 632–34.
5. Joseph A. Yager, *Transforming Agriculture in Taiwan; The Experience of the Joint Commission on Rural Reconstruction,* Ithaca, NY: Cornell University Press, 1988, pp. 265, 272. Also, T.H. Shen, *The Sino-American Joint Commission on Rural Reconstruction: Twenty Years of Cooperation for Agricultural Development,* Ithaca, NY: Cornell University Press, 1970.
6. Yager, *Transforming Agriculture,* pp. 127–34.

7. Peter R. Moody, *Political Change in Taiwan: A Study of Ruling Party Adaptability,* New York: Praeger, 1992, p. 185. Tun-jen Cheng and Stephen Haggard, "Regime Transformation in Taiwan: Theoretical and Comparative Perspectives," in *Political Change in Taiwan,* Tun-jen Cheng and Stephan Haggard, eds., Boulder, CO: Lynne Rienner, 1992.

8. Thomas B. Gold, *State and Society in the Taiwan Miracle,* Armonk, NY: M.E. Sharpe, 1986. Moody, *Political Change in Taiwan.* Tun-jen Cheng and Haggard, "Regime Transformation," p. 7.

9. Neil H. Jacoby, *U.S. Aid to Taiwan,* New York: Praeger, 1966, p. 38.

10. Jacoby, *U.S. Aid,* pp. 38, 53.

11. Regarding Taiwan, see Moody, *Political Change in Taiwan,* pp. 180–82. Hung-mao Tien and Chyuan-jeng Shiau, "Taiwan Democratization: A Summary," in *World Affairs,* vol. 155, no. 2 (Fall 1992), p. 59. Gold, *State and Society,* pp. 124–29.

12. Andrew J. Nathan and Helena V.S. Ho, "Chiang Ching-kuo's Decision for Political Reform," in *Chiang Ching-kuo's Leadership in the Development of the Republic of China on Taiwan,* Shao-chuan Leng, ed., New York: University Press of America, 1993.

13. Jacoby, *U.S. Aid,* pp. 33, 39, 43.

14. Ibid., p. 34.

15. W.W. Rostow, *Eisenhower, Kennedy, and Foreign Aid,* Austin: University of Texas Press, 1985. Also Jacoby, *U.S. Aid,* pp. 56–57.

16. Rostow, *Eisenhower, Kennedy,* pp. 46–50. As one of the principals of the 1957–58 reconceptualization, Rostow had an interest in casting his theory in the best, "most democratic" light. His account does, however, fit with his writings of the time. See W.W. Rostow, *The Stages of Economic Growth: A Non-Communist Manifesto,* Cambridge, England: Cambridge University Press, 1960.

17. Jacoby, *U.S. Aid,* p. 136.

18. Chen-Kuo Hsu, "Ideological Reflections and the Inception of Economic Development in Taiwan," in *The Role of the State in Taiwan's Development,* Joel D. Aberbach et al., eds., Armonk, NY: M. E. Sharpe, 1994, pp. 308–11.

19. Jacoby, *U.S. Aid,* pp. 136–37.

20. Stephan Haggard and Chien-kuo Pang, "The Transition to Export-Led Growth in Taiwan," in *The Role of the State in Taiwan's Development,* Joel D. Aberbach et al., eds., pp. 67–68.

21. Haggard and Pang, "Transition," pp. 68–69.

22. Jacoby, *U.S. Aid,* pp. 137–38.

23. Haggard and Pang, "Transition," p. 60.

24. Jacoby, *U.S. Aid,* pp. 50–51.

25. Ibid., p. 81.

26. Haggard and Pang, "Transition," p.74.

27. Ibid., p. 79.

28. Ibid., pp. 80–81.

29. Hung-mao Tien and Chyuan-jeng Shiu, "Taiwan's Democratization: A Summary," in *World Affairs,* vol. 155, no. 2 (Fall 1992), p. 58.

30. Haggard and Pang, "Transition," p. 64.

31. Ibid., p. 63.

32. Jacoby, *U.S. Aid,* pp. 133, 135.

33. Ibid., pp. 61, 138. Haggard and Pang, "Transition," p. 63. Moody, *Political Change in Taiwan.*

34. Gold, *State and Society,* p. 124.

35. Allan B. Cole, "Political Roles of Taiwanese Enterprisers," *Asian Survey* (September 1967), pp. 645–54.

36. Jacoby, *U.S. Aid,* pp. 111–14.
37. NSC 146/2, 6 November 1953, in *FRUS,* 1952–54, vol. XIV, pp. 309–14.
38. Ibid., p. 314.
39. *FRUS,* 1952–54, vol. XIV, pp. 206–10.
40. Ibid., p. 207.
41. Ibid., p. 253.
42. NIE, 14 September 1954, in *FRUS,* 1952–54, vol. XIV, pp. 632–34.
43. George Kerr, *Formosa Betrayed,* Boston: Houghton Mifflin, 1965, p. 422–25.
44. Ibid.
45. *FRUS,* 1955–57, vol. III, pp. 69–70.

14

The 1971 Debacle at the United Nations

The Betrayal of Taiwan?

An analysis of the Nationalist China–U.S. alliance must include a consideration of the exit of the ROC from the United Nations in September 1971, because Taiwan representatives have charged that that episode represented U.S. "betrayal" of America's alliance partner. This charge was conveyed in the title and content of the memoir of Taiwan's ambassador to the United States in 1971.[1] It was also a charge echoed by conservative Republican critics of Richard Nixon and Henry Kissinger at the time.[2]

"Betrayal" is a loaded term, implying the breaking of promises. It is thus essential to unpack that term, breaking it down into specific operationizable meanings. One meaning of "betrayal," as used by James Shen and others, is that the United States decided to terminate the alliance. U.S. leaders decided that their nation's interests were no longer best served by that alliance. In terms of U.S. use of Nationalist China as an instrument for pressuring and containing Communist China, the alliance did indeed end in 1971–72. Yet most alliances are not eternal and, while bitterness by one side upon termination of an alliance is perhaps inevitable, that in itself does not constitute evidence of U.S. breaking of faith.

Another meaning of "betrayal" is that the United States would no longer help protect Taiwan from the PLA. It was widely feared in Taiwan at the time of U.S.-PRC rapprochement that the Nixon-Kissinger objective was achievement of a "decent interval" between the end of U.S. responsibility for Taiwan's defense and the final conquest of Taiwan by the PLA. This fear was strengthened, of course, by South Vietnam's experience. After twenty-some years, however, it seems fair to dismiss this fear. The end of the U.S.-Nationalist alliance did not mean that the United States abandoned Taiwan to its fate at PLA hands.

A final operationalization of "betrayal" is that the United States did not do all it could do, or all it had promised to do, to keep the ROC represented in the United Nations. This chapter will demonstrate that this charge is half true, but only half. U.S. leaders did apparently default on a promise to use the United States veto power in the fight over China representation. They also declined to modify the process of U.S.-PRC rapprochement to gain tactical advantage in the UN debate. But these U.S. actions must be placed alongside those of Taipei itself. Taiwan's own representatives did not work to secure, or to support U.S. efforts to secure, ROC representation in the UN General Assembly. To Taipei this was a variant of an unacceptable two-Chinas policy. Taiwan's leaders simply refused to accept and adapt to the changing international situation. A major responsibility for the outcome of the 1971 UN debate must be laid at the doorstep of Taipei.

Evolution of the U.S. Position in Chinese Representation

By the early 1960s, support for continued exclusion of the PRC from the United Nations was eroding. Throughout the 1950s, the United States was able to mobilize a majority in the General Assembly to prevent consideration of the question of China's representation in the United Nations. The entry of many newly independent African and Asian nations into the United Nations during the 1950s resulted, however, in a steady increase in the number of countries voting against this U.S.-sponsored moratorium. As a result of this erosion of support, in 1961 the United States, Australia, Colombia, Italy, and Japan proposed that any change in the representation of China in the United Nations be deemed an "important question" that required a two-thirds majority for approval. The "important question" device allowed a U.S.-led simple majority to require that Beijing's proponents had to mobilize a two-thirds majority. The important question proposal was adopted in 1961 by a vote of 61 to 34, a support ratio of 1.79 : 1. Thereafter, there were annual votes, with support for the U.S.-GRC position falling steadily. By 1970, the support ratio had fallen to 1.2 : 1.[3]

In October 1970, for the first time, a simple majority voted in favor of the usual Albanian resolution to seat the PRC and expel the ROC. This was still far short of the required two-thirds majority, but U.S. officials felt that an important symbolic turning point had been reached. Although procedural maneuvers might work for a while longer, they felt such tactics would bear the onus of being "antidemocratic" and would concede the moral high ground to PRC friends. Following the 1970 UN vote, Japan, Britain, and Belgium told the United States that they doubted the PRC could be kept out of the UN much longer. Canada went further, recognizing the PRC in October. Canada's action sent ripples through pro-American capitals around the world. If even America's closest friend recognized the PRC, how could such an action be construed as anti-American?[4]

Confronted with eroding support, Washington began to look for a new UN strategy. In November 1970, Nixon directed Kissinger to study the question of "Red China's" admission to the United Nations. Nixon's objective was to "keep our commitments to Taiwan" and "not be rolled over by those who favor admission of Red China."[5] Nixon felt that the national security interests of the United States required better relations with the PRC, which dictated, in turn, an end to U.S. efforts to keep China out of the UN Nixon hoped to allow the PRC into the UN, however, while keeping the ROC in the General Assembly. From Nixon's perspective, dual representation, if it could be achieved, would allow the United States to retain the geopolitical advantage of keeping the island of Taiwan in friendly hands, while allowing the United States to achieve cordial relations and diplomatic leverage with the PRC. It also had the domestic political advantage of allowing Nixon to please the liberal wing of Congress, which was increasingly challenging him over Vietnam, without alienating congressional conservatives whose support Nixon needed.[6] Even if the dual representation plan were doomed to failure, Nixon felt that he had to try it for domestic reasons; at least, this was the situation according to Kissinger. Otherwise, conservatives would accuse him of not trying a potentially fruitful way of saving Taiwan's UN seat.[7]

In April 1971, a commission established to mark the twenty-fifth anniversary of the United Nations, and chaired by Republican Party elder Henry Cabot Lodge, submitted a report on the UN to Nixon. It contained the recommendation that the United States seek the early entry of the PRC to the United Nations, but under no circumstances agree to the expulsion of the "Republic of China on Taiwan."[8] By early 1971, the State Department had also concluded that representation of both the PRC and Taiwan in the United Nations would best serve U.S. interests and principles.

Kissinger opposed "dual representation" for several reasons. In the first place, since it was unacceptable to both Taipei and Beijing, he felt dual representation had little chance of success. Even if Taiwan could be persuaded to support it, the PRC was certain to object. Moreover, given the fact that more and more nations wanted better relations with the PRC because of that country's growing political weight, those countries were unlikely to wish to antagonize China by supporting dual representation. Kissinger also feared that U.S. support for dual representation would undermine the new and still fragile opening to the PRC. Beijing might conclude that the United States saw China's opening to the United States as a sign of Chinese weakness, and might conclude that U.S. support for dual representation was an attempt to exploit this weakness. This could well prompt Beijing to break off its developing relationship with the United States, Kissinger feared.[9]

Nixon shared Kissinger's apprehensions that U.S. support for dual representation might induce Beijing to abort the incipient rapprochement with the United States. Throughout the first half of 1971, he therefore prevented the State Department from pursuing its program of dual representation. He nonetheless moved to line up Taiwan's support behind such a plan, in case it became apparent that such a plan would not torpedo the new opening to Beijing. In April 1971, Nixon sent veteran diplomat Robert Murphy to Taipei to propose that Washington and Taipei work toward dual representation. According to James Shen (who sat in on the discussions between Murphy and Chiang Kai-shek), Murphy proposed that both the ROC and the PRC be seated in the General Assembly and that *the ROC would retain China's seat in the Security Council.* The logic of this bid for continued ROC representation of China on the Security Council is unclear. Murphy and Nixon certainly understood that such an arrangement had no chance of success, because both Beijing and an absolute majority of the General Assembly would reject it. Presumably, this element of Murphy's proposal was intended as a face-saving measure for Chiang, allowing him to go down to "principled defeat" in the General Assembly, side by side with his American allies. In any case, Chiang Kai-shek was dissatisfied with Murphy's plan but agreed to go along if the United States promised not to sponsor the PRC's admittance to the United Nations, and if the United States attempted, once again, to rally a majority behind the "important question" formula.[10] In other words, it was Chiang Kai-shek himself who insisted that the United States make its stand at the forthcoming U.N. session primarily over the important question issue. The United States would comply with both of Chiang's requests during the subsequent General Assembly debate. The idea that the ROC would represent China in the Security Council quickly went by the wayside.

Shortly after the Murphy-Chiang talks, James Shen traveled to Washington to become ambassador to the United States. He quickly met with U.S.

officials to reiterate Taipei's demand that the United States rely on the "important question" tactic at least one more year. U.S. officials were reluctant, fearing that this would fail. They agreed to try, however, with the proviso that this be coupled with a resolution on dual representation.

On 19 July 1971, four days after Kissinger's first visit to Beijing was publicly announced, Ambassador Shen met with Secretary of State William P. Rogers. Although Shen was primarily interested in discussing Kissinger's visit to Beijing, Rogers turned the conversation toward the United Nations. Inquiries with North Atlantic Treaty Organization (NATO) countries indicated, Rogers said, that unless the ROC agreed to yield her seat in the Security Council to the Chinese Communists, the dual representation formula would have no chance whatsoever of being adopted in the General Assembly. Shen did not think much of this suggestion: "We were being asked to give up our seat in the Security Council to the Chinese Communists in return for an American promise to do what it could to enable us to retain our seat in the General Assembly—without any guarantee, however, that this would work."[11] There are few guarantees in politics; the real problem was that the GRC simply could not bring itself to agree to accept Communist China's entry into the United Nations, since this implied acceptance of the legitimacy of the Beijing regime and abandonment of the quest to recover the mainland.

Kissinger's first secret visit to Beijing in July 1971 and the announcement of Nixon's forthcoming visit to China further eroded support for exclusion of the PRC from the United Nations. But Kissinger's visit also cleared the way for the United States to move forward with its plan for dual representation. Following Kissinger's discussions with Zhou Enlai, Nixon concluded that neither Taiwan nor the UN issue was high on Beijing's agenda and that, therefore, the State Department could move forward with its dual representation scheme without derailing the opening to Beijing. Zhou had confirmed to Kissinger that the PRC would not accept dual representation and would refuse to enter the United Nations on such terms. But the PRC had waited a long time for UN membership, Zhou said, and could wait several years more.[12] The United Nations question was not central to the new Sino-U.S. relationship. Thus assured that pursuit of dual representation would not abort U.S.-PRC rapprochement, Nixon authorized Secretary of State Rogers to launch his long-delayed push for dual representation.

This was done on 2 August 1971, when Rogers made a statement calling for seating both the PRC and the ROC in the UN General Assembly. Such a move, Rogers insisted, "need not prejudice the claims or views of either government" regarding its "claims to be the sole government of China and representative of all the people of China." Accordingly, the United States would "support action at the Assembly this fall calling for seating the People's Republic of China," and at the same time would "oppose any action to expel the Republic or China or otherwise deprive it of representation in the United Nations." Representation in the Security Council was a separate matter which "in the final analysis" the Security Council and the "members of the United Nations" would decide.[13] Rogers' statement did not take a position on whether Beijing or Taipei should hold China's permanent seat on the Security Council. It implied, however, that the United States was prepared to see this question decided by *all* UN members, that is, by the General Assembly, where neither the ROC nor the United States had veto power. In hopes of mobilizing majority support behind keeping Taiwan in the General Assembly, Washington quietly began recommending that China's Security Council seat go to Beijing.[14] Taipei was very angry about this shift in U.S. position and about the abandonment of what it took to be the U.S. pledge that had been conveyed during Murphy's April 1971 visit. Taipei refused to accept Washington's new line. When the issue came before the United Nations, the United States and the ROC had no common policy.

The 1971 General Assembly Debate

The first major battle in the 1971 United Nations debate came on 22 September at the 191st meeting of the General Committee of the General Assembly. The General Committee sets the agenda for the General Assembly's deliberations. On 15 July, well before the United States decided to launch its drive for dual representation, Albania submitted to Secretary-General U Thant its perennial resolution providing for seating the PRC and expelling Taiwan. Thant received the Albanian proposal well before he received the American proposal calling for PRC assumption of China's Security Council seat and dual representation in the General Assembly. He therefore placed the Albanian proposal before the U.S. proposal on the proposed agenda he submitted to the General Committee on 22 September.

The sequence of the two proposals ultimately had a decisive influence on the Assembly's deliberations about the U.S. and the Albanian resolutions. Approval of the Albanian resolution might mean that the U.S. proposal on dual representation would never come to a vote or even get a full hearing. To avoid this, U.S. representative George Bush proposed at the 191st General Committee meeting that the Albanian and U.S. proposals be combined into a single item, to be entitled "Question of China" and to be considered together by the Assembly. Combination of the two proposals into a single item, Bush argued, would ensure a full debate of both proposals before either one was voted upon. Leaving the two separate, as two agenda items, Bush warned, could mean that Assembly debate and action on the first-scheduled proposal might prejudge or preempt consideration of the second item.[15] This, of course, would eventually be the case.

Supporters of the Albanian resolution packed the 191st General Committee meeting. Representatives from Albania, Iraq, Guinea, the Democratic Republic of the Congo, Algeria, Pakistan, Romania, Syria, and Yugoslavia asked and were permitted to participate in the proceedings, even though they were not members of the General Committee. The representatives of each of these countries spoke at length against Bush's proposal to merge the two proposals into a single agenda item. The only non-General Committee member that participated and also supported the U.S. proposal to merge the two proposals into a single agenda item was Saudi Arabia. Throughout the UN debate in 1971, Saudi Arabia was, along with the United States, Taiwan's most active supporter.

The ardently pro-PRC non-General Committee members participating in the 191st General Committee meeting took the lead in arguing against the U.S. proposal. Their main argument was that since the two proposals "had nothing in common," they could not logically be joined. Nor was the U.S. proposal "aimed at facilitating the Assembly's deliberations of the [China] problem or at finding an adequate solution to it," according to the Yugoslav delegate. Rather, it sought to "prolong the myth of the existence of two Chinas by maintaining the representation of the Chiang Kai-shek regime." The Iraqi representative pointed out that, at the General Assembly meeting in 1970, a clear majority had favored the PRC's admission to the United Nations. The 700 million Chinese people had to be represented, the Iraqi said. Syria denounced the U.S. proposal as a new "procedural trick" similar to the "important question trick" that it had used for years to keep China out of the United Nations. Pakistan's representative maintained that the practical effect of the U.S. proposal would be to prevent the PRC from entering the United Nations.

The Belgian representative on the General Committee supported the U.S. proposal "in a spirit of fair play." The question of China was intrinsically a political one, he said, and should therefore be decided by the General Assembly, not the General Committee. The General Committee should concern itself only with procedural matters, not with substantive ones, the Belgian said. It should not structure the agenda in such a way as to prejudice or even determine the resolution of a particular issue. This view was seconded by the Greek representative, who noted that the opponents of the U.S. proposition were acting on the premise that the PRC should be seated. This, however, was a substantive issue and was beyond the competence of the General Committee. The U.S. proposal had the merit, the Greek representative said, of allowing a full debate of all sides of a highly complicated issue.

The participation of the ROC delegation in the debate of the 191st General Committee meeting was remarkably unrealistic. Taiwan, like the United States, was a member of the General Committee. ROC representative Liu Chieh said that his government *was against the inclusion of the Albanian resolution on the General Assembly's agenda.* This was remarkable: Liu was actually speaking against the U.S. proposal to combine the two resolutions into a single agenda item. The Albanian proposal, Liu said, should not even be on the agenda. When it came to a vote, however, Liu did vote for the U.S. proposal.

The U.S. proposal to combine consideration of the Albanian and U.S. proposals into a single agenda item was defeated by a vote of 12 to 9, with 3 abstentions. Could the United States have swayed the three or four votes necessary to ensure consideration of its proposal for dual representation? Perhaps. Among those abstaining were Belgium and Ireland, whose delegates had earlier spoken in favor of the U.S. proposal. Among those voting against the proposal was Britain. The United States may not have gone all out to secure a majority during the 191st session of the General Committee because it believed there would be other occasions when it could achieve the desired debate and vote over the question of dual representation. Moreover, according to Kissinger, U.S. officials believed that they could win one more vote on the "important question" issue which would have forced a debate and a vote on the U.S. dual representation resolution.

The next battle came in the full General Assembly on 25 October 1971, over whether the question of China's representation was an "important question." The United States proposed that this was the case and that consideration of this "important" issue should be given priority over consideration of the Albanian proposal. This proposal was approved by a substantial majority. This meant that before voting on the Albanian resolution, the General Assembly would first decide whether a simple majority or a two-thirds majority vote would be required to adopt the Albanian resolution.

The central thrust of the U.S. argument presented on 25 October by George Bush was that the issue before the Assembly was whether or not to expel a member state, the ROC, from the United Nations, and that since this had never before been done, it clearly was an important question. The issue was not, Bush said, the seating of the People's Republic of China in the United Nations. There was agreement on this. The question was rather, "Shall we expel forthwith the Republic of China from the United Nations, or shall it continue to be represented here? This is the heart of the matter."[16]

As the Australian representative Sir Laurence McIntyre pointed out during the 25 October debate, the Albanian resolution explicitly used the word "expel" in reference to Taiwan, and Article 18 of the Charter specified expulsion as one of the "important questions" requiring a two-thirds majority. Regarding the substantive issue, Bush advanced several reasons Taiwan should not be expelled. The first was "realism." Dual representation in the General Assembly reflected "the plain facts regarding who governs in Taiwan as well as who governs the Chinese mainland," Bush said. "For 20 years the United States has been accused of ignoring reality. Today I submit to you that it is the sponsors of the Albanian resolution who are ignoring reality." "Universality" was Bush's second reason. The ROC government was the spokesmen for a population of some fourteen million, and they should not be denied a voice in the General Assembly. To expel because of ideological disagreements a state that in fact exercised effective control over its territory and population would run counter to the principle of "universality." It would also, Bush warned, set a dangerous precedent. This may have been an allusion to Israel. "Practicality" was Bush's third argument. The U.S. proposal of joint representation contained nothing prejudicial to the claims of either Taipei or Beijing regarding the "ultimate solution" of the China question. Representation of both the PRC and the ROC in the General Assembly would neither preclude nor favor either Taipei's or Beijing's proposed solution of the China question. A number of member states had merged together or divided into two without considerations of UN membership constituting any obstacle. The merger of Egypt and Syria (and their subsequent divorce into two independent countries) and the merger of Tanganyika and Zanzibar were examples cited by Bush. By expelling the ROC, the General Assembly was, in fact, prejudging the "ultimate solution" of the China question.

Once again, during the debate on 25 October, ROC delegate Liu Chieh did not support the U.S. position and contradicted it in several important ways. A major thrust of Liu's comments regarded the "indivisibility of the Chinese nation," undercutting the U.S. argument about "universality" and dovetailing with the argument advanced by the proponents of the Albanian resolution that the question facing the Assembly was simply one of *which* government, Taipei or Beijing, represented "China." Liu indicated that he was in "complete agreement" with Albania about "the indivisibility of the Chinese nation" and "the fact that Taiwan is Chinese territory."[17] Liu also insisted on trundling out the theory that the CCP regime would soon be overthrown, and he contended that this eventuality should influence the votes of Assembly members. While there is no doubt that this thesis reflected the deeply held beliefs of ROC leaders, in the context of the 1971 General Assembly debate it contributed to a sense that the U.S.-ROC position was unrealistic. The PRC had been kept out of the United Nations for twenty years on the basis of the theory, at least in part, that the CCP regime was destined for the dustbin of history. By 1971, this view was a distinctly minority view in the General Assembly.

Most amazingly, the Taiwan delegation did not demand that it be allowed continued representation in the General Assembly. Taipei insisted that the General Assembly make an either-or choice between it and Beijing. Taiwan representatives failed to use several arguments that might have had some effect in the General Assembly debate of 1971. They could have appealed to the small countries of the General Assembly for protection against large, powerful neighbors who had designs on them. Many of the 131 members of the General Assembly were small states—indeed, "microstates"—that were apprehensive about the ambitions of more powerful neighbors, and that looked to the United Nations as an instrument for help in checking expansionist ambitions. Had Taipei cast the issue in terms of a small country threatened by absorption by a powerful neighbor, this appeal might have had some persuasive effect. Of course, this would have required acceptance of the fact that the ROC was confined to Taiwan and did not represent all of China. But "two Chinas" was unacceptable to Taipei.

Taipei could also have appealed to the principle of "universality." Taipei could have argued that no government that effectively controlled a substantial population and a substantial territory should be denied representation in the General Assembly because of objections by a great power. Taipei did not resort to these arguments, because to do so would have meant conceding the legitimacy of the Beijing government and tacitly accepting the PRC's right to be seated in the United Nations, or rather, to exist. Nationalist beliefs were unrealistic, but they were at the core of Nationalist self-identity and regime legitimacy. Nationalist leaders simply could not countenance any action accepting, implicitly or explicitly, the continued existence of the PRC, even though this doomed the ROC on Taiwan to expulsion from the United Nations.

Taipei could have won goodwill and enhanced its aura of reasonability by clearly stating its willingness to give up "China's" Security Council seat. By continuing to insist that it represented all of China, Taipei undercut the U.S. appeal to "realism," and made it seem that the United States, contrary to George Bush's assertions, wanted to continue the "unrealistic" policy of the previous twenty years. Finally, as remarkable as it may seem, the ROC delegation apparently had no guidance from its government about how to respond to the U.S. dual representation proposal when the China issue was decided at the United Nations on 25 October. Ambassador Shen's memoir says of the U.S. public endorsement of dual representation on 2 August:

> This put our government in a dilemma. Obviously we could not support any move to seat the Chinese Communists in the General Assembly, despite the fact that the resolution would also call for retention of the Republic of China's seat in the same body. When asked by governments friendly to us how we would wish their representatives to vote, we did not know what to say. Instead, we could only explain our dilemma and ask them to be guided by their own judgment in the balloting. As a result, many of our friends were in a quandary. In the end this proved to be our undoing because they did not know what we really wanted them to do.[18]

Although Taipei had nearly three months to formulate a response, it was unable to do so. This meant that ROC representatives at the United Nations did not go all-out to rally support for the ROC's continuing representation in the General Assembly. Had Taipei reacted differently, had it decided to alter its opposition to any PRC participation in the U.N. and to work in tandem with the United States and other friendly countries at the U.N., the outcome on 25 October 1971 could well have been very different. The failure of the Albanian resolution to muster the required two-thirds majority would then have opened the way for deliberation on the U.S. dual representation proposal. Had this proposal passed, Beijing would well have been presented with the choice of entering or not entering the U.N. with the ROC still seated in the General Assembly. Had Beijing refused, the status quo would have been maintained for at least another year. Once starting down the road of dual representation, however, Taiwan would have had to accept the legitimacy of the PRC. It was Chiang Kai-shek's unalterable determination to overthrow the Communist regime and, as he saw it, his adamant refusal to become the agent of a partition of China that condemned the ROC to expulsion from the UN in October 1971. Ironically, the convictions that made Chiang so valuable as an ally against Communist China condemned him to isolation once the United States decided on rapprochement with China.

The "important question" resolution failed by 4 votes; the tally was 59 to 55, with 15 abstentions. Among those abstaining were such NATO allies as Italy, the Netherlands, Belgium, and Turkey. Every NATO ally but Luxembourg, Greece, and Portugal voted "no" or abstained. According to Kissinger, "The essence of the matter was that friendly nations changed their positions."[19]

After losing the "important question" vote, Bush immediately raised a "point of order," proposing to delete the clause "and to expel forthwith the representatives of Chiang Kai-shek from the place they have unlawfully occupied at the United Nations and in all the organs related to it" from the Albanian resolution. As Bush pointed out, if this clause were deleted, the

Albanian resolution would have the effect of welcoming the PRC into the General Assembly and the Security Council without affecting the representation of the ROC in the General Assembly. The president of the Assembly, the Canadian representative at that point, ruled the U.S. proposal out of order on grounds that voting on the Albanian resolution had already begun—a point disputed by the U.S. delegation. Liberia then proposed a separate vote on various provisions of the Albanian resolution—a "vote by division." Bush seconded this proposal, arguing that members should be allowed a separate vote on the question of expelling a member state. This proposal was rejected 61 to 51 with 19 countries abstaining. It was at this point that Liu Chieh announced that the ROC was leaving the General Assembly. The ROC's final words to the General Assembly were:

> The rejection of the ["important question"] draft resolution is a flagrant violation of the Charter, which governs the expulsion of Member States. In view of the frenzied and irrational manners that have been exhibited in this hall, the delegation of the Republic of China has now decided not to take part in any further proceedings of this General Assembly. I should like to take this opportunity to express the profound gratitude of my Government to those friendly Governments which have lent us their unstinting support throughout the years. My Government will further strengthen these relations in the years to come. We shall continue to struggle with like minded Governments for the realization of the ideals upon which the United Nations was founded and which the General Assembly has now betrayed.[20]

By withdrawing before the critical vote, the ROC was able to assert that, technically, it was not expelled from the United Nations, but withdrew of its own volition. After the ROC delegation withdrew, the Albanian resolution came to a vote and passed by a vote of 76 to 35 with 17 abstentions amidst great jubilation by representatives of third world countries. The session closed at 11:25 P.M. with the words of the Albanian representative: "In the great People's Republic of China the peoples [of the world] see the great citadel of socialism, the firm and resolute support essential to the peoples struggling for national and social liberation, the resolute defender of the principles of justice, the opponent and impregnable barrier to the policy of hegemony and world domination of the two great imperialist powers."[21] The next day, when the U.S. resolution on dual representation came before the Assembly, its Canadian president proposed that "In view of the action taken by the General Assembly" the day before, "may I assume that it is the wish of the Assembly not to consider the United States proposal?" "It was so decided," reads the official transcript.[22]

Taipei's performance during the 1971 UN debate was not directed toward retaining the ROC's General Assembly seat in the context of PRC entry into the UN and accession to China's seat on the Security Council. This was in spite of the discussions between Chiang and Murphy in April 1971. Chiang Kai-shek had a choice between continued ROC representation in the General Assembly as a "little China," or expulsion from the United Nations and continued adherence to the doctrine of ROC representation of all China. He chose the latter and this choice contributed very substantially to the outcome of the UN debate of 1971. On this critical issue, the two alliance partners failed to cooperate. Indeed, they did not even pursue parallel policies. Each went its own way. George Bush's concluding words during the Assembly debate of the Albanian resolution implicitly recognized this divergence in U.S. and ROC policy when he said:

> Let the United Nations take the affirmative road—not the road of exclusion. . . . And *let this decision be made not in Taipei*, let it be made not in Peking, but here in New York. *Let it be made, not according to the demands of either party,* but according to the interests and the spirit of the United Nations. And having made our decision in that spirit, then we can in good conscience say to both parties: the halls of the United Nations are big enough for you both, the doors of the United nations are open to you both for the urgent and creative work of building a more peaceful world. [Emphasis added.][23]

As part of his "betrayal" hypothesis, James Shen argued that various U.S. actions associated with the U.S.-PRC rapprochement severely undermined Taipei's UN battle in October 1971. Shen stresses in this regard Kissinger's July and October 1971 visits to Beijing. The volte-face in U.S. policy reflected by Kissinger's July 1971 visit and the announcement of Nixon's forthcoming trip cast a shadow over Taipei in the United Nations. Even more egregious, in Shen's view, was Kissinger's presence in Beijing in October for a second set of discussions, just when the General Assembly was debating the China question. Shen suspected that this "unbelievable lack of coordination" between Bush, "who was doing his best to defend our interests in the UN," and Kissinger was by design.[24] Nixon was aware of the possible impact Kissinger's visit to Beijing might have on UN deliberations and ordered Kissinger to stop over in Alaska for a day, as he returned to the United States, so as not to arrive on the day of the UN vote.

Kissinger essentially agrees with Shen regarding the impact of his trips to Beijing immediately prior to the General Assembly's deliberations, but argues that his visits to Beijing were only an expression of a new, more basic U.S. policy toward the PRC, and that it was that policy, more fundamentally, that determined the UN vote. Many nations wanted to improve relations with China for broad political reasons having to do with their own national interests. But they also wanted good relations with the United States, and as long as the United States was adamantly opposed to the PRC and PRC entry into the UN, those countries hesitated to antagonize the United States. Once the United States itself began improving relations with the PRC, these countries no longer feared that the United States would impose heavy penalties on them for dealing with China.[25]

It must also be noted that the United States abstained from using all available leverage to influence UN deliberations in 1971. In the lead up to the China debate, the Nixon Administration deliberately renounced fiscal leverage. The United States contributed a large portion of the UN budget, yet on 15 October 1971, well after the General Committee's critical decisions regarding the agenda, but ten days before the decisive General Assembly debate, George Bush told the Administrative and Budgetary Committee of the General Assembly that, while he could not know how the debate over China's representation would proceed, nor could he foresee how the U.S. people would react in the event of the expulsion of the ROC, he wanted "to assure this committee that the administration of President Nixon is not threatening the United Nations or planning financial reprisals for any political contingency here." "On the contrary," Bush said, "we want the UN's finances to be rescued from their present precarious state."[26] Six weeks before the China debate, Nixon also ruled out a proposal by former Congressman Walter Judd that the United States insist the expulsion of the ROC require a recommendation by the Security Council to the General Assembly.[27] Such an arrangement would have allowed both the United States and the ROC to use their veto power.

A 1971 memorandum for the president on a new China policy for the United States, written by Rand Corporation Consultant Richard Moorsteen and retired diplomat Morton Abramowitz, explained why the United States did not use all available influence to keep Taiwan in the General Assembly.[28] This highly influential memorandum worked through many of the complex issues of China policy. Among the questions it dealt with was the feasibility of either a "two-Chinas" or a "one-China–one-Taiwan" arrangement in the United Nations. While a one-China–one-Taiwan arrangement was attractive to many people in the United States, the study noted, U.S. pursuit of such a policy would "seriously aggravate relations with Peking, rather than improve them. It would take a bold man to predict that such a deterioration in relations would lead to improvements later on." "The mere prospect of our moving toward" a "one China, one Taiwan position, however obliquely . . . produces a response from Peking verging on paranoia." In other words, if the United States wanted an overall improvement in relations with Beijing, it should not support a one-China–one-Taiwan pol-

LIVERPOOL
JOHN MOORES UNIVERSITY
AVRIL ROBARTS LRC
TEL. 0151 231 4

icy. Tactically, the United States "should fight hard enough to show our heart is in the right place. But we should not expect to find an ingenious route to victory." Therefore,

> We should not stake too much prestige nor arouse the United States public on a matter this risky. In the long run, the intensity with which we push our position may have a greater effect on our large interests than the details of the position itself. Peking is likely to gauge the seriousness of our opposition (and the United States public the seriousness of any defeat we risk) mainly from the magnitude of our efforts.[29]

In short, the United States did not go all-out to force a vote on its proposal of "universal" representation and to win majority support for that proposal, because the exercise of the instruments of influence necessary to achieve this would have run counter to the basic objective of rapprochement with Beijing.

Was this, then, a U.S. "betrayal" of its ally? I would argue that it was not. Taipei itself did not desire dual representation. Taipei acquiesced to the U.S. proposal of dual representation only because American representatives persuaded it that any other solution was doomed to failure, and insisted that, in this event, Taipei would have to bear responsibility for the failure. Again, reference to the Moorsteen and Abramowitz book is useful. The United States "should not coerce or bribe [Taipei] to adopt a formulation of ours," the report stated. "Should Taipei insist, we should even consider staying with our previous position" of insisting on an either-or choice. Taipei would then have to "accept responsibility for the outcome and our publicly playing down the importance of the issue, given the probability of losing."[30] Taipei probably agreed to go along with Washington's plan because the United States felt strongly that continued adherence to the old approach was doomed to defeat, whereas a proposal of dual representation at least had a chance of success. Rather than assume responsibility for likely failure, Taipei reluctantly endorsed the United States plan, but Nationalist hearts were not behind the dual representation plan that implied abandonment of the goal of destroying Communist power on the mainland. Rather than accommodating to the realities of the PRC's growing international prominence, and struggling to stay in the General Assembly in cooperation with its allies on the basis of that pragmatic accommodation, Taipei clung to its dogma. This contributed directly and significantly to the outcome of the UN contest in 1971. Given that Taipei did not struggle to stay in the General Assembly and even refused to work in tandem with the United States to this end, it is difficult to conclude that the United States "betrayed" Taipei on this issue.

Notes

1. James C.H. Shen, *The U.S. and Free China: How the U.S. Sold Out Its Ally,* Washington: Acropolis Books, 1983.

2. See the essays in *About Face: The China Decision and Its Consequences,* John Tierney, ed., New Rochelle, NY: Arlington House, 1979.

3. *China, U.S. Policy Since 1945,* Washington: Congressional Quarterly, 1980, p. 365.

4. Henry Kissinger, *White House Years,* Boston: Little Brown, 1979, p. 772.

5. Richard M. Nixon, *The Memoirs of Richard Nixon,* vol. 2, New York: Warner Books, 1978, p. 10.

6. Kissinger, *White House Years,* p. 719.

7. Ibid., p. 773.

8. *Department of State Bulletin,* 2 August 1971, pp. 132–33.

9. Kissinger, *White House Years,* p. 773.

10. Shen, *The U.S. and Free China,* pp. 5, 58.

11. Ibid., p. 73.

12. Kissinger, *White House Years,* p. 773.

13. Shen, *The U.S. and Free China,* pp. 60–61.

14. Kissinger, *White House Years,* p. 774.

15. *Official Records of the General Assembly Twenty-Sixth Session, General Committee,* Summary Records of Meetings, 22 September–9 December 1971, New York: United Nations, 1974, pp. 4–11.

16. *United Nations General Assembly Twenty-Sixth Session Official Records,* 1,976th Plenary Meeting, 25 October 1971, pp. 12–13.

17. Ibid., pp. 10–11.

18. Shen, *The U.S. and Free China,* p. 62.

19. Kissinger, *White House Years,* p. 784.

20. *United Nations General Assembly Twenty-Sixth Session Official Records,* 1,976th Plenary Meeting, 25 October 1971, pp. 40–41.

21. Ibid., pp. 41–42.

22. *United Nations General Assembly Twenty-Sixth Session Official Records,* 1,977th Plenary meeting, 26 October 1971, p. 8.

23. Ibid., 1,976th Plenary Meeting, 25 October 1971, pp. 12–13.

24. Shen, *The U.S. and Free China,* p. 6.

25. Kissinger, *White House Years,* pp. 784–85.

26. *Department of State Bulletin,* 15 November 1971, p. 557.

27. *Department of State Bulletin,* 4 October 1971, pp. 341–42.

28. Richard Moorsteen and Morton Abramowitz, *Remaking China Policy: U.S.-China Relations and Governmental Decision Making,* Cambridge, MA: Harvard University Press, 1971.

29. Ibid., pp. 15–16.

30. Ibid., p. 16.

15

The Alliance and U.S.-PRC Rapprochement

Contradictions in the Alliance

By the early 1960s, the U.S. policy of keeping the Sino-Soviet alliance in the pressure cooker began to have visible effect. The tension that erupted in 1958–59 between Moscow and Beijing over Taiwan and over policy toward the United States quickly intensified. By 1960, polemical battles were under way, and by the next year, these battles were beginning to divide the international Communist movement. The direction of China's movement under the impact of the Sino-Soviet split was not what had been anticipated by U.S. leaders, however. Rather than moving toward accommodation with the United States, Beijing became ultramilitant, confronting both the United States and the Soviet Union. By 1961, most U.S. leaders recognized the reality and the significance of the Sino-Soviet split. It took seven years, however, for the United States to develop a strategy that could effectively exploit that conflict to U.S. advantage. Not until Richard Nixon took office in 1969 did U.S. leaders formulate the strategy of balancing between Beijing and Moscow so as to increase American leverage with both.

Inducing Moscow to adopt a more cooperative policy toward the United States and isolating North Vietnam from Soviet and Chinese support were among the most important objectives of Nixon's triangular strategy. Implementation of this strategy led Nixon to open contacts with Beijing and to slightly ease U.S. containment of China. The implicit offer, which was being made explicit in confidential U.S.-PRC talks by 1970, was the abandonment of containment altogether. The key question was whether Taiwan was to be sacrificed on the altar of great-power politics, as the strategic triangle replaced containment as the dominant paradigm inspiring U.S. policy toward China.

In certain regards, Nixon's triangular strategy was a return to the doctrine of the offshore perimeter that had been embraced briefly in the transitional period before the Sino-Soviet alliance and North Korea's strike to the South. While trying to minimize conflicts with Beijing so as to better exploit Sino-Soviet tensions, the United States drew its defense perimeter along the fringe of the western Pacific where U.S. maritime power held a substantial comparative advantage. There were several major differences between President Harry S. Truman's strategy of early 1950 and President Richard M. Nixon's similar strategy of 1969. One had to do with Nationalist China on Taiwan. While Truman was prepared to sacrifice Taiwan to the PRC for the sake of drawing Beijing away from Moscow, Nixon was not.

Considerations of U.S. credibility as an ally and a friend weighed heavily in Nixon's calculations regarding Taiwan. Nixon recognized that two decades of close cooperation between the two countries as allies had substantially changed the nature of the U.S.–Nationalist China relationship. A sacrifice of Taiwan in early 1950 would have meant only the loss of that island as a military platform. A sacrifice of Taiwan in the 1970s would mean the abandonment of a long-term, important, and valued ally on the altar of great-power politics. Nixon was firmly convinced that such a move would deeply damage the credibility of the United States as an ally. If the United States gained a reputation for sacrificing its allies when such a move became convenient, the United States would lose the trust and confidence of its friends—trust and confidence that Nixon felt was essential for a superpower.

Nor was such a sacrifice of Taiwan necessary to achieve better relations with Beijing, Nixon believed. In spite of Beijing's rhetoric, Nixon was convinced that Taiwan was not the issue of deepest concern to it. The United States and the PRC shared a range of convergent issues touching on relations with the USSR which, if used properly by U.S. diplomacy, could compel Beijing to shelve the Taiwan issue on terms acceptable to the United States. Of course, Beijing would push for U.S. recognition of Beijing's sovereignty over Taiwan and for the revocation of the mantle of U.S. military protection from Taiwan. But if the United States held firm, offered cooperation in other areas of greater urgency to Beijing, and could work out a verbal formulation that saved Beijing's face over Taiwan, the United States might gain the triangular leverage it desired without sacrificing Taiwan.

With these strategic calculations went a strong sympathy for Chiang Kai-shek and his deeply anti-Communist Nationalists. In this regard, Nixon was the counterpoint of Truman. Nixon had begun his career as a politician in the late 1940s attacking Truman's "abandonment" of Chiang Kai-shek. During his eight years as vice-president, Nixon had frequent contact with Nationalist leaders and communed with them on both strategic and ideological levels. During his years of exile after his Presidential loss to John Kennedy, Nixon continued to be warmly received in Taipei. Nixon had strong, warm sympathies for Taiwan when he took office. Like most leaders, he was able to achieve a congruence of sentiment and strategic calculations. There would be no sacrifice of Taiwan. Management of the contradictions between rapprochement with Beijing and a continued but looser relation with Taiwan was a major concern for the Nixon Administration.

Throughout the 1950s and 1960s, Taipei opposed all official contact between the United States and the People's Republic of China. Each time a meeting took place between U.S. and PRC ambassadors in Geneva or Warsaw, Taipei would reiterate its opposition by delivering a diplomatic protest or having a foreign ministry spokesman make a statement.[1] Nationalist concern led Secretary of State John Foster Dulles to give assurances, during the ratification of the mutual defense agreement in March 1955, that "the United States will not enter into negotiations dealing with the territories or rights of the Republic of China except in cooperation with the Republic of China."[2] This did not mean that Taipei had a veto on talks between the United States and China. It all depended on what was being discussed, Dulles told the press. If discussions touched on issues related to the ROC, then "We are not going to talk about the interests of the Republic of China behind its back."[3] U.S. diplomats subsequently briefed Nationalist officials whenever the Warsaw ambassadorial talks touched on topics related to the ROC.

Taipei was dismayed by any movement in the United States toward improving relations with Communist China. Hearings by the Senate Foreign Relations Committee in February 1966 on U.S. policy toward China, for example, drew sharp attacks from Taipei. Nationalist criticism focused on calls by professors John King Fairbank and A. Doak Barnett for a policy of "containment without isolation" toward the PRC.[4] In effect, these critics were urging that the U.S. deal with the PRC as it did with the USSR. Now that differential approaches to the two Communist powers had secured the U.S. objective of undermining the alliance between them, this made sense. Yet the freezing of U.S.-PRC relations during the Vietnam War spared Taipei major concern for several years.

When Richard Nixon took office as president in January 1969, he had already committed himself in a *Foreign Affairs* article of October 1967 to bringing China into the community of nations while reducing American responsibilities as the "policeman" of Asia.[5] Yet he rejected the notion that Taiwan should be given to Beijing as part of this process. Conceding to China a "sphere of influence" "embracing much of the Asian mainland and extending even to the island nations beyond" was an unworkable course, according to Nixon. "Taiwan" was included in the list of Asian nations that had to pull together to cope with the China threat in the coming era of diminished American involvement. "The primary restraint on China's Asian ambitions," Nixon wrote, "should be exercised by the Asian nations in the path of those ambitions, backed by the ultimate power of the United States."

During his first year as president, Nixon received a crash course in Soviet-Chinese conflict as he and his advisers pondered how to respond to the brink-of-war crisis between those countries. He and National Security Advisor Henry Kissinger emerged from those deliberations with some good ideas about how to use Sino-Soviet conflict to America's advantage. A critical juncture came in August 1969, when the administration helped prevent a preemptive Soviet attack on China's embryonic nuclear facilities.[6] By mid-1969 the Nixon Administration was signaling Beijing of its desire to end the U.S.-PRC confrontation. Key among these signals was the discontinuation of Seventh Fleet patrols of the Taiwan Strait in December 1969. To ensure that Beijing did not mistakenly conclude from this move that the United States no longer intended to protect Taiwan, Kissinger told Beijing, via Pakistani President Yahya Khan, that the basic U.S. commitment to Taiwan's defense remained unchanged. The termination of the Strait patrols was merely a gesture intended to remove an irritant in relations.[7] About the same time, Nixon also ordered the termination of CIA involvement with the Tibetan resistance, which was still soldiering on, with Nationalist support, from Nepal's Mustang plateau.

Taipei noted these moves and understood that their purpose was to foster a general improvement in Washington-Beijing relations.[8] The Nationalists issued their standard denunciations and warnings.[9] In February 1970, the long-delayed 135th PRC-U.S. ambassadorial meeting at Warsaw took place. Beijing's representative stressed that U.S. disengagement from Taiwan was the prerequisite for improvement of U.S.-PRC relations. Taiwan, he said, was the "crucial issue" preventing improvements in Sino-American relations.[10] What Taipei found most alarming about the February 1970 Warsaw meeting was that the Nixon Administration broke with precedent by failing to inform Taipei in advance of what the United States planned to bring up at the Warsaw talks. Moreover, when ROC representatives asked subsequently for a briefing on what had transpired, they were given only vague and evasive replies. This led ROC officials to suspect that the United States was discussing questions relating to Taiwan behind its back.[11] They were not wrong in this regard. U.S. policy had changed. The process of alliance termination had begun.

In an effort to gauge just how far Nixon intended to go, Vice-Premier Chiang Ching-kuo flew to Washington in April 1970. What concessions was the United States prepared to make to Beijing in the process of improving relations with China, Chiang asked? Did the United States intend to reach some sort of peaceful coexistence or nonaggression agreement with Beijing, which would be tantamount to the recognition of Beijing as the legitimate government of the Chinese mainland? Chiang also wanted to know whether the United States still intended to honor the 1958 Formosa Resolution, and whether it would support Taipei in the event of another PRC attack on Jinmen and Mazu.[12]

Nixon reassured Chiang Ching-kuo that he did not intend for the United States to withdraw from Asia, but merely to deal with regional problems in a new way. Nixon downplayed the significance of the recently resumed Warsaw talks and assured Chiang that they would not fundamentally alter America's protective relation toward Taiwan: "I can assure you that the United States will always honor its treaty obligations and, to use a colloquial expression, I will never sell you down the river."[13] In a separate conversation, Kissinger asked Chiang Ching-kuo for his reaction should the U.S. government decide to move the U.S.-PRC ambassadorial talks from Warsaw to either Washington or Beijing. In effect, Kissinger was asking about the establishment of Sino-U.S. diplomatic relations. Chiang objected strongly.

After the April 1970 discussions in Washington, Chiang Ching-kuo was left with no doubt that the Nixon Administration intended to undertake a broad improvement of relations with Beijing. U.S. leaders were also plain about their intention of not abandoning Taiwan to Communist China. ROC leaders did not, however, accept U.S. professions at face value. They increasingly feared that the Taiwan pawn might be sacrificed in the great power game of the strategic triangle.

A new ROC ambassador to the United States, James C.H. Shen, arrived in Washington on 10 May 1971. Shen had studied journalism at the University of Missouri and had worked as Chiang Kai-shek's English language interpreter for many years. He was thus both au courant with Chiang Kai-shek's thinking and well versed in American ways. When Shen presented his credentials to Nixon a week after his arrival, Nixon assured him that the United States would continue to honor its obligations under the 1954 treaty, and that it would continue to support the ROC both in and outside the United Nations.[14]

Shortly after assuming his new post, Ambassador Shen learned of Kissinger's earthshaking July 1971 secret visit to Beijing. Shen, like the Australian and Japanese ambassadors, was informed of Kissinger's visit only when Secretary of State William P. Rogers telephoned him twenty minutes before Nixon announced it on television. In explaining developments to Shen, Rogers asked Shen to tell Chiang Kai-shek that the United States would never forsake its friends and would continue to stand by the mutual defense treaty. Several hours later, ROC Vice–Foreign Minister H.Y. Yang lodged a strong protest with Ambassador Walter McConaughy in Taipei, calling Kissinger's visit "a most unfriendly act" that was bound to have serious consequences. Ambassador Shen met with Assistant Secretary of State for East Asia Marshall Green to stress how "indignant," "bewildered," and "shocked" "everyone in Taipei" was by the United States' opening to Communist China. Shen pointed to Taiwan's underlying fear when he asked, "Where is all this going to end?"[15]

The Taiwan Question and U.S.-PRC Rapprochement

The U.S. relation with Taiwan was *the* most sensitive and difficult issue to resolve during the process of Sino-U.S. rapprochement in the 1970s. This is not to say that it was the most *important* issue. Both sides were primarily concerned with the global geopolitical threat presented by the Soviet Union. Yet, for both sides, the Taiwan issue was extremely sensitive in terms of basic principle and domestic politics. For Mao the Taiwan issue involved the completion of China's "national liberation" and the final blotting out of its "national humiliation." Taiwan was a core issue on the patriotic agenda that had fueled China's twentieth-century politics. Mao was also extremely sensitive to being taken advantage of by the Americans on this issue as he entered into a new relationship with the Americans. Mao feared that because the Americans believed China needed U.S. help in dealing with Soviet pressure, Washington would try to take advantage of China on the Taiwan issue.[16] This was unacceptable to Mao.

Nixon confronted far less amorphous domestic constraints on the Taiwan issue. The conservative wing of the Republican Party was strongly supportive of Taiwan and suspicious of liberal Republican Nelson Rockefeller's protégé, Henry Kissinger. Any endangerment of the security of Taiwan would condemn Nixon's opening to China in the eyes of these Republicans, and this, in turn, would diminish Nixon's prospects for a second term as president.

On 9 December 1970, Nixon received his first message from Zhou Enlai. It focused on Taiwan. A representative of the president would be welcome in Beijing for a discussion of the question of Taiwan, Zhou said. Nixon replied by widening the scope of potential discussion. Any meeting should not be limited to a discussion of Taiwan. A range of global issues should be discussed, Nixon said.[17] Regarding Taiwan, the United States was willing to reduce its military presence on Taiwan "as tensions diminish in East Asia and the Pacific region." In an oral comment to the Pakistani intermediary who carried these messages, Kissinger remarked that the withdrawal of U.S. forces from Taiwan was not a difficult problem.[18] Nixon and Kissinger took the absence of any reference to the Vietnam War as an encouraging indication that Beijing did not consider the war an insurmountable obstacle to U.S.-PRC rapprochement.

In his next message, in April 1971, Zhou Enlai reiterated Beijing's insistence that the Taiwan issue be at the center of the forthcoming talks. The Taiwan issue was the principal and prerequisite problem that had to be resolved before relations between the United States and China could be restored, Zhou insisted. In order to reach a settlement with the United States, however, Beijing was interested in direct discussions and, therefore, reaffirmed its willingness to receive a special envoy from the president. Nixon believed that Zhou's reference to Taiwan was "ritual," and felt that the important thing was that Beijing was now ready to open direct and high-level contacts with the United States. Zhou's insistence on the Taiwan issue, Nixon believed, was primarily a way of guarding the opening to Washington from criticism by more militant elements within the CCP and of keeping on record Beijing's stance on Taiwan.[19] Nixon therefore gave a go-ahead for Kissinger's visit to Beijing on the condition that "each side would be free to raise the issues of principle concern to it." Zhou's reply agreed to this but specified that China's first concern was Taiwan. Zhou also picked up the U.S. concession of the previous December by adding that China's prime interest was to find a "concrete way" for the withdrawal of all U.S. forces from Taiwan and the Taiwan area. Kissinger maintained that U.S. forces would be withdrawn as Sino-U.S. relations improved, thus establishing an implicit link between withdrawal and PRC nonuse of force against Taiwan.[20]

The Taiwan issue did not dominate the three days of discussions during Kissinger's first visit to Beijing in July 1971. During the first formal meeting of Kissinger and Zhou, Taiwan was mentioned only briefly. During the second meeting, symbolically held in the Fujian room of the Great Hall of the People, Zhou delivered a strident presentation which included Beijing's claim to Taiwan. Later, when the Chinese side presented its draft of the communiqué announcing the forthcoming U.S. presidential visit to China, it asserted that the purpose of the visit was to discuss the Taiwan issue as a prelude to normalization of relations. Kissinger rejected this, insisting that Taiwan could not be the sole agenda item of the forthcoming presidential visit.[21] Zhou then said that while topics other than Taiwan might be discussed, this should not be mentioned in the joint communiqué to be issued at the conclusion of Nixon's forthcoming visit. Kissinger rejected this too and insisted, successfully, that the communiqué make references to discussions of global issues.[22] While giving ground on these issues, Zhou upped Beijing's demands by insisting that the United States recognize that Taiwan was a province of China, in addition to withdrawing its armed forces.[23] Finding a way around this demand became a major focus of the process of drafting the communiqué during Nixon's visit to Beijing. Kissinger also indicated during his July visit that the United States would not support Taiwan independence.[24]

During Kissinger's second visit to China in October 1971, the Taiwan issue dominated the first round of negotiations over the communiqué to be issued during Nixon's forthcoming visit. Zhou led off with a tough speech, which was delivered, Zhou said, at the express instructions of Mao. The speech demanded, inter alia, that the United States renounce its ties to Taiwan. Kissinger answered in kind with an "unusually hard" reply. China would not respect the United States if it started its new relation by betraying old friends, Kissinger said. The United States would not renounce its ties with Taiwan, Kissinger told Zhou.[25] The two sides then agreed that the joint communiqué would follow the unusual format of allowing the two sides to state contradictory positions on various issues, including Taiwan. There was much negotiation about exactly what each side would say regarding Taiwan. The two sides eventually agreed to this formulation of the American position: "The United States acknowledges that all Chinese on either side of the Taiwan Strait maintain there is but one China and that Taiwan is a part of China. The United States Government does not challenge that position." The phrase "and that Taiwan is a part of China" was added at Chinese insistence.[26] This verbiage was a diplomatic masterpiece that accommodated both the United States' insistence that it would not remain disinterested if Beijing used force against Taiwan and the PRC's insistence that relations between the mainland and Taiwan were purely an internal affair of China. The use of the word "acknowledge" (*renshidao* in Chinese) rather than "recognize" (*chengren* in Chinese) in the Shanghai communiqué, together with attribution of the view that "Taiwan is a part of China" to "all Chinese on either side of the Taiwan Strait," provided a legal basis for continuing U.S. relations with Taiwan not subject to Beijing's veto. In diplomatic usage, "recognition" implies acceptance of a state or government's claims to sovereignty. The term "acknowledge" does not carry this implication. Had the United States "recognized" that "Taiwan is a part of China," it would have given Beijing standing to regulate relations between the United States and Taiwan. By attributing the idea that "there is but one China and Taiwan is a part of China" to "all Chinese on either side of the Taiwan Strait," U.S. negotiators put additional legal distance between the United States and acceptance of the PRC claim to sovereignty over Taiwan. In effect, the United States took no position over whether or not Taiwan was a part of China but merely acknowledged that other governments did so. The United States promised only not "to challenge" the position that Taiwan was a part of China. This corresponded to the pledge that the United States would not support Taiwan independence. The equally critical paragraph of the joint communiqué regarding the American defense relationship with Taiwan was not negotiated until Nixon's arrival in Beijing in January 1972.

Four days before Nixon left for Beijing, his third annual foreign policy report was published. It reaffirmed all U.S. existing alliance relations, spoke of the United States' "friendship, our diplomatic ties, and our defense commitment" to Taiwan, and stressed that "a peaceful resolution of this problem by the parties would do much to reduce tension in the Far East."[27] This put on record the U.S. position for the upcoming talks in Beijing, and was intended to reassure Taiwan and other U.S. friends in the region.

According to Nixon's account, "Taiwan was the touchstone for both sides" during the 1972 summit. "We were committed to Taiwan's right to exist as an independent nation," Nixon said, while "The Chinese were equally determined to use the communiqué to assert their unequivocal claim to the island."[28] Nixon used arguments about building a political basis within the United States for U.S.-PRC rapprochement to persuade Zhou and Mao to mute their claim to Taiwan in the communiqué:

> We knew that if the Chinese made a strongly belligerent claim to Taiwan in the communiqué, I would come under murderous crossfire from all the various pro-Taiwan, anti-Nixon, and anti-PRC lobbies and interest groups at home. If these groups found common ground on the eve of the presidential elections, the entire China initiative might be turned into a partisan issue. Then, if I lost the election, whether because of this particular factor or not, my successor might not be able to continue developing the relationship [with] Peking. In the official plenary sessions with Chou, therefore, I spoke very frankly about the practical political problems a strongly worded communiqué on Taiwan would cause me.[29]

After "lengthy discussions," Zhou's "common sense" led him to agree to "sufficiently modified language." The two sides would agree to disagree over Taiwan and those differences would be reflected, in moderate language, in the communiqué. Mao Zedong made the final decision.[30] When meeting with Mao, Nixon repeatedly said that he could make no "secret deal" regarding Taiwan. This implied that the United States should not be understood, by Mao, as abandoning Taiwan for the sake of anti-Soviet cooperation with the PRC.

Regarding the joint communiqué's treatment of U.S. military relations with Taiwan, the Chinese pushed for the United States to say that peaceful solution of the Taiwan question was a U.S. "hope." The U.S. side insisted, however, that this was not merely a "hope" but an "interest," and, moreover, insisted on "reaffirming" it. "Reaffirmation" connoted a long-standing, and therefore basic, interest. China also pushed for a U.S. commitment to total and unconditional withdrawal of U.S. military forces from Taiwan. Nixon resisted this and would go no further than saying that such a withdrawal was the *ultimate* U.S. objective. Even then, he insisted on linking such withdrawal to both a peaceful solution of the Taiwan problem and an easing of tensions in Asia in general. Kissinger and Qiao Guanhua spent many hours debating these terms, with Kissinger rejecting repeated attempts to weaken the U.S. position. Moreover, while including the Chinese demand that "all U.S. forces and military installations must be withdrawn from Taiwan," the joint communiqué contained neither Chinese condemnation of, nor indeed any reference to, the 1954 U.S.-Taiwan defense treaty—this in spite of the fact that Nixon's foreign policy report of only a few days before had reiterated the continuing validity of that treaty commitment. The same point was reiterated by Kissinger while still on Chinese soil at a press conference on 27 February 1972.[31] In the communiqué, the United States "affirmed" that its "ultimate objective" was "the withdrawal of all U.S. forces and military installations from Taiwan." "In the meantime," it was to "progressively reduce its forces and military installations on Taiwan as the tension in the area diminishes."

Nixon and Kissinger left Beijing confident that they had achieved their objective of reassuring the U.S. Congress that the United States was still committed to defending Taiwan against attack from the PRC—that they had not "abandoned" Taiwan. They did not, however, achieve the same objective vis-à-vis Taiwan itself. Nationalist leaders were deeply suspicious that Nixon and Kissinger had made a secret agreement with Beijing to sacrifice Taiwan on the altar of the strategic triangle. Ambassador Shen met with President Nixon shortly after Nixon's return from China. Nixon assured Shen that the United States had not made a "secret deal" regarding Taiwan and would not negotiate the fate of other countries behind their backs. He also told Shen, "Between our two countries we have a Mutual Defense Treaty. Please tell your government that the United States is determined to abide by its commitments to the Republic of China."[32] Nixon pointed out that the Shanghai communiqué had not reached agreement on a number of issues, but had merely allowed both sides to state their own positions. One of these issues was Taiwan. Shen put the question to Nixon, "Did Chou En-lai promise not to use force against Taiwan?" And Nixon answered, "No." Shen cited this failure to explicitly renounce use of force against Taiwan as proof of his thesis that the United States had "sold out its ally."

It is likely that Zhou and Mao *did* actually hope to drive a wedge between Taipei and Washington via rapprochement with Washington. By drawing the United States away from Taiwan, by securing gradual U.S. political-military disengagement from Taiwan, Beijing hoped to lay the basis for the eventual "liberation" of Taiwan and its incorporation into the PRC. A document justifying the opening to America that was circulated within the CCP in 1973 advanced exactly such a rationale. The "wise strategic decision of Chairman Mao" to open ties to the U.S. imperialists was significant in four ways, the document said. The fourth way dealt with Taiwan:

> Fourthly, it benefits our liberation of Taiwan. . . . For over 20 years the [Chiang Kai-shek] gang has relied on U.S. imperialism and signed all sorts of military and economic treaties with it. The gang depends entirely on "U.S. aid" as a means of survival. Taiwan is in reality forcibly occupied by U.S. imperialism. . . . The Shanghai communiqué . . . forced U.S. imperialism to take cognizance of the fact that Taiwan is a part of Chinese territory and that the ultimate objective is the withdrawal of all U.S. forces and military installations from Taiwan. This keeps U.S. imperialism from making a further intervention in Taiwan. Simultaneously with the improvement in the Sino-U.S. relations, there will arise a gradual alienation in the relations between the United States and the Chiang gang. This is beneficial to our settlement of the Taiwan question without foreign intervention. Meanwhile, the Chiang gang, when formerly banking on the support of U.S. imperialism, appeared to be quite tough. Now, in the wake of the improvement in relations between China and the United States, with the U.S. Army to be withdrawn from Taiwan, the Chiang gang is no longer able to get tough. We can exploit this by urging them to come over for talks in order to strive for the liberation of Taiwan and the unification of the fatherland by peaceful means.[33]

Mao and Zhou did not recognize any trade-off between opening to the United States for the sake of security objectives and the compromise with the United States over the issue of Taiwan. Rapprochement with Washington would serve *both* objectives, they concluded. They believed that Washington wanted cooperation with Beijing for broad regional and global reasons, and as long as China kept up the pressure over the Taiwan issue and insisted that Washington disengage from Taiwan, the United States would eventually accede to China's demands on Taiwan. The Soviet Union would thus be deterred *and* Taiwan would return to the embrace of the Motherland. This dual strategy succeeded in 1979, when the United States did withdraw militarily from Taiwan. Beijing failed to secure Taiwan's incorporation into the PRC after 1979 because the United States refused to withdraw its military and political protection from Taiwan. This seems clear enough in retrospect. It was not at all clear at the time, especially from Taipei's perspective.

Shortly after the Shanghai communiqué was issued, Taipei reiterated its unequivocal denial of the legitimacy of the CCP regime and its commitment to the overthrow of that regime.[34] Taipei objected deeply to Nixon's 1972 trip to China in part because they believed it contributed to the legitimization of the CCP regime. Chinese leaders from Taiwan understood very well the role that foreign leaders traveling to the Forbidden City to pay obeisance to the emperor played in making the emperor's rule acceptable to ordinary Chinese. Nixon's trip demonstrated to ordinary Chinese that even the ruler of America, the great outer country far across the seas, respected and recognized China's modern emperor, Mao. In this context, Taipei also found objectionable many of Nixon's actions, words, and mannerisms. Nixon seemed "obeisant," "self-demeaning," and "too anxious to please."[35] ROC leaders steeped in China's cultural tradition probably understood this aspect of Nixon's visit much better than did U.S. leaders. Yet, even had American leaders understood better the internal dynamics of Mao's need for international recognition, it is difficult to see what significance this would have had. The U.S. objective was not, and had never been, the overthrow of the CCP regime. The Nationalists were committed to this goal, and, indeed, this commitment was a large part of the reason for its taking umbrage at Nixon's conferring legitimacy on Mao's regime. The United States, however, had never shared this objective. Throughout the U.S.-Nationalist alliance, the U.S. objective was to contain Communist China, not to overthrow Communism in China.

Nixon's reliance on secret diplomacy when engineering Sino-U.S. rapprochement exacerbated GRC suspicions. Nixon was well known for his obsession with secrecy. In the case of China policy, secrecy may well have been necessary. The China question was an extremely controversial issue in the United States. Given Nationalist China's many close supporters in the U.S. Congress, liaison with Taipei would probably have led in short order to congressional opposition to Nixon's bold, new policy. Had Nixon been forced to concentrate on defending policy before Congress and the media rather than engineering ties with China, he could easily have lost the initiative. Recognition of the strength of pro-Taiwan sentiment in Congress was one reason for Nixon's reliance on secret diplomacy during his engineering of rapprochement with Beijing. He felt that unless final arrangements for his upcoming visit to China were kept entirely secret, "conservative opposition might mobilize in Congress and scuttle the entire effort."[36]

U.S. Demonstrations of Support

Taipei's apprehensions about possible betrayal by Washington were also based on an understanding that Beijing's immediate objective was to divide the United States and the ROC via "smiling diplomacy" toward Washington, while simultaneously building up military superiority in the Taiwan Strait. Taipei feared that once this was accomplished, the PLA would launch a large scale assault on Jinmen and Mazu. In November 1971, ROC planning posited the PLA as using between 8 and 11 infantry armies; 9 artillery, armor, and amphibious divisions, 109 warships, 322 cargo vessels, and 425 junks; and 1,036 fighter aircraft.[37] U.S. leaders, with their knowledge of the depth of PRC-USSR antagonisms in 1971, probably discounted the realistic possibility of a PLA assault in the Taiwan Strait, but they also knew that since these fears were real, they could have real consequences in terms of Taiwan's actions. Thus Washington took a number of moves designed to reassure Taipei as the United States moved toward rapprochement with the PRC. In April 1971, the Pentagon approved the lease of two submarines to the ROC navy. These were Taiwan's first submarines, weapons which Taipei had long sought to acquire. They were transferred to Taiwan in 1973 after ROC navy personnel had completed training in the United States.[38] From 20 August to 24 August 1971, about a month after Kissinger's first visit to Beijing, the flagship of the Seventh Fleet, the guided missile cruiser *U.S.S. Oklahoma City,* visited northern Taiwan's Keelung. Representatives of the local media were allowed to tour and photograph the ship. For its part, the MND arranged a "troop cheering" show including singers, dancers, and acrobats, to welcome the *Oklahoma City's* crew. This was the first such welcoming ceremony in a number of years. The U.S. Navy's air demonstration team, the Blue Angels, also performed in Taiwan during November 1971 as part of a multicountry tour of the western Pacific.[39]

More substantively, elements of the U.S. military conducted joint exercises with the ROC military—exercises with the hypothetical purpose of repulsing a PLA attack. As we saw in chapter 6, throughout the 1960s joint U.S.-ROC exercises were typically premised on unconventional warfare on the mainland. The last such exercise was in 1968. The termination of these exercises was apparently part of the architecture of U.S.-PRC rapprochement. By 1971, joint exercises carried out under the 1954 treaty were purely defensive. The November 1971 joint exercise envisioned repulse of a PLA assault on Jinmen and Mazu, with CINCPAC supplying an aircraft carrier with destroyer escorts, plus reconnaissance, fighter, and antisubmarine warfare (ASW) aircraft. The exercise also envisioned U.S. authorization to attack and destroy airbases, missile-launching sites, logistics lines, and supply dumps supporting the PLA assault.[40] Similar annual exercises continued throughout the 1970s: in May 1973, May 1974, May 1975, March–May 1976, April–May 1977, and May 1978. The last joint exercise envisioned a surprise attack by three PLA armies, including a full-scale invasion of the Pescadores combined with a blockade of Jinmen and Mazu, plus air attacks and infiltration of Taiwan by land and by sea.[41]

Taipei was not completely reassured by Washington's professions of continuing concern for Taiwan's security and its residual military cooperation with Taiwan. Balanced against these moves were a series of American moves to disengage from Taiwan and the Far East. In 1974, Congress repealed the Formosa resolution of 1955 as part of a series of moves to limit presidential discretion regarding the use of military force.[42] More momentously, the United States remained passive in 1975, as South Vietnam collapsed before a massive, conventional invasion by Hanoi's forces. The spectacle of the United States washing its hands of a once-close ally in which it had invested such energy and treasure was profoundly disturbing to Taipei. The prediction of the pessimists seemed to be coming to pass.

Taipei's Nuclear and Soviet Gambits

As U.S.-PRC rapprochement accelerated during the first Nixon Administration, Taipei toyed with two options: rapprochement with the Soviet Union and development of nuclear weapons. Although consideration of the second option, especially, takes us beyond the time frame of this book, it is nonetheless appropriate, because these moves were consequences of the momentous realignment of Taiwan, the PRC, and the United States in 1971–72.

Taipei's Soviet gambit began in October 1968, when Victor Louis, Moscow correspondent for the *London Times* and unofficial Soviet plenipotentiary, paid the first visit by a Soviet citizen to Taiwan since 1949. While there, Louis talked with Defense Minister Chiang Ching-kuo regarding the possibilities of improving Soviet-Taiwan relations, and extended an invitation to ROC journalists to visit the USSR.[43] In the spring of the following year, in the midst of the spiraling Sino-Soviet border confrontation, several unofficial ROC representatives showed up for events in Moscow and Sofia.

Another flurry of symbolic actions came on the heels of the ROC's expulsion from the United Nations. In November 1971, Foreign Minister Chow Shu-kai announced that since the ROC was no longer in the UN, it would trade with all Communist countries other than Communist China. There would be no "political ties" to Taiwan's trade, Chow said. About this time, there were also repeated reports that the Soviet Union was covertly contributing money for the development of various industrial enterprises in Taiwan.[44] The following March, Chow was explicit with a group of U.S. reporters who were touring Asia to determine the reaction of Asian leaders to Nixon's recent visit to the PRC. During the interview Chow said that, although he did not envision formal diplomatic relations between the USSR and the ROC, he did anticipate a further development of relations. While not compromising its anti-Communist philosophy, Chow said, Taiwan would explore what it could do with the Soviet Union. Chow envisioned "secret talks" between Taiwan and the Soviet Union, similar to the U.S.-PRC talks in Warsaw. Taipei would study the "possibilities" that arose from such talks, and were the United States to make important concessions to Beijing, or to disengage completely from the Western Pacific, "The Free nations of Asia would begin turning toward the Soviet Union," Chow warned.[45] Two days after Chow's provocative remarks, the Foreign Ministry issued an "explanation" that diluted them a bit. Still, the message had been conveyed. Soviet actions indicated that it too saw utility in signaling the possibility of a Soviet-Taiwan link. In May 1973, two days before the head of the newly established U.S. Liaison Office in Beijing was scheduled to assume his post, Soviet warships passed through the Taiwan Strait and then turned back north to circumnavigate Taiwan.

The ROC leadership was divided in the early 1970s over possible links with the USSR. Chow Shu-kai felt that signals about possible links with Moscow were useful as a way of warning Beijing not to push too hard. A more powerful group of leaders believed that contacts with Moscow would be morally wrong and would undermine support for the ROC in the United States. Many Americans who supported Taiwan did so because of Taipei's uncompromising anti-Communism, and they would be alienated by Taiwanese flirtation with Moscow. Moreover, those opposed to playing the Soviet card argued, dependence on Soviet protection would be extremely foolish, for Moscow was certain to dump Taiwan unceremoniously whenever it served its purposes. Chow Shu-kai's resignation as foreign minister in May 1972 represented a victory for the opponents of the Soviet card.[46]

Regarding Taipei's nuclear gambit, Taiwan began developing nuclear expertise under a U.S.-ROC agreement that was signed in 1955, and which provided for cooperation.[47] Under this agreement, the United States provided U-235 and research reactors for use in scientific, engineering, and medical programs, while Taiwan agreed to abstain from non-civilian-related activities and to accept various safeguards stipulated by the U.S. Atomic Energy Commission to ensure compliance. By the early 1970s, Taiwan had accumulated a substantial store of nuclear expertise. Over 700 Taiwanese had studied nuclear technology in U.S. government laboratories and universities.[48]

During the late 1960s, Taiwan began an ambitious atomic energy program, planning to meet half of its electricity requirement by atomic-powered generators by the mid-1980s. In 1969, Taipei purchased a large (40-megawatt) heavy water reactor from Canada. The sales contract contained no clause prohibiting reprocessing of spent fuel to obtain plutonium and the Canadian reactor became the core of a nuclear system independent of International Atomic Energy Agency (IAEA) safeguards. The Canadian reactor was similar to the one (also Canadian-supplied) used by India to produce the plutonium used in the bomb it exploded in 1974.[49] Even more ominously, in 1969 Taiwan began construction of a reprocessing laboratory with components obtained from around the world. The United States refused to cooperate with Taiwan's reprocessing efforts, and made clear its determination to oppose such activities. In the U.S. view, Taiwan's civil power program did not justify a reprocessing program.[50] The reprocessing facility was operational by 1975. By the next year, Taiwan had four nuclear generating units under construction and another two in the planning stage.[51]

In mid-1975 Taipei decided to begin extracting plutonium. In October it informed the United States of its intention to reprocess spent fuel from its U.S.-supplied research reactor. During the first half of 1976, U.S. intelligence learned that Taiwan had begun the secret reprocessing of spent uranium fuel from the Canadian and other smaller research reactors.

The accelerating pace of U.S.-PRC rapprochement, plus the U.S. debacle in Indochina, reportedly caused a "hawk" faction to insist that the United States was unreliable and that nuclear weapons were a necessary last-resort defense against attack by China. Other Nationalist officials were reportedly opposed to such a course because of the fiscal burden it would impose, but may well have agreed to move in that direction in order to signal to Washington that U.S. interest would not be served if Taiwan felt compelled to rely entirely on itself for defense.[52]

Nuclearization of Taiwan could have prompted similar developments in Japan, in South Korea, and elsewhere in Asia—a development adverse to U.S. and PRC interests. It would also have diminished the prospects for a peaceful resolution of the Taiwan question; at least, U.S. analysts seem to have concluded this would have been the case.[53]

On 14 September 1976, U.S. Ambassador Leonard Unger met with Premier Chiang Ching-kuo to underline U.S. opposition to Taiwan's reprocessing activities. The American message was that continuation of the present course would "seriously jeopardize" cooperation in civilian uses of nuclear energy. The United States supplied all of Taiwan's enriched uranium fuel for its nuclear power plants. Taiwan could have purchased uranium fuel from South Africa. The United States warned, however, that continued reprocessing by Taiwan would make impossible any further economic or military assistance by the United States.[54] Early in October 1976, Taipei capitulated to U.S. demands. A note promised that Taiwan had "no intention whatsoever to develop nuclear weapons, or a nuclear explosive device, or to engage in any activities related to reprocessing purposes." Taipei also stated its intention of abiding by the Non-Proliferation Treaty and its willingness to open *all* nuclear facilities on Taiwan to IAEA inspections.

Both Taipei's nuclear gambit and its Soviet gambit were intended to limit U.S.-PRC rapprochement, or failing that, to prepare various options in case Taiwan found itself truly abandoned before a PRC threat. Neither ploy succeeded in blocking Sino-U.S. rapprochement. Both, however, did influence Washington's and Beijing's handling of their new relationship. On the American side, there was recognition of common U.S. and PRC interests vis-à-vis avoiding a nuclearized or Soviet-linked Taiwan. As an editorial in the *Washington Post* said on 31 August 1976 (just as the US-ROC confrontation over nuclear reprocessing was coming to a head):

> The impulses which make a bomb seem attractive or even compelling to some officials on Taiwan are not, we would emphasize, frivolous. Taiwan looks across the Pacific at the United States, and back over its shoulder at Peking, and is bound to wonder what its future holds. If the United States will not stand still while Taiwan builds its own bomb, then Taiwan has a strong claim on alternative security arrangements based on clear political understandings in Washington, Peking, and Taipei.... Those who would have the United States shift its diplomatic allegiance forthwith from Taipei to Peking, by the way, would do well to bear in mind the impetus to proliferation which such a switch would impart. There is a delicate strategic and diplomatic equation to be written. A way must be found to do it.[55]

A series of statements by the PRC's top leaders in the early 1970s suggest that they took seriously the possibility of collaboration between Moscow and Taipei. In January 1973, for example, Zhou Enlai accused the Soviets of harboring ambitions to occupy Taiwan. Zhou also noted that Soviet ambitions would be opposed not only by the PRC but also by the United States. PRC leaders also reiterated the idea that Beijing and Washington shared an interest in preventing a Taiwan-USSR linkup.[56] From this perspective, Beijing's interests would be served by allowing Taiwan to remain under loose and relatively benign American influence, rather than forcing it beyond the pale of the American sphere with possibly adverse nuclear and Soviet consequences. Beijing's fear of Soviet involvement, exacerbated by Taipei's moves, may have been one factor in persuading Mao to compromise with Nixon over Taiwan during the delicate negotiations of 1971 and 1972.

Notes

1. James C.H. Shen, *The U.S. and Free China: How the U.S. Sold Out Its Ally,* Washington: Acropolis Books, 1983, p. 66. Shen was Taiwan's ambassador to the United States from 1971 to 1978. This is his memoir of that service.

2. Statement to press in Taipei, 3 March 1955, in *Department of State Bulletin,* 14 March 1955, p. 421.

3. Press conference, 26 April 1955, in *Department of State Bulletin,* 9 May 1955, p. 755.

4. Melvin Gurtov, *Taiwan in 1966,* Rand Corporation, AD 641 665, October 1966, Defense Documentation Center, Defense Supply Agency, Naval Historical Center.

5. Richard Nixon, "Asia After Vietnam," *Foreign Affairs,* vol. 46, No. 1 (October 1967), pp. 116–23.

6. See John W. Garver, *China's Decision for Rapprochement with the United States, 1968–1971,* Boulder, CO: Westview, 1982, pp. 55–79.

7. Henry H. Kissinger, *White House Years,* Boston: Little Brown, 1979, p. 187.

8. Shen, *The U.S. and Free China,* p. 66.

9. *Statements and Answers to Press Queries by the Spokesman for the Ministry of Foreign Affairs* (July 1969–June 1970), Taipei: Ministry of Foreign Affairs, 1970, pp. 24–25.

10. Richard H. Solomon, *Chinese Negotiating Behavior, 1967–1984: An Interpretative Assessment* (hereafter cited as Solomon, *An Interpretative Assessment*), R-3299, Rand Corporation, December 1985, p. 32.

11. Shen, *The U.S. and Free China,* p. 66.

12. Ibid., pp. 48–54. Shen was vice foreign minister at the time of Chiang's trip.

13. Ibid., p. 51.

14. Ibid., pp. 56–57.

15. Ibid., p. 72.

16. Solomon, *An Interpretative Assessment,* p. 3.

17. Richard Nixon, *The Memoirs of Richard Nixon* (hereafter cited as *Memoirs*), vol. 2, New York: Warner Books, 1978, p. 10.

18. Richard H. Solomon, *U.S.-PRC Political Negotiations, 1967–1984: An Annotated Chronology* (hereafter cited as Solomon, *An Annotated Chronology*), R-3298, Rand Corporation, December 1985, p. 12.

19. Nixon, *Memoirs,* vol. 2, p. 14.

20. Solomon, *An Interpretative Assessment,* p. 33. Solomon, *An Annotated Chronology,* p. 14.

21. Kissinger, *White House Years,* pp. 749–52.

22. Solomon, *An Interpretative Assessment,* p. 33.

23. Solomon, *An Annotated Chronology,* p. 14.

24. Ibid.

25. Kissinger, *White House Years,* p. 782.

26. Ibid., p. 783. The text of the final Shanghai communiqué is in *China, U.S. Policy Since 1945,* Washington: Congressional Quarterly, 1972, pp. 21–23.

27. Kissinger, *White House Years,* p. 1053.

28. Nixon, *Memoirs,* vol. 2, p. 407.

29. Ibid., pp. 40–41.

30. Ibid.

31. Kissinger, *White House Years,* pp. 1073, 1075–80.

32. Shen, *The U.S. and Free China,* p. 8.

33. "Reference Materials Concerning Education on Situation," prepared by the Political Department of the Kunming Military Region, 4 April 1973, in *Chinese Communist Internal Politics and Foreign Policy,* Taipei: Institute of International Relations, 1974, pp. 136–37.

34. *Statements and Communiqués (July 1971–June 1972),* Taipei: Ministry of Foreign Affairs, 1972, p. 26.

35. Shen, *The U.S. and Free China,* p. 79.

36. Nixon, *Memoirs,* vol. 2, p. 14.

37. *Meijun zaiHua gongzuo jishi (xiefang zhi bu)* [Record of U.S. military activities on Taiwan (defense assistance section)] (hereafter cited as *Xiefang zhi bu*), Taipei: Historical Bureau, Ministry of National Defense, October 1981, pp. 13–18.

38. *Meijun zaiHua gongzuo shiji (haijun guwen zhibu)* [Record of U.S. military activities on Taiwan (naval advisory section)], Taipei: Historical Bureau, Ministry of National Defense, 1981, pp. 220–22.

39. Commander U.S. TDC, *Command History, 1 July–31 December 1971,* Public Affairs Office, Headquarters U.S. TDC, Taipei, Taiwan, 1972, pp. III-23.

40. *Xiefang zhi bu,* p. 23.

41. Ibid., p. 65.

42. The text of the relevant congressional action is in Ralph N. Clough, *Island China,* Cambridge, MA: Harvard University Press, 1978, pp. 114–15.

43. John W. Garver, "Taiwan's Russian Option: Image and Reality," *Asian Survey,* vol. XVIII, no. 7 (July 1978), pp. 751–66.

44. Garver, *China's Decision,* p. 757.

45. Garver, "Taiwan's Russian Option," p. 765.

46. Clough, *Island China,* pp. 169–70.

47. *Treaties Between the Republic of China and Foreign States (1927–1957),* Taipei: Ministry of Foreign Affairs, 1958, pp. 831–35.

48. Edward Schumacher, "Taiwan Seen Reprocessing Nuclear Fuel," *Washington Post,* 29 August 1976, pp. 1, 3.

49. Don Oberdorfer, "Atomic Fuel in Taiwan Not Inspected," *Washington Post,* 5 June 1976, pp. 1, 6.

50. Testimony by Assistant Secretary for East Asia Arthur W. Hummel, Jr., before Subcommittee on Arms Control, Senate Foreign Relations Committee, 22 September 1976 (hereafter cited as Testimony by Hummel), in *Department of State Bulletin,* 11 October 1976, pp. 454–56.

51. Ibid.

52. Schumacher, "Taiwan Seen Reprocessing Nuclear Fuel." Also see "A Nuclear Taiwan?" *Washington Post,* 31 August 1976, p. 14.

53. Schumacher, "Taiwan Seen Reprocessing Nuclear Fuel." "A Nuclear Taiwan?"

54. Testimony by Hummel.

55. "A Nuclear Taiwan?"

56. Clough, *Island China,* p. 169.

16

Conclusions

All Means Short of War

Nationalist China played a central role in the political war waged by the United States. The U.S. program of political warfare against the PRC was multifaceted, systematic, and sustained. A central focus of that effort was to undermine the authority of China's Communist state. To this end, U.S. policy encouraged and assisted antigovernment movements. It infiltrated cadre, and it air-dropped arms and communications equipment to anti-Communist rebels. It provided training, munitions, and (presumably) money for anti-Communist "dissidents" within China. It encouraged and supported ethnic rebellions, most importantly in Tibet. It established radio stations to broadcast news detrimental to Beijing's authority and prestige. It attempted to isolate the Communist regime internationally, denying it the prestige and international legitimacy that derive from international interactions. Economically, it sought to constrict the international commerce of Communist China through a number of means.

The U.S. objective in doing all this was not to overthrow China's Communist-led state, but to weaken and constrain that state, to enhance its sense of vulnerability, and to increase the demands it made on its Soviet ally. Overthrow of China's Communist state might be a desirable objective, but it was an unrealistic one, most U.S. leaders concluded. American propaganda talked about the overthrow of the Communist regime, and Nationalist Chinese leaders certainly took this objective seriously. U.S. leaders were skeptical about whether this could be accomplished through any means

283

short of an all-out U.S. military effort against China. A more realistic objective inspired U.S. strategy of political warfare: keeping the Sino-Soviet alliance in a pressure cooker until it split apart. Once that objective was achieved, which happened by 1960, the strategy continued, partly as a result of inertia and partly as a response to the growing revolutionary militancy of China.

In the context of this program of political war, Nationalist China provided ideologically dedicated and ethnically Chinese personnel for a broad range of U.S.-sponsored covert, intelligence, and special operations. By the late 1950s, the standing threat of invasion by large and well-trained Nationalist armies, supported by U.S. military air and naval forces, contributed to balance of power favorable to U.S. victory should the Cold War turn hot. Nationalist China also provided a surrogate China, support of which allowed the United States to restrict the PRC's international diplomatic influence for two decades. Politically, the example of an increasingly prosperous, relatively free China stood as an alternative to the Communist model of development being implemented by the CCP. Washington did everything possible to persuade Chinese everywhere, including communities of Chinese living outside China, that the government in Taipei, not the government in Beijing, deserved their loyalties.

Most U.S. measures of covert involvement in China's internal affairs seem to have been suspended about 1965. Most covert operations ended by the middle of the 1960s, although the Tibetan operation apparently continued to the end of that decade. It is possible that this conclusion is inaccurate, due to the thirty-year declassification rule of the U.S. Department of State. As records for the late 1960s are declassified, and more especially as the U.S. Central Intelligence Agency loses its aversion to the Freedom of Information Act, it may become apparent that U.S. covert operations against China continued until 1972, or possibly even later. More probably, however, the suspension of these operations was related to the escalation of the Vietnam War in 1965–66 and to Washington's desire to prevent the expansion of that conflict into another direct Sino-U.S. war. In 1972, with U.S.-PRC rapprochement, the United States dropped the last of its covert operations against the mainland.

The CCP waged a similar political war against the United States. Although this book has focused on U.S.-Nationalist efforts against Communist China, the fact that Beijing was simultaneously doing all it could to injure and punish the United States must not be overlooked. To do so would be to severely distort history. The CCP did all that it could to encourage the USSR and the international Communist movement to adopt militant, anti-U.S. policies. Torrents of anti-American propaganda were generated and distributed around the world. Beijing gave encouragement and substantial material assistance to a wide array of anti-American dissident and revolutionary movements. Anti-imperialist parties and movements from Southeast Asia to Africa to Latin America received Chinese training, arms, money, and political support. Anti-American forces from Charles de Gaulle to Japan's Communist Party were courted and encouraged. Most important, Beijing gave large-scale and crucial support to Kim Il Sung's war to conquer South Korea and to Ho Chi Minh's war to take over South Vietnam. In short, the Cold War between the PRC and the United States was a deep confrontation in which *both sides* used all means short of war. Each side gave as good as it got.

The U.S. campaign of pressure against the PRC can be seen as an attempt to socialize the new Chinese state, the People's Republic of China, to the norms of international society. A recent study of this phenomenon by David Armstrong develops a theoretical analysis of this issue and presents a series of case studies in the socialization of revolutionary states.[1] In the early years of their existence, states that emerge out of the ideologically inspired social upheavals we call revolutions often reject the norms of the old international order into which they are born. That old order is based on legal norms of mutual respect for sovereignty among states. The state is the highest authority, and states entering that society pledge themselves to respect the legal rights of sovereignty of other states in return for respect of their own claims of sovereignty. Revolutionary states, however, typically envision a universal community of humanity whose claims to loyalty supersede those of states. This grand community of humankind requires solidarity of like-minded comrades across interstate boundaries. Indeed, such boundaries, along with the many other practices of the old state-centric order, are seen as obstacles to the march of humanity toward the grand community of the future.

The revolutionary states' violation of the norms of the state-centric order lead other members of that society to impose sanctions. These range from refusal to recognize the deviant revolutionary state (i.e., refusal to confer the rights of a sovereign state on the new entity) to war. The sanctions by the norm-abiding members of the state-centric society impose costs on the revolutionary state. Over a period of time, these costs persuade the new states' leaders to modify their behavior. As this socialization progresses, as the new state conforms more and more to the norms of the state-centric system, other members of that society make available the rewards that flow from lawful participation in the established order: commercial and financial benefits, diplomatic recognition and status, and a degree of protection that comes from being a law-abiding member of a legal order. Eventually the new state is socialized.

In his case study of the PRC, Armstrong dates the PRC's socialization to the 1970s and 1980s. The early PRC had little regard for the norms of the established state-centric order. While claiming its rights as a sovereign state, the PRC refused to recognize its obligations as a member of state society. It violated the immunity of U.S. diplomats and diplomatic facilities in China. It seized the legal property of the U.S. government. It de facto confiscated foreign commercial property through a campaign of escalating squeeze. It delivered massive amounts of aid to Ho Chi Minh's forces struggling against the French colonial state in Indochina. It gave similar support to Kim Il Sung's effort to obliterate the South Korean state. Most egregious, China's new rulers linked their state to the USSR's global drive to topple the existing interstate order, and to replace it by a community of Leninist Party states.

From this perspective, the protracted political war waged by the United States consisted of sanctions imposed by a major beneficiary of the state-centric order to socialize a deviant state. As China began assimilating the norms of the interstate order, those sanctions were dropped. With them ended the U.S. alliance with Nationalist China.

Rapprochement with Beijing entailed suspension of the United States' political war against the PRC. Nationalist China thereby lost much of its utility to Washington. Twenty years of close cooperation prevented a return to the December 1949 policy of sacrificing the Taiwan pawn for the sake of exploiting USSR-PRC relations. Instead, the mantle of U.S. protection continued to cover Taiwan, though ever less directly, predicated on the continuing utility of Taiwan in the maintenance of U.S. thalassocracy in the western Pacific and on Taiwan's accelerating evolution toward liberal and democratic politics.

Costs and Benefits of the Alliance with the Nationalists

As noted in the introduction to this book, many analysts have maintained that the United States' alliance with Nationalist China was a mistake—that it injured more than it benefited the United States. Having reviewed the U.S.-Nationalist alliance in detail, it is now possible to return to this question by assessing the costs and gains to the United States from the alliance with Nationalist China.

The costs of the alliance were many and heavy. Severe strain was put on U.S. alliances with Britain and Japan. London believed that the Anglo-American powers would be best served by washing their hands of Taiwan and the Nationalist regime there, as part of an effort to reach a modus vivendi with the PRC. This approach was modified somewhat by recognition of military exigencies arising out of the Korean War, but London believed that links with the Nationalists should be kept to a minimum and that the Cairo Declaration's transfer of Taiwan to China should be unequivocally upheld. London was dismayed by the Eisenhower Administration's embrace of the Nationalists.[2]

Anglo-American disagreements over China policy were genuine, and generated tensions within that alliance. Those tensions and disputes did not, however, impair the Anglo-American alliance. Common British and American interests in Europe were so overwhelming, and the bonds of fraternity forged in two world wars against Germany were so strong, that disagreements over China policy remained a secondary irritant in London-Washington relations.

Regarding U.S.-Japanese relations, the United States' embrace of Nationalist China also created sharp disagreements. The imperative of trade with the China mainland led Japan's postwar governments to desire normal relations with the PRC. There was also substantial popular and left-wing resentment about Japan's being tied to the anti-China policies of the United States. But these tensions too remained secondary and did not prevent the evolution of a close Japan-U.S. alliance. Japan's need of U.S. support in other areas was great: It was needed to recover sovereignty and end the occupation, to develop Japan's economy through participation in the postwar system of free trade, and to defend Japan against the USSR. Because of these overriding common interests, Japan's government went along with the United States' China policy despite disagreement with key aspects of it.

U.S. strategic interests defined in terms of dealing with the Sino-Soviet alliance were not identical to the interests of key members of the American-led coalition. The United States' problem was to pull together and to hold together a coalition of disparate powers (including Britain and Japan), so as to pressure the Sino-Soviet alliance. Coalition partners sometimes had divergent interests. The United States had to persuade those partners to more or less go along with U.S. strategic policy, and not to pursue divergent policy interests too substantially, directly, or openly. U.S. leaders were able to achieve this and keep together a fairly coherent coalition around a policy which had as a centerpiece use of the U.S.-Nationalist alliance as an instrument of pressure. The United States was able to properly manage secondary, intracoalition contradictions so as to keep together a coalition directed against the primary enemy, first the Sino-Soviet alliance and then China alone. Intracoalition tensions over Nationalist China were real, but did not fundamentally undermine the coalition.

The adverse impact of U.S.-Nationalist operations on Burma must be placed squarely in the debit column of the U.S.-Nationalist ledger. U.S.-

Burma relations were soured, and warm PRC-Burma relations were fostered. U.S.-Nationalist activities in northern Burma worked counter to the greater U.S. interest in the emergence of the stable Union of Burma. Washington was lucky that this state survived in spite of the problems inflicted on Rangoon by U.S.-Nationalist activities. U.S. activities in Burma also inadvertently contributed to Burma's emergence as a narcotics production center. In 1996, a U.S. congressional study found that Burma accounted for 94 percent of all opium production in Southeast Asia, with much of that heroin being transported to the United States by ethnic Chinese criminal organizations.[3]

Another cost of the U.S.-Nationalist alliance was increased conflict with the PRC. The U.S. protectorate over Taiwan was the major bone of contention during the ambassadorial talks at Warsaw. It played a key role in the 1958 confrontation that took the two countries to the brink of war. It is not enough, however, to recognize that Taiwan was a source of conflict on U.S.-PRC relations. We must also ask whether U.S.-PRC relations would have been qualitatively better if the United States had not denied Taiwan to the PRC. An answer to this question depends fundamentally on one's beliefs about the sources of the U.S.-PRC confrontation. If, as I argued at the outset, that confrontation involved a clash over the future path of development in a large part of Asia, then conflict over Taiwan becomes proportionately less significant. While Mao and his comrades ardently desired the "liberation" of Taiwan, there were deep conflicts of interest and perspective between Beijing and Washington in a dozen other regions of Asia around China's periphery. These conflicts were rooted in the differing ideologies of the ruling elites of both the PRC and the United States, and in the determination of both to shape Asian development along lines compatible with their national ideologies and interests. In this context, U.S. nonengagement and sacrifice of Taiwan to Beijing would not have averted deep U.S.-PRC conflict. It would, however, have substantially diminished the United States' ability to maintain a balance of power favorable to the shaping of Asia's development along liberal, capitalist lines of development while foiling the efforts of the revolutionary PRC to direct Asia along Leninist, socialist lines of development. Intense U.S.-PRC conflict would have continued, but with the United States holding a less favorable hand.

Utilization of the island of Taiwan by U.S. military forces contributed substantially to the military position of the United States in the region. Naval and air reconnaissance from Taiwan helped the United States keep track of air, surface, and submarine movements off the coast of Asia and in the western Pacific. Taiwan provided an important staging area for large-scale operations in the area. The massive U.S. logistical effort in Vietnam during 1967–72, for example, would not have been possible without a network of forward staging areas—of which Taiwan was an important part. Most fundamentally, U.S. development of the military potential of Nationalist China, and the standing U.S. threat to support a Nationalist return in the event of a general U.S.-PRC war helped ensure that the PRC moved cautiously in pursuing its goals in Asia.

Given the U.S. decision to use covert operations as an instrument of the struggle with the PRC, cooperation with Taiwan gave the United States distinct tactical advantages. Nationalist China offered a substantial cadre of dedicated anti-Communist Chinese who could provide the personnel to conduct these operations. Americans, with their largely European and African heritages, would have been at a severe disadvantage in attempting to conduct operations inside China. Whereas Americans could and did undertake underground operations inside Nazi-occupied Europe, racial and cultural differences made it impossible for Americans to operate clandestinely inside China. Even Chinese Americans, who were far fewer in number in the 1950s than in the 1990s, would have faced substantial difficulties of cultural familiarization. On Taiwan, however, there were many thousands of young Chinese raised in families that spoke the dialects of mainland Chinese provinces and were zealous about destroying Communist power on the mainland.

Political camouflage for covert operations was another American gain. The ROC was in a state of war with the PRC. Although the war was undeclared, as most civil wars are, neither side thought it necessary to hide its hostile acts toward the other. Nationalist newspapers routinely announced commando or air raids against the mainland, while Communist newspapers proudly affirmed Beijing's right to use military force to liberate Taiwan. In such a situation, should various actions be publicized, it would be difficult to distinguish Nationalist from American actions. In the argot of intelligence operations, the Nationalists acted as a "cutout," obfuscating by their presence the true perpetuator of various actions. In a strict legal sense, since the United States recognized the ROC as the legitimate government of all of China, whatever it did inside China with the approval of that government did not, again in a strict legal sense, constitute interference in the internal affairs of another sovereign state.

In weighing the costs and gains of the U.S.-Nationalist link, probably the single most important criterion is its impact on the PRC-USSR alliance. Driving a wedge between Beijing and Moscow was a major U.S. objective. If the U.S.-Nationalist alliance contributed to this objective, this must be deemed a major gain. If it helped to hold the PRC-USSR link together, this must be deemed a heavy cost. Many scholars have argued that the latter was the case—that the U.S. link with Nationalist China pushed Beijing closer to Moscow. This proposition seems dubious to me. The fact is that the Sino-

Soviet rupture began and intensified while the U.S.-ROC bond was most strong. Disagreements between Mao and Khrushchev can be traced back to Khrushchev's 1956 denunciation of Stalin at the Twentieth Congress of the Soviet Communist Party, and they intensified over the next several years. During 1958 and 1959, the approaches of Mao and Khrushchev toward relations with the United States gradually diverged, with Mao favoring more militant, confrontational tactics toward the United States and Khrushchev fearing that such tactics would lead to war. By 1960, the rupture was open and was widening rapidly.

This deterioration of Sino-Soviet relations occurred against a background of a continuing strong U.S.-Taiwan alliance. The beginning of the disagreement between Mao and Khrushchev was preceded by the conclusion of the U.S.-ROC mutual security treaty, and it intensified while U.S.-ROC military and economic relations were becoming steadily deeper. Nor was there any weakening of U.S. support for the ROC in the United Nations or in other international forums. Mao's institution of direct policies against Moscow on the occasion of Lenin's Centenary in April 1960 more or less coincided with the first (and only) visit by a seated U.S. president to Taiwan in September 1960. It thus seemed clear that there was no direct correlation between closer U.S.-ROC relations and closer USSR-PRC relations. Indeed, the chronology of events in the 1950s suggests an *inverse* relationship: that closer U.S.-Taiwan ties led to Sino-Soviet tension.

A U.S. sacrifice of Taiwan after the formation of the PRC-USSR alliance would have confirmed to Beijing the utility of that alliance. The Chinese Communist interpretation of a U.S. sacrifice of Taiwan after February 1950 almost certainly would have been that the United States had not dared to intervene on Taiwan because it feared the power of the Sino-Soviet bloc. As it was, the obstinate U.S. engagement with Taiwan during the 1950s precipitated deep disagreements between Beijing and Moscow. Because of U.S. refusal to budge from Taiwan, policy toward Taiwan was a major source of disagreement between Mao and Khrushchev. When Washington moved to sign the mutual security treaty with Nationalist China in 1954 and then proved unwilling to accept Beijing's demands and move away from its close relation with Taiwan in 1957–58, Mao and his comrades decided military force would have to be used to sober the American imperialists. Mao was quite willing to precipitate military confrontations with the United States to achieve various goals vis-à-vis Washington-Taipei relations: to force Washington to reconsider its close association with Taipei, to exacerbate Taipei-Washington contradictions, to retaliate for U.S.-Nationalist operations against the mainland, and so on. The two Strait crises resulted. Khrushchev felt that Mao's willingness to open fire on the U.S. imperialists was reckless. The 1958 crisis seems especially to have been a turning point in this regard, with Khrushchev emerging from that crisis convinced of Mao's recklessness. Such distrust contributed directly and substantially to Moscow's 1959 decision to cancel the nuclear technology agreement with China—a pivotal event in the evolution of the Sino-Soviet dispute. Mao concluded that only a strategy of uncompromising ideological struggle would force the USSR to abandon its "revisionist" policy of appeasing U.S. imperialism. Khrushchev feared the consequences of Mao's militancy and moved steadily to disassociate the USSR from it.

The close U.S. link with Taiwan, it seems, played an important role in the U.S. strategy of exploiting contradictions in the PRC-USSR relation. By tightly integrating Nationalist Formosa into the containment structure in Asia, and by refusing all entreaties and threats to abandon this policy, Washington moved Beijing toward militancy. Taiwan, however, was an issue far removed from Soviet interests. Moreover, there was nothing comparable to the Taiwan question in Soviet-American relations. The USSR was not prepared to risk war to overturn the status quo, with which (under Krushchev) it was essentially satisfied. Beijing's dissatisfaction with the status quo led it to favor a more militant policy. By denying Taiwan to Beijing, Washington fostered divergence between Beijing and Moscow.

Was this intentional? To some degree it was. As we have seen, even after embracing Nationalist Formosa in June 1950, the Truman Administration kept Taipei at arm's length, in anticipation of some sort of accommodation with Beijing after the end of the Korean War. Had this approach been continued into the mid-1950s, the U.S.-PRC ambassadorial talks might have had rather different results. The Eisenhower Administration dropped Truman's policy of maintaining political distance, however, and began treating Taipei as a full-fledged ally. This new approach was intended to break apart the PRC-USSR bond by keeping it in a pressure cooker. As the United States stepped up pressure on China, Beijing would be encouraged to make demands on Moscow—demands that Moscow would be unwilling and unable to satisfy. This, in fact, is pretty much what happened, with Taiwan becoming the key issue of Chinese discontent. Moreover, the conduct of political war against the PRC was a central part of the differential policy toward the PRC and the USSR. That differential policy was, in turn, designed to foster divergent perspectives between Beijing and Moscow. Without U.S. pressure on China, the Sino-Soviet alliance might have endured a good while longer.

Yet we should avoid claiming too much prescience for U.S. strategists. None of the documentary evidence thus far declassified indicates that U.S. leaders foresaw in the 1950s that Taiwan itself would become a major bone of Sino-Soviet contention. Taiwan was merely one part of a larger policy of stepping up the pressure on China. And, of course, U.S. leaders bungled efforts to benefit from the collapse of the Sino-Soviet alliance. If Washington's tough line on Taiwan helped drive a wedge between Beijing and Moscow by pushing Beijing toward a more militant policy, one immediate expression of China's new militancy was support for Hanoi's renewed effort to take over South Vietnam. Once having split apart the Sino-Soviet bloc, U.S. leaders proved spectacularly inept at using that leverage to isolate North Vietnam—at least until Nixon.

As argued earlier, the most important objective sought by the United States in Asia was the containment of Communism in that region. In this regard, U.S. policy was relatively successful. There were major defeats, most prominently in Vietnam, but overall the United States prevailed in East Asia. Today East Asia is home to several vibrant liberal, democratic capitalist states—South Korea, Taiwan, Japan, and the Philippines—and Southeast Asia is home to several other countries that show promise of moving along a similar path—Thailand and Malaysia. Had it not been for the United States' exercise of near-maximum political, economic, and military power over the course of three decades, a number of these countries would have fallen to Communism: certainly South Korea and Taiwan, almost certainly Indonesia, and perhaps the Philippines and Thailand. U.S. political warfare against Communist China lessened China's ability and inclination, and the ability and inclination of the Sino-Soviet bloc, to support revolution in these countries. Had the costs to the PRC incurred by supporting Communist takeovers in various Asian countries been minimal, had such efforts not been met by counterexercise of U.S. power, and had the USSR-PRC alliance not split apart by the pressure cooker of U.S. containment, a much wider swath of Asia would have been subjected to the rigors of the Communist experiment of the twentieth century. The point is that the U.S. alliance with Nationalist China played an important role in the achievement of these successes, and that to a considerable degree this victory justifies the suffering wrought by the political war producing that victory.

It may ultimately turn out that the rejection of Communism in China itself was due, to some degree, to the U.S. policies of political warfare, including those implemented in association with Taiwan. Clearly the primary reasons for rejection of the tenets of Communism in China in the 1980s had primarily to do with the internal problems of the system itself. Moreover, it can be argued that U.S.-Nationalist subversive efforts encouraged and justified the repression that perpetuated the system longer than would otherwise have been the case. Against this, however, would have to be weighed the impact that the model of successful Taiwanese development had on China. It may still be too soon to judge the full impact of U.S. policies on China's evolution. Yet it does seem clear that Taiwan is the first instance of a democratic polity in China's long history. Taiwan, like Japan before it, has apparently succeeded in the immensely difficult task of grafting together Western-derived values and institutions with Confucian-derived culture and psychology. Communism is intellectually dead on the mainland, and many Chinese there are asking fundamental and long-repressed questions about how China is to modernize. The impact of the Taiwan model in this regard may ultimately be substantial.

Intra-Alliance Bargaining

The U.S.-ROC alliance of 1954–71 involved substantial bargaining over policies and levels of support. Chiang Kai-shek attempted repeatedly to persuade Washington to adopt more militant, more confrontational policies toward the PRC, including support for a Nationalist invasion of the mainland. Chiang also used the offshores to engineer situations which promised to draw the United States and the PRC into military conflict. Chiang's interest was in rollback. He was adamantly opposed to American efforts to legally separate Taiwan from the mainland, and he used various techniques, including defection via collapse from demoralization, to foil American two-Chinas schemes and to persuade Washington to countenance more aggressive policies toward the mainland. Thus, Chiang insisted that the United States support the Nationalist engagement of the Chinese Communists at Jinmen, that it not formally reject the possibility of a Nationalist return to the mainland, and that it allow the Nationalists to conduct limited covert war against the mainland.

The United States also used its leverage to modify ROC policies. Taipei was compelled to accept restrictive scope-of-application clauses in both the 1952 peace treaty with Japan and the 1954 U.S.-ROC mutual security treaty. The treaty itself was a quid pro quo for Taipei's acceptance of an effort to secure U.N. sponsorship of the neutralization of the Taiwan Strait. The United States repeatedly rejected Nationalist entreaties for a return and refused to support a Nationalist military force capable of independent military operation. Yet it did agree to a wide range of limited offensive operations demanded by the Nationalists. Washington periodically considered, but always ultimately rejected—though not without concessions—Nationalist rollback proposals. When Nationalist actions periodically threatened to persuade Beijing that the alliance had offensive aims, Washington would reassure Beijing that this was in fact not the case. Thus, early in 1955 after

Chiang succeeded in rejecting U.S. pressure to evacuate Jinmen and secured a private U.S. commitment to its defense, the United States publicly rejected the idea of U.S. support for a Nationalist invasion. Again, after the 1958 crisis, which was precipitated in part by Chiang, U.S. officials publicly denigrated prospects for a Nationalist return and pressured Chiang into endorsing peaceful methods of liberating the mainland. Finally, after the Nationalist invasion drumroll of 1962, Washington informed Beijing that it would not support any Nationalist invasion attempt. Through these actions, Washington signaled Beijing that it would not allow Taipei to define the aims of the alliance and that, in the U.S. view, those aims were defensive.

Both Nationalist efforts to maneuver the United States into conflict with the PRC and U.S. efforts to maneuver the ROC into acceptance of two Chinas caused substantial resentment. From the U.S. perspective, a small and extremely vulnerable ally completely dependent on the United States for protection was attempting to maneuver the United States into a potentially catastrophic war with China—a war initiated without the support of the U.S. people or U.S. allies. Nationalist attitudes were frequently unrealistic and parochial, U.S. leaders believed. The Nationalist counterpart to this American resentment was bitterness at U.S. refusal to live up to its professions of hatred for Communism and its willingness to reach pragmatic compromises with Communist powers. Paramount among such unprincipled compromises was Washington's willingness to come to terms with the PRC while continuing to deny Taiwan to Communist China. The separation of Taiwan from China was as deeply despised by Chiang Kai-shek as was indefinite perpetuation of Communist rule over mainland China. Neither was acceptable. These fundamental differences in perspective and the animosity they generated were kept in bounds by agreement regarding the virtue of the anti-Communist struggle of the Cold War—and by the joint desire to keep Taiwan out of CCP hands.

There were strong similarities between the U.S.-ROC alliance of 1954–71 and the earlier 1941–45 alliance against Japan. The World War II alliance also involved a fundamental divergence of Chinese and American perspectives and sharp bargaining between the two sides over policies. The 1941–45 alliance was marked by the clash between Washington's Europe First and Chongqing's Asia First perspectives. After Pearl Harbor, Chiang's interest lay in fighting Japan less (conserving his strength for the coming showdown with the CCP), whereas the United States' interest lay in persuading Chiang to fight Japan more, while concentrating American strength on the defeat of Germany. The result was continual confrontation between Washington and Chongqing over levels of support and levels of fighting. Basically, Roosevelt agreed to support the ROC's establishment as a major power, in return for Chiang's agreement to keep his country in the war and fighting against Japan. In the 1941–45 alliance, as in the 1954–71 alliance, threatened defection was Chiang's preferred instrument of leverage. If U.S. support for ROC territorial or diplomatic development was inadequate, the ROC armies might cease fighting Japan, freeing large numbers of Japanese troops to confront U.S. forces elsewhere. Similarly, during the 1954–71 alliance, if the United States dropped its support for Nationalist "return," then it faced the possibility of a Nationalist-Communist accommodation that would have withdrawn Taiwan from the western Pacific island perimeter, which was then deemed essential to U.S. security. By subtly threatening to cause such a breach in Washington's ring of containment, Taipei was able to force Washington to go beyond a strict policy of containment and to endorse elements of rollback.

The 1941–45 and the 1954–71 alliances differed considerably in terms of their overall success. In the first, both American and Nationalist goals were substantially achieved. Nationalist armies fought Japan (though not as much as the United States would have liked) until V-J Day. China won great-power status, as reflected in the abrogation of the unequal treaties, the recovery of Manchuria, Xinjiang, and Taiwan; and a permanent seat on the UN Security Council. The 1954–71 alliance was much less successful *from the Nationalist perspective.* The Nationalists were able to extract certain rollback concessions from their allies, but were never able to induce Washington to abandon containment. Nor was Taipei able to thwart Sino-American rapprochement. From the Nationalist perspective, the second alliance, therefore, fundamentally failed. It was only in the 1970s and 1980s that Nationalist leaders began to embrace the view, long held by American leaders, that the ROC should emphasize its authority over Taiwan. By that point, U.S. leaders had already accommodated to the international reality established by the two Chinese governments in Taipei and Beijing by formally promising not to support Taiwanese independence.

Impact of the Alliance on Subsequent U.S.-Taiwan Relations

Association as allies over a period of twenty years during the Cold War transformed the nature of U.S. and Taiwanese relations. This transformation seems to have worked at three levels: the strategic, the sentimental, and the political.

At the strategic level, the alliance with Taiwan paid off. As previous chapters have demonstrated, important American objectives were achieved through the alliance with Taiwan and the Nationalist regime there. While there were multiple failures and serious difficulties, overall the U.S.-Nationalist Chinese alliance worked satisfactorily. While what is useful in one situation may not be useful in another, prudence suggests that instruments of demonstrated utility not be casually discarded. This is especially true if, as this book has argued, the overarching strategy of the United States in the Asia-Pacific region since 1949 has been that of a maritime power countering hostile continental powers, or a coalition of such powers.

In terms of sentiment, many analysts have noted the strong moral streak of U.S. politics and diplomacy. As a result of two decades of association as allies, many Americans came to feel a sense of moral obligation toward Taiwan. Many Americans developed the image of Taiwan as a loyal friend and ally. Small but brave Taiwan was seen as a country willing to stand by the United States in times of adversity, and to do some of the unpleasant, dirty work that sometimes needed to be done. Taiwan was also seen as a friend willing to learn from the United States—a perspective that appealed to American vanity. As bilateral ties proliferated, so did personal friendships. Robust military and civilian governmental links, advisory programs and exchanges, trade and economic ties, cultural ties, and growing emigration from Taiwan to the United States translated into personal friendships between many Americans and many Chinese from Taiwan. Nationalist representatives worked assiduously to cultivate these American images and sentiments toward Taiwan. Understanding how American politics works, Nationalist representatives early on began courting American public opinion.

One common American belief, which developed during the alliance, was that the United States owed continuing friendship to Taiwan because Taiwan had been a loyal friend of the United States. The United States should repay friendship and loyalty in kind; it should not "betray" Taiwan. When the United States unilaterally terminated the alliance and began making friends with the PRC in 1971, there was a strong sense of guilt among Americans. While Americans might understand and approve of the diplomatic rationale for rapprochement with Beijing, many simultaneously felt guilty for "betraying" Taiwan. Members of the U.S. foreign policy elite might be able to dispose of Taiwan dispassionately. This was not so for many ordinary Americans. There was a sense that the United States had undeservedly wronged Taiwan. Power politics might require a divorce with Taiwan, but sentimental bonds of friendship remained. At a minimum, many Americans concluded, the United States should not abandon Taiwan to the tender mercies of the Chinese Communist Party.

Politically, the two decades of alliance and cooperation represented a very substantial U.S. investment in Taiwan's development as a liberal, capitalist democracy. As documented earlier, the United States used its robust aid program with Taiwan to nudge the Nationalist regime in the direction of an open market economy and more liberal politics. In the first area, the United States secured substantial success. In the second, success was much more modest. Yet even in the political sphere, by the time the alliance ended in 1971, a large class of native Taiwanese entrepreneurs and professionals had emerged; they provided the basis for an increasingly powerful challenge to the KMT's monopoly of power.

The full fruits of the U.S. investment in Taiwan's democratic development did not mature during the U.S.-Nationalist alliance. Only in the 1980s would Taiwan move toward a "soft authoritarian" system, and not until the early 1990s did Taiwan complete its transition to full-blown liberal democracy. But by the mid-1990s, that transition was complete. It can be traced in a very substantial and direct fashion to U.S. efforts of the 1950s and 1960s. The United States' investment in the evolution of a democratic Taiwan was very substantial, and that investment paid off.

At the close of the twentieth century, America can look across the Pacific at a string of dynamic, successful, liberal, capitalist democracies along the western littoral of that ocean: Japan, South Korea, Taiwan, the Philippines, and Australia. The fundamental compatibility of systems and ideologies between these polities and the United States is a source of great strength and security for America. This situation was not achieved without substantial U.S. effort.

Notes

1. David Armstrong, *Revolution and World Order: The Revolutionary State in International Society,* New York: Oxford University Press, 1993.

2. Regarding Anglo-American differences, see Qiang Zhai, *The Dragon, the Lion, and the Eagle: Chinese-British-American Relations, 1949–1958,* Kent, OH: Kent State University Press, 1994.

3. *Drug Control: U.S. Heroin Program Encounters Many Obstacles in Southeast Asia,* General Accounting Office, GAO/NSIAD-96–83, March 1996.

Index

Information contained in tables or figures is identified by italicization of the page number.

John W. Garver is Professor in the School of International Affairs at the Georgia Institute of Technology. He is the author of four books—*China's Decision for Rapprochement with the United States* (1982), *Chinese–Soviet Relations, 1937–1945: The Diplomacy of Chinese Nationalism* (1988), *The Foreign Relations of the People's Republic of China* (1993)—and over fifty articles dealing with China's foreign relations.

LIVERPOOL
JOHN MOORES UNIVERSITY
AVRIL ROBARTS LRC
TEL. 0151 231 4022